Introduction to Sport Marketing

Introduction to Sport Marketing is an accessible and engaging introduction to key concepts and best practice in sport marketing. Aimed at students with little or no prior knowledge of marketing, the book outlines a step-by-step framework for effective sport marketing, from conducting market analysis and developing a strategy, through to detailed planning and implementation. The book has a wider scope than other sport marketing textbooks, recognising that students are just as likely to have to employ their marketing skills in community sport or the not-for-profit sector as in professional sport, and therefore represents the most realistic and useful sport marketing text currently available.

Now in a fully revised and updated second edition, the book has expanded coverage of digital and social media, product innovation, services and relationship marketing, and key contemporary issues such as social responsibility and sustainability. It features a much wider range of international cases and examples, covering North America, Europe, and the vibrant and rapidly developing sport markets in Asia-Pacific, the Middle East and Latin America. Every chapter includes a range of useful features to help the reader to engage with fundamental principles and applied practice, such as problem-solving exercises and review questions. *Introduction to Sport Marketing* is an essential textbook for any degree-level sport marketing course.

Aaron C.T. Smith is a Professor in the Graduate School of Business and Law at Royal Melbourne Institute of Technology (RMIT) University, Australia. Aaron has research interests in the management of psychological, organisational and policy change in business, sport, health, religion and society, and has authored fifteen books and consulted to more than 100 clients concerning these issues. Aaron's qualifications include two doctorates, the first in management and the second in cognitive science.

Bob Stewart is director of the sport management and policy research program at Victoria University, Australia. Bob is one of Australia's most experienced sport studies scholars, and has taught a range of sport management subjects at both undergraduate and postgraduate level, including sport finance, sport policy, sport strategy, sport organisation performance, sport economics and sport and globalisation. Bob has also written widely on the commercial evolution of sport, and his theories of hyper-commercialisation and post-modernisation in sport are used as templates for the analysis of the sport–business nexus.

Sport Management Series

Series Editor: Russell Hoye, La Trobe University, Australia

This **Sport Management Series** has been providing a range of texts for core subjects in undergraduate sport business and management courses around the world for more than 10 years. These textbooks are considered essential resources for academics, students and managers seeking an international perspective on the management of the complex world of sport.

Many millions of people around the globe are employed in sport organisations in areas as diverse as event management, broadcasting, venue management, marketing, professional sport, community and collegiate sport, and coaching as well as in allied industries such as sporting equipment manufacturing, sporting footwear and apparel, and retail.

At the elite level, sport has moved from being an amateur pastime to one of the world's most significant industries. The growth and professionalisation of sport has driven changes in the consumption and production of sport and in the management of sporting organisations at all levels.

Managing sport organisations at the start of the twenty-first century involves the application of techniques and strategies evident in leading business, government and non-profit organisations. This series explains these concepts and applies them to the diverse global sport industry.

To support their use by academics, each text is supported by current case studies, targeted study questions, further reading lists, links to relevant web-based resources, and supplementary online materials such as case study questions and classroom presentation aids.

Also available in this series:

Sport Management
Principles and applications (Fourth edition)
Russell Hoye, Aaron C.T. Smith, Matthew Nicholson, Bob Stewart

Sport and Policy
Barrie Houlihan, Chris Auld, Matthew Nicholson, Russell Hoye

Sports Economics
Paul Downward, Alistair Dawson, Trudo Dejonghe

Sport and the Media
Matthew Nicholson

Sport Governance
Russell Hoye, Graham Cuskelly

Sport Funding and Finance (Second edition)
Bob Stewart

Managing People in Sport Organizations
A strategic human resource management perspective (Second edition)
Tracy Taylor, Alison Doherty and Peter McGraw

Introduction to Sport Marketing (Second edition)
Aaron C.T. Smith and Bob Stewart

Introduction to Sport Marketing

SECOND EDITION

Aaron C.T. Smith and Bob Stewart

Routledge
Taylor & Francis Group

LONDON AND NEW YORK

First published 2015
by Routledge
2 Park Square, Milton Park, Abingdon, Oxon OX14 4RN

and by Routledge
711 Third Avenue, New York, NY 10017

*Routledge is an imprint of the Taylor & Francis Group,
an informa business*

British Library Cataloguing-in-Publication Data
A catalogue record for this book is available from the British
Library

Library of Congress Cataloging in Publication Data
Smith, Aaron, 1972–
    Introduction to sport marketing/Aaron C.T. Smith and Bob
    Stewart. – Second edition.
    pages cm. – (Sport Management Series)
    Includes bibliographical references and index.
    1. Sports – Marketing. I. Stewart, Bob, 1946– II. Title.
    GV716.S56 2015
    796.0688 – dc23
    2014029402

ISBN: 978-1-138-02295-9 (hbk)
ISBN: 978-1-138-02296-6 (pbk)
ISBN: 978-1-315-77676-7 (ebk)

Typeset in Berling and Futura
by Florence Production Limited, Stoodleigh, Devon, UK

Printed and bound by CPI Group (UK) Ltd, Croydon, CR0 4YY

Contents

Figures

Tables

Abbreviations

ABS	Australian Bureau of Statistics
AEG	Anschutz Entertainment Group
AMA	American Marketing Association
B2C	business-to-consumer
C2C	consumer-to-consumer
CEP	customer experiential pathway
CSF	critical success factor
EPL	English Premier League
ESPN	Entertainment and Sports Programming Network
FA	Football Association
FIA	Fédération International de l'Automobile
FIFA	Fédération International de Football Association
IOC	International Olympic Committee
MCFC	Manchester City Football Club
MLB	Major League Baseball
MMS	multimedia messaging service
NFL	National Football League
PWC	PricewaterhouseCoopers
SIT	Sequential incident technique
SMS	short message service
VE	Volleyball England
VNZ	Volleyball New Zealand
WADA	World Anti-Doping Agency

CHAPTER 1

Sport marketing introduction

LEARNING OUTCOMES

At the end of this chapter, readers should be able to:

- explain what the terms 'marketing' and 'sport marketing' mean
- describe how sport marketing can be represented by a philosophy, a process, a set of principles, and a suite of tools
- understand the relationship between the philosophy, processes, principles, and tools of sport marketing
- identify the two different 'angles' of sport marketing
- explain the difference between selling and marketing
- identify the components of the Sport Marketing Framework.

OVERVIEW

A sound knowledge of sport marketing enables sport professionals to successfully position their sport, association, league, team, players, venue, or event so that it can secure a competitive edge. This chapter begins by discussing the concept of sport marketing, before explaining how its principles and tools can be applied to the marketing of sport organisations both professional and amateur. That is, sport leagues, governing bodies, players/athletes, sporting equipment and merchandise suppliers, and anyone running sport events. It also makes the distinction between two types of sport marketing. The first type involves the marketing of sport itself, while the second 'type' involves the use of sport to market some other, sometimes non-sport, products. It also introduces the basic marketing concepts, and outlines the 'Sport Marketing Framework' that will be used to guide the structure and content of the remaining chapters in this book.

WHAT IS MARKETING?

The beginning of marketing

Marketing as a business concept is quite young. There were a few references to the marketing of household products in the late nineteenth century, but it did not really emerge as a serious business issue until the early part of the twentieth century. It all started with the initiatives of Frederick Winslow Taylor, who later became known as the father of scientific management as the result of his now famous publication *Principles of Scientific Management* in 1911. Taylor was the first industrialist to examine the production of material goods from a scientific perspective using tools such as time and motion studies. One of Taylor's most cited studies involved the shovelling of coal, where he determined the most efficient way of undertaking physical labour and manual tasks. His maxim that the principal object of management should be to secure the maximum prosperity for the employer, coupled with the maximum prosperity for each employee, provided a catalyst for other business theorists and practitioners to move further down the production and distribution chain, and see how salesmanship and retailing could also become better organised and more efficient. W. Hoyt, in his 1913 publication, *Scientific Sales Management*, explained how sales management could be made more productive, and most of the ideas he outlined revolved around the 'Taylorist' principle of standardisation. This involved breaking down sales jobs into their component parts, and discovering 'new tools' to secure more customers and consequently increase sales volume. Sales management techniques could, for example, be made more effective if sales territories and travel routes were rationalised, and the salesperson's 'sales talk' could be placed within a standardised framework. Advertising was also made subject to standardisation.

The major philosophical shift in the idea of selling came when industrial societies became more affluent, more competitive, and more geographically spread out during the 1940s and 1950s. This forced business to develop closer relations with buyers and clients, which in turn made business realise that it was not enough to produce a quality product at a reasonable price. In fact, it was equally essential to deliver products that customers actually wanted. Henry Ford may have gotten away with producing his best-selling T-model Ford in one colour only (black) in 1908, but in modern societies this was no longer possible. The modernisation of society led to a marketing revolution that destroyed the view that production, and the accompanying salesmanship, would create its own demand. Customers, and the desire to meet their diverse and often complex needs, became the focal point of business.

Today the term 'marketing' has universal currency, although it still tends to be used in a variety of ways. Some think of marketing as the use of advertising, publicity and personal selling techniques to make others aware of a product, or to attract more consumers to buy it. That is, it's all about making a sale. However, marketing is now far more comprehensive than this narrow and mechanistic interpretation. Put simply, and in the most general of ways, marketing is all about satisfying the needs of customers and consumers. In the case of sport marketing, it is about meeting the needs of sport customers and sport consumers. These customers and consumers include people who play sport, but it goes much further than this. It also includes people who watch or listen to sport programmes, buy merchandise, collect memorabilia, purchase sports goods such as clothing and shoes, and additionally 'surf' sport-related websites to find out the latest gossip surrounding their favourite team, player or event.

Readers may have already noted that the terms 'consumer' and 'customer' have been used to describe those people who buy sports products. A sport consumer is someone who generally uses sport products or services. A sport customer is someone who pays for the use of a specific product or service. In the light of the very slight difference in meaning, it is legitimate to use the terms interchangeably to refer to those people who use and pay for sport products and services.

> *Chapter principle 1.1*: Marketing is more than promotion, advertising, personal selling or sales gimmicks.

Satisfying the needs of consumers obviously involves more than just putting together a slick advertisement or offering a temporary discount. For example, marketing involves making decisions about what different groups of consumers may need or want: the most effective way of selling a product or service, the best way of making the product or service available, the idea behind a product or service, the unique features of a product or service, and ultimately, its price. Marketing demands a process where a range of issues are considered in order to maximise the likelihood that a customer will first of all be attracted to the product, will second, make the decision to buy it, and third, be satisfied by the product or service once it has been consumed and used. These processes can then be combined in order to construct a workable definition of marketing.

The marketing process

Marketing is generally described as the process of planning and implementing activities that are designed to meet the needs or desires of customers. Marketing pays attention to the development of a product, its pricing, promotion and distribution. It aims to create an exchange, where the customer gives up something (usually money), for a product or service they believe is of equal or greater value. Although the term 'product' directly refers to tangible items, it is quite common to use it to represent the entire offering to consumers including services. Thus, it is conventional to speak of the 'sport product' in a global sense as a representative term for all offerings associated with sport, whether in physical form, such as sport equipment, or as a service, such as entertainment. Marketing aims to not only entice people to try products or services, but also keep them as long-term customers.

> *Chapter principle 1.2*: Marketing aims to create an exchange where the customer gives up something for a product or service.

What is sport marketing?

Sport marketing is a relatively new phenomenon. In the 1940s and 1950s most sport was not heavily commercialised, and was thus seen as an activity people just 'did'. Sport was taken for granted, and the attitudes young people had about sport were usually shaped by tradition, family values, and peer-group influence. Tennis, for instance, was for the most part a middle class activity that attracted both males and females. It had no body contact, and thus was not a sport most working class males got excited about. These highly energised young people wanted a bit more rough-and-tumble in their leisure time practices, and hence football was their preferred pursuit. On the other hand tennis had a strong connection to women who wanted something athletic and moderately vigorous, but not heavily masculinised. There was, if you like, a type of natural selection operating, where people gravitated to the sport on the basis of its structure, stereotypical image, and aesthetics. No marketing or heavy sales pitch was needed to motivate people to join tennis clubs. It just happened. The proximity of clubs also played a part in driving demand. Tennis clubs were everywhere in Australia, they had a relatively strong presence in New Zealand, but were far more dispersed in Britain and the United States. The game's social status also had a role to play in shaping demand. In Britain and the USA it had a slightly snobbish image, and it was played mostly within the confines of private clubs. In Australia, on the other hand, tennis clubs were spread across the nation, and every small country town had its own public tennis court. It came as no surprise to find that not only was tennis one of Australia's most popular sports, but also that Australia produced most of the world's most successful players at this time.

Today things are completely different. National governing bodies for tennis operate in a majority of nations around the world, and in every case are fighting for the hearts and minds of every young person with an interest in sports. What is more, they are competing against scores of national governing bodies for a range of other sports. Every national governing body for sport now has a modified games unit, schools support unit, a player development unit, a promotions unit, a marketing unit, a media unit, and a partnership and sponsorship unit. Each unit is expected to use appropriate marketing strategies to attract more junior players, get more parents involved as volunteers, keep everyone in the game for longer, build up the public image of the game, attract more spectators to the big events, get a lucrative sponsorship deal, and, in a best case scenario, secure a massive broadcast rights agreement. Every sporting body around the world now recognises that its 'product' can only grow if it is underpinned by a professionally run marketing campaign.

INTERACTIVE CASE

Have a look at the following two websites:

www.volleyballengland.org
www.volleyballnz.org.nz

The first website contains information on Volleyball England (VE), the governing body for volleyball across England. The second website does the same thing for Volleyball New Zealand (VNZ), which controls the organisation and operation of volleyball for both its north island and its south island. The websites are quite different. They not only look different but they are also delivering different messages. These differences raise a few questions:

Questions

1 From a marketing perspective which homepage is the most impressive and most watchable?
2 Can you explain what makes one homepage more attractive than the other?
3 What marketing messages are you picking up from the VE website?
4 How do the VE website messages differ from messages contained in the VNZ website?
5 What is the marketing significance of the 'kiwi volleyball' section?
6 What could be done to improve the 'game marketing' strategies of each website?

Points of interest

Websites are a powerful marketing tool for national sporting bodies. Their role is to grow and develop the game, so it makes sense for them to make their marketing campaigns as strategic and focused as possible. However, there are many ways of going about this process. Volleyball is a case in point. The first thing to note is that volleyball comes in different shapes and sizes. There is, in fact, a range of volleyball products, with each product having a special appeal to different parts, or segments, of the population. The second thing to note is that sport consumers have a broad spread of needs and wants, and it is often impossible for a single product to meet all these needs simultaneously.

MULTIDIMENSIONAL NATURE OF SPORT MARKETING

The above discussion suggests that sport marketing is multidimensional. First, it involves the application of marketing concepts to sport products and services, and second, it involves the marketing of non-sport products through an association to sport. Sport marketing therefore has two key features, which we will subsequently refer to as 'angles'.

The first angle is the application of general marketing practices to sport-related products and services. The second angle is the marketing of other consumer and industrial products or services through sport. Like any form of marketing, sport marketing seeks to fulfil the needs and wants of consumers. It achieves this by providing sport services and sport-related products to consumers. However, sport marketing is unlike conventional marketing in that it also has the ability to encourage the consumption of non-sport products and services by association. It is thus important to understand that sport marketing means both the marketing of sport itself, and the use of sport as a tool to market other products and services.

These two angles of sport marketing are central to understanding the full range of ways in which sport is managed from a marketing perspective. However, this is not the full story, since the previous dual-angle discussion tends to emphasise the selling part of sport marketing. This is a far too simplistic approach to the sport marketing issue. Before any transaction can occur, a lengthy strategic analysis must be performed in order to determine what sport consumers want, why they want it, and how these wants can be best delivered to them. As a result, sport marketing should also be seen as the collection of planning and implementation activities associated with the delivery of a sport product or service.

Prior to any sales, a sport product or service must hold a place in the mind of a consumer. In practice, this demands that a consumer is aware of the sport product or service and has responded to it in some – hopefully positive – way. The process of cultivating such a response is known as branding, and when a sport brand has grasped a firm place in consumers' minds, then it is said that it is positioned. The consequence of successful branding and the acquisition of strong market positioning is not merely a single transaction. Rather, sport marketing reflects the establishment of an ongoing relationship between a sport brand and its users.

With the introduction of these three further points, it is possible to devise a simple working definition of sport marketing.

> *Chapter principle 1.3*: Sport marketing is the process of planning how a sport brand is positioned and how the delivery of its products or services are to be implemented in order to establish a relationship between a sport brand and its consumers.

DIFFERENT ANGLES, DIFFERENT INTENTIONS

With a working definition of sport marketing specified, it is useful to return to the idea that there are two angles to sport marketing. To repeat, the first is that sport products and services can be marketed directly to the consumer. The second is that other, non-sport products and services can be marketed through the use of sport. In other words, sport marketing involves the marketing *of* sport and marketing *through* sport. For example, the marketing *of* sport products and services directly to sport consumers could include sporting equipment, professional competitions, sport events and local clubs. Other simple examples include team advertising, designing a publicity stunt to promote an athlete, selling season tickets, and developing licensed apparel for sale. In contrast, marketing *through* sport happens when a non-sport product is marketed through an association to sport. Some examples could include a professional athlete endorsing a breakfast cereal, a financial-services business sponsoring a tennis tournament, and a beer company securing exclusive rights to provide its products at a sport venue or event.

> *Chapter principle 1.4*: Sport marketing has two angles: one is the marketing *of* sport products and services, while the other is marketing *through* sport.

INTERACTIVE CASE

Have a look at the Ducati website, www.ducati.com

This is an example of the marketing *of* sport.

Questions

1   How does Ducati market its product *to* sport consumers?
2   What sort of sport consumers do you think would be interested in Ducati products?
3   How does Ducati emphasise that its product is a sport product?

Now have a look at the Shell website, www.shell.com

This is an example of marketing *through* sports. Go to 'Shell Motorsport', then select 'Shell and Ducati'.

Consider the following questions:

1   How does Shell market its motorcycle oil products to sport consumers?
2   How does the Shell association with Ducati influence sport consumer perceptions about Shell motorcycle oils?
3   What promotional techniques has Shell used to market its products?

Points of interest

The products offered by Ducati are not limited to motorcycles. It also sells merchandise, promotes Ducati clubs, organises the 'Ducati Week' for motorcycle enthusiasts, and provides sports information press releases. It encourages consumers to become enthusiastic about Ducati products. The Shell website offers many 'products' to the sport consumer, while also advertising its range of oils, and providing bike travel guides, bike tips, downloads, and Ducati videos. It can thus be said that while Ducati motorcycles are clearly definable sport products, the success of Shell's motorcycle oils is dependent on the sale of more Ducati motorcycles.

A PHILOSOPHY OF SPORT MARKETING

While thinking about what sport marketing encompasses, it is helpful to understand that it is a hierarchical concept. That is, there are levels at which sport marketing can be considered. At the broadest level, sport marketing embraces a *philosophy* – a set of beliefs, if you like – about how to *do* marketing. It is not just marketing managers or the marketing department of a sport organisation that can think in marketing terms. A marketing philosophy is about putting the needs and wants of the customer at the centre of all decisions. It is important to add that the needs of the customer must complement the goals of the enterprise. In business, the goal is to make a profit, but in sport organisations the most important goal is usually to win or attract attention to the sport or organisation. Marketing philosophy is concerned with creating a win–win situation for both the organisation and sport consumers, but it recognises that no one will win if consumers' needs are not met. This sport marketing philosophy threads its way through the text. Each chapter provides a sharp reminder of the importance of understanding and targeting customers' needs, and working out the best alignment between an organisation's goals, the sport product's features, and the expressed needs of consumers.

> *Chapter principle 1.5*: The *philosophy* of sport marketing is to deliver products that best satisfy the needs of sport consumers.

At a second level, sport marketing may be considered a *process*. It is a process because it involves a series of activities and steps. For example, sport marketing involves research, analysis, planning, development, implementation and evaluation. These processes are a common property of sport marketing and feature as the structural framework around which this text is written.

> *Chapter principle 1.6*: The *process* of sport marketing is the series of steps required to find opportunities, devise a strategy, plan the tactics, and implement and evaluate a sport marketing plan.

At the third level, sport marketing may be summarised as a set of principles because it adopts numerous ideas and concepts that provide specific guidance to those undertaking sport marketing activities. In each chapter, a set of sport marketing principles are highlighted in order to provide clear guidance as to how the processes of sport marketing can be used in practice.

Finally, at the most operational level, sport marketing principles can be implemented with the aid of tools, which are devices and activities used in day-to-day practice. Direct selling is a tool, and so are price discounting, targeted advertising, and press conferences.

> *Chapter principle 1.7*: *Sport marketing* can be described as a philosophy (a set of values that drive the marketing function), a process (a linked series of activities), a set of principles (rules and guidelines) and tools (techniques).

To summarise, this text adopts the sport marketing *philosophy* that consumers' needs are met when they match features of a product or service where the ultimate goal is to cultivate an ongoing relationship between a sport brand and consumers. The remainder of this book structures this philosophy around a sequence of sport marketing *processes* that reflect the organisation of the chapters. Within each chapter, sport marketing *principles* are presented to help steer the implementation of sport marketing processes. In addition, *tools* are offered as specific, recommended techniques. The four levels are represented in Figure 1.1.

> *Chapter principle 1.8*: The *principles* of sport marketing provide the rules and guidelines for the implementation of the Sport Marketing Framework *process*, while the *tools* of sport marketing are specific activities designed to help execute the *principles*.

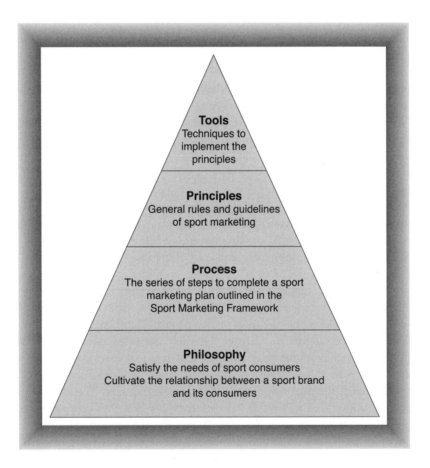

FIGURE 1.1 The structure of sport marketing

WHAT IS TO FOLLOW?

The marketing of sport may appear at first to be similar to general marketing. However, sport marketing does have differences to other forms of marketing. For example, the sport product is often highly inconsistent and unpredictable because it is not possible to predict the outcome of a sporting match or control the quality of play. In many other industries, the failure to guarantee the quality of a product would be disastrous. Another significant difference is that few products can evoke the emotional attachment and personal identification that sport commands. To be successful in sport marketing, it is necessary to understand general marketing as well as the unique circumstances of sport.

There are two aspects of sport that are pivotal to understanding its unique circumstances: the sport market and the sport consumer. Chapter 2 introduces the special features of sport with an emphasis on the three sectors associated with sport: the government, the not-for-profit, and the corporate sectors. Chapter 3 introduces the various types of sport consumers including those who utilise sport as a consumer product and those who actively engage in sport. The chapter will also reveal the idiosyncratic motives and behaviours of sport consumers as well as the factors that influence their behaviour.

Once the sport market and the sport consumer are described, it is possible to move on to the process of sport marketing. Chapter 4 provides an overview of the four stages of the sport marketing process: (1) identify sport marketing opportunities; (2) develop a sport marketing strategy; (3) plan the marketing mix; and (4) implement and control the strategy. Figure 1.2 illustrates the Sport Marketing Framework. It is helpful because it offers a structure through which the logical sequence of sport marketing is implemented. A detailed guide to stage one is contained in Chapter 4. Stage two is provided in Chapter 5.

> *Chapter principle 1.9: The Sport Marketing Framework* provides a detailed explanation of the four stages of the sport marketing process: (1) identify sport marketing opportunities; (2) develop sport marketing strategy; (3) plan the marketing mix; and (4) implement and control the strategy.

Chapter 6 explores the first elements of the sport marketing mix. It introduces the key elements of the sport product, and outlines product-related marketing strategies. Chapter 7 specifies the second element in the sport marketing mix. The chapter is structured around a step-by-step pricing approach. Chapter 8 tackles the third dimension of the sport marketing mix. It highlights the basic concepts and issues of sport distribution and pays particular attention to the centrality of the sport venue, and media and broadcasting. Chapter 9 highlights the final component of the marketing mix. The chapter identifies the purpose of promotions, reviews its key elements, and describes promotions planning. Building on the promotion of sport, Chapter 10 presents the process of locating sponsors, the nature of sponsorship associations, the management and leveraging of relationships, and the evaluation process. Chapter 11 augments the sport marketing mix by examining sport services. This chapter introduces the specific aspects of services marketing and the idiosyncrasies of the sport service. It describes the techniques of quality service and customer satisfaction management as well as customer relationship marketing.

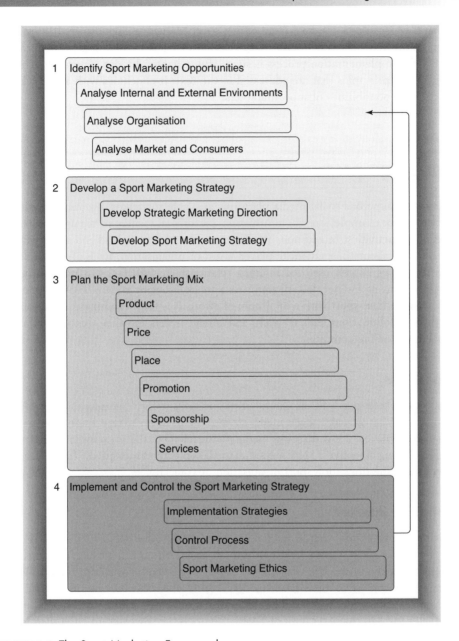

FIGURE 1.2 The Sport Marketing Framework

The world of sport marketing is changing rapidly, and the way in which the marketing mix and sponsorship are deployed is subject to constant new media platforms, technologies and opportunities. Chapter 12 focuses on the current marketing context relevant to sport. This includes the key social and digital media technologies and their implications for the way in which sport consumers engage in the marketing process.

Chapter 13 explains the final stage of the Sport Marketing Framework. It introduces readers to the activities associated with setting up feedback mechanisms for determining whether the implementation process is successful. Chapter 13 also summarises the key processes and principles that are addressed in the text. It concludes with a discussion of the ethical responsibilities of sport marketers.

INTERACTIVE CASE

There are numerous social media platforms available for teams, events, or players. Facebook, for example, streams information, pictures and videos of the user's current and future activities. In addition, YouTube enables fans to upload and share videos with others about their favourite player, team or organisation. Each of these social media options is well used for building relationships with fans but not nearly as instantaneous as Twitter or Instagram. As a micro-blogging service Twitter quickly links fans to their sport with a minimum of effort. It is fast becoming commonplace for fans to follow their idols or team, and spread tweets to other fans as soon as it reaches the online community.

Questions

A sport marketer needs to ask a number of questions before engaging through social networks. What would a social media strategy be used for? What business benefits are to be achieved? How do social media platforms meet the organisation's business and marketing objectives? How are social media objectives measured? Try to answer these basic questions for a sport organisation of your choice.

Points of interest

Twitter embraces viral trends much more readily than other social media platforms. As a no-frills social networking platform, it enables many sport organisations to interact quickly. In the US, many of the major leagues use Twitter in some way to connect consumers to their brand and to teams. It serves the purpose facing all businesses, that is, to break through the information clutter efficiently. For the sport marketer the 140 character limit of Twitter compels the 'Tweeter' to pitch their idea succinctly and creatively. If successful it can establish stronger links to fans and they in turn, can re-tweet the message to others. The spread of information is an economical means of connecting fans and maintaining a bond to the sport brand. One prominent source (www.statisticbrain.com) reports that there are over 640 million active registered Twitter users with over 40 per cent of them accessing Twitter via their mobile phones. The annual advertising revenue in 2013 for Twitter exceeded US$400 million, making it a viable platform for sport organisations and their associated sponsors. Twitter can bring the fan closer to their idol than ever before. The most popular athlete Twitter account belongs to Portuguese footballer, Cristiano

Ronaldo with over 25 million followers. During the 2011 Fédération International de Football Association (FIFA) Women's World Cup, many of the players started to use Twitter to communicate with fans before, during, and well after the competition's end, generating increased interest for individual stars, such as 2011 FIFA World Cup Golden Glove winner Hope Solo. However, in 2014 *Forbes Magazine* claimed that only one per cent of the Twitter community are represented by celebrities, athletes or journalists who engage in breaking or sharing news of their exploits.

PRINCIPLES SUMMARY

- Chapter principle 1.1: Marketing is more than promotion, advertising, personal selling or sales gimmicks.

- Chapter principle 1.2: Marketing aims to create an exchange where the customer gives up something for a product or service.

- Chapter principle 1.3: Sport marketing is the process of planning how a sport brand is positioned and how the delivery of its products or services are to be implemented in order to establish a relationship between a sport brand and its consumers.

- Chapter principle 1.4: Sport marketing has two angles: one is the marketing of sport products and services, while the other is marketing *through* sport.

- Chapter principle 1.5: The *philosophy* of sport marketing is to satisfy the needs of sport consumers.

- Chapter principle 1.6: The *process* of sport marketing is the series of steps required to find opportunities, devise strategy, plan the tactics, and implement and evaluate a sport marketing plan.

- Chapter principle 1.7: *Sport marketing* can be described as a philosophy (a set of values that drive the marketing function), a process (a linked series of activities), a set of principles (rules and guidelines) and tools (techniques).

- Chapter principle 1.8: The *principles* of sport marketing provide the rules and guidelines for the implementation of the Sport Marketing Framework *process*, while the *tools* of sport marketing are specific activities designed to help execute the *principles*.

- Chapter principle 1.9: The *Sport Marketing Framework* provides a detailed explanation of the four stages of the sport marketing process: (1) identify sport marketing opportunities; (2) develop sport marketing strategy; (3) plan the marketing mix; and (4) implement and control the strategy.

REVIEW QUESTIONS

1   What is the basic philosophy of all marketing?
2   How does marketing differ from selling?
3   When and why did marketing emerge as a crucial management competency?
4   How is sport marketing different from general – that is, generic – marketing?
5   Explain the difference between marketing *in* sport and marketing *through* sport.
6   What are the steps in the Sport Marketing Framework?
7   Provide a definition of sport marketing in your own words.
8   What do you think is the ultimate goal of sport marketing?
9   Does this 'ultimate' goal generally deliver more benefits than costs to society?

RELEVANT WEBSITES

www.volleyballengland.org
www.volleyballnz.org.nz
www.shell.com
www.ducati.com

CHAPTER 2

Sport markets

LEARNING OUTCOMES

At the end of this chapter, readers should be able to:

- describe the scale and scope of the sport industry
- identify the differences between the three sport sectors and their roles in sport marketing
- explain the unique features of sport products
- describe how the special features of sport impact upon sport marketing theory and practice.

OVERVIEW

This chapter provides an overview of the structure and operation of sport markets. It does this by first discussing the nature of the sports industry in general, and its three core sectors in particular. They are the government sector, the not-for-profit sector, and the corporate sector. A review of the scale and scope of different sport markets is undertaken, while the chapter ends with an examination of sport's special features, and how they present such a unique marketing challenge.

THE SPORT INDUSTRY

What is an industry?

To understand the sport industry it is instructive to first explain what an industry is. The term industry can be defined as an assembly of markets where similar, or closely related, products and services are offered to consumers. Industries are often categorised according to the types of products and services they offer. The result is that there can be a wide range of organisations involved in an industry, including commercial or corporate entities, non-profit organisations, associations, manufacturers, wholesalers, retailers, government agencies and small businesses. From a sport marketing perspective it is useful to remember that in a single industry the products and services produced satisfy similar consumer needs and wants. As a result, the sport industry includes all the suppliers of products and services that satisfy the needs of sport consumers. The important point is that the sport industry constitutes a marketplace where consumers can acquire products and services that are associated with a multitude of sports, with each sport offering a different and often quite unique experience to its participants and fans.

It is easy to get caught in the trap of thinking narrowly about what the sport industry comprises. For example, on first impressions the sport industry may appear to be little more than sport venues, gymnasiums, clubs and teams, leagues, athletes, sporting apparel and shoes, merchandise, sporting associations, the Olympic Games, and government sport departments. While this is a good start, there are many other organisations that form part of the sport industry. Some examples include:

- government departments of sport and recreation, at state or county, and federal or national level;
- the media, including print, television, cable, satellite and the Internet;
- educational organisations such as universities and private providers that teach sport management programs;
- researchers and consultants who study the sport market or consumers, as well as exercise physiology and sport medicine;
- the transport and construction sectors that contribute to the building of sporting venues;
- corporations and private enterprises that contribute to sport through sponsorship;
- volunteers who assist in the operation of sport clubs and associations by talking on administrative, coaching and officiating responsibilities.

One way of thinking about the composition of the sport industry is to imagine it as a series of steps that begin with the supply of raw materials that are used to create sport products and services, through to their delivery and marketing at a specific place or destination. Figure 2.1 provides an example of a 'value chain' for the sport industry. It is called a value chain because at each step there is the addition of new value to the sport product. This diagram shows that government has a broad impact across all areas of the sport industry. Not only do they provide money to support sport organisations, they also help to create many of the physical facilities and venues in which sport activities take place. In addition, governments create legislation and policies that affect sport in many ways. For example, they set laws that regulate how and when media can cover sport events. Many other types of government legislation can affect the individuals and groups involved in the sport industry, such as company law, taxation, patents and copyright, contract law and income tax law.

The next level down in the diagram shows seven different categories of producers, suppliers, consumers and others who are involved in the sport industry. Underneath each is a list of examples for that category. The shaded area shows the activities and groups

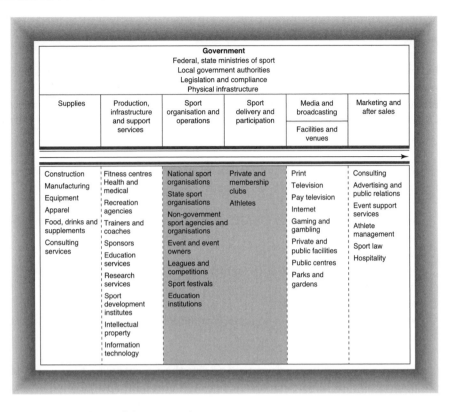

FIGURE 2.1 Value chain of the sport industry

that are most commonly associated with the sport industry. These may be seen as the core sport products and services. Figure 2.1 shows that there is a lot more to the sport industry than just the core. For example, to the left of the shaded core are input activities contributing to the development of the core sport products and services. To the right of the shaded area are activities related to the distribution and marketing of sport products and services.

The size of the sport industry can be measured in a number of ways. For example, one way is to count how much money is spent on sport, such as sporting goods, the building of venues and organised sporting activities. Another approach involves determining how much money government and private organisations such as corporations contribute to sport by way of grants and sponsorships. Another approach still would be to examine how much consumers spend on sport-related products and services per year, how many people participate in sport, how many people are employed in the sport industry and even how many volunteers provide their services. However, it is extremely difficult (if not impossible) to calculate accurate statistics on these aspects of sport. The sport industry is just too large, and it is also so fragmented that it is not practical to locate and study them all.

INTERACTIVE CASE

The four PricewaterhouseCoopers (PWC) websites listed below provide a lot of figures on the scale and scope of the global sports industry. Each website belongs to a business consulting group whose job is to provide advice to clients on industry trends. In this case the focus is the global sports industry.

- www.pwc.com/en
  (www.pwc.com/en_GX/gx/hospitality-leisure/pdf/changing-the-game-outlook-for-the-global-sports-market-to-2015.pdf)
- www.statista.com
  (www.statista.com/statistics/194122/sporting-event-gate-revenue-worldwide-by-region-since-2004/)
- www.atkearney.com.au
  (www.atkearney.com.au/documents/10192/6f46b880-f8d1–4909–9960-cc605bb1ff34)
- www.plunkettresearch.com
  (www.plunkettresearch.com/sports-recreation-leisure-market-research/industry-and-business-data)

We all know that consulting groups tend to give their clients what they would like to hear and read, but despite the mandatory optimism built into these reports, the global outlook for sport is very impressive. But, there are also a number of questions that need to be asked about the details contained in each of these reports.

Questions

- What are the key points made in the PWC report?
- What does the PWC report say about the scale of the global sport industry in American dollar terms?
- Does the Statista report add much to the PWC report? If not, then why not?
- What industries and markets does the Plunkett Group report focus on? Would you class the report and the results it contains as narrow or broad?
- The AT Kearney report gives a global sport annual revenue figure that is four times the number provided by PWC. How can this be explained?

The following website houses the Australian Bureau of Statistics (ABS). Unlike the websites listed above, it is government owned rather than privately owned. The ABS gathers a lot of data on the sports sector. This particular site looks at the Australian sports sector from a customer perspective. It focuses on household spending. What does the data tell us about the Australian sport industry?

www.abs.gov.au
(www.abs.gov.au/AUSSTATS/abs@.nsf/Lookup/AE59C66187F4E58DCA257C0D0
00F91A9?opendocument)

Points of interest

When reading industry reports it is important to look at the fine print, and especially the conditions and assumptions that are being applied to the study. In this case, it is important to understand how the reports define their terms. So, the question you need to ask is: 'What makes up the industry, are its parameters clearly explained, and what markets are in, and what markets are out?

The multi-sector nature of the sport industry

In looking at the sport industry value chain, it becomes clear that three different kinds of industrial activities are involved. First, there are those associated with the government, which are collectively referred to as the public sector, including national, state/county/provincial, regional and local governments, as well as quasi-government institutions and agencies that are involved in the development of sport, determining government sport policy, bolstering competitive performance or in health promotion or drug compliance. The second kind of activity is undertaken by the non-profit or voluntary sector. This group is made up of local clubs, community-based associations, universities and colleges, governing organisations and international federations. In the non-profit sector, the focus is on the development of sport through organised competition and participation, with a heavy emphasis on the regulation and management of sport. The final set of activities is the purview of the professional or corporate sport sector. This group is commercially focused, comprising professional clubs, leagues and major events. In addition, this group includes a vast number of corporations that have a financial interest in sport, such as equipment and apparel manufacturers, sport retailers, broadcasting companies, telecommunications providers and sponsors. In fact, any organisation with the primary purpose of making a profit from an association with sport may be placed in this category.

As Figure 2.1 shows, the three sectors mix and mingle, their activities intersecting regularly. In fact, sport could not be produced without the collusion of all three sectors. To begin with, the government or public sector provides the context in which sport is undertaken. Often this includes financial support and the provision and maintenance of sport venues and facilities for non-profit sector activities. Equally, non-profit sport is expected to deliver social and community benefits. The regulatory environment created by government also affects corporate sport because professional leagues generally require the use of public venues. Corporate sport is also dependent on community sport because they provide the playing, coaching and administrative talent to leagues and associations. Reciprocally, parts of the corporate sector seek marketing benefits through an association with non-profit sport by providing much needed funding through sponsorships. In general, it is important to remember that the activities of the three sectors bleed into each other. For example, some high-profile non-profit sport organisations are professionally managed and behave as corporate entities. There is also some ambiguity about where large non-government, non-corporate entities such as the International Olympic Committee, or large universities in North America, fit in. The next sections focus on the marketing implications that are connected with each of the three sectors and their primary activities.

Government sport sector

In general, governments get involved in sport because of its potential to deliver social, economic and political benefits. For example, sport can provide health benefits for participants as well as social cohesion. It can also stimulate economic activity and bolster civic pride. For some governments, sport is advantageous because it can cultivate national identity and solidarity, which tends to be helpful for the re-election of politicians and in developing national goodwill. Although the policy approach taken by a government towards sport can change radically depending on its ideological orientation, all governments influence sport in at least four ways.

First, governments at various levels provide funding and facilities for sport. This includes funding for national sport organisations and Olympic campaigns, and the construction and maintenance of major and local sport, recreation and leisure facilities. Second, governments can be directly involved in the development of sport via training institutes and elite testing facilities. Third, governments can deliver sport-, health- or physical activity-related programs, or just promote lifestyle campaigns. Finally, governments can take responsibility for aspects of sport compliance, such as anti-doping, as well as the composition of the general regulatory environment. A few further comments on this last element are warranted.

The term 'regulatory environment' refers to the nature of competition within an industry. Unlike more traditional industries, the sport industry is often allowed by government to pursue anti-competitive practices, including significant restrictions on the rights of players. This occurs because many governments accept that sport performs poorly under normal market conditions. As a result, although league regulation may be anti-competitive, it is generally not considered unreasonable, or against the public interest. While member teams are highly competitive and concerned with on-field dominance, they also understand that their long-term viability depends on a high-quality and well-balanced competition where teams are of comparable strength and ability.

Governments regularly employ marketing principles to support their sport objectives. Typically, governments do not get directly involved in marketing sport, but often spend considerable money on promoting the benefits of sport or its locations. For example, governments use marketing to attract large sport events to specific cities. They also employ marketing to promote the social and health benefits of sport participation or an active lifestyle.

Non-profit sport sector

In the Western world, where economies are centred on the interaction of capitalist enterprises and their customers, it is generally accepted that government will never be responsible for the bulk of the production, distribution and sale of sport products and related services. The result has been the emergence of non-profit sport organisations that make up the gaps in between profit-oriented business and government. Non-profit sport organisations are therefore concerned with the public good rather than making money.

However, since they are not administered by the government, non-profit sport organisations must find resources and expertise for themselves, and must comply with government regulations about their legal status and conduct. As a rule, non-profit sport organisations are highly specialised in that they tend to evolve to fit a particular community sporting need. They are also administered mainly by volunteers. Non-profit sport organisations are the backbone of sport.

Non-profit sport organisations develop communities, social networks and local groups through the provision of specialised sport products and services. Typically, these services revolve around the organisation of sport competitions and the subsequent development and management of players, coaches and administrators, along with the code itself. However, there are also professional service organisations, lobby groups, event organisers and governing bodies. Sport and recreation organisations can be classified into three different kinds of non-profit groups. The first includes amateur sport, training, fitness and sport facilities, and sport competitions and events. The second includes recreation and social clubs, such as country clubs and leisure clubs. The third includes service clubs that use sport as a vehicle for social development. Of these three groups, the first is the largest as it incorporates a vast number of sport clubs and their associations. In some countries, and particularly in the United States, school and college sport is the most prevalent form of non-profit sport.

Non-profit sport organisations face numerous marketing challenges. To begin with, they are often cash-poor, which means that they cannot pursue expensive advertising or other major promotional activities. Another challenge is that they do not necessarily have access to sport marketing expertise as they heavily rely on the goodwill and service of volunteer staff. A final problem is that many non-profit sport organisations have rich but cumbersome amateur traditions that do not lend themselves to attractive marketing. Non-profit sport organisations consequently focus their marketing initiatives on low-cost activities that emphasise the benefits of participating in sport. Some have recognised the importance of differentiating their products and services from others, and work hard to create a relationship between their brand and sport consumers. In addition, some non-profit sport organisations are taking advantage of new technology and new media platforms to inexpensively position themselves distinctively in a cluttered sport marketplace.

Corporate sport sector

The corporate or professional sport sector is characterised by the commercial imperative; the desire to make a profit from sport. As Figure 2.1 demonstrates, there are numerous places in which commercial enterprises can provide value-adding products or services associated with sport that can generate money. At the hub of corporate sport are professional clubs and teams that compete in large national or international leagues, or athletes and teams that participate in large events. Although these organisations and athletes may not be profit-seeking, they nevertheless provide the core content that other profit-based businesses wish to associate with.

Professional sport teams produce a product that is sold to four groups: first, fans who support leagues by attending games, following games on television and other media and purchasing league- and team-related merchandise; second, television and other media or broadcasting companies that purchase the right to show games as a programming option;

third, communities that build facilities and support local clubs; and fourth, corporations that support leagues and clubs by increasing gate monies, purchasing teams outright or providing revenues through sponsorships or other associations.

Professional sports leagues are just one part of the corporate sport sector. There is also an enormous amount of money to be made in the manufacture of sport-related products and services. The tangible product sector is growing at every turn, and includes areas such as stadium construction, equipment manufacturers, sport apparel and fashion labels. The equipment needed to play ice hockey, go sailing, and even compete in competitive cycling events can cost participants many thousands of dollars. There are also professional sport services to be considered, which include advertisers, athlete and player managers, sport nutrition and supplement consultants, sport physicians, physiotherapists, event and sport tourism promoters, hospitality services, sponsors and team franchise owners.

An increasingly important part of corporate sport is branding, since in such a competitive sports world it is crucially important to establish lasting relationships with sport fans and consumers. For example, sport equipment and apparel manufacturers need to convince consumers that using their brand has benefits over using a competitor's brand. Much of the branding emphasis of corporate sport revolves around the spectacle and entertainment value of the sport experience, and all the symbolism and images that go with it.

INTERACTIVE CASE

Forbes, America's best-known business magazine, does a regular update of the world's major sport brands. Go to the following website for more details.

www.forbes.com
(www.forbes.com/pictures/mlm45jemm/the-most-valuable-company-brands)

Questions

Based on your reading of the Forbes article, how would you respond to the following questions?

- What are the names of the most highly valued sports brands?
- What makes for a strong sports goods brand?
- From a marketing perspective, what can be done to strengthen a sub-standard sports brand?
- The Forbes article says nothing about sports goods suppliers. If sports goods suppliers were included, then what two businesses would need to be included, and why?
- Are highly valued brands just about the image that marketers project to the public, or is there something else behind the brands that drives up their value?

Points of interest

The strength of a sports brand is dependent on the ability of marketing campaigns to draw more public awareness, more media coverage, more members, more supporters, and more corporate partners. But, of course, one crucial determinant of brand-value is missing. For a professional sport club its win–loss record is critical. Real Madrid, Barcelona and Bayern Munich have massively valued brands, and they don't come from just having a nicely designed stadium, a lovely combination of club colours, a highly distinctive club logo and motto, or even a well-respected chairman of the governing board. Ultimately high brand values, especially in professional football, are built on a foundation of winning and success. This is why Crystal Palace and the Hull City Tigers will never have the same brand value as Manchester United and Liverpool FC. Good marketing will make a difference at the margins, but a marketing campaign will only be effective in the long run if the product is also of high quality.

Sport markets

Within each of the three sectors described above there are a multitude of markets. Take, for example, the non-profit sport sector. Around the world there are hundreds of sports being played, and in most instances these sports are governed by international associations, national associations, and in some cases state and provincial associations. Each of the sports can be viewed as a market where the suppliers of the services are seeking customers – that is, participants – to use their services. This means that there are markets for services associated with athletics, badminton, basketball, cricket, exercise programs, football, field hockey, horse racing, ice hockey, rock-climbing, rugby, tennis and volleyball. The list goes on. And, within each market, there are clubs and venues offering an array of different experiences. Tennis clubs, for instance, may offer weekend competitions, weekday competitions, competitions with modified rules, gender-specific competitions, or mixed-gender competitions. The point to make here is that while sports markets are unified by their emphasis on physical activity of one sort or another, they can also be very different. Participation can involve playing the game, but it can also involve watching others play. It can involve the use of complex technologies such as motorcycles and sailboats on one hand, and simple technologies such as running shoes and footballs on the other.

THE SPECIAL FEATURES OF SPORT PRODUCTS

Sport, whatever its features and idiosyncrasies, has an extraordinary ability to command attention, interest and loyalty. In some extreme instances, where injury is common, or violence is excessive, it can lead to abhorrence. Most people, however, value sport. Some people go further by claiming that sport is a sacred space because it takes people out of their ordinary existence and transports them to a world where anything is possible. Others are more circumspect and merely suggest that sport is character-building, provides participants with a solid moral compass, and thus its purpose is far loftier than doing business and making profits. For these people sport is special and unlike other activities that our daily lives offer up to us.

Some sport commentators believe that when sport becomes a business it loses its most important qualities, which includes a sense of history, tradition and continuity, a passionate connection to clubs and players, and even just the belief that sport gives life a little more variety and a lot more meaning. Sport marketers who accept the view that sport has an emotional resonance missing in most other products, and is additionally framed by a plethora of rules and ethical standards, tend to believe that managing sport is a difficult task, and that standard business and marketing practices do not translate easily to sport. This is because the emotions inherent in sport force managers to avoid decisions that could compromise long-standing traditions, cause fan dissatisfaction or reduce volunteer participation. Additionally, sport often has a moral aspect to it, and thus notions of fair play and cheating are always front and centre. People who believe sport is a unique enterprise also argue that the commercialisation and professionalisation of sport have damaged its community foundations and ethical base.

On the other hand, to some commentators sport, whether played at the elite and professional level or at the local-community level, remains just another form of business. They argue that sport expresses a form of leisure that, like any other product, is valued because it not only delivers a fit and healthy body if played on a regular basis, but also provides an entertainment experience. In each case the product will have a benefit, and in order to secure this benefit the users of a sport product will be prepared to pay a specific price. And, more sales mean that the supplying organisations will make more money by keeping more customers happy and satisfied. This is the market at work.

From such a viewpoint, good business practices are needed to help keep sport organisations alive; any benefits that sport might confer (e.g. health benefits, character-building opportunities, and a sense of belonging) will be lost forever if an organisation cannot remain profitable by operating in a business-like manner. As a result, those who believe sport operates as just another business take the view that standard marketing practices are the most appropriate way of dealing with the operation of sport. Instead of seeing sport as a unique enterprise, they believe that sport is a client-based service business, operating within a specific, but not necessarily unique business marketplace. This means they also take a corporate view of volunteers and traditions. For example, volunteers are a 'human resource' of an organisation, who must be inducted, rewarded, trained and counselled like any other member of staff in any other commercial enterprise.

Our belief is that both of these perspectives are true. Sport is a special kind of product, but it still operates in a business context that demands professionalism and accountability. Most sport marketers hold the view that sport organisations, whatever their size or scope, can no longer be managed as fun and games, or separated from the wider commercial world. Even non-profit clubs, for example, must perform financially if they want to survive in the highly competitive world of sport and alternative entertainment products. Sport is not so unique that it cannot be put in a commercial framework. But it is not just another form of commercial entertainment either. Sport is business, but it is a special form of business. The key is to understand the special features of sport and their relevance to meeting the needs of sport consumers.

In the next section, the special features of sport products and sport experiences are discussed. It emphasises the point that those factors that make sport appealing to consumers, can in other situations make the products extremely unattractive. For example, going into a volleyball game as a spectator or player is more exhilarating when the result is uncertain. However, buying a washing machine on the basis that the outcome of the wash will be uncertain does not make any sense, since the expectation for reliability and certainty drive what really matters. As a result, sport's features are important for sport marketers to understand. From a marketing perspective there is a continual demand to balance sport's need for uncertainty on one hand, against the need for rules that will provide a regular quality outcome on the other.

> *Chapter principle 2.1*: Sport is a special form of business. A standard marketing approach does not always work in sport, so sport marketers must also understand the special features of the sports market.

Emotion and passion

Sport can stimulate an emotional response in its consumers of the kind rarely elicited by other products. Imagine bank customers buying memorabilia to show allegiance with their bank, or consumers identifying so strongly with their car insurance company that they get a tattoo with its logo. We know that some sport followers are so passionate about players, teams and the sport itself that their interest borders upon obsession. This addiction provides the emotional glue that binds fans to teams, and maintains loyalty even in the face of on-field failure.

While most marketers can only dream of having customers that are as passionate about their products as sport fans, the emotion stimulated by sport can also have a negative impact. Sport's emotional intensity can mean that organisations have strong attachments to the past through nostalgia and club tradition. As a result, they may ignore efficiency, productivity and the need to respond quickly to changing market conditions. For example, a proposal to change club colours in order to project a more attractive image may be defeated because it breaks a link with tradition. Similarly, a coach or manager can be appointed on the basis of his/her previous loyalty to the club rather than because of a capacity to manage players better than the other applicants.

> *Chapter principle 2.2*: Sport can elicit an emotional response in its consumers that is rarely found in other businesses. It can stimulate immense loyalty, but also strong attachments to nostalgia and club tradition.

On-field versus off-field success

One of the most significant differences between not-for-profit sport organisations – especially those that participate in competitive sport settings – and commercial businesses, are the ways in which they measure performance. Commercial businesses may have many goals, but their main purpose is to maximise profits. For example, British Petroleum and Shell are fierce retail competitors, but in the same year they could both produce a profit, and claim it a success. That is, they can all win, with no losers. However, sport is different. Sport club members and fans judge performance on the basis of trophies, championships, premierships, pennants, cups and rankings. For every winner there are many more losers. Moreover, a large annual profit might not seem like a success to sport clubs if they finished the season at the bottom of the ladder. For the most part sport clubs value winning over expanding profits. It is also important to note that on-field and off-field successes do not always go together. A sport club may bankrupt itself by paying high salaries for players and coaches in an effort to secure a championship. On the other hand, they may succeed financially by placing a ceiling on player payments, but not perform on the field of play because of their scarcity of playing talent.

Competitive sport clubs and organisations have to manage competing demands. On the one hand, they need to maximise profit in order to invest in their competitive activities. On the other hand, they need to perform on the field of play no matter what the cost. However, as the sport and leisure industry becomes increasingly competitive, and more alternative entertainment options are available to sport consumers, sport organisations become more pressured to focus on profits and cash flow. Marketing is one avenue to help support revenue without compromising an emphasis on sport performance.

Chapter principle 2.3: Sport organisations measure their success both on and off the field of play. On-field success refers to achievement within sport competition. Off-field success refers to financial stability and profitability.

A level playing field

In most business settings it is desirable to put competitors out of business. Both British Airways and Qantas would be better placed if Ryanair and Virgin respectively were either available for takeover, or were pushed into insolvency. Fewer competitors mean more available customers, which in turn leads to higher profits. Paradoxically, and despite our observations in the previous section, this is not always the case in sport. In fact, sport organisations that compete in leagues demand the opposite. That is, they rely on the health of their competitors for their own success. This is because most fans are more attracted to a close contest where the winner is unknown in advance. Dominating a league or competition can be self-defeating because the interest of fans can fade. It is therefore often in the interests of the big teams to prop up the operations of the less powerful teams. The New York Yankees is the wealthiest club in American baseball, but it also understands that its long-term sustainability depends upon the playing strengths of its competitors.

Overall then, sport leagues attract higher attendances and viewers when it is difficult to predict who will win a match. Ironically, in order to remain successful, leagues and competitions need as many of their clubs to be competitive as possible. When the outcome of a match is highly predictable, it will not attract large crowd numbers and eventually it will reduce ticket, media and sponsorship revenue. A healthy, competitive balance between teams remains essential. Sometimes this will require a radical transfer of resources from wealthy clubs to poorer clubs, which of course rarely happens in the private business sector.

Chapter principle 2.4: Sport organisations that compete in leagues and competitions rely on the health of their competitors for their own success. Sport consumers are more attracted to attend games where there is a balanced competition.

Collaboration and cartels

As noted earlier, teams and clubs depend on the continued on-field and off-field success of their opponents. If a league becomes divided into two groups, one group of wealthy and high performing teams and another group of poor and low performing teams, this will ultimately damage all the clubs involved and the competition. In practice, clubs must cooperate with their rivals in order to deliver what their consumers want. Sport clubs need their opposition to remain successful, and may cooperate to share revenues and trade player talent to maintain competitive balance. In most industries, businesses would not be allowed to cooperate in this way; it is considered anti-competitive, or *cartel-like* behaviour, and there are often laws that prohibit it. But in sport, cartel arrangements are common. For example, clubs may share revenue, prevent other clubs from entering the market, collectively fix prices and generally limit the amount of competition.

Some sport codes and leagues have pursued a balance in their competition, and have implemented policies to encourage it. Sport regulators commonly believe that a balanced competition will produce exciting and close results, which will increase the level of public interest in the sport and generate larger attendances and broadcast rights fees. For example, salary caps for players, rules about sharing revenues, and regulations regarding how players are to be drafted to teams, are all designed to maintain a competitive balance between teams.

The idea of regulating sport leagues in order to keep a fair and balanced competition has become common in sport. To achieve this, regulators often adopt three key structural principles. First, they establish an independent decision-making body to regulate the member teams or organisations, such as the Fédération International de l'Automobile (FIA) for motor sport, and the English Football Association for football. This decision-making body makes rules that address how players or teams are recruited and allocated, the number of teams allowed in the competition, where the teams are located, the length of the playing season, the design of the fixtures, and admission charges. Such rules can help to ensure that no one team monopolises the best players, and that each team has a reasonable chance of winning. Other regulations set by the central body may even involve changing the rules of the game itself to make the sport more attractive to new markets or different forms of distribution (such as free-to-air or pay television). For example, the Atlanta Organising Committee for the Olympic Games in 1996 infamously decided to schedule the marathon in the hottest part of the day in order to maximise prime-time television viewing. The regulating body is usually able to enforce disciplinary action upon those who breach the regulations.

Second, sport regulators impose rules designed to minimise costs and maximise profits. For example, they enforce policies to restrict the ability of teams to bid for players, set limits on player salaries, and determine the distribution of shared revenues such as broadcasting rights. In principle, policies are designed to ensure that teams cannot only acquire their fair share of quality staff, coaches and players, but can also retain them.

Third, sport regulators aim to increase revenue through marketing efforts. They may try to expand the consumer base for their sporting product, improve the overall attractiveness of the product, or generally try to improve the image of the league in the community. The market, for example, could be expanded by admitting new teams to the league, extending the playing season, or playing games at different times of the week. Regulators may also spend money on improving the quality of the game through programs to develop player skills, or by upgrading venues to make them more fan-friendly, or safer for athletes. Governing sport bodies also use their market power as sole owners of the sport competition (or monopolists) to maximise broadcast and sponsorship rights fees by negotiating as a single entity rather than through individual teams.

> *Chapter principle 2.5*: Sport leagues and competitions implement policies to encourage competitive balance. Policies often include salary caps for players, rules about sharing revenues and regulations regarding how players are to be shared between teams.

Variable quality

Commercial businesses aim for predictability and certainty, especially when it comes to product quality. But predictability and certainty are not always valued in the sporting world, especially when it comes to the delivery of professional sport competitions. From a spectator's perspective the sport experience is better experienced when unpredictable. Sport events actually depend on that unpredictability in order to attract people to the game. When the results of games cannot be predicted, attendances at sporting contests are likely to be higher, as are the profits of leagues. However, the lack of predictability also leads to significant variability in the quality of sporting performances. Many factors can contribute to the variability of the sport product, including the weather, player injuries, the venue, the quality of the opponents, the closeness of the scores and even the size of the crowd. A cricket match can be exhilarating, boring or even frustrating, but fans still have to pay the same price. Sport marketers may attempt to overcome this by 'improving' the product in systematic ways, such as including a star player, offering premium seating or providing other forms of entertainment and attractive facilities. The uncertain nature of sport contests is just one element of a total experience, although it is an important element for financial success.

> *Chapter principle 2.6*: Unpredictability can be advantageous in the competitive sport product because it makes sport more attractive.

Product and brand loyalty

Strong loyalty to sport products and brands accompanies the emotional attachments that sport consumers develop for their favourite teams, events, players and equipment. A good test of loyalty for conventional products can be seen in whether consumers are prepared to keep purchasing the product even when the price of competing products falls. For the most part this occurs in sport as fans invest an enormous amount of time and energy in their favourite sport products, creating a lifetime bond. In fact, sport fans often see their team as an extension of themselves; a part of their self-identity.

When sport consumers passionately support a particular kind of sport, a specific competition or a specific team (or brand), a low cross elasticity of demand exists. This is an economic term that means it is difficult to substitute (or replace) one sport product for another. Most sport competitions have an inelastic demand and a high degree of product loyalty. Even if fans are unhappy about the result of a game, the winning margin or the standard of refereeing, it is unlikely that they would change their sporting preferences. If, for instance, a supporter's football team is playing away and the match is not televised, he or she would probably not go to a hockey or bocce game instead, regardless of whether the venue was attractive and the ticket was free. The situation is quite different for most other products. If a consumer bought a computer but felt unsatisfied with its quality, he or she would be likely to change brands or retail outlets next time. In team sports the substitution of products occurs infrequently, although it can be more common for sport products such as equipment.

It might seem that the low degree of product substitution in sport could only be an advantage to sport organisations. However, there are drawbacks. For example, it can be difficult for a new sport, team or brand to enter the marketplace and wrestle fans away from their existing loyalties. Another obstacle is that sport consumers maintain a reluctance to increase their sport watching as a result of reduced ticket prices, or increased personal income levels. This means that marketing efforts need to be innovative about how to attract and convert fans as some conventional marketing tactics are ineffective.

> *Chapter principle 2.7*: In competitive sport there is a low cross elasticity of demand where it is difficult to substitute (or replace) one sport league, team, brand or competition for another.

Identification

Some sport consumers identify so strongly with their sporting heroes that they seek to emulate them. Supporters may wear the same club 'uniforms', colours and sport clothing brands as their heroes. Many businesses such as sport equipment and clothing manufacturers have recognised the power of sporting identification, and regularly market their products through successful athletes. Of course, sport identification is the driving power behind sport sponsorship. By seeking an association with sport, sponsors try to claim some of the loyalty that fans possess for sports, teams and players. The issue of fan identification is discussed further in Chapter 3.

> *Chapter principle 2.8*: Product loyalty is strong due to the emotional attachments that sport consumers develop to sport products and brands.

Blind optimism

Despite their allegiance to tradition and history there are some situations where sport consumers and marketers have a high tolerance for change, particularly when they involve personnel (such as players and coaches) and competitive success. For example, even when a star player moves from one club to another, his or her supporters are likely to remain loyal to the original club. Usually, the emotional bond that joins fans to their clubs means that they will put up with countless changes to its personnel. This is an important variable for sport marketers to understand, since sport organisations rarely pass up the opportunity to trade players and remove coaching and support staff where it might lead to more competitive performance.

Chapter principle 2.9: Sport consumers identify with teams, clubs, brands and athletes, and see them as extensions of themselves.

Fixed supply schedules

A supply schedule refers to the ability of a business to change their production rates to meet the demand of consumers. Some businesses are able to increase their production level quickly in order to meet increased demand. However, sporting clubs have a fixed, or inflexible (inelastic) production capacity. They have what is known as a *fixed supply schedule*. It is worth noting that this is not the case for sales of clothing, equipment, memberships and memorabilia. But clubs and teams can only play a certain number of times during their season. If fans and members are unable to get into a venue, that revenue is lost forever. Although sport clubs and leagues may have a fixed supply schedule, it is possible to increase the number of consumers who watch. For example, the supply of a sport product can be increased by providing more seats, changing the venue, extending the playing season or even through new television, radio or Internet distribution.

Chapter principle 2.10: The competitive sport product is restricted by a fixed supply schedule making it difficult to change production rates in order to meet the demand of customers, but can be overcome through alternative distribution channels.

This chapter observed that sport requires professional marketing, but with an appreciation of the special features of the sport market. The financial and business sides of the sport product need to be balanced with an understanding of its emotional power. Sport is a business, but a special kind of business. It is important for sport marketers to understand the unique features of the sport market because they have an influence on the development of a marketing programme.

INTERACTIVE CASE

The following two websites discuss the factors that drive people to become sports *fans*, and thus consume the sports of sport-related products we were talking about above.

www.sportsbusinessdaily.com
(www.sportsbusinessdaily.com/Journal/Issues/2010/04/20100419/SBJ-In-Depth/What-Makes-Fans-Crazy-About-Sports.aspx)

www.sportsnetworker.com
(www.sportsnetworker.com/2012/02/15/the-psychology-of-sports-fans-what-makes-them-so-crazy/)

Questions

1   What are the five to ten most important motives for consuming sport products as a sports fan or sports spectator?
2   Can we distinguish between individual factors and social factors?
3   Is there an aesthetic factor? Please explain if there is.
4   Is there an entertainment factor?
5   What type of sports markets and sport products would best meet the desires and motives of sports fans?

Points of interest

The factors that motivate people to become fans, and to become spectators, are often going to be different from the factors that motivate people to participate in sport as active players. People will participate as players because they want to get fit, and keep their bodies in shape. They want to consume a 'physical activity experience'. Being a fan will not deliver these outcomes. Fans are more interested in consuming a 'sports watching experience', or maybe a 'sport entertainment experience'. But, when you think further on this matter, there are in fact some motivational overlaps. The main overlap is the social connectedness that comes from both playing sport and watching others play it. There is also the escape factor, which means both playing and watching provides a way of getting away from the stresses of life and throwing oneself into a world quite different from work or the family home. Some sports markets do this better than others, as we will see in the following chapters.

PRINCIPLES SUMMARY

- Chapter principle 2.1: Sport is a special form of business. A standard marketing approach does not always work in sport, so sport marketers must also understand the special features of the sport market.

- Chapter principle 2.2: Sport can elicit an emotional response in its consumers that is rarely found in other businesses. It can stimulate immense loyalty, but also strong attachments to nostalgia and club tradition.

- Chapter principle 2.3: Sport organisations measure their success both on and off the field of play. On-field success refers to achievement within sport competition. Off-field success refers to financial stability and profitability.

- Chapter principle 2.4: Sport organisations that compete in leagues and competitions rely on the health of their competitors for their own success. Sport consumers are more attracted to attend games where there is a balanced competition.

- Chapter principle 2.5: Sport leagues and competitions implement policies to encourage competitive balance. Policies often include salary caps for players, rules about sharing revenues and regulations regarding how players are to be shared between teams.

- Chapter principle 2.6: Unpredictability can be advantageous in the competitive sport product because it makes sport more attractive.

- Chapter principle 2.7: In competitive sport there is a low cross elasticity of demand where it is difficult to substitute (or replace) one sport league, team, brand or competition for another.

- Chapter principle 2.8: Product loyalty is strong due to the emotional attachments that sport consumers develop to sport products and brands.

- Chapter principle 2.9: Sport consumers identify with teams, clubs, brands and athletes and see them as extensions of themselves.

- Chapter principle 2.10: The competitive sport product is restricted by a fixed supply schedule making it difficult to change production rates in order to meet the demand of customers, but can be overcome through alternative distribution channels.

REVIEW QUESTIONS

1   What does it mean to say that sport is a special form of business?

2   In what ways can sport products be differentiated from other products?

3   Why is it important for sport competitions to have competitive balance?

4   What are some of the ways in which sport organisers can encourage competitive balance?

5   Why are some sport products unpredictable?

6   Explain why corporate sponsors want to be associated with sport.

7   What does it mean to say that sport has a low cross elasticity of demand where it is difficult to substitute (or replace) one sport league, team, brand or competition for another?

8   What are some of the ways in which sport organisations can get around the fixed supply schedules associated with sport competitions?

RELEVANT WEBSITES

www.pwc.com/en	PricewaterhouseCoopers
www.statista.com	Statista
www.atkearney.com.au	AT Kearney
www.plunkettresearch.com	Plunkett Research
www.abs.gov.au	Australian Bureau of Statistics
www.forbes.com	*Forbes* magazine
www.sportsbusinessdaily.com	*Sports Business Daily*
www.sportsnetworker.com	Sports Networker

FURTHER READING

Robinson, L. and Palmer, D. (2010). *Managing Voluntary Sport Organisations*. London: Routledge.

Wakeland, K. (2011). *Team Sports Marketing*. London: Routledge.

CHAPTER 3

Sport consumers

LEARNING OUTCOMES

At the end of this chapter, readers should be able to:

- identify the different motives consumers have for buying sport products and services
- explain the effects of each motive on sport consumption
- highlight the external factors that can influence the behaviour of sport consumers
- specify how the external factors can be influenced by sport marketers to change consumer attitudes and behaviours, and enhance product usage.

OVERVIEW

Sport consumers are driven by a range of aspirations, incentives, and benefits to join clubs, compete in tournaments, attend games, buy merchandise, and watch sport on television. This chapter explains the factors that motivate sports participants and fans, and provides advice on how to best communicate with consumers through marketing processes. It also distinguishes between two different categories of motivation, one of which is internal to the consumer, and one of which is external to the consumer. Both factors are important to understand since they can radically change the ways in which sport consumers might perceive the utility of a sports product, and can thus lead to quite different patterns of sport goods consumption.

BECOMING A CONSUMER

We are all consumers. We all have needs, wants and desires, and will do all that it takes to satisfy them. We also like to think that we are rational when making decisions to purchase goods and services, and acting out our consumption preferences. Economists make this assumption when they construct their models of consumer behaviour. They propose that consumers are continually seeking product information, and regularly weigh up the costs and benefits of buying one brand over another. And this is also the way we like to see ourselves. That is, we are ruggedly autonomous individuals, shrewd and street-smart, but also intellectually hard-headed with an innate ability to identify false claims, expose exaggerated proclamations, and pick out fictitious testimonials. However this myth was destroyed many years ago. In 1957 Vance Packard wrote *The Hidden Persuaders*, an exposé of the advertising industry. Packer claimed that advertisers, who preferred to snobbishly call themselves 'symbol manipulators' and 'motivation analysts', actually knew more about consumers than consumers knew about themselves. These symbol manipulators and motivation analysts did not share the economic viewpoint that we are all rational human beings in charge of our buying behaviour and consumption practices. Instead, as Packard noted, the advertisers viewed consumers in terms of day dreams, hidden yearnings, guilt complexes, irrational emotional blockages, and image loving, while susceptible to a confronting array of impulsive and compulsive decisions and behaviours. More than 50 years later, little has changed. Indeed consumption has now become an industry in itself. Consumption has gone beyond the purchase of goods and services to meet our daily needs. People now use consumption to create a lifestyle, and build an identity. In short, we are what we consume. Sport consumption is no exception.

SCOPE AND SCALE OF SPORT CONSUMPTION

Consumption takes place in markets, and sport consumption is no different. Sport markets, like all other markets, will function only if there are some people who are willing to sell goods and services, and other people who are prepared to buy those exact same goods. There are multitudes of sellers in sports markets, some of whom are intent on maximising profits, and others who are more interested in delivering something of value to members of their community. The Nike sportswear business wants to produce high quality shoes, clothing and related equipment, but it also aims to build its profits and increase its share price and net worth. The International Olympic Committee (IOC) is also a large and powerful global business, but its goal is not to maximise profits, instead seeking to build the Olympic movement, and deliver high quality sport competitions for the world's best athletes. Both Nike and the IOC operate in the supply side of different sports. One market is focused on sporting gear, while the other is more concerned with mega sport events.

Of course markets have another side, which is all about demand. Demand is crucial to the operation of markets, since without demand there will be no supply. Nike has become successful because it has convinced people that its sports gear delivers value, both functionally and symbolically. Its functional value is built on a foundation of comfort and durability, while its symbolic value arises from the belief that Nike's products provide social status. The IOC has become successful because people believe its biennial sport event delivers fans the highest quality athletic performance in an array of sports.

INTERACTIVE CASE

The website below contains a detailed analysis of professional sport in the United States. It was prepared by the PERFORM Consulting Group, Kantar Media Sports, and TV Sports Markets in 2013.

http://prod.talentleague.com
(http://prod.talentleague.com/wp-content/uploads/2013/09/Global_Sports_Media_report_2013.pdf)

This next website also contains an analysis of sport consumption in the United States. However this report focuses its attention on direct sport participation, which means it is mainly about people 'playing' different types of sports.

(www.physicalactivitycouncil.com)
www.physicalactivitycouncil.com/PDFs/2012PACReport.pdf

Questions

Based on your reading of these reports, how would you respond to the following questions?

1   How do consumers go about consuming professional sport in the United States? Do any of the figures surprise you?
2   How much time does the average sport fan in the US spend consuming sport?
3   Which particular group or cohort of sport fans has the highest level of consumption?
4   How important is consuming sport through an online source? Which is the most popular? Is it PC, mobile phone, or tablet?
5   What sports have the highest levels of consumption when it comes to playing?
6   What proportion of Americans consumes very little sport as players? Is it fair and reasonable to label these people as sedentary?
7   What are the main items of spending when it comes to the consumption of sport through playing it?
8   Does sport consumption around 'playing' fall away with age? Is the drop-off significant, and if it is, then how can it be explained?

Points of interest

Without consumers there is no sport. It becomes nothing more than an idea, an imaginative state, and an unrealised aspiration. It is not a practice, there is no material impact, and there will be no market. In reality, though, there are hundreds of millions of sports consumers around the world. Moreover, these sport consumers have a wide variety of sporting preferences they ultimately express as the desire to purchase a sporting good or service. One of the main ways of differentiating one type of sport consumption from another is to distinguish between participation in sport as players and athletes, and participating in sport as spectators, listeners, readers and viewers.

The reports confirm that consumers are the lifeblood of sport since they are prepared to pay suppliers to deliver them a sport good or sport experience. At the same time, sport consumers are not a homogeneous group. That is, they are really heterogeneous, which means they have different social backgrounds, life-course experiences, religious and cultural traditions, educational attainments, patterns of employment, dispositions, desires, aspirations and personalities. Consequently, no simple formula describes how and why sport consumers behave as they do. Take, for instance, the attitudes and behaviours of sport fans. Some fans may use teams and players to help them construct a sense of self and social identity, but others may only follow sport to fill in their spare time with a pleasurable, but often quite ephemeral form of entertainment. Sport consumers can be remarkably loyal, but they can also be fickle and critical. Consumers who play at sport can also be idiosyncratic. Some play on for years, but others drop out early. Some are forever updating their clothing and equipment, while others keep them until they no longer become usable. There is, as someone once said, no accounting for taste.

Sport consumers thus exhibit an enormous variety of behaviours. Some of it is easily explainable, such as when people join an exercise class to keep fit. This is a logical response to concerns that they are gaining weight rapidly, and want to maintain a healthy lifestyle. Some sport consumption is less easily explainable, however. For instance it is difficult to understand what motivates middle aged men to spend thousands of dollars on a state-of-the-art-racing cycle when all they intend to do is engage in weekend riding along quiet countryside roads. Many weekend golfers also get caught up in the assumption that the more expensive the equipment, the greater the likelihood of playing well. In order to better understand what motivates sport consumers, a useful starting point is to identify the different kinds of sport consumers, and to highlight the motives that drive them to buy.

CATEGORIES OF SPORT CONSUMERS

There are numerous ways of defining sport consumers, most of which revolve around identifying different kinds of sport products or services. However, the first point to make is that there is a difference between sport consumers and sport stakeholders. A consumer is an individual or group who uses a sport or sport-related product or service in exchange for a direct (such as cash to buy a ticket to a game) or indirect (such as purchasing a television in which sport is one form of entertainment) payment. A stakeholder is an individual or group who has an interest or agenda in a sport product or service. For example, the government and corporate sponsors are stakeholders in that they have an interest in sport products and services, but they are not consumers. Sport consumers are the end-users. Sport consumers can be differentiated into four categories.

First are *sporting goods consumers*. These retail consumers buy sport products including, for example, equipment, apparel, books, magazines, nutritional and health supplements, games, merchandise, memorabilia and licensed products. A sporting goods consumer is anyone who purchases a physical product that has a sport-related aspect or purpose. This may range from the direct, such as a tennis racquet, to the indirect, such as a computer or console game.

Second are *sport services consumers*. These consumers utilise a sport-related service or experience excluding viewing or participating in sport directly. Sport-related services include education, gambling, specialised coaching, medical services and recreational and health activities such as those offered by pools, gymnasiums and leisure centres.

Third are *sport participants and volunteers*. These consumers are actively engaged in sport as participants or in unpaid organisational and support roles. This includes all participants in school, recreational and organised club sport.

Fourth are *sport supporters, spectators and fans*. These consumers take an active interest in the performance of sport mainly, but not confined to, the elite or professional level. The activities of sport supporters, spectators and fans include attendance at live sport, or viewing sport on television, via the Internet, or on DVD. These sport consumers are highly complex because they may use sport products and services in ways that other, less intense consumers do not. For example, fans may actively engage in online chat rooms or fantasy league games about sport. In some instances, particularly committed fans may become 'fanatical' when their behaviour and level of engagement steps outside of normal social expectations. Of course, most sport participants and volunteers are sport fans as well, and also utilise different kinds of sporting goods and services. For this reason, it is best to assume that sport consumer motivations are multi-variable and complex. It is easier to categorise kinds of sport consumption than kinds of sport consumers. Furthermore, based on these categories of consumption, it is clear that the motives of sport supporters, spectators and fans are the most complex, and need to be explored further.

> *Chapter principle 3.1*: A sport consumer is an individual who purchases sporting goods, uses sport services, participates or volunteers in sport and/or follows sport as a spectator or fan.

SPORT CONSUMER MOTIVES

Even though the topic of sport consumer motives can be complex, it is pivotal to understanding sport marketing in the current, competitive environment. Sport marketers need to appreciate the many reasons why consumers are motivated to buy sport-related products and services. Without this knowledge, tailoring products to consumers' needs becomes difficult. The more a marketer understands about sport consumers, the easier it is for them to design enticing marketing.

Sport consumers attend games, follow clubs and teams, and buy products for a multitude of reasons. As a result, we may look at sport consumer behaviour from a range of perspectives. One common approach in business, but typically outside of a marketing orientation, is to consider sport consumption behaviour from an *economic* viewpoint. This view suggests that people behave rationally and use sport products and services that meet their quality and value needs. The problem with this view, of course, is that sport consumers do not necessarily behave in rational ways because they have an emotional connection to the sport products they consume. As noted previously, considering consumer behaviour from a *psychological* and *social* point of view can prove rewarding. A psychological perspective suggests that people's attitudes and motivations (or desires) will predict what they buy. A social perspective suggests that people may be influenced by their social circumstances. The forthcoming section examines sport consumer behaviour mainly from a psychological and social perspective. It also focuses on the fourth group of consumers identified in the previous section because their consumption decisions are the most complex and furthest removed from rational expectations based on economic factors. This group of sport supporters, spectators and fans will simply be referred to as sport fans.

BECOMING A SPORT FAN

There are many possible benefits that sport fans may experience through watching, talking, reading and thinking about sport. This section considers what it is about sport that has captured the attention and passion of so many people for so long. There has been a considerable amount of research examining the psychological and social reasons (often called *psycho-social* motivations) why sport fans consume sport products. Here, the reasons are summarised into three different groups of motives: (1) psychological motives, (2) socio-cultural (social and cultural) motives, and (3) self-concept motives.

> *Chapter principle 3.2*: Sport fan motives for consuming sport products and services can be summarised into three categories: (1) psychological motives, (2) socio-cultural motives, and (3) self-concept motives.

Psychological motives

The psychological reasons (or motives) that drive sport fans to consume sport products and services are connected to the interest and enjoyment that they derive from sport. Sport can fulfil a number of emotional and intellectual needs for the sport consumer. For example, sport can be stimulating, can help to release stress, can be an escape, and can provide entertainment and visual pleasure. In other words, sport can stimulate positive feelings and thoughts for the sport consumer. Each one of these motives is explained further next.

Stimulation

Sport can be a stimulating, psychologically energising activity. It generates excitement and even anxiety, both of which can encourage the body to produce adrenaline. It also allows fans to shout and vent aggression in a socially acceptable way and to experience intense sensory stimulation.

Escape

The stimulation provided by sport can provide consumers with a distraction from the ordinary routine of everyday life. The collisions, body contact and action offered by many sports can attract fans who want to escape from their highly organised and regulated work environments into a world of passion, spontaneity and uncertainty. After all, sport gives spectators an acceptable place to shout, scream and sing or dance, where their normal work or family roles might not. Sport can also provide a release and a diversion from a stressful lifestyle. For many fans, sport watching is the ultimate 'escape experience'.

Aesthetic (visual) pleasure

Sport watching offers aesthetic (or visual) pleasure to fans. Sport fans are often prepared to pay to witness excellence, such as skilful play or memorable moments. In some sports (although not all) fans may also be attracted by the 'sex appeal' of the participants; bikini-clad beach volleyball players are an obvious example of this, as are the physique-hugging Lycra uniforms worn by track and field athletes.

Drama and entertainment

Sport can provide entertainment and drama. Through watching an engaging contest, fans can be part of a theatrical experience. The scale of many sporting venues, the sight of thousands of fans in club colours, and the use of lively half-time entertainment all enhance sport's dramatic qualities. Some events, such as horse racing for example, have blended sport performance with fashion, theatre and a carnival feel to maximise the dramatic atmosphere.

> *Chapter principle 3.3*: Psychological motives for sport fans include the opportunity for stimulation, escape, aesthetic pleasure and a sense of dramatic entertainment.

Socio-cultural motives

In addition to the psychological interest and pleasure that sport fans receive from consuming sport, they may also experience social and cultural benefits. Sport encourages fans to gather into groups, such as families, fellow team supporters, and state and national 'cheer' squads. It provides fans with a social gathering place, as well as activities to share and common topics to talk about.

Family and social interaction

Sporting events and activities provide an opportunity for families and friends to spend time together in an organised and pleasurable way. A sport experience can help sport fans fulfil family needs, or spend time with friends. It is important for sport marketers to realise that if a spectator is motivated to attend a match because of these reasons, then the type of game they attend or the teams that are playing may be irrelevant. Alternative activities may easily substitute for the sport experience, and still allow the consumer to meet their family and social needs.

Cultural connections

Fans use sport as a form of cultural connection and celebration. Sport can help fans connect to their national, racial or ethnic culture, or even a subculture that they belong to (a social group that shares beliefs and behaviours). Spectators may like to attend games that are relevant to their heritage, or where the majority of athletes are from ethnic or racial groups they identify with. Sport can also provide meaningful symbols, rituals and 'mythical images'. The Olympic Games, for example, use a number of important rituals and symbols, such as the lighting of the flame, the Olympic oath and the closing ceremony, all of which have special meaning to participants and spectators. For sporting clubs, the theme song, club colours, insignia and mottos fulfil the same function by providing powerful images representing belonging to the group. Watching, reading and talking about sport can create a feeling of familiarity that comes from participating in a seasonal ritual. There are also weekly cycles that include the dramatic match, the post-game argument, the mid-week review, and the pre-match media analysis, which are repeated reliably from season to season.

Economic benefit

Another kind of socio-cultural benefit for sport fans is the possibility of gaining money through gambling on sport. This is a potential advantage that is not part of the game itself, but one of the 'extras', or an external benefit that needs a social and cultural system to operate.

> *Chapter principle* 3.4: Socio-cultural motives for sport fans include the opportunity for family and social interaction, cultural connections, and even economic benefit.

Self-concept motives

While psychological and socio-cultural motives help describe why a fan is attracted to sport, it is clear that not all fans experience the same degree or strength of identification. The degree to which a fan identifies with a team is an important issue, since it may predict their loyalty. It is therefore useful to differentiate between psychological and self-concept motives, as the former describes attraction, and the latter strength of sport identification. Psychological motives are internal to individuals whereas belonging motives are a function of a sport consumer's interaction with sport. Fans with a stronger identification have sport more deeply embedded in their self-concept. A fan's identification with a team could be motivated by a need to belong to a group or a tribe, or by a desire for vicarious achievement.

Belonging and group affiliation

Sport consumers may feel a need to belong to a group. They may also be motivated to develop a sense of identity that is connected to the group, or to identify with something bigger than themselves. These fans want to feel part of a tightly bound community that shares a common interest. They may also develop a sense of personal identity partly through a connection to teams and athletes. If a sport fan develops a strong feeling of connection to a successful team or player, they may use that success to pretend that they too are successful; they share the warm after-glow of victory. It is important to note, however, that the depth of identification fans possess can vary significantly. On the one hand, there may be 'fair-weather' fans whose attendance at events will match team success. On the other hand, there are the passionate supporters who will remain loyal to their favourite teams and clubs even when the teams are performing poorly.

Tribal connections

Sport fandom can also be used to recreate ancient ceremonies and primitive social rituals. For example, team sports such as football provide strong tribal connections, with athletes acting as the tribal heroes, and rituals such as pre- and post-game ceremonies. The fans themselves are the tribal followers who have conflicts with other tribes (other team's fans) and show their tribal colours and loyalty by wearing club colours. Of course, there are also tribal chants and team songs that help to bind the fans together and to intimidate rival tribes.

Vicarious achievement

Sport fans can develop a psychological attachment to sports, teams and players. This connection can assist fans to develop a feeling of being strong, important and successful. The term vicarious achievement refers to a sense of accomplishment that is felt second hand, through the success of someone else. Some fans may experience an increase in self-esteem when their team is winning. Others may feel a sense of confidence and skilfulness by learning team statistics and club history. Given that sport fans feel successful when their team is successful, the reverse occurs when they must deal with the disappointment of scandals and poor team performances. In these situations fans may be a little less eager to publicly announce their support of the team, and they might even downplay the failure of the team. Fans can compensate for a team's poor performance by developing strong feelings of closeness with fellow fans, being critical of other successful teams, voicing criticism of umpiring or refereeing decisions, or by being blindly optimistic that things will get better.

> *Chapter principle 3.5*: Self-concept motives for sport fans include the opportunity for belonging and group affiliation, tribal connections and vicarious achievement.

INTERACTIVE CASE

Sport watching has always had a tribal element to it. Over recent years it has taken on another dimension. View the following sport fan websites to get a clearer picture of what is happening:

The Fanatics website: www.thefanatics.com
www.thefanatics.com and www.thefanatics.com/gallery.php

The Fans Voice website: www.fansvoice.com
Look at the 'Sports Fan Bill of Rights' page.

Questions

1   What is the Fanatics, and what is the overall purpose of this 'collective'?
2   What might motivate a sports follower to join the Fanatics collective?
3   What might the Fanatics add to the tone and flavour of a sport event?
4   How might the Fanatics motivate players and teams to enhance their performance?
5   What is the Fans Voice all about?
6   What do you think of the Fans Voice Bill of Rights?
7   Is there much evidence to confirm the Fans Voice aims have been achieved?
8   What does the current status of the Fans Voice website say about success in getting others on board?

Points of interest

The Fanatics began in 1997 as a loose collective of like-minded sports fans who thought it would be a good idea to form an organised, passionate and patriotic support group that would follow Australian sports teams around the world. Its main role is to organise international travel and group seating for like-minded fans. It also provides a focal point for fan support, and is thus able to orchestrate a collective support-base at many events and tournaments. The Fanatics is still going strong, but tends to be the subject of criticism because its members are viewed as disruptive and unruly. They are also often accused of painting a very poor image of sports followers, and of perpetuating a stereotype of fans as loud, crass, short on civility and subtlety, and big on belligerence.

INFLUENCES ON SPORT CONSUMER MOTIVES

The motives just described help to explain why a fan may be driven to consume sport. But it is clear that not all sport fans will be motivated by the same reasons. Some may be motivated by a desire for entertainment while others may be motivated by deep feelings of connection to a group.

Research on sport consumer behaviour has revealed some of the variables that influence the motives that fans hold. This research indicates that a sport fan's reasons for buying a sport product may be affected by demographic variables, or their age, education, income, gender and race. For example, older fans are less likely to be motivated towards sport through the desire to belong to a group than younger fans. Fans with higher levels of education are less likely to be motivated for economic gain, bolstering self-esteem, stimulation or group affiliation.

Other research suggests that males and females may be motivated to consume sport for different reasons. Males, for example, are more likely to be motivated by economic factors than females, as well as for reasons of escapism, psychological stimulation, aesthetic pleasure and self-esteem. Females, however, are more strongly motivated to consume sport for family and social reasons.

While research into these kinds of factors can be informative, as a sport marketer it is important to remember that not all research provides the same result. For example, not all researchers agree that gender makes a significant difference to fan motivation. In addition, some researchers have found that gender differences may be more pronounced in some cultures or racial groups than others. There may also be other reasons to think carefully about the results of research. After all, it is likely that the sport fans targeted in one research study are different to those that have been studied in others.

The key issue to remember is that different sport fans will be motivated to consume sport for different reasons. Some reasons for consuming sport will lead to greater loyalty than others. Self-concept motives in particular may stimulate stronger feelings of allegiance. Also, fans' reasons for buying a sport product may be affected by their age, education, income, gender and race, although there is enough evidence to suggest that these demographic variables do not influence motivation in a uniform way. One approach to assist in understanding sport fans better is to examine and classify their behaviour rather than their motivations. This is easier because behaviour is tangible and measurable irrespective of the motivation that stimulated it.

> *Chapter principle 3.6*: Fan motives for consuming sport are affected by their age, education, income, gender and race, but these demographic variables do not always influence motivation in a uniform or predictable way.

UNDERSTANDING SPECTATOR BEHAVIOUR

Some fans watch sport for no other reason than to see their favourite team contest the game. These *passionate partisans* are loyal to their team and get despondent when their team loses and elated when it wins, and are prepared to incur inconvenience (a wet day, or a long, slow trip to the stadium) to savour the fruits of success. They form the hard-core support base of sport, and their moods and identities are bound up with the successes and failures of their favourite teams. Such fans are heavy purchasers of memorabilia and club merchandise and will be great defenders of club history and traditions. They also possess a significant personal investment in their preferred club and its season-to-season performance.

There are also many sport fans who are more interested in supporting a winning team than blindly following their team through 'thick and thin'. These *champ followers* share some of the emotional highs and lows of the passionate partisan, but are less reliable and fanatical. The champ follower's allegiance will change according to whatever team happens to be the top performer. Alternatively, champ followers often remain hidden from public view (are non-attendees) until their favourite team starts winning and they become vocal and active supporters, but drop off when their team begins to lose again.

A third category is the *reclusive partisan*, whose interest in the game and commitment to the team is strong, but who attends infrequently. The reclusive partisan is opinionated, and apparently loyal to his or her team, and could become a passionate partisan again if others can influence them or through media-saturation coverage of the event.

The common motive shared by each of the above categories is fans' desires to see their team win. Their dominant concern is not whether it is likely to be a close contest or whether it will be skilful, dramatic or entertaining, but the likelihood of success. They are attracted to team performance or team quality. Such sport fans are parochial.

There are at the same time many sport fans who, while notionally committed to a particular team, are more interested in the game or sport itself and attend more frequently than the reclusive partisan, but less frequently than the passionate partisan. These fans may be considered *theatregoers*. The theatregoer is motivated to seek entertainment through a pleasurable experience. However, entertainment from this viewpoint involves more than drama and half-time shows. It also includes comfortable and proximate viewing conditions, easy access, the availability of complimentary services, a close contest, and the participation of star performers. The theatregoer is attracted to comfort, enjoyment, excitement, sensory stimulation and uncertainty of outcome. Since their team and game loyalty initially begins at a low level, most theatregoers will attend less frequently than passionate partisans unless the likelihood of exciting and pleasurable contests continues throughout the season. At the same time, a few theatregoers will put such high value on their sporting experiences that they will become regular patrons. In this respect, theatregoers may be described as either *casual* or *committed*.

Like the theatregoer, the *aficionado* will be attracted to games that are expected to be exciting, and contain star performers. However, unlike most theatregoers, aficionados attend frequently because of their strong attachment to the structure of the game and its athletic practices. They will attend games that provide high skill levels, tactical complexity and aesthetic pleasure, even if they are likely to be one sided or unexciting. Some aficionados would call themselves purists because they would attend their match of the day, which may or may not include the top performing teams. The aficionado will also be attracted to a quality venue since it will accentuate a quality performance. Both the aficionado and the theatregoer will show only moderate concern about who wins or loses. Their dominant concern is game performance or game quality, and not the likely success or failure of a particular team.

While each of the fan categories has an interest in the game or sport, there are significant differences in the ways in which their interest is expressed. Different incentives will activate different segments. A change to the structure or conduct of the competition that attracts more of one type of fan may be resisted by another type. For example, while theatregoers are likely to attend more games where the stadiums are comfortable, games are expected to be close and competitive, and where complimentary entertainment is provided, passionate partisans and champ followers may think that such changes undermine the essential nature and traditions of the game, and lessen the expectation of success. Similarly, while theatregoers may be excited about the sensory delights that they see arising from new rules designed to speed up the game, an expanded league, or the relocation of one team to another city, passionate and reclusive partisans are likely to view such adjustments as treachery, and in extreme cases sever their relationship with their club. It should be noted that all fans could vary according to their personal profile and depending on the sport in question. Thus, one individual may be a casual theatregoer when it comes to cricket, but a passionate partisan when observing volleyball. Table 3.1 summarises the five categories of spectators, their motivations and behaviour.

TABLE 3.1 Sport fan categories

Type of spectator	Motivation	Behaviour
Aficionado	Seeks quality performance	• Loyal to game rather than team, although will usually have a preferred team • Attends on regular basis • Puts emphasis on aesthetic or skill dimension
Theatregoer (casual and committed)	Seeks entertainment, close contest	• Only moderate loyalty to team • Frequent losses create lack of interest only in team • May attend other games
Passionate partisan	Wants team to win	• Loyal to team • Short-term loyalty undiminished by frequent losses • Strongly identifies with, and responds to, team's success and failure
Champ follower	Wants team to win	• Short-term loyalty • Loyalty a function of team success. Expects individual or team to dominate otherwise supports another team or spends time elsewhere
Reclusive partisan	Wants team to win	• Loyalty not always translated into attendance • Strong identification but provides latent support only

MARKETING IMPLICATIONS

For the sport marketer, the previous categories highlight the different segments that comprise the sport fan market. In particular, they reinforce the importance of supporting the passionate partisan and the aficionado. However, it is clear from the categories that the motivations of partisans and aficionados are quite different. The categories also demonstrate the potential for increased attendances provided by the theatregoer, champ follower and reclusive partisan. In each case, the provision of appropriate incentives may be used to generate greater frequency of attendance. The theatregoer would be attracted to comfortable seating arrangements, colour and drama, the availability of appropriate food and drink, and the expectation of an exciting contest, whereas the reclusive partisan and champ followers would be most attracted to games in which their teams had a good probability of winning and were in the championship race. For champ followers to maintain interest, in contrast to passionate partisans, it would be necessary to have a competition where playing talent was distributed equally among the teams, and where the championship race was close for most of the season. Reclusive partisans would also be influenced by the social context in which the sport operates, and a strong media campaign emphasising the cultural significance and fashionability of the event may be effective in this case.

Sport marketers are faced with the difficult task of ensuring that the sport product provides for good watching conditions, a balanced competition, uncertainty of game and seasonal outcome (exciting high-quality games played in attractive surroundings), and that the loyalty of partisan fans is maintained (by ensuring the ongoing viability of teams within strategically positioned regions and districts that fans can use to establish a sense of identity and community). While changes to the structure of a sport competition (such as new recruiting laws, the relocation of teams or the merger of clubs) are likely to weaken the loyalty of partisan supporters, it must be weighed against the attraction that such changes have for the other spectator categories, particularly the theatregoers.

Chapter principle 3.7: Sport fans can be classified according to the sources and dimensions of their attraction to the sport, and their frequency of attendance.

EXTERNAL FACTORS THAT INFLUENCE SPORT CONSUMPTION

Even when fans are strongly connected to their team or club, they will not always regularly attend games or watch them on television. The reasons for attending matches and events may also be influenced by other factors, such as the type of sport involved, the balance of the competition, the uncertainty of outcome and the likelihood of a certain team winning. Other important factors include the venue and facilities, weather conditions, prices, income levels, special experiences, promotional factors, and the availability of alternative activities. Each of these factors will be briefly examined along with its potential influence on sport fan behaviour.

Type of sport

Different sports attract different types of fans, and different fans are motivated by different factors. The type of sport that a fan follows reveals something about his or her motivations. Fans of individual sports such as tennis and motor racing are more likely to be motivated by an interest in particular athletes, compared with fans of team sports such as football, soccer and volleyball who are more likely to be motivated by a sense of personal belonging to a team. In addition, fans who prefer non-aggressive sports such as baseball are more likely to be motivated by aesthetic concerns than fans of aggressive sports such as American football and boxing who are more interested in vicarious escapism.

Balance and uncertainty

Some fans will be influenced by the anticipated closeness of the competition. More fans will attend games when they expect a close contest, which will be affected by the quality of the opposing team or athletes. Closer contests tend to be expected later in the season or event when semi-finals and finals are played. Generally, the closer the expected result of the match, the more attractive a game will be to fans. When fans are uncertain about who might win, they are likely to be more enthusiastic about attending, and tend to have more intense experiences when they do.

The likelihood of winning

Although some fans appreciate a close contest, others are preoccupied with winning. Since fans can receive a sense of personal satisfaction in identifying with a winning team, they will attend or watch games more frequently if they believe their team has a strong chance of winning. In contrast, a team that consistently loses will have difficulty attracting a large following. In general, winning teams and athletes will attract more spectators than losing teams and athletes. There are some instances, however, where fans enjoy watching teams that they dislike lose.

The venue

Sport venue features and facilities can have a strong impact on a fan's decision to attend a sport event. A facility will attract fans if it is able to provide an attractive setting, a convenient layout, good signage, a visually appealing scoreboard, comfort, a better view of the contest and easy accessibility. Parking, the quality of food and beverages, childcare facilities and other entertainment options can also have an effect on a fan's decision to attend. The expectation of a large crowd can also be a motivating factor.

Weather

The weather can affect match attendances by influencing both the conditions under which fans watch the game, and the quality of the game itself. A waterlogged ground will not only inconvenience many fans, but may also produce slow-moving and boring games. This has encouraged many venues in rain-prone cities to construct retractable roofs or provide undercover seating. However, good weather may also be a problem if it means that people may be attracted to alternative leisure activities. For example, a temperate climate and close proximity to water-based activities may lure fans away from sport.

INTERACTIVE CASE

In general, sport consumers are attracted to products that deliver positive and enjoyable experiences. Poor weather conditions will nearly always make an outdoor sport even less attractive, even where a close and exciting contest is anticipated – hence the construction of stadia with retractable or permanent roofs. Log on to the following website to look at the biggest stadium in the world with a retractable roof.

www.millenniumstadium.com

Questions

1 Cardiff is in the heart of Wales, which is part of the British Isles. Why have a stadium with a retractable roof in Cardiff?
2 What sports are the main sports played at the Cardiff Millennium Stadium?
3 What makes an enclosed-roof sports game more satisfying than a no-roof game?
4 Under what conditions might a no-roof game be more satisfying than an enclosed-roof game?
5 What design features in the stadium are likely to enhance the sport fan experience?

Points of interest

The Millennium Stadium opened its gates in 1999. It replaced the National Stadium at Cardiff Arms Park, which was built in 1962 but by the early 1990s it was clear that its best days were behind it. The standing room areas had become decrepit, sight lines were poor, safety and security standards were frighteningly low, and the venue in general was becoming increasingly costly to maintain. Funds were secured from the National Lottery endowment, and a five star UEFA rated facility was constructed. It now hosts a range of elite sport events – with an emphasis on rugby and football – as well as motorcycle racing. It delivers spectators a quality experience, and offers a prime example of how venues can be used to successfully market sport events.

Price

To some extent admission prices to sport events can have a predictable effect. While admission prices are typically fixed during the regular season, between seasons and during finals they can change significantly, impacting on a fan's decision to attend. Broadly speaking an increase in admission prices will lead to a reduction in crowd numbers. However, some evidence suggests that price increases have only a minor influence because sport fans are unusually loyal consumers. This relates to the point made earlier that sport has a low cross elasticity of demand. Sport fans may be unlikely to substitute one sport league, team or competition for another, even if the price of their preferred competition rises.

Income levels

The income levels of fans can have a direct effect on what kind of leisure they prefer. As the income of fans rises, there is often a decrease in match or event attendances. More income usually means people have more choices to participate in alternative leisure activities, such as travel, restaurants and the theatre.

Special experiences

Special experiences will generally gain the attention of fans. The experience may involve the participation of a star player or personality, or the likelihood of a record-breaking performance. It may also involve the expectation of a dramatic or even violent encounter, or the anticipation of highly skilled and aesthetically pleasing play. These experiences can give sport fans a feeling that they are getting value for money. Special experiences can also include the availability of reserved seating, access to a private box, and the opportunity to meet a celebrity. The contest itself is just part of the total package.

Promotional factors

Promotional strategies, particularly when accompanied by admission concessions, sales vouchers and merchandising discounts, are important influences on fans' decisions to attend sport. Advertising, direct mail outs, give-away prizes, the promotion of upcoming games, entertainment and the provision of premium seating can all increase crowd sizes.

Alternative activities

The availability of alternative activities will also influence sport fan decisions. While this factor is unlikely to explain week-to-week variations in attendances, it can explain a decline in attendance over a longer period of time. Fans have become increasingly mobile and are able to choose between a huge number of leisure and entertainment alternatives. In addition, home entertainment options such as computers, game consoles and pay television are the biggest threats to live sport. The choice between competing leisure activities has never been more expansive.

> *Chapter principle 3.8*: Fans' decisions to attend or view sport may be influenced by external factors, such as the type of sport involved, the balance of the competition, how uncertain the outcome is, the likelihood of their team winning, the venue and facilities, weather conditions, prices, personal income levels, special experiences that are being offered, promotional factors and the availability of alternative activities.

INTERACTIVE CASE

The Barmy Army has become a permanent feature of international cricket matches between England and Australia. For more details go the following website.

www.barmyarmy.com

English sports fans have a reputation for being actively engaged in the games they watch. They have a colourful history of collective chanting, cheering, singing and scarf waving. In many instances they become an integral part of the event. The ways in which Liverpool FC fans set the tone for what is to come provides a case in point. Sometimes English football fans become too involved. Some male fans in particular like to ritualistically get drunk, abuse anyone in sight, release flares into the crowd, and fight opposition supporters. They add sound, movement and colour, but most of it is ugly. They are generally known as 'football hooligans'.

English cricket also has its fair share of supporter and fan collectives. The Barmy Army is a good example. It all started during the 1994–95 Ashes series. The English Cricket team was not achieving great success against Australia, but they had a loyal group and highly visible fans who attracted a significant amount of media attention. The Australian media labelled this lively group England's Barmy Army. The group became so popular that it became a registered trademark in late 1995.

The Barmy Army entourage comprises a colourful ensemble of fanatical cricket supporters who liven up the game with their songs, merchandise and banter, and who are prepared to travel to all of England's overseas matches in support of their team. Like all supporter groups, they have created occasional antagonism. This is to be expected since the combination of a large gathering of sport fans and the over-abundance of alcohol encourages critics of sport to focus on the negative side of fandom. The passionate vocal support can be considered intimidating and disruptive behaviour that resembles a kind of mob mentality. A large group of sport fans, dominated by males, in a stadium environment, and projecting insults at opposition supporters can quickly diminish the spectator experience to something approaching terrifying.

However, the Barmy Army has tried to project a different identity. Regardless of race, age or gender, any fan of English cricket can be a part of the Barmy Army. Although there is no official membership scheme, a mailing list of 25,000 subscribers reveals strong interest levels. Barmy Army marketing focuses on recruiting people by emphasising the fun of being involved, the social connectivity, their vibrancy and colour, and most vividly of all, the cleverness and catchiness of their songs and chants.

Barmy Army emblazed cricket merchandise has become a successful business venture and the group has enhanced their exposure with guest appearances on television. These entrepreneurial activities have been criticised, but they provide a unifying influence on fans. On balance, the Barmy Army has added an attractive dimension to the game. Cricket is a commercialised commodity and its coverage on television focuses not only on the game, but also on the overall atmosphere.

Broadcasters can easily identify the animated Barmy Army, and the guaranteed attention provides an attractive location for perimeter advertisers.

Realising the potential to attract media attention, the Barmy Army has progressed beyond rigid commercial interests, and has assumed a benevolent persona, demonstrating social sensitivity through charity work. One of its best-known acts of charity was to support the victims of Pakistan's earthquake in 2005. Operating through the Islamic Relief Organisation, the Barmy Army has also played in charity matches and used the funds from shirt sales to support those in need. In the United Kingdom, they donated 6,000 Barmy Army bottles of water during the Leukaemia Research Fund's fun run. They also collected funds for tsunami victims at the Boxing Day test in South Africa in 2004.

Questions

1   What is the Barmy Army and what is its overall purpose?
2   What led to the formation of the Barmy Army?
3   What makes the Barmy Amy so idiosyncratic?
4   Does the Barmy Army enhance or detract from the sport consumer's experience?
5   How do the Barmy Army 'performances' compare with the Fanatics 'displays'?
6   Could sport do with more Barmy Army-styled fan collectives?

Points of interest

The Barmy Army has become an integral part of England–Australia cricket matches. It has become part of the product offering, if you like. It is now so successful and well known that it can attract its own sponsorship. The Barmy Army has also become a social entrepreneur by getting involved in philanthropic causes. Although some of its behaviour will offend some fans, the Barmy Army has created its own style of fandom that is highly appealing. The Barmy Army has subsequently become a permanent fixture of the international cricket scene, and is now part of the cricket experience.

PRINCIPLES SUMMARY

- Chapter principle 3.1: A sport consumer is an individual who purchases sporting goods, uses sport services, participates or volunteers in sport and/or follows sport as a spectator or fan.

- Chapter principle 3.2: Sport fan motives for consuming sport products and services can be summarised into three categories: (1) psychological motives, (2) socio-cultural motives, and (3) self-concept motives.

- Chapter principle 3.3: Psychological motives for sport fans include the opportunity for stimulation, escape, aesthetic pleasure, and a sense of dramatic entertainment.

- Chapter principle 3.4: Socio-cultural motives for sport fans include the opportunity for family and social interaction, cultural connections, and even economic benefit.

- Chapter principle 3.5: Self-concept motives for sport fans include the opportunity for belonging and group affiliation, tribal connections, and vicarious achievement.

- Chapter principle 3.6: Fan motives for consuming sport are affected by their age, education, income, gender and race, but these demographic variables do not always influence motivation in a uniform or predictable way.

- Chapter principle 3.7: Sport fans can be classified according to the sources and dimensions of their attraction to the sport, and their frequency of attendance.

- Chapter principle 3.8: Fans' decisions to attend or view sport may be influenced by external factors, such as the type of sport involved, the balance of the competition, how uncertain the outcome is, the likelihood of their team winning, the venue and facilities, weather conditions, prices, personal income levels, special experiences that are being offered, promotional factors and the availability of alternative activities.

REVIEW QUESTIONS

1 Identify and describe the different kinds of sport consumers.
2 Define and distinguish between (1) psychological motives, (2) socio-cultural motives, and (3) self-concept motives.
3 Choose one variable from age, education, income, gender or race, and speculate on how it might influence sport consumption.
4 Why are sport fans often distinguished on the basis of their consumption behaviour?
5 List the five different types of sport fans and provide a brief comment on the best way to market sport to each.
6 What is the difference between an internal factor and an external factor when it comes to their influence on sport consumption?

RELEVANT WEBSITES

http://prod.talentleague.com   Talent League
www.physicalactivitycouncil.com   Physical Activity Council

www.thefanatics.com	The Fanatics
www.millenniumstadium.com	Millennium Stadium
www.barmyarmy.com	Barmy Army

FURTHER READING

Earnheardt, A.C., Haridakis, P. and Hugenberg, B. (2013). *Sports Fans, Identity, and Socialization: Exploring the Fandemonium*. New York: Lexington Books.

Simons, E. (2013). *The Secret Life of Sports Fans: The Science of Sports Obsession*. New York: Overlook Press.

CHAPTER 4

Sport marketing opportunities

LEARNING OUTCOMES

At the end of this chapter, readers should be able to:

- identify the key marketing activities required to identify sport marketing opportunities
- explain the elements and purpose of a SWOT analysis
- conduct a macro and micro environmental analysis
- describe the process and importance of a competitor analysis
- identify some of the introductory issues associated with market research, including its application and importance to identifying marketing opportunities.

OVERVIEW

This chapter examines the ways in which sport marketing opportunities can be identified and exploited. This will be done by constructing a Sport Marketing Framework. The Sport Marketing Framework begins by identifying marketing opportunities and then proceeds to developing a strategic marketing strategy that involves planning the sport marketing mix, and implementing and controlling the sport marketing strategy. This chapter provides detailed guidance for undertaking the first stage of the Framework: identifying sport marketing opportunities. Included are details on the three parts of stage one: (a) analyse internal and external environments; (b) analyse organisation; and (c) analyse market and consumers.

THE SPORT MARKETING FRAMEWORK

The Sport Marketing Framework describes the stages and activities of sport marketing. It is the backbone of all sport marketing efforts. The Sport Marketing Framework is made up of four stages and is illustrated in Figure 4.1, with stage 1 of the process, 'Identify Sport Marketing Opportunities', highlighted. Stage 1 involves three parts. First is the analysis of

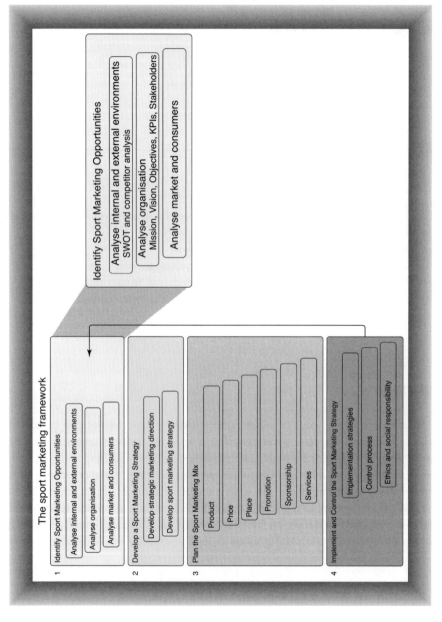

FIGURE 4.1 Identify sport marketing opportunities

conditions in the external marketplace (such as competitors' activities, technology, legal restrictions and the economic climate) as well as the internal environment of a sport organisation (such as its strengths and weaknesses). Second is the analysis of the sport organisation's unique position, such as its mission, vision, objectives, performance measures and stakeholders. Third is the analysis of the market and its consumers via market research.

Once stage 1 is completed, the assembled information is used to undertake stage 2 of the Sport Marketing Framework – 'Develop a Sport Marketing Strategy'. Stage 2 involves making key decisions about the strategic direction a sport marketing programme should take in light of the analysis performed in stage 1. During this stage, it is important to establish the strategy within the boundaries of both objectives and performance measures in order to later evaluate whether the marketing programme has been successful. Stage 2 also involves determining the specific tactics that will be used during the strategy, such as how it will position (differentiate) the sport product or service in the market, exactly who it will be targeted towards (segmentation), and what marketing mix decisions (this is a term covering the elements of product, pricing strategies, promotional strategies and distribution systems) will be employed to implement the strategy. In stage 3 of the process, the sport marketing mix is documented in detail. Finally, stage 4 involves putting the plan into action and making sure it remains on track through systematic evaluation and modification.

> *Chapter principle 4.1*: The Sport Marketing Framework describes the four stages of sport marketing: identifying sport marketing opportunities, developing a sport marketing strategy, planning the sport marketing mix, and implementing and controlling the sport marketing strategy.

STAGE 1: IDENTIFYING SPORT MARKETING OPPORTUNITIES

The first step of the Sport Marketing Framework recognises the importance of conducting preliminary research and analysis before it is possible to make sensible marketing decisions. For example, it is essential to know what opportunities exist in the marketplace, what competitors are doing, what a sport organisation is good at doing, and what consumers actually want. The first stage of the sport marketing process is therefore to identify sport marketing opportunities. This involves analysing the market and consumers, as well as the organisation for which the plan is being constructed. It is important to realise that the three parts of stage 1 should be conducted at approximately the same time, as the three analyses are interconnected.

Analyse internal and external environments

The first activity in stage 1 prescribes an analysis of the internal and external environments in which a sport organisation is placed. The internal environment refers to the unique circumstances of the sport organisation for which the plan is developed. A sport marketer must therefore determine the strengths and weaknesses of his or her sport organisation. For example, a local football club may be strong in terms of its positive community profile and the support it receives from a regional association providing access to a well-organised competition structure. However, the club may be weak in financial terms and may have difficulty in attracting young players.

The external environment refers to the marketplace in which a sport organisation operates. This includes the immediate sport industry as well as the national and international context. In fact, it is important to understand the industry-related external environment, the nature of competitors, and the broad national and global environment. In the example of a local soccer club, an analysis of the external environment may reveal that soccer is not a popular sport in the region, or that there is limited government support for its development. These external factors may also have a strong influence on the specific strengths and weaknesses of a sport organisation.

In the following section, the tools for conducting an internal and external analysis will be explained in detail. These tools include SWOT analysis (with external environment analysis) and competitor analysis (with the Five Forces Analysis).

> *Chapter principle 4.2*: The first step in identifying sport marketing opportunities is to analyse the internal and external environment using the tools of SWOT analysis (with external environment analysis) and competitor analysis (with the Five Forces Analysis).

INTERACTIVE CASE

Many professional sport organisations undertake a marketing audit to identify current organisational strengths and weaknesses relative to their rivals. They also look towards the future in relation to exploring environmental opportunities and reducing threats. In the face of the considerable appeal of professional sport and the accessibility to a wider range of sport and leisure opportunities, financial and participative support for sport at a local club level is always a challenge. One of the most common planning tools used by organisations is a SWOT analysis.

Questions

1   Conduct a quick SWOT analysis of extreme sports.
2   Identify the most important strength, weakness, opportunity and threat.
3   Explain why the previous were selected.

Points of interest

Extreme sports are having a renaissance in recent years. One of the key factors influencing this resurgence is the shift forward from the global recession. Extreme sports have a broad customer base with different demographic, psychographic and behavioural characteristics and include activities such as in-line skating, snowboarding, paintball and mountain bike riding. The increased interest in Internet access to visually exciting sporting quests and the appeal of sporting apparel as fashion, makes the extreme sport industry ripe for expansion. A SWOT analysis of companies in the industry can reveal numerous gaps from which marketing objectives can be developed.

SWOT analysis: An analysis of the internal and external environments

One of the basic tools in this stage of the sport marketing process is known as the SWOT analysis. The term SWOT is an acronym for the words *strengths, weaknesses, opportunities, threats*. A SWOT analysis examines the strategic position of an organisation from the inside (strengths and weaknesses) and the outside (opportunities and threats).

The SWOT analysis can be divided into two parts. The first part represents an internal analysis of an organisation, which can be summarised by its *strengths* and *weaknesses*. An organisation has control over its strengths and weaknesses. The strengths of an organisation include those areas in which an organisation does well, and can be considered capabilities. The weaknesses of an organisation can include those areas in which it does poorly, and can be seen as deficiencies. The second part of the SWOT technique concerns external factors. These constitute elements that the organisation has no direct control over and can be summarised as *opportunities* and *threats*. Opportunities include environmental circumstances that can be used to an organisation's advantage, while threats include unfavourable situations in the external environment that need to be avoided.

The strengths and weaknesses of a sport organisation, along with the opportunities and threats it faces, will influence the options available for a marketing plan. As a result, SWOT analysis is used to identify the major issues that mitigate strategic options. A good rule of thumb is to look for no more than five factors under each of the four headings so that the most important issues are given the highest priority. One of the most common mistakes made when conducting a SWOT analysis is getting caught in needless detail, and losing sight of the 'big picture'. It is also important not to focus only on sport-related matters, but to consider general organisational and business factors.

Strengths and weaknesses

The analysis of strengths and weaknesses should be focused on present-day circumstances. To recap, strengths can be defined as resources or capabilities that a sport organisation can use to achieve its strategic ambitions. Common strengths may include committed coaching staff, a sound membership base, a good junior development program, or management staff with sound business skills and knowledge. Weaknesses should be seen as limitations or inadequacies that will prevent or hinder the strategic direction from being achieved. Common weaknesses may include poor training facilities, inadequate sponsorship, a diminishing volunteer workforce, or a weak financial position.

Opportunities and threats

While strengths and weaknesses should be focused on the present-day situation, opportunities and threats should be future-oriented. Opportunities are favourable situations or events that an organisation can use to its advantage in order to enhance its performance. For example, common opportunities include new government grants, the identification of a new market or potential product, or the chance to appoint a new staff member with unique skills. Threats, in contrast, are the unfavourable situations making performance more difficult in the future. Common threats include inflating player salaries, potential new competitors, or unfavourable trends in the marketplace such as the increased popularity of gaming consoles. Table 4.1 summarises the SWOT technique.

The next section will introduce the many factors that need to be considered when evaluating the external environment in order to determine the opportunities and threats an organisation faces. This is followed with an explanation of how to perform a competitor analysis and Five Forces competitor analysis.

TABLE 4.1 SWOT guidelines	
Strengths	• Resources (e.g. finance, staff, volunteers)
	• Skills (e.g. talents of management, staff and volunteers)
	• Advantages (compared with competitors)
Weaknesses	• Lack of resources (e.g. finance, staff, volunteers)
	• Lack of skills (e.g. among management, staff and volunteers)
	• Disadvantages (compared with competitors)
Opportunities	• Favourable situations in the external environment
	• Weaknesses of competitors
Threats	• Unfavourable situation in the external environment
	• Unfavourable trends in leisure and entertainment

INTERACTIVE CASE

Lawn bowls is played around the world, but enjoys its highest popularity in nations that were once part of the British Commonwealth. Older age groups traditionally played the sport, although it is now beginning to attract younger adults. Go to the following websites for more information on the game. The BBC site gives a clear and succinct description of the rules of the game, and how to play it.

www.bowlsaustralia.com.au
www.bowlsengland.com
www.bowlsnz.co.nz
(www.bowlsnz.co.nz/Category?Action=View&Category_id=1182)
http://news.bbc.co.uk
(http://news.bbc.co.uk/sport2/hi/other_sports/bowls/4747148.stm)
www.bowlsaustralia.com.au
(www.bowlsaustralia.com.au/Portals/9/Media/Final-Report.pdf)

Questions

1 What are the most attractive aspects of lawn bowls?
2 Does the game have any weaknesses, and if so, what are they?

3 What sports and games are its main competitors?
4 Is there a specific group of people whose demographic profile might sit well with both the demands and pleasures of lawn bowls?
5 What new markets and new players could lawn bowls target?
6 How might lawn bowls go about seeking out these new markets and new players?
7 What sort of material would you place in a brochure that aims to promote the game to people aged 18–30?

Points of interest

Lawn bowls has a lot going for it. It is played outdoors on beautifully manicured grass. It is easy to play, but also requires skill to perform at a high level. It provides a strong after-game experience, where friendships are formed and social networks are established. Its customs and protocols deliver an appropriate level of discipline, while also allowing creativity to thrive. It is inclusive, and is one of the few sports that have impeccable gender balance. Neither does it discriminate between social classes. So, why has it faced so many problems in attracting new members over recent years?

The core problem revolves around the average age of club members. Lawn bowls has a history of attracting older adults, and as a result, anyone in his or her fifties is considered young. This is the public image of the game, and despite the fact that more young adults are becoming involved, and doing well at the elite level, this stereotype persists. From a marketing perspective the challenge revolves around rebranding the game, and recasting it as a whole-of-life sport for all demographics where equity, inclusivity and social connectedness are its key values.

External environment analysis

The external environment is made up of a number of factors, including an organisation's competitors, the sport industry, and the wider environment. These are illustrated in Figure 4.2.

The largest circle in Figure 4.2, the macro (or broad) external environment, comprises the political, economic, legal, technological, social and physical environments. Imagine for example that there has been a change over time in the demographic make-up of a region. Such changes may impact the kinds of sports that are considered most popular and likely to attract participants. In a population with a greater proportion of older people, sports such as lawn bowls and golf may have an improved opportunity to expand their participation bases.

Figure 4.3 summarises the six factors that form the macro external environment of a sport organisation. It is important to understand the demands, constraints and possibilities that each of these elements might bring to the sport organisation. Each of these will be described next.

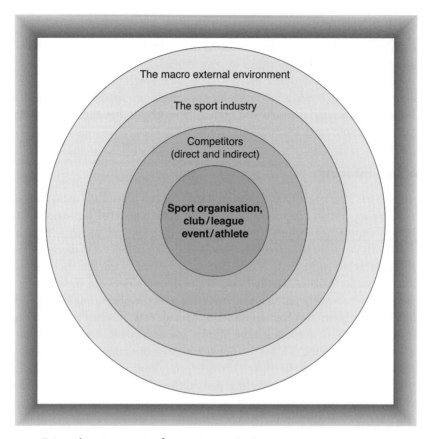

FIGURE 4.2 External environments of a sport organisation.

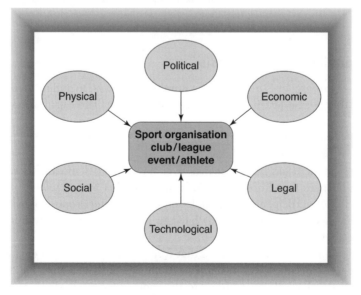

FIGURE 4.3 The macro external environment

Political environment

Government policy influences the ways in which sport organisations are able to operate. For example, sport policy in some countries such as England put a high priority on the development of elite sport, which may be supported by millions of pounds of funding. Government influence can also be relevant in attracting major events to cities.

INTERACTIVE CASE

Most Western nations now have government agencies that administer the national government's sports development policies. Canada is a case in point. Log on to the Sport Canada website.

www.pch.gc.ca
(www.pch.gc.ca/progs/sc/index_e.cfm)

Questions

1 What is the overall responsibility of Sport Canada?
2 Is Sport Canada only concerned with elite sport development?
3 What kinds of sports does the government support?
4 Are some sports more favoured than others?
5 Which sports get the most funding and why?
6 What does this say about the priorities that the Canadian government has for sport?
7 Why would the government want to fund sport anyway?

Points of interest

Sport Canada is a branch of the Canadian government. Its job is to manage sport programs, implement the government's sport policy, and assist in the conduct of major sport tournaments and events. Sport Canada's brief is not only to help Canadians to participate in sport, but also to assist them to excel. Sport Canada operates under the bureaucratic umbrella of the Department of Canadian Heritage. It thus has an explicit role to play in 'strengthening the unique contribution that sport makes to Canadian identity, culture and society'. From a marketing perspective this is a good thing for sport and the people who consume it. That is, sport will not only make people fit and healthy, give them a lot of pleasure, and build up their stocks of social capital, but also consolidate Canada's national identity and sense of national pride.

Economic environment

The economic environment is made up of two elements: the macroeconomic and the microeconomic. Macroeconomic elements represent the big picture as they describe the economy on a national level. Microeconomic elements represent the detailed picture at the organisational or consumer level.

Macroeconomic factors provide a broad picture of economic issues that might affect a sport organisation. When employment levels and consumer spending are higher (in times of prosperity), consumers tend to spend more money on sport. During times of recession or depression, consumers may not be as likely to spend money on sport. However, it is possible that during these low economic times consumers will still choose to spend money on sport for entertainment and distraction. The way that sport organisations will be affected may vary greatly from one organisation to another.

One of the most important microeconomic elements relevant to sport organisations is consumer income levels. Naturally, a consumer's income level will have an influence on whether they can afford to purchase a sport service or product. When economists talk about income, they often use the terms gross income, disposable income, and discretionary income. Gross income is how much money people earn before any tax or expenses are taken out. Disposable income is how much money is left over after tax has been paid. Finally, discretionary income is what remains after tax had been paid and all the necessities of living have been bought (e.g. rent, food, transportation). As sport is not a necessity of life, consumers pay for sport products out of their discretionary income. Therefore, the greater the amount of discretionary income that a consumer has, the more money they have to potentially spend on sport if they wish. It is true, however, that some sport fans are so dedicated that they consider spending on sport as important as spending on the essentials of living.

Legal environment

The legal aspect of the macro external environment can include legislation passed by government, as well as the regulations set down by sport associations, and national and international sporting bodies. Governments create legislation (laws) designed to implement and enforce the policies they set (see Political Environment section). For example, the government sets laws that regulate how and when broadcasters can cover sport events. Many other types of government legislation can also affect the individuals and groups involved in the sport industry, such as company law, taxation, patents and copyright, and contract law. The smaller regulatory bodies relevant to sport organisations can include associations, leagues and international federations. The International Olympic Committee, for example, sets rules about how Olympic competitions should be run. WADA (the World Anti-Doping Agency) is another international example. WADA sets regulations regarding the types of substances athletes are permitted to use in sanctioned sport competitions, and also establishes the standards of punishment for non-compliance.

Technological environment

Technology has had a substantial impact on the way sport organisations operate. For example, email has revolutionised communication, medical technology has improved sport medicine techniques and webstreaming has made sport accessible from almost anywhere in the world. Technological developments are so important to the marketing of sport that Chapter 12 is dedicated to exploring its implications.

INTERACTIVE CASE

Consider the case where the BBC web-streamed the 2014 Sochi Winter Olympics. Look at the following web link:

www.bbc.com/sport

You may also want to view:
http://blog.buttermouth.com/2012/05/top-10-websites-to-sports-streaming.html

Questions

1   What is web-streaming?
2   Of what value is web-streaming to sport consumers?
3   What sports lend themselves best to web-streaming?
4   Does web-streaming adversely alter the sport consumption experience?
5   What are the costs of web-streaming?

Points of interest

Web-streaming occurs when media – be it video or audio – is sent in compressed form over the Internet and played immediately, rather than being saved to a hard drive. As a result users do not have to download a file in order to play it. The other benefit of web-streaming is that users can pause, rewind or fast-forward, just as they can with a downloaded file. It also has advantages for the content deliverers, since it enables them to monitor which visitors are watching and work out how long they are watching the content for. Content creators also have more control over their intellectual property because the video file is not stored on the viewer's computer. Once the video data is played, the media player discards it.

Social environment

The social environment can include the culture of a region as well as its prevalent social trends and demographics. Different cultures and changing cultural trends can have an influence on whether sport is a valued activity, what kind of sport is appreciated, and even how sport and competition should be organised. Cricket, for example, enjoys great strength in England, Australia, New Zealand, India, South Africa and the West Indies (all previous colonies of the British who introduced the game). It is common for sport consumers from other countries, however, to report that the game is too slow and boring. Social issues may also include demographic trends, which refer to the changing composition of a population in an area.

Physical environment

The physical environment can include the unique geographical features of a region, the weather, and the built facilities available. On the east coast of the United States, for example, the temperate climate and accessible coastline offer the opportunity to participate in water sports. In many European countries, in contrast, the Alpine formations and cold environment during winter provide ample options for a variety of snow sports to be enjoyed. Weather factors, such as the availability of water, can directly impact on the kinds of sporting surfaces that can be easily managed. For example, golf courses and other turf surfaces require significant water resources to be maintained. Changing weather patterns may represent a significant threat to sport grounds and events, with drought being an obvious example. Finally, the availability of sporting facilities can also present unique opportunities and threats to a sport organisation. In a country such as England, for example, there are numerous facilities and grounds available for Polo to be played, whereas few such facilities exist in China and Indonesia.

INTERACTIVE CASE

A rich oil-producing nation on the Arabian Peninsula has a snow resort. You have got to be joking! Log on to the website for Ski Dubai.

www.skidubai.com
www.visit-dubai-city.com/dubai-ski-resort.html

Questions

1   What motivated the city of Dubai to build a ski run?
2   Who is their target market?
3   What aspects of the ski run would attract sport consumers?
4   Why would a sport consumer with an interest in snow sports visit Dubai, and not a 'real' snow resort such as the ones in the Swiss or Italian Alps?
5   What additional value would a sports consumer get from a few days at the Dubai ski run that could not be secured at a traditional ski resort?

Points of interest

This is an unusual case. But, it starkly shows how a sport facility can provide a service that operates in direct contrast to the geographical features and weather of the local environment. This is an example of a ski resort in the desert! The average daily temperature in Dubai during January is 24°C/75.2°F. The average daily temperature rises to 41°C/105.8°F in July. This hardly seems like the kind of environment for snow sports, but despite this massive climatic constraint, a 400-metre indoor ski slope has been built. There are 23 mega-scale air conditioners to help keep the temperature at around 2°C/30°F. The Dubai-desert ski resort is the ultimate novelty sport experience. However, it has a major drawback. It is costly to run, and these costs will only escalate as the Dubai authorities aim to win their 'fight' against the environment. This fantasy sporting escape may enhance the city's image as a 'can do' place, but at what cost?

The sport industry environment

Sport organisations should look at how the general external environment influences their specific industrial environment. Figure 4.4 provides a summary of the specific sport industry environmental factors that may influence a sport organisation's marketing decisions. The combination of an analysis of broad, external environmental factors and the sport industry external environment should complement the opportunities and threats component of the SWOT analysis.

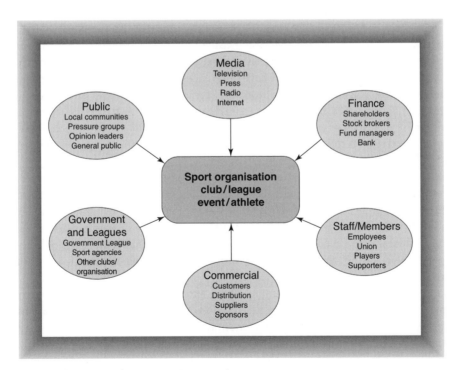

FIGURE 4.4 The sport industry (micro) external environment

Chapter tool 4.1 SWOT and external environment analysis: A SWOT analysis is used to examine the strategic position of an organisation from inside (strengths and weaknesses) and outside (opportunities and threats). The OT part of the analysis is supported by examining the macro (or broad) external environment, which is made up of the political, economic, legal, technological, social and physical environments, as well as the sport industry environment, which is made up of media, finance, staff and members, commercial, government and leagues, and public groups.

Direct and indirect competitors

Although direct and indirect competitors are external factors, their assessment is so important that it typically constitutes a separate activity. Competition occurs when numerous sport organisations attempt to meet the needs of the same group of consumers. The sports shoe sector offers an example of an extremely competitive sport market where large numbers of manufacturers and sellers try to attract the same consumers to buy their products.

A sport organisation must understand its competition for several reasons. First, competitors may have weaknesses to be exploited. Second, competitors may have strengths that could represent a threat, or alternatively provide helpful lessons. Third, competitors change over time. By analysing the competition, a sport organisation considers some of the opportunities and threats that it needs to manage.

There is a difference between direct and indirect competition. Direct (or immediate) competition can be defined as the competition that occurs between sellers who produce similar products and services. The example of sporting shoe manufacturers provides a good illustration. Direct competition can also exist between two products that consumers consider substitutable. Instead of purchasing Nike shoes, a sport consumer might choose to buy adidas instead. These products have differences to one another, but they are similar enough that the consumer could substitute (replace) one for the other. Secondary competition occurs when sellers produce substitute products that meet consumer needs in a different way, such as going to a basketball game instead of a rugby match. Here, the consumer need reflects the desire for entertainment rather than the experience of watching a particular sport.

Indirect competition occurs between sellers who produce *different* products and services that either satisfy similar consumer needs or encourage consumers to seek the satisfaction of different needs. In the case of sport, other forms of entertainment are a strong source of indirect competition. For example, movie theatres, music concerts, cafés, shopping centres, restaurants and even television offer alternative ways that consumers could choose to spend their leisure time. Figure 4.5 illustrates the levels of direct and indirect competition.

The level of intensity in competition, where entry into the market is dependent on timing and speed, and understanding the response from competitors is very important, has made the gathering of intelligence an advantageous commodity for sport organisations. No sport can operate in a vacuum. The diversity of competition whether it is direct or indirect is much more complex than it first appears. Direct competition in most professional sports leagues is similar in terms of a specific product offering, technology or

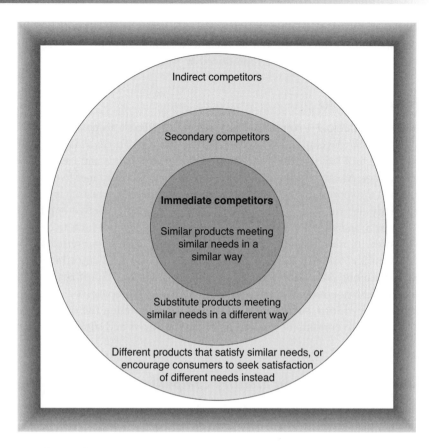

FIGURE 4.5 Types of competitors

target markets. Direct competition can also be more general in that the product or technology may be the same but different segments of the consumer market are targeted. For example, women's and men's World Cup tournaments are generally the same but target different consumer and sponsor segments of the market. On the other hand, indirect competition is often different and overlooked in a competitor analysis. When women's netball in Australia developed their semi-professional league in 2008 there was a notable increase in interest and attendance from male sports fans, satisfying a sport consumer's need differently. Alternatively, it can shift the sport consumer's discretionary spending elsewhere, such as the purchase of digital devices and services to support an individual training strategy rather than employing the services of a personal trainer. Latent competition can take the sport marketer by surprise and change the competitive playing field appreciably. Understanding where the competition is, where your customers are going and where they access information are all part of building strategic intelligence.

Competitor analysis

Because competitors can have a large impact on the strategy a sport organisation develops, sport marketers must analyse competitors in a careful and systematic manner.

In conducting a competitor analysis, it is critical to assess competitors' strategies, strengths, vulnerabilities and resources, as well as their forthcoming actions. The recommended aspects of a competitor analysis are reproduced in Table 4.2.

Five Forces Analysis

In addition to conducting a competitor analysis, it is advisable to conduct a Five Forces Analysis. Originally developed by Michael Porter, the Five Forces Analysis is the most commonly used tool for describing the competitive environment, and can be adapted to the sport industry. As can be seen from Figure 4.6, this analysis examines five forces driving competition in the sport industry. Understanding the competitive situation in a sport sector is a particularly helpful way of determining whether it is an attractive one in which to conduct business, and whether there is scope for existing or new products to be developed. In other words, it may help to identify future opportunities and threats. Although businesses would consider a lower level of competition better than a higher one, the situation is often not as straightforward for sport organisations. Sport organisations rely on close on-field competition to keep consumers interested. Competitive threats, however, may come in many forms, such as new leagues or sports entering the market, substitute products available to consumers, and the potential for buyers and suppliers to exert their bargaining power.

Intensity of rivalry among industry competitors

In general, greater rivalry will be present where there are more sport organisations offering similar products and services. The rivalry between Nike and adidas is an excellent example of extreme rivalry. College football teams in the United States are another example, as

TABLE 4.2 Dimensions of a competitor analysis

Dimension	Description
Geographic scope	What region or location do they operate in with emphasis on overlap?
Mission and vision	Do they intend to maintain their current market position, or do they have a vision to change their situation? What are their ambitions for the future?
Objectives	What are their short- to medium-term goals?
Market share and position	Are they a small player, a medium player or a virtual monopolist?
Strategy	What methods are they using to gain an advantage over their competition?
Resources	What are the amount and availability of resources?
Target market	To whom do they market their products and services?
Marketing mix approach	What products and services do they offer? What promotions, pricing and distribution strategies do they use?

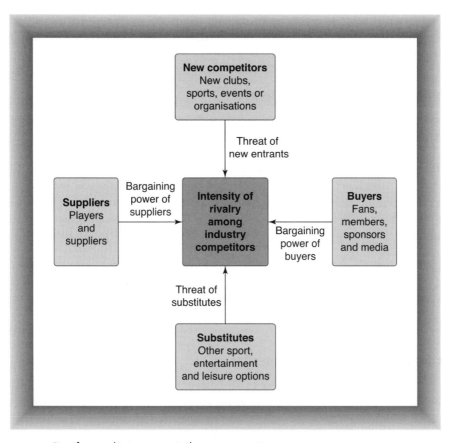

FIGURE 4.6 Five forces driving sport industry competition

would be different soccer clubs in any one country's professional soccer league. While one club is unlikely to be able to 'steal' supporters from the other, there would be significant competition between them for media exposure, corporate sponsorship, players and coaches/managers. Intensity of rivalry appears at the centre of the diagram not only due to its significance, but because the other four forces can all contribute to its magnitude. Typically, the outcome of a Five Forces Analysis is represented in terms of the intensity of rivalry among industry competitors.

The threat of new entrants

Every sport organisation is faced with the possibility that at any time new competitors can enter their industry sector and offer substitute products. Of course, in some forms of professional sport, it seems unlikely that new clubs or teams could enter the competition. There are typically regulations dictating how many teams are allowed in the competition, and it may be difficult to generate a supporter base if fans hold strongly to the history and traditions of the competition. However, in other segments of the sport industry, there are often new organisations entering the marketplace, such as new sport facilities, leisure and recreational centres, events, sport apparel companies, and new equipment manufacturers. In general, the greater the threat of new entrants, the higher the intensity of rivalry among industry competitors.

The bargaining power of buyers

Buyers of sport products and services include individuals, groups and organisations. Fans, sport club members, corporate sponsors, and the media are all examples of parties that purchase sporting goods and services. The nature of competition in the environment will be affected by the strength of the bargaining power of buyers. The term 'bargaining power' refers to the influence that buyers have to exert pressure on suppliers in order to reduce prices. For example, judging by the high ticket prices of some professional leagues, fans have little bargaining power. Also, when the bargaining power is low for media broadcasters, they may have to pay extravagant sums of money to secure the rights to broadcast an event. In contrast, when bargaining power is higher, the costs of rights will be lower. For most sport organisations, however, the main buyers are fans, and since fans do not usually work together to increase their bargaining power, it remains limited. In general, the greater the bargaining power of buyers, the higher the intensity of rivalry among industry competitors.

The bargaining power of suppliers

Like buyers, suppliers may also be able to use bargaining power to force sport organisations to pay more for the inputs they require. When suppliers of raw materials threaten to raise prices or withdraw their products or services, they are attempting to improve their bargaining power. For example, suppliers of inputs to sport organisations include equipment and materials manufacturers. The most significant example of suppliers using bargaining power in sport has come about in relation to players, who can be thought of as suppliers of sport talent. As some professional player groups have become unionised, they have tried to put pressure on leagues and clubs to raise their salaries and salary caps. This has been successful in some instances where the player groups have been well organised. In 2002 in the United States, for example, players in Major League Baseball threatened to strike if their salary demands were not met, which forced the league into negotiations. In contrast, a similar dispute led the US National Hockey League to cancel the entire 2004–05 season. In general, the greater the bargaining power of suppliers, the higher the intensity of rivalry among industry competitors.

The threat of substitute products and services

Some competitors may not provide exactly the same product, but may offer alternatives or substitutes. As the sport industry expands, it is more common for different sports to compete with one another to meet similar needs of sport consumers. Other forms of leisure and entertainment also threaten to attract sport consumers' time. In general, the greater the threat of substitute products and services, the higher the intensity of rivalry among industry competitors.

Chapter tool 4.2 Competitor and Five Forces Analyses: In order to conduct a competitor analysis it is important to be mindful of the three different categories of competitors: immediate/direct competitors, secondary competitors and indirect competitors. When considering the *what* and *how* of competitors, it is important to consider their geographic scope; vision, mission and objectives; market share and position; strategy; resources; target market; and marketing approach. It is also advisable to conduct a second type of competitor analysis: the Five Forces Analysis which comprises: (1) the intensity of rivalry among industry competitors, (2) the threat of new entrants into the marketplace (for example new clubs or leagues), (3) the threat of substitute products in the marketplace (such as other forms of entertainment), (4) the bargaining power of buyers (such as the media, sponsors and spectators) and (5) the bargaining power of suppliers (including players/athletes).

ANALYSE THE ORGANISATION

The second stage in identifying sport marketing opportunities is to analyse the organisation. In order to do this, it is necessary to understand the purpose, aims and goals of an organisation in addition to the needs of its stakeholders. There are four tools that help to analyse the organisation. They are: mission statement; vision statement; organisational objectives; and stakeholder analysis.

An analysis of the organisation will provide important information about the strategic direction it intends to pursue. It is important, for example, to understand the mission, vision and objectives of an organisation, which indicate why an organisation exists, and what it is aiming to achieve. After all, the marketing efforts of an organisation are designed to fulfil its mission and achieve its objectives. It is possible that the information acquired during the organisational analysis may be considered useful to the internal (SW) analysis that contributes to the SWOT evaluation. This is one of the reasons why the three parts of stage 1 should be conducted at around the same time.

Chapter principle 4.3: The second step in identifying sport marketing opportunities is to conduct an analysis of the organisation. This requires four tools: mission statement; vision statement; organisational objectives; and stakeholder analysis.

Mission statements

A mission statement identifies the purpose of an organisation. It should describe why an organisation was set up, what services and products it provides, and to whom they are provided. If a mission statement is not documented in writing, it can be easy for organisational members to be confused about the purpose of the organisation, or to have different ideas about what it should be. It is not uncommon for players, members, spectators, staff, coaches, media, sponsors and government representatives to have different ideas about what constitutes the 'right' purpose. When it is recorded as a single, short statement (preferably a single sentence), this mission delivers a powerful declaration of the organisation's intentions. When developing a marketing plan, the mission statement offers fundamental guidance in the development of a strategy, as it should be consistent with the stated purpose of the organisation. For example, imagine that a community sport organisation states that its mission is to provide access to physical activities for people with an intellectual disability in a given area. This basic guidance would be a useful starting point in developing a marketing plan. Many sport organisations possess mission statements, so their consideration is a simple task within an organisational analysis.

> *Chapter tool 4.3 Mission statement*: The sport organisation's mission statement should be reviewed in order to guide the identification of sport marketing opportunities. The mission statement reveals the purpose of an organisation: why it was created, what services and products it provides, and to whom they are provided.

Vision statements

Having a vision for the future is an important part of an effective sport organisation. A vision for the future is like a clear mental image of how a sport organisation would like to see itself in approximately three to five years' time. A vision statement is a written record of this future image, usually no longer than a sentence. It states the medium- to long-term goals of a sport organisation, or in simple terms, what it wants to achieve in a given time. The vision is, of course, essential information before a marketing strategy can be devised. For example, if a sporting apparel manufacturer has the vision 'to be the number one brand of quality sporting clothes to the luxury market', it would be inappropriate to develop a marketing plan that involved providing budget goods and discount prices.

> *Chapter tool 4.4 Vision statement*: The sport organisation's vision statement should be reviewed in order to guide the identification of sport marketing opportunities. A vision statement is a written record of the desired achievements of an organisation in the future.

INTERACTIVE CASE

Mission and vision statements are important for organisations at all levels to define their reason for being and what the organisation's intentions are. Check out these statements reflecting the intentions of a sport at local (www.carolinespringsfc.com), state (www.redsrugby.com.au/AboutUs), government (www.dsr.wa.gov.au/vision-statements) and professional level (www.footballaustralia.com.au/insideffa). A well-written mission statement should articulate the direction the organisation is heading. Understanding what is 'in scope' for an organisation based on its capabilities and what is 'out of scope'.

Questions

Value statements are increasing in popularity and generally reflect a number of key themes. Provide examples about how would you include the following:

- creating value for stakeholder groups;
- member or customer focus;
- recognising an ethical and social responsibility;
- advocating teamwork and unity;
- priorities to be delivered;
- core beliefs;
- appreciating diversity and inclusivity.

Points of interest

Writing down ideals may be easy for some. Having values that are distinct and reflective of a unique sport organisation may be more problematic. The challenge is to put words into practice. How well is the organisation fulfilling its mission or reflecting its values?

Organisational objectives

If a vision statement shows the medium- to long-term ambitions of an organisation, organisational objectives are the stepping stones along the way to this destination. They are the targets that must be reached in order to make the vision a reality. For example, imagine that a hockey club sits at the bottom of the championship ladder but has a vision to finish in the top three. As might be expected, achieving this vision within one season is unrealistic. Therefore, an objective might be set to improve by three places in the following season, as a stepping stone to the ultimate goal. It is essential that these objectives are measurable, which means that they must be specific enough to be able to determine with certainty that they have been achieved. For example, the objective 'to be the best team' is not measurable, as this goal does not clearly state what being the best means. For example, does it mean the team that wins the most games, the team with the greatest number of new players joining, or the team with the most amount of money in the bank? In sporting clubs, objectives are normally set in each of the major operational areas, such as on-field performance, youth development, finances, facilities, marketing, and human resources. Just as with mission and vision statements, the objectives of an organisation help sport marketers to know where exactly to target their efforts so that they align with the broader goals of the organisation. In fact, they should provide marketers with more specific information about how to apply the mission and vision to the marketing plan.

> *Chapter tool 4.5 Organisational objectives*: A sport organisation's objectives should be reviewed in order to guide the identification of sport marketing opportunities. Organisational objectives are targets that must be reached in order to make the vision a reality.

Stakeholder analysis

Before an analysis of the organisation is complete, its stakeholders need to be considered. Stakeholders are all the individuals, groups and other organisations that have an interest in a sport organisation. These stakeholders might include employees, players, members, the league, association or governing body, government, community, facility owners, sponsors, broadcasters and fans. The obvious question this list raises is: Who is the sport marketer going to try to make happy? The needs of different stakeholders will vary, and each will lead to corresponding implications for a marketing strategy. An interesting example is the case of some professional sport clubs, such as football clubs, that tend to focus on winning to the exclusion of all other priorities, including sensible financial management. While this may make members and fans happy in the short term, other stakeholders may not be happy, such as governing bodies, leagues and employees, who are more likely to be interested in the financial sustainability of the organisation. In a stakeholder analysis, the bargaining power of the different stakeholders should be weighed up. For example, some stakeholders, such as sponsors and government departments, may withdraw their funding if their needs are not met.

A careful analysis of the goals and objectives of each stakeholder in their affiliation with the sport organisation must therefore be completed before a strategic direction can be set. A marketing strategy can be strongly influenced by the beliefs, values and expectations of powerful stakeholders. It should be noted that sport consumers might also be considered stakeholders of sport organisations. However, an analysis of customer needs is part of market research, which is outlined in the forthcoming section.

> *Chapter tool 4.6 Stakeholder analysis*: A stakeholder analysis involves assessing the diverse agendas of all individuals, groups and organisations that have an interest in a sport organisation.

ANALYSE MARKET AND CONSUMERS

The third step in identifying sport marketing opportunities refers to gathering information about the market and the consumers it contains. Market research is the process of learning about the marketplace and what consumers want, assessing their desires and expectations, and determining how to entice consumers to use a sport product. Market research is also used to ascertain whether sport consumers have reacted to a marketing plan as expected. In other words, market research is a way of evaluating the success of a marketing program.

Market research is concerned with answering a number of general questions about the market, such as:

- Who are the sport organisation's customers?
- What do these customers need and want?
- In what manner and how often should customers be contacted?
- Which marketing strategies elicit the most favourable responses from customers?
- What responses will each type of marketing strategy elicit?
- What mistakes have been made?

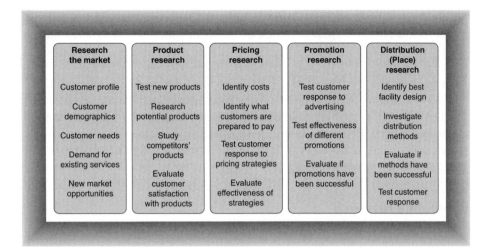

Research the market	Product research	Pricing research	Promotion research	Distribution (Place) research
Customer profile	Test new products	Identify costs	Test customer response to advertising	Identify best facility design
Customer demographics	Research potential products	Identify what customers are prepared to pay	Test effectiveness of different promotions	Investigate distribution methods
Customer needs	Study competitors' products	Test customer response to pricing strategies	Evaluate if promotions have been successful	Evaluate if methods have been successful
Demand for existing services	Evaluate customer satisfaction with products	Evaluate effectiveness of strategies		Test customer response
New market opportunities				

FIGURE 4.7 Applications of market research

These questions are only a starting point because market research can have quite specific uses. Figure 4.7 highlights the potential applications of market research. As Figure 4.7 indicates, there are five applications of market research. The first is to determine specific information about the market: who are the customers, and what do they want? The other four areas represent what is known as the *marketing mix* (product, price, promotion, place). Market research can help not only to identify the best strategies in these areas, but also to evaluate how successful they have been once implemented.

The more detailed the information obtained from market research, the easier it is to design an effective marketing program. However, the more the detail, the greater the cost of the market research. Thus, the difficulty facing small and resource-challenged sport organisations is that market research can often prove expensive, time-consuming and expertise intensive. For these organisations, the answer lies with finding a rapid and inexpensive approach, while avoiding the pitfalls of poor research, which include:

- using an unrepresentative sample;
- asking irrelevant questions;
- ignoring selected answers;
- 'stacking' questions so that they force certain types of responses that are 'leading' and include biases;
- failing to accept criticism.

Different types of market research

There are two types of market research: *quantitative* and *qualitative*. Quantitative research involves numerical information. This information tends to be superficial and is usually gathered from a diverse and large sample of people. Qualitative research involves non-numerical information (such as words from an interview with a consumer). Qualitative information tends to be more in-depth, and is usually gathered from a narrow and relatively small sample of consumers. In order to better understand the differences between quantitative and qualitative research, it is helpful to consider some examples of each.

> *Chapter principle 4.4*: The third step in identifying sport marketing opportunities involves acquiring information about the sport market and consumers. Market research is the process of collecting information in order to learn about the marketplace and what consumers in general, and a sport organisation's customers specifically, want. It involves two kinds of information: quantitative or numerical and qualitative or non-numerical.

Quantitative research

The most common method for gathering quantitative information is to use a survey or questionnaire. A survey/questionnaire may use multiple choices or scaled responses (see below) questions. This means that the consumers can give brief responses to set questions regarding specific topics. It is possible to survey a large group of consumers this way, and to analyse the results with the help of a computer spreadsheet. Questionnaires may be conducted via mail outs, one-on-one interviews or over the phone or Internet.

An example of a scaled response survey question

Question: How would you rate the seating quality at this venue?

(please circle the number that best represents your response)

1	2	3	4	5	6	7
Poor		Average		Outstanding		

Quantitative research should be used when a sport organisation already knows something about its customers and would like to refine this knowledge with greater precision. For example, if a sport organisation already knows that there are four main reasons why their customers employ their services, then they can use questionnaires to establish the relative importance of each. In addition, questionnaires can help to estimate how many customers actually share each of these reasons for using the service. Quantitative research can also be used to evaluate how satisfied customers are with the product, pricing, promotion and place (distribution) strategies of a sport organisation. Furthermore, quantitative research techniques are valuable for constructing demographic profiles of customers (e.g. gender, age, marital status, education, etc.) or of a general segment of consumers.

There are obviously situations in which quantitative research is not a useful method. If a sport organisation does not know anything about its customers, it is not advisable to give them a survey with inflexible questions to try to get to know them. This is because the set questions and topics on a survey may miss the mark altogether, and may not give customers the opportunity to share their unique perspectives. Also, it is often desirable to find out about complex issues, such as the motivations behind customers' consumption behaviours, which cannot be revealed using the relatively superficial information that a survey elicits. Circling a number or ticking a box on a questionnaire will not help a sport marketer get to the heart of consumer opinion and behaviour. For example, a survey may show that a netball club has a married, middle-aged female player with three children who plays because she enjoys the game and wants the exercise, and is relatively happy with the quality of service. However, it is unlikely to tell us that she is thinking about taking up basketball because her kids play, it is less stressful on her knees, that she will not play next season because a business commitment will take her overseas for several months, that her sister is an expert in marketing and specialises in non-profit organisations, that she would like to try coaching a junior netball team, that she finds it annoying that the showers in the changing rooms constantly leak, and that weekends are not a very convenient time to play games after all. While some of these questions can be answered by questionnaires and surveys, designing a survey that is so comprehensive would be impractical. For these reasons, a sport organisation may choose to undertake a qualitative approach as a first step in its market research process.

> *Chapter tool 4.7 Quantitative market research*: Quantitative research involves the collection of numerical information through a survey or questionnaire and should be used when a sport organisation already knows something about its customers and would like to refine this knowledge with greater precision.

Qualitative research

Qualitative research is a method of acquiring information that is non-statistical but in-depth. Because qualitative information is more detailed, complicated and time-consuming to collect, it is usually gathered from a narrow and relatively small sample of sport consumers. The results obtained through qualitative research can also be used later to help construct a quantitative survey, if required. There are a number of effective and inexpensive approaches to qualitative market research that can provide rich and detailed information about the market and its consumers. They include:

1   interviews and focus groups
2   suggestion boxes
3   complaint analysis.

Interviews and focus groups

One of the fundamental tools of qualitative market research is the interview, which can be conducted in a one-to-one situation or with numerous respondents at the same time. One efficient method is known as the focus group where a group of customers from the group being studied are gathered in an informal setting, and encouraged to talk about specific issues. To be successful, the focus group should be conducted by an interviewer who has the skills to coordinate the group without inhibiting, intimidating, or leading the respondents, so that ideas can flow freely and all opinions are expressed. Sessions should always be audio-recorded so that they can be evaluated for important themes after the event.

Suggestion boxes

A suggestion box is a simple tool that can work if taken seriously. It is important to both the research process and good relationships with customers that the suggestions are read regularly and acted upon. It is usually best to document all suggestions (anonymously) and responses in a prominent place within the organisation where readily accessible to all customers, members and staff. It is also best not to make excuses if there is a genuine problem, and the actions taken to improve the situation should also be identified. Nothing is worse than a suggestion box with a rusty lock, so there is no point in pursuing this form of customer feedback without the commitment to deal with the suggestions promptly and systematically.

Complaint analysis

This method is cheap and relatively easy to implement. Customer complaints can provide an insight into the elements of the product or service that are not meeting customer needs. With this information, it is possible to consider how to change and improve the situation, hopefully leading to improved customer satisfaction. Complaint analysis involves encouraging customers to contact employees directly if they have a problem or a complaint. It is advisable to respond to every complaint with a personal and formal letter or email thanking customers for highlighting the problem and providing them with information about how the problem will be resolved.

> *Chapter tool 4.8 Qualitative market research*: Qualitative research involves the collection of non-statistical, but in-depth information through interviews and focus groups, suggestion boxes or complaint analysis.

SPORT MARKET OPPORTUNITIES

The information that was obtained in stage 1 of the Sport Marketing Framework, and its subsequent analysis, should highlight potential market opportunities. A market opportunity is a situation where a new or modified product or service can be introduced that meets an unfulfilled sport consumer need. However, it is first necessary to establish whether the opportunity is worth capitalising upon. Once decided, the target consumer group can be identified, along with a solid idea of where the sport product or service can be placed within the context of a marketplace that already contains sport products and services.

> *Chapter principle 4.5*: A market opportunity is a situation where a new or modified product or service can be introduced that meets an unfulfilled sport consumer need.

A useful tool for examining the marketing opportunities available is the Product-Market Expansion Grid. The grid provides a summary of the opportunities available for

TABLE 4.3 Product-Market Expansion Grid

	Existing product	New product
Existing markets	Market penetration	Product development
New markets	Market development	Diversification

'selling' a particular product or service. The Product-Market Expansion Grid is shown in Table 4.3.

Market penetration is the first possible type of market opportunity. It is an opportunity to increase 'sales' by attracting more consumers without sacrificing the old. An example of a market penetration opportunity in the horse-racing industry would be to attract even more males over the age of 50 to attend race meetings. It is therefore a 'more of the same' approach.

Market development is similar to market penetration in that the product remains the same. However, with market development the aim is to expand the target market to reach a wider range of consumers. A market development approach therefore promotes the product or service to existing markets as well as to a wider range of consumers. In the horse-racing example, a market development opportunity could be to attract more of the existing customers (males over the age of 50) as well as a wider range of consumers (such as women over 50 as well).

The third category, *product development*, involves marketing to the same consumers with a new version of the product or service. This new or modified product is 'sold' to the same target market as the existing product, such as Twenty20 Cricket and beach volleyball.

The final category, *diversification*, involves marketing a new product to a new target market. It is an attempt to 'start-over'. Examples of diversification include indoor cricket, mixed netball and modified rules versions of sport for children.

The Product-Market Expansion Grid provides alternatives to consider when going through the process of setting a strategic market direction, which is examined in the next chapter.

> *Chapter tool 4.9 Product-Market Expansion Grid*: The Product-Market Expansion Grid provides a summary of the opportunities available for 'selling' a particular product or service. It highlights four possibilities: (1) *market penetration* is an opportunity to increase 'sales' by attracting more consumers without sacrificing the old; (2) *market development* is an opportunity where the product remains the same but seeks to expand the target market to reach a wider range of consumers; (3) *product development* is an opportunity involving marketing to the same consumers with a new version of the product or service; and (4) *diversification* is an opportunity involving marketing a new product to a new target market.

INTERACTIVE CASE

The idea that clever people and smart businesses will always turn a problem into an opportunity has become the 'correct' thing to say at business forums, strategic planning meetings and professional development seminars. Nike is a case in point. You are invited to take a look at the company's latest annual report at the website below. Its latest sustainability report is also listed. This should also be viewed.

http://investors.nikeinc.com/Investors/Financial-Reports-and-Filings/Annual-Reports/default.aspx
www.nikeresponsibility.com/report

Nike is one of the world's best-known corporate brands. It has revolutionised the sportswear market, and during the 1980s and 1990s it could do little wrong. Its frequent successes were reflected in its massive brand equity, highly rated balance sheets, and impressive profit and loss statements. But Nike has not always had things all its own way.

Seizing opportunities is part of innovative advancement in most sport equipment manufacturing companies, but there is more to it than releasing the latest and most faddish design. Sport consumers seeking the latest fashion and equipment readily accepted Nike's mass-produced sporting products. But this all changed in 1997 when the media highlighted the 'sweatshop' conditions imposed upon offshore factory workers. Nike was immediately subjected to boycotts and protests, and suffered a decline in its share value. Nike's image and brand equity had taken a severe hit, and its reputation for looking after its stakeholders, and especially its workers, had been shredded.

At the same time, Nike understood the power of a good reputation, and it made significant changes to its social and environmental practices. From the buildings they operated to the materials they used, Nike introduced sustainable design principles. 'Reuse-a-shoe' was one successful initiative illustrating Nike's ability to turn an environmental problem into a strategic opportunity. In 1993, Nike developed a recycling program to 'close the loop'. Instead of athletic shoes being sent to landfill, consumers could deposit worn out athletic shoes, regardless of the brand, at any Nike factory around the world. The shoes were recycled into a granulated rubber for use as sports-surfacing material. In 2004 Nike claimed it had recycled more than 20 million pairs of shoes and contributed to over 250 sport surfaces, including running tracks, basketball courts and playgrounds.

Nike also got involved in health promotion, and collaborated in programmes to combat obesity and poverty. 'NikeGO' targeted inactive youths from age eight upwards to motivate them to become involved in physical activity while also having fun. Nike also worked with non-government organisations to address the substandard working conditions in its offshore factory suppliers. In 2007 it reorganised its soccer ball manufacturing in Pakistan, and as a result all manufacturing plants had to provide fair wages and social benefits for workers.

In 2002 Nike partnered with Lego to develop a 'BIONICLE' shoe. The shoes had interchangeable toe caps designed to emulate the masks of Lego BIONICLE characters. Targeting children's imaginations, Nike saw this as an opportunity to further encourage children to become physically active, while cleverly getting the brand even deeper into the community psyche. Nike's opportunistic values also led it to partner up with the Apple iPod. In 2006 Nike released the Nike1 shoes, which allowed wearers to embed an iPod transmitter in the sole. As participants walked or ran, the sensor relayed information to their iPod Nano, logging their time, distance, pace and calories burned.

Nike have now gone the next step and documented all their social development initiatives. They are contained in an impressively thick and glossy responsibility report. The latest report covers everything from waste management to people and culture. It concedes that it still has 'lessons to learn', but then immodestly goes on to say that it succeeds because 'we're obsessed with innovation'. It then says it is 'relentlessly curious about our world and how we can make it better'. It finally notes that it applies this curiosity to its sustainability efforts, and 'continue[s] to learn what is required for real, meaningful progress'.

Questions

1   How did Nike come to be such a successful business?
2   Was it just about image, or was it something more tangible?
3   What happened in the 1990s that tarnished the Nike brand, led to a fall in its share price, and squeezed its market share?
4   How did Nike turn things around and protect its brand?
5   How do you rate this turnaround as an example of corporate opportunism?
6   How did you respond to the Nike responsibility report?
7   What does the report tell you about Nike's ability to adapt to its political environment?

Points of interest

Nike is the most popular athletic shoe brand in the world. The company sells millions of shoes and items of apparel every year. Nike does not actually manufacture any of these products in its own plants or factories. Instead, the company contracts-out with manufacturing facilities located offshore. Around 800,000 people work in these factories, which are primarily in low income Asian nations. In 2002 Nike issued a company Code of Conduct to all its factories, which was used to regulate working conditions and safety requirements. The company's first 2004 Responsibility Report, which established further health and labour standards, was considered a major victory for both workers and international human rights groups. Nike also included a full list of its factory locations, and undertook to enable independent monitoring and investigation to take place.

PRINCIPLES SUMMARY

- Chapter principle 4.1: The Sport Marketing Framework describes the four stages of sport marketing: identifying sport marketing opportunities, developing a sport marketing strategy, planning the sport marketing mix, and implementing and controlling the sport marketing strategy.

- Chapter principle 4.2: The first step in identifying sport marketing opportunities is to analyse the internal and external environment using the tools of SWOT analysis (with external environment analysis) and competitor analysis (with the Five Forces Analysis).

- Chapter principle 4.3: The second step in identifying sport marketing opportunities is to conduct an analysis of the organisation. This requires four tools: the mission statement; vision statement; organisational objectives; and stakeholder analysis.

- Chapter principle 4.4: The third step in identifying sport marketing opportunities involves acquiring information about the sport market and consumers. Market research is the process of collecting information in order to learn about the marketplace and what consumers in general, and a sport organisation's customers specifically, want. It involves two kinds of information: quantitative or numerical, and qualitative or non-numerical.

- Chapter principle 4.5: A market opportunity is a situation where a new or modified product or service can be introduced that meets an unfulfilled sport consumer need.

TOOLS SUMMARY

- Chapter tool 4.1 SWOT and external environment analysis
- Chapter tool 4.2 Competitor and Five Forces Analyses
- Chapter tool 4.3 Mission statement
- Chapter tool 4.4 Vision statement
- Chapter tool 4.5 Organisational objectives
- Chapter tool 4.6 Stakeholder analysis
- Chapter tool 4.7 Quantitative market research
- Chapter tool 4.8 Qualitative market research
- Chapter tool 4.9 Product-Market Expansion Grid

REVIEW QUESTIONS

1 Differentiate between the four stages of the Sport Marketing Framework.

2 Identify the three parts of identifying sport marketing opportunities. Provide a general explanation of their respective functions.

3 For a sport organisation you know well, write a brief mission statement and vision statement.

4 What are the different kinds of sport marketing objectives?

5 Under what circumstances would it be advisable to use a qualitative approach to collecting market research information?

6 Devise an original example for each category in the Product-Market Expansion Grid.

RELEVANT WEBSITES

http://news.bbc.co.uk/sport	BBC Sport
www.pch.gc.ca	The Department of Canadian Heritage, including Sport Canada
www.skidubai.com	Ski Dubai
www.visit-dubai-city.com	Dubai City
www.bowlsaustralia.com.au	Bowls Australia
https://www.bowlsengland.com	Bowls England
https://www.bowlsnz.co.nz	Bowls New Zealand
http://investors.nikeinc.com	Nike Investor's Centre
www.nikeresponsibility.com/report	Nike Corporate Social Responsibility

FURTHER READING

Veal, A.J. (2011). *Research Methods for Leisure and Tourism* (4th edn). London: Pearson Education.

CHAPTER 5

Sport marketing strategy

LEARNING OUTCOMES

At the end of this chapter, readers should be able to:

- explain the process of determining a strategic marketing direction
- identify the main considerations when developing strategic marketing objectives
- outline the factors critical to setting performance measures
- describe the importance of determining a core marketing strategy
- define the terms market positioning and market segmentation
- discuss the importance of market segmentation
- identify the main approaches to market segmentation
- describe the process and importance of market positioning
- outline the major elements of the marketing mix.

OVERVIEW

This chapter explains stage 2 of the Sport Marketing Framework, which comprises two parts: (a) develop strategic marketing direction and (b) develop sport marketing positioning. The chapter includes guidance on the process of setting marketing objectives and performance measures, developing a sport marketing strategy, determining market positioning and market segmentation strategies, and preparing to devise the marketing mix.

STAGE 2: DEVELOP A STRATEGIC MARKETING STRATEGY

The second stage of the Sport Marketing Framework is to 'develop a sport marketing strategy', and is highlighted in Figure 5.1. The first step of stage 2 requires the development of a strategic marketing direction by identifying marketing objectives and performance measures.

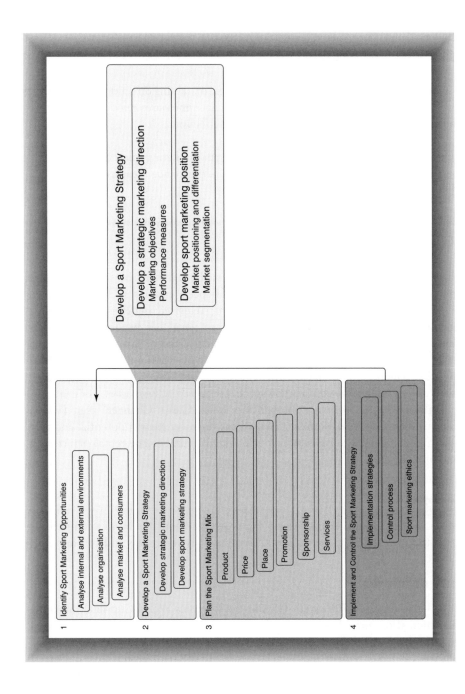

FIGURE 5.1 Develop a sport marketing strategy

Chapter principle 5.1: The second stage of the Sport Marketing Framework is to develop a sport marketing strategy. This requires two steps: (a) to develop a strategic marketing direction, and (b) to develop a sport marketing position.

DEVELOP A STRATEGIC MARKETING DIRECTION

There are two steps involved in developing a strategic marketing direction. First, marketing objectives need to be developed. Second, performance measures need to be assigned to these objectives. Both are outlined in the following section.

Chapter principle 5.2: Developing a strategic marketing direction involves constructing marketing objectives and setting performance measures.

INTERACTIVE CASE

How difficult is it to position sport positively in the minds of consumers? Picture this: a soccer World Cup; competing powerful soccer nations such as Germany, Spain, Sweden, Brazil; capacity filled stadiums; televised matches; social media furore; women! Women's football at the highest level has become increasingly popular. In 1977 international women's football consisted of three teams and two matches. By 2010 it had grown to 141 teams playing over 500 matches. Today there are over 29 million female players globally. A critical aspect of positioning a product lies with understanding the competitive space it occupies in the market. For example, The England FA for women's football five year 'Game Changer' plan (www. thefa.com) recognises that women's football has the most growth potential and that there is a pressing need to reposition it as England's number one female sport both on and off the field.

Questions

How can women's football capitalise on this growing fervour and build a competitive position that will appeal to participants, consumers, governments and corporates?

Points of interest

In 2011 Japan defeated FIFA giant USA in the women's World Cup final. Japanese participation at the time was a meagre 25,000 (www.nadeshikoleague.jp) compared with more than 1.7 million in the United States (www.nwslsoccer.com). Most elite players in Japan remain amateurs compared to the semi-professional players of the United States. Yet in order to play the US in the final, Japan became the giant killer, defeating defending champions Germany and all powerful Sweden. At the end of the FIFA final, Twitter was logging over 7,000 posts per second, a figure that surpassed the Super Bowl tweets for the same year. Host country Germany filled its stadiums, and the Entertainment and Sports Programming Network (ESPN) television ratings for the final nearly doubled its previous best for a World Cup match. On field skills and behaviour were exemplary and the rise of Japan, France and Australia reinforced the decision to extend team entries to 24 teams for the 2015 World Cup. The timing is now perfect for Japan and women's soccer generally to position themselves in a competitive space that will attract and captivate a global audience.

Marketing objectives

The word objective means an aim or goal. A marketing objective is a goal that a sport organisation may realistically achieve as the result of its marketing strategy. It is typically summarised in the form of a short sentence that describes what will be achieved as a result of marketing activities. Marketing objectives represent a guide through all of the coming stages of the marketing framework. They should offer a clear direction to follow when it comes to conceiving the rest of the marketing plan. This means that the importance of marketing objectives cannot be underestimated. It is critical to think about marketing objectives carefully, and to document them clearly. They should provide everyone in a sport organisation with a clear direction so that all marketing activities are carried out in line with predetermined goals. As recorded in Table 5.1, there are four broad categories of marketing objectives that sport organisations may pursue: participation, performance, promotion and profit.

Privately owned sport facilities such as gymnasiums and recreation centres will have *profit* as their main objective. This would also be the main aim for sport equipment and apparel manufacturers such as FILA, and professional sport clubs that operate as franchises such as in North America, and as public companies. In fact, the corporate or professional sector of sport is interested primarily in profits. Any other objectives that these organisations might develop would remain subservient, or a means to achieving a greater profit. In theory, a privately owned professional club may want to sign up more club members, but only so that they can make more money. However, most business managers understand that the fastest route to profit in professional sport is to win.

On the other hand, many sport organisations will not have profit as their main objective. For example, sport clubs and community-based clubs will have *performance* and *participation* objectives. National sport associations and government sport agencies may also be interested in *promoting* messages about healthy lifestyles. Generally speaking, sport organisations that are member-based are set up as non-profit organisations and therefore will not pursue profit as their main objective. It is still important for them to make sure they are earning enough money to cover their costs, or perhaps a little more to spend on developing new services or buying new equipment. However, for them, profit should be a means to an end, not their primary objective. Some recommendations when it comes to writing good sport marketing objectives follow.

TABLE 5.1 The four main categories of sport marketing objectives	
Category	Examples of marketing objectives
Participation	• To increase the number of members in a club
	• To increase the number of clubs in a sport or competition
	• To increase the number of consumers using a service
	• To improve spectator levels at a competition or event
	• To expand the number of club administrators or officials
	• To expand the number of volunteers involved
	• To increase the volume or frequency of consumer use of the product or service
Performance	• To increase market share
	• To increase the range of products or services on offer to consumers
	• To improve customer satisfaction and service quality
Promotion	• To promote a health and well-being message
	• To improve the public 'image' of the organisation
	• To increase customer awareness of the product/service
Profit	• To increase product or service sales
	• To increase profit margins
	• To acquire new sponsorships or grants
	• To increase annual profit or surplus (or decrease expenses or deficit)
	• To increase the amount that sales revenue exceeds costs
	• To improve the ratio of cost to revenue

Writing good marketing objectives

1 *Marketing objectives should match organisational objectives.* Marketing objectives should help the sport organisation to achieve its overarching organisation objectives. In fact, marketing objectives should be stepping stones along the way that will help the organisation to realise its overall vision.

2 *Objectives should be realistic.* Marketing objectives should be plausible and within reach, especially considering the resources available to a sport organisation.

3 *Marketing objectives should focus on action.* Marketing objectives should say what is going to be done. This is why the examples in Table 5.1 begin with the word 'To'.

4 *Marketing objectives should be narrowed down to the most important.* By narrowing objectives down to as few as possible, the sport organisation will be better at focusing its energy on what really matters. Five or less is a good ambition.

5   *Marketing objectives should be prioritised and ranked from the most important to the least important.* An organisation should know which objectives are the most important. To do this it will need to discuss and consult within the marketing department, and with the other managers of the sport organisation.

6   *Marketing objectives should be documented.* There should be a record to review at any time in order to ensure that focus remains on the objectives and so that they can be evaluated at a later stage of the Sport Marketing Framework.

7   *Marketing objectives should be clear, specific and measurable.* If objectives are not clear, it becomes difficult to know exactly what is wanted. For example, the objectives in Table 5.1 are clear, such as the aim 'to increase membership levels'. But, if it was 'to improve participation', then this would not be clear, as the kind of participation desired is left unsaid (membership numbers, spectator levels, number of volunteers etc.). An unclear objective also makes it difficult to determine whether an organisation has achieved what it wanted. As a result, all marketing objectives need to be measurable.

8   *Marketing objectives should be time-focused.* Without a time focus it is impossible to determine when further marketing activities should be undertaken.

Chapter tool 5.1 Marketing objectives: A marketing objective is a goal that a sport organisation wants to achieve as the result of its marketing strategy. There are four different categories of marketing objectives that sport organisations may pursue: participation, performance, promotion and profit. All marketing objectives should be consistent with organisational objectives, realistic, action-oriented, narrowed down and ranked in order of importance, documented, clear, specific and measurable, and time-focused.

Performance measures

Once objectives have been set, it is important to add performance measures. The word measure refers to a way of estimating, calculating or assessing whether an objective has been achieved. It usually involves finding a way to quantify or put a number to an objective. For example, imagine that one organisational objective is 'to increase profit'. A possible performance measure would nominate the amount of the increase and the time period in which it is to be accomplished, say $10,000 in one year. This performance measure has added a quantity to the objective, and has also made it easy to determine whether it has been reached or not. Some further examples appear in Table 5.2.

Chapter tool 5.2 Performance measures: Performance measures quantify or put numbers to objectives in terms of magnitude and time so that their specific achievement is transparent.

TABLE 5.2 Examples of performance measures	
Common examples of marketing objectives	*Possible performance measures*
To increase club membership	To increase membership from 70 to 100 members by January 2010
To increase the number of people who use our service	To increase the number of people who use our service to 50 customers per month by July 2016
To improve spectator levels at a competition	To increase spectator levels to an average of 25,000 spectators per game, by December 2009, as measured by ticket sales
To increase customer satisfaction levels	To increase customer satisfaction levels to 7/10 as rated by them on an annual customer satisfaction survey
To increase profit	To increase profit to $120,000, calculated at the end of the 2016 financial year
To increase awareness of our sport product	To increase the number of people who have heard of our product in India to 100,000, as measured by market research

INTERACTIVE CASE

Parachute payments are a relatively new strategy used in managing professional sports. In sports leagues such as the English Premier League (EPL) the rules allow that at the season's end the bottom three finishers on the League table are relegated to the division below. For relegated clubs this Football Association (FA) inducement is around £40 million over four seasons if the club is demoted and fails to return to the Premier League.

Question

Do parachute payment systems create a level playing field and is it inappropriate to reward failure as an objective?

Points of interest

EPL players are highly paid and despite many of the contracted players having relegation clauses of a 50 per cent pay cut written into the playing contract, teams such as Arsenal have a wages bill of over £180 million primarily spent on the manager (coach) and playing 11. With no relegation clause for player payments, a fall into a lower division could send a club into administration. Well-managed teams failing to finish in the top four or bottom three of the Premiership League receive no incentives.

Poorly managed teams with poor success in the drop zone have an inducement to relegate. Portsmouth Football Club received inducements for relegating to the Championship League in 2012 greater than the incomes of other existing teams. Burnley Football Club has had a joy ride effect on their financial situation in consecutive seasons with revenues jumping from £11.5 million to nearly £46 million in 2009/10, to then reduce to £28 million in 2010/11 (including a £15 million parachute payment). Many clubs across numerous sport leagues are now looking elsewhere, such as foreign ownership, for financial backing. The EPL sets objectives aiming to allow clubs to secure a financial position where they can entice top level players to the league and compete at the highest level. But, as this case reveals, some objectives require strategies that do not produce consistent effects.

Developing sport marketing positioning

The process of constructing a sport marketing position involves four steps. Steps 1 and 2 involve market segmentation, step 3 introduces a market positioning strategy, and step 4 leads to a marketing mix. This section overviews these steps, including a detailed explanation of market segmentation and market positioning. The development of the marketing mix is examined in detail over the six forthcoming chapters. Figure 5.2 illustrates the four steps of developing sport marketing positioning.

> *Chapter principle* 5.3: Developing a sport marketing position involves four steps: market segmentation (1, 2), market positioning tactics (3) and devising the marketing mix (4).

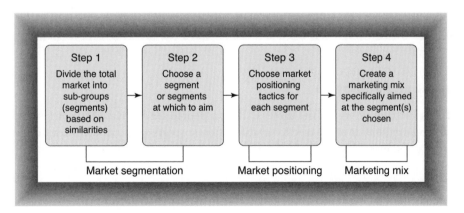

FIGURE 5.2 Develop sport marketing positioning

INTERACTIVE CASE

The World Tourism Authority claims that sport tourism is an emerging market with a projected 1.6 billion participants by 2020 (www.tourism.gov.ph). Individual involvement in sport tourism can occur from three broad perspectives. First, a person may travel to a destination to take part in a sport activity such as the London (www.facebook.com/londonmarathon) or Boston Marathon (www.facebook.com/TheBostonMarathon). Second, many people plan their trips around a significant sporting event such as a World Cup, Olympic Games or Grand Prix. Finally, for other tourists the nostalgia of visiting a significant sports venue such as the Melbourne Cricket Ground (www.mcg.org.au) in Australia, All England Club (www.wimbledon.com) in Britain or even the Colosseum in Rome classifies them as a sport tourist.

Questions

What are the issues (both within the managing organisations and the external environment) affecting the development of a 'sportainment' destination for the twenty-first century.

Points of interest

Spanish Football Club giant, Real Madrid, has ventured down this pathway with the building of a 'sportainment' destination on Al-Marjan Island in Ras Al-Khaimah in the United Arab Emirates. Real Madrid has identified a very strong fan base in the Middle East and positioning an innovative sport service supports a strategic intention to simultaneously attract local and 'Real' fans from Europe and Asia. Success of the joint project is dependent upon a number of factors such as the stability of the region and the accessibility of the location. Appealing to the traditional Real Madrid fan base can also impact on the marketing strategy.

Market segmentation

Not all sport consumers are the same. Different people are motivated to consume sport for different reasons. It is also true to say that different sports or events will attract different kinds of consumers. For example, Formula 1 motor racing appeals to a different crowd than synchronised swimming. This means that sport marketers must have an understanding of the kind of consumers that are currently attracted to their products and services, as well as the kind of consumers they might like to attract in the future.

Market segmentation is the process of categorising groups of consumers together, based on their similar needs or wants. A market is the total group of potential consumers for a product, and can include retailers, businesses, government, media and individuals. Market segmentation therefore involves breaking down this total group into smaller groups based on something that the consumers have in common, such as their age, gender, interests, behaviours or needs. Market segmentation recognises that it is not possible for a sport organisation to be all things to all consumers. Once a sport organisation has selected a particular segment or segments of the market, it can customise its product and marketing strategies to meet their specific needs. By breaking down sport consumers into different segments (or sections), it is possible for a sport organisation to use its limited marketing resources more effectively.

Imagine the marketing situation of a large fitness and recreation centre with swimming facilities. A forthcoming Olympic Games might provide an opportunity for them to market their facility at a time when many people are watching and thinking about sport and fitness. One non-segmented (mass marketing) approach would involve advertising the facility on television, thereby reaching a large but diverse group of people. However, television advertising is extremely expensive and may not be the best use of money. Another disadvantage of this idea is that many people who will see the promotion will not be interested in the facility's services because they live some distance away. The advertisement is wasted on these consumers. The alternative approach would be to target a specific segment (or a couple of segments). For example, some research undertaken by the facility might reveal that stay-at-home mothers with young children who live within 20 kilometres of the facility have a strong interest in getting fit and meeting other mothers. A marketing program could be tailored to these consumers by offering a special off-peak rate during the day, creating a space for coffee and socialising, and advertising the facility through all the kindergartens in a 20-kilometre radius. Depending on the facility's resources, it may also be possible to consider developing childcare facilities or negotiating an agreement for casual childcare to be provided by a local business.

The process of segmentation

Market segmentation comprises two parts. First, the market must be divided into sub-groups based on a common feature. This can be done with the help of market research, as discussed earlier in the chapter. Second, the target segment must be determined in order for the segment(s) chosen need(s) to be substantial enough to justify all the efforts associated with developing and implementing the marketing strategy. It is equally important that the segment identified is different from the general market. If the needs of all the consumers in the total market are very similar, it might not be necessary or profitable to try to break them down any further.

Ways of segmenting sport consumers

There are six ways of grouping consumers together for segmentation, illustrated in Figure 5.3. Consumers are often grouped together into the following categories: demographic, socio-economic, lifestyle (psychographic), geographic, product behaviour and benefits. Each is described in the following paragraphs.

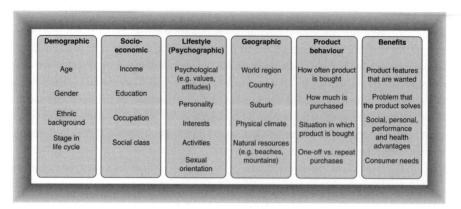

FIGURE 5.3 Categories for segmenting sport consumers

Demographic segmentation

Demographic segmentation is the most conventional and common in sport marketing. Demographic variables include age, gender, ethnic background and what stage of their working 'life cycle' a consumer occupies. Sporting apparel, for example, is often targeted towards consumers based on their gender and age. For example, a popular age demographic that has been recently recognised is known as the 'tweenies': young people aged between 10 and 12 who are not yet teenagers, but are no longer children. Many fashion and music products in particular have been marketed specifically to this high growth consumer segment, and sport products such as gaming consoles and fashion sporting shoes are also targeted towards the burgeoning tweenies segment.

The life cycle category is less obvious than age and gender. Traditionally, life cycle refers to the conventional stages of life from being single, married with children, 'empty-nesters' (couples with adult children who have left the family home), retired, and the elderly. In addition to these traditional stages, sport marketers recognise relatively new categories such as: married without children, same-sex couples, single parents, blended families, and the separated or divorced. The life cycle stage of a consumer will naturally make a difference to how, when and why they spend money on sport products. A single, working adult may have more income to spend on expensive tickets to high-profile sport events, whereas parents of young children may prefer to buy a membership to the local club so that their daughter can participate in sport every week.

A consumer's ethnic background refers to their race, nationality or religion. It is important for sport marketers not to think of the ethnic background of different groups in stereotypical ways, but to try to understand their unique behaviours. The major national soccer leagues in Australia and the United States possess a strong ethnic fan base. Both of these countries have large numbers of immigrant populations, with Melbourne's Italian community the largest outside Italy itself, for example. For a person who emigrates to a new country, the sport that they enjoyed in their country of origin can become an important link for them. It connects them not only to their personal history, but also to a new community, which may share similar experiences of settling in a new country.

Socio-economic segmentation

Socio-economic segmentation refers to aspects of a consumer's social or economic circumstances, such as their income, the highest level of education they have achieved, and their occupation. These kinds of factors are often grouped together under demographic segmentation. However, they have been separated out here for clarity.

Income is a popular way to segment markets. How much money a consumer earns (and their disposable income) is likely to have an influence on their purchasing behaviour. A family living on a tight budget is unlikely to buy box seats to a football match. The sport apparel industry is another example where discount department stores offer lower income customers easy access and budget products. On the other hand, there are higher priced speciality stores that offer middle-income customers brand names with the latest imported fashion colours and designs.

A person's education, income and occupation are often strongly related. The higher the level of education a person achieves, the more likely they are to earn more and work in jobs with higher status. It can also be true that the higher a consumer's or their family's wealth, the more likely they are to be able to afford an education that can lead to more prestigious employment. Some sports have been associated with certain social class segments. For example, football has traditionally been seen as a working class game, golf and tennis as middle class activities, and polo and yachting are perceived as sports of the rich. Of course, the popularity and accessibility of these sports can shift and change over time. In Western countries the average income is significantly higher than in developing countries, and many consumers spend significant sums of money on the technologies necessary to access sport and entertainment.

Lifestyle (psychographic) segmentation

Lifestyle factors refer to consumers' day-to-day routines and their general way of life. These can be influenced by a consumer's personality, their interests, activities, and their opinions. For example, a consumer's activities include what they do for leisure, socialising, sport, hobbies and holidaying. Their interests may include family, home, recreation, fashion and/or a desire to achieve. It is possible to segment consumers based on lifestyle factors as Table 5.3 demonstrates.

Geographic segmentation

Sport consumers can be segmented according to their geographical residence. Geographical segments might include local (such as a suburb or state/county/province), national and international regions. A local baseball club, for example, might target their services to players who live in a 5–10 kilometre radius. The environment, climate and natural resources in a region can also provide the basis for segmentation. For example, the high mountains in Switzerland mean that there are a large variety of snow sports available to residents (and tourists of course), while the beaches in Thailand provide plenty of opportunity for warm water sports.

TABLE 5.3 Segmentation examples			
Opinions (about)	Interests	Activities	Personality
Politics	Family and children	Work	Values
Education	Home	Leisure and entertainment	Attitudes
Environment	Career	Self-care	Beliefs
The future	Art and culture	Holidays	Hopes
Religion	Sport and leisure	Hobbies	Habits
Social issues	Achievements	Home tasks	Expectations
Money	Travel and languages	Volunteering	Temperament
Morality	Community support	Social events	Reactions to situations
War	Charity	Community activities	Ways of thinking

Product behaviour segmentation

It is possible to segment sport consumers on the basis of their buying behaviour. For example, consumers may display similarities in how much and how often they purchase certain sport products, the situations in which they buy sport products, and how loyal they are to certain sport brands (such as whether they repeat purchase, or just buy once-off). Sport consumers who have a strong emotional connection to a brand or team, and who see it as an extension of themselves, are more likely to be loyal. This means that they are more likely to repeatedly buy tickets to games and purchase memberships and memorabilia, even if the team is performing poorly. Other consumers may be more interested in sport as a form of entertainment or socialising. These consumers will probably engage with sport in situations where their friends are involved, where special events and promotions are offered, and where additional entertainment options are available. Another example of behaviour segmentation in sport may be found in the consumers who buy life memberships or season tickets, compared with those who attend games casually. Consumers who sign up for season tickets are buying sport on a 'heavy usage' basis. Those who rarely attend are light users in comparison. Chapter 3 provided a detailed set of sport fan categories based on sport consumption behaviour.

Benefits segmentation

A final way that sport consumers can be segmented is based on the similar benefits that they seek from using a sport product or service. For example, a particular sport shoe brand might have shock-absorbing qualities that are appealing to one group of consumers, while another group of consumers may be more interested in the colours and fashion appeal of another brand. Different sport products offer different advantages, such as social, personal, performance, or health benefits. Some of the consumers who are interested in one aspect of a brand's features or benefits can be grouped together, usually on the basis of the underlying needs that are being met, such as fitness, entertainment or belonging.

Approaches to using segmentation

In addition to the six kinds of segmentation, there are three main ways of using segmentation. In step 2 of the segmentation process, it is possible to choose one or more than one segment. It is also possible not to choose any at all. The three ways of using segmentation are: focused segmentation, multiple segmentation, and undifferentiated segmentation. Focused segmentation occurs when only one segment is chosen with one corresponding marketing mix. Multiple segmentation involves the selection of more than one segment, with a unique marketing mix for each. Finally, undifferentiated segmentation occurs when a sport organisation decides not to choose a segment at all, but rather considers the total market as a single and unvarying consumer group. Figure 5.4 highlights where these three approaches fit within the four-step process of developing marketing positioning. Each is explained in further detail next.

Focused segmentation

Focused segmentation involves selecting only one of the market segments that has been identified and developing just one marketing mix with which to communicate to that segment. The result is that all of an organisation's focus targets one segment, an approach sometimes called niche marketing, or concentrated segmentation. For example, a

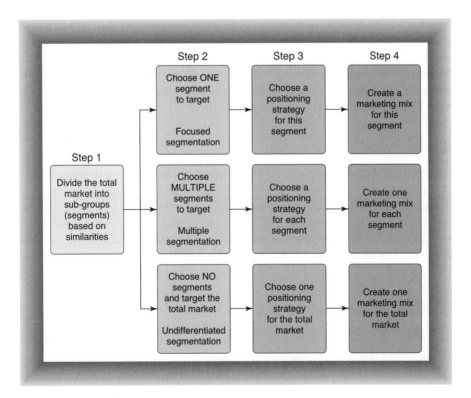

FIGURE 5.4 Sport marketing segmentation approaches

government agency might focus their efforts on a single segment of the market, such as encouraging smokers to quit.

There are some advantages to focused segmentation. By choosing one segment to emphasise it is possible to develop a highly specialised marketing mix perfectly tailored to meet the segment's needs. It also means that a sport organisation can direct all of its resources towards the single market segment, making it more cost effective. However, there are also disadvantages to focused segmentation. There are dangers if the market segment turns out to be too small, or if it shrinks over time. Also, another sport organisation might start to market to the same focused segment, but with more resources. Focused segmentation is powerful but risky.

Multiple segmentation

Multiple segmentation means choosing more than one segment, and developing a separate and unique marketing mix for each one. However, not all the elements of the marketing mix need to be changed for each market segment. For example, different promotions may be employed for each segment, but the same product, price and distribution options may remain. Multiple segmentation can help to spread the risk in the event that one of the segments is too small, shrinks in size over time, or was a poor choice in the first place. However, there are also disadvantages to using multiple segmentation. The main disadvantage is that it can be expensive. This is because it takes money, time and resources to create a new marketing mix for each segment. For example, it might mean that a sport organisation has to develop new products, invest in a number of different promotional programmes, distribute its products in different ways and research different pricing strategies. It is often wise to limit the number of segments chosen, particularly for smaller sport organisations with constrained resources. With the exception of large national or multinational organisations, it is probably imprudent to choose more than two or three segments.

Undifferentiated segmentation

Undifferentiated segmentation reflects the decision not to choose a segment at all, but rather to consider the entire market as a group of potential consumers. A sport organisation employing this strategy would develop one marketing mix for all consumers. Sometimes this approach is called mass marketing. It may seem uneconomical to follow the three steps of the segmentation process if only to decide not to proceed with any segmentation. However, one of the benefits of the segmentation process is that it reveals important information about consumers. Regardless of which segment is selected, or even none at all, it is always helpful to know as much about the market as possible. Another reason to follow the segmentation process is that it will help to decide whether choosing one, more than one, or no segment at all will be most advantageous. For example, if a sport marketer discovered that there is little difference between segments in the market, it might be best to use undifferentiated segmentation.

As with the previous two approaches to segmentation, undifferentiated segmentation has advantages and disadvantages. Like focused marketing, it can be more resource effective because it requires an investment in the development of only one marketing mix.

One of the disadvantages of undifferentiated segmentation is that it is harder to stand out from competitors.

Target market

Target marketing is a term used in sport marketing in reference to the way an organisation chooses one or more segments in which to target or aim its marketing mix. The segment(s) selected are like the numbers on a dartboard, where marketers take aim with a marketing mix. When the segmentation process is complete, a target market (or segment) should be the outcome.

> *Chapter tool 5.3 Market segmentation*: Market segmentation describes the process of categorising groups or segments of consumers together, based on similar needs or wants. There are several important elements to the effective use of segmentation as a marketing sport tool. First, the segment(s) chosen need(s) to be big enough to justify the effort of developing and implementing a marketing mix. Second, the segment chosen should be different enough from the other segments in the market to justify the effort and resources. If they are not different enough (and all the consumers in the total market are very similar already), then it may be more advisable to use an undifferentiated approach. In addition to these suggestions, there are four relevant issues to consider when choosing a segmentation approach:
>
> 1   It is important to estimate how easy it will be to reach the chosen segment. Is there a way to communicate with them? Can it be done via the media, Internet, newspapers or another means? Is there a way of getting the sport product to them? If they cannot be reached, or there is no way to distribute the sport product to them, then they are not the right segment to choose.
> 2   A sport organisation must consider the resources it can apply to the marketing process. Multiple segmentation can be expensive and time consuming, and it therefore may not be the best approach for a small and/or new organisation to employ.
> 3   The segmentation approach should also reflect how much a sport organisation knows about consumers. If it is a new enterprise, and/or offering a new product, it may not know much about its consumers yet, and its potential consumers may not yet be aware of the sport organisation and its products. Such circumstances would make it difficult to follow a multiple segmentation approach, which would demand considerable information about consumers.
> 4   The level of competition a sport organisation has in the market is likely to influence the choice of segmentation approach. If there is little competition, an undifferentiated approach might be satisfactory and, of course, cost less. However, in a market with fierce competition, multiple segmentation or concentrated segmentation would be helpful. This is not the only way to deal with competition. The way a product is positioned in the market helps to separate it from competitors.

Market positioning and differentiation

After the target market has been identified, a positioning strategy must be devised for use with each segment. Market positioning refers to how a sport brand is perceived by consumers relative to its competitors. For example, do consumers consider a sport brand as a luxury and high-quality product, or as a basic and value-for-money product? Do they see it as conservative and reliable, or exciting and dynamic? Positioning takes into account the fact that consumers will compare a product with others in the market. It assumes that they will put each product into a position in their minds; they will find a place where it fits compared to others.

The outcome of successful market positioning is a *differentiated* sport brand or product. If a sport brand or product has been differentiated it means that each target market segment attributes a specific value or set of features to it that are unique and special compared to competitors. In short, a differentiated sport brand or product stands out from the rest.

As reproduced in Table 5.4, there are numerous different positioning tactics that a sport organisation can choose from in order to best appeal to the target segment. Each positioning strategy will create a different perception in the minds of consumers. A positioning strategy is strongly connected with the concept of branding, where it is reinforced, amplified and extended. Sport branding is considered in Chapter 6.

Chapter tool 5.4 Market positioning: Market positioning is the process of attributing a sport brand or product a distinctive value or set of features for each target market segment compared to its competitors. The outcome of market positioning should be a differentiated sport brand or product. There are eight tactics of market positioning that a sport marketer might consider:

1 product features
2 product benefits
3 specific product use
4 product user
5 price and quality
6 against competitor
7 product class
8 hybrid positioning.

INTERACTIVE CASE

Traditional sport marketing is driven by top down direction and authority. That is, the vision, goals and marketing strategy are devised by senior administration and pushed through the organisation to the various stakeholders. In recent years, however, as the economy shifts from industry-based to knowledge-based, some sport businesses are embracing a new way of thinking about strategy development. A 'flipped' model

TABLE 5.4 Positioning tactics

Positioning tactics	Method	Examples
Product features	Focus on the unique features of the product	Unique features of sport shoes couldinclude a comfortable fit, shock-absorption qualities or a cutting-edge fashion design
		Most sport codes have unique features in the way a game is played, such as soccer, cricket, tennis and football
Product benefits	Tell customers what they will get out of the product or service	Health, fitness, social contact, fun, entertainment
Specific product	How can consumers use or apply the product?	Consumers could go to a game in order to socialise with friends
		What does the product do in specific situations?
Product user	Focus on the personality of the user	Show women enjoying the catwalkfashion at a horse-racing event to encourage more women to attend
		Show how the product can be used by people whom the user relates to
Price and quality	High price may reinforce quality, and low price may reinforce value	Making sport accessible for families or appealing to those with high disposable income because it is exclusive
Against competitor	Show consumers how the product or service is better than its competitors	Position the product or service as a market leader, an innovator; emphasise a superior product or better price
Product class (associate or disassociate)	Position the product as belonging to a particular class or category of products. Tell consumers it is associated or connected to this category. Or, highlight the product as being revolutionary or innovative, and in a class of its own. It is incomparable with other products	Promoting a sport event as a once-off experience
Hybrid positioning	Using a number of elements of different types of positioning	High-quality and innovative product; a unique experience

for marketing strategy is taking hold across numerous sectors. A shift has occurred from what the organisation perceives stakeholders want from them, to flipping the responsibility onto the stakeholder groups and having them drive the strategic focus. Added to this is a relatively new opportunity to leverage technology to enable stakeholders to provide input into marketing strategy and to deliver output back to the wider sport community.

Questions

By looking at an existing strategic plan such as www.sportnz.org.nz, is it really possible for a sport organisation to apply the 'flipped' metaphor in sport marketing to its strategic planning today?

Points of interest

A flipped marketing requires a new way of thinking and learning; an innovative way of capturing ideas with the use of technology and stakeholder engagement. A flipped strategy implies that the end-user, the sport consumer is in control of the purchasing situation. Buying a product or service is far more self-directed than ever before. Without doubt a sport consumer no longer wants to receive an organisation-driven solution to their sport consumption desires. Sport consumers are seeking to control their relationship and interactions with the seller. New technologies give sport marketers an unprecedented opportunity to cultivate deeper customer relationships. Flipping marketing to this mindset means that strategy formulation comes from the expectations buyers have of the organisation. It's their ideas, their learning and their demands that drive strategy.

Introduction to the marketing mix

The final part of this chapter is a brief introduction to the marketing mix, which is explained in detail in the six subsequent chapters. After a sport organisation has divided the total market into subgroups (step 1), chosen a segment(s) (step 2), and identified a positioning strategy for that segment (step 3), it must then develop a marketing mix for each segment. The marketing mix is a set of strategies and activities that cover product, price, promotion and place (distribution). These are commonly referred to as 'The Four Ps'. The fact that these four elements are grouped into a set, or a 'mix', is important, because they should be coordinated together in an integrated fashion. In this text, further to the four Ps, services and sponsorship each receive a chapter of their own. This is because sport services and sponsorship demand quite unique marketing strategies. Table 5.5 illustrates the marketing mix and their composition.

TABLE 5.5 Marketing mix composition

Product	Price	Promotion	Place
Service/product/facility	Level	Advertising	Location
Quality	Concessions	Sponsorship	Distribution
Features and options	Special offers	Event signage	Availability
Design and packaging	Season tickets	Exhibitions	Sport facilities
Benefits	Payment methods	Sales promotions	Accessibility
Ideas and intangibles	Social costs	Personal selling	Public transport
Licensing/merchandise	Customer time	Publicity	Parking
Brand name	Market sensitivity	Direct marketing	Media distribution
Product image	Legal constraints	Promotional licensing	Internet distribution
Resource management	Pricing objectives	Branding	Manufacturers/wholesalers/retailers
Staff	Break-even analysis	Public relations	Ticket distribution

Product

It is easy to think of the word *product* as referring to a physical, manufactured item. For example, Wilson produces sport equipment. However, the term product can also refer to services, ideas and the benefits that a sport organisation offers consumers. Many sport organisations offer a service, such as a form of physical activity, entertainment, or an experience. There is often no physical product to take away, but a sport organisation might offer some intangible benefits such as a lifestyle, a social group or even a belief system. The product can also include design, packaging and merchandise. Marketing the sport product is explained in detail in Chapter 6, and is heavily associated with branding. Sport services are considered exclusively in Chapter 11.

Price

The price refers to the cost that a consumer must pay to receive a product or service. This is usually thought of as the literal cost in monetary terms. In order to develop a pricing strategy it is important to consider pricing goals and match them to pricing techniques. Devising a pricing approach is considered in Chapter 7.

Place

Place is concerned with where consumers access the sport product or service. It is another word for distribution. Place is therefore about the way a product is made available to consumers; how it gets from the place where it is produced to the place where the consumer buys and consumes it. For physical, concrete products, place is concerned with the practical issues of getting a product from producers to consumers, along with any other stops along the way such as wholesalers and retailers. In recent years the Internet has provided a new way of distributing products. With the Internet or other forms of mail order, there does not necessarily need to be a retail outlet or shop, as consumers can buy directly from wholesalers, manufacturers or even just individual people (such as on eBay).

When it comes to services, sport may be delivered to people via pay, cable or satellite television, free-to-air television or other media. It may also be delivered in person by a sport organisation, such as local competitions and sports health practitioners. Place also includes different ways of getting tickets for a game or event, and decisions about where to locate sport facilities. Perhaps the most important aspect of place marketing is the way the sporting venue is used to augment the sport consumption experience. Place is considered in Chapter 8.

Promotion

Promotion is about communicating with consumers, getting a message across to the marketplace. Promotion therefore includes advertising, sponsorship, signage, exhibitions, sales promotions, personal selling and publicity. These are examined in Chapter 9. Chapter 10 examines sport sponsorship as part of a promotional strategy.

INTERACTIVE CASE

An excellent example of sport strategy can be seen in the recent acquisition of Australian A-League football (soccer) club Melbourne Heart by English Premier League side Manchester City. With the A-League growing as a genuine Asian league presence, Manchester City secured an Asian stronghold from which to launch their global branding objectives.

www.footballaustralia.com.au/melbourneheart
www.mcfc.com

Questions

Also of note, the strategic investment assumes part ownership of the National Rugby League team the Melbourne Storm, previously held by the Melbourne Heart ownership group. Why would Manchester City be interested in an Australian rugby league club?

Points of interest

The football boom intensifying across the massive Asian marketplace represents a significant opportunity for Manchester City to diversify its brand and gain the attention of a new generation of technologically savvy, globally oriented football fans who are gaining an interest in following the EPL. Marketers for Manchester City know very well that there is little chance of growing their market share in the cluttered domestic space, but are prepared to make strategic forays into the nascent sporting riches of Asia.

PRINCIPLES SUMMARY

- Chapter principle 5.1: The second stage of the Sport Marketing Framework is to develop a sport marketing strategy. This requires two steps: (a) to develop a strategic marketing direction, and (b) to develop a sport marketing position.

- Chapter principle 5.2: Developing a strategic marketing direction involves constructing marketing objectives and setting performance measures.

- Chapter principle 5.3: Developing a sport marketing position involves four steps: market segmentation (1, 2), market positioning tactics (3) and devising the marketing mix (4).

TOOLS SUMMARY

- Chapter tool 5.1 Marketing objectives
- Chapter tool 5.2 Performance measures
- Chapter tool 5.3 Market segmentation
- Chapter tool 5.4 Market positioning

REVIEW QUESTIONS

1 How is the information acquired from stage 1, identifying sport marketing opportunities, used for stage 2, developing a sport marketing strategy?

2 Identify the key criteria in devising a good sport marketing objective.

3 What is the relationship between sport marketing objectives and performance measures?

4 What are the different kinds of market segmentation options?

5 When should each kind of market segmentation be used?

6 What is the purpose of market positioning?

7 How does market positioning influence the marketing mix?

RELEVANT WEBSITES

www.thefa.com — English Football Association
www.nadeshikoleague.jp — Japan Women's Football League
www.nwslsoccer.com — US National Women's Soccer League

www.tourism.gov.ph	World Tourism Authority
www.facebook.com/londonmarathon	London Marathon Facebook site
www.facebook.com/TheBostonMarathon	Boston Marathon Facebook site
www.mcg.org.au	Melbourne Cricket Ground
www.wimbledon.com	All England Lawn Tennis Club
www.sportnz.org.nz	Sport New Zealand
www.footballaustralia.com.au/melbourneheart	Melbourne Heart Football Club
www.mcfc.com	Manchester City Football Club

FURTHER READING

Gómez, S., Kase, K. and Urrutia, I. (2012). *Value Creation and Sport Management*. Cambridge: Cambridge University Press.

Hoye, R., Smith, A., Stewart, B. and Nicholson, M. (2015). *Sport Management: Principles and Applications* (4th edn). Oxford: Elsevier.

CHAPTER 6

Sport products and branding

LEARNING OUTCOMES

At the end of this chapter, readers should be able to:

- define the term sport product
- outline the key characteristics of sport products
- explain the sport product continuum
- define the term product augmentation, and describe augmentation strategies
- identify the process of new product innovation and development
- explain the concept of the product life cycle
- describe the process of building a sport brand.

OVERVIEW

The purpose of this chapter is to explore the first of the six elements of the marketing mix: the sport product. It will introduce the key components of the sport product and will outline product strategies that can be used within the marketing mix, including product augmentation, new product innovation, and sport branding.

STAGE 3: PLAN THE MARKETING MIX

Sport product: Goods and services

Chapters 4 and 5 explained the first two stages of the Sport Marketing Framework. This chapter concentrates on the first of six elements in stage 3, Plan the sport marketing mix: the concept of the sport product, and product strategies that can be used in sport marketing. The additional elements of stage 3 are presented in the forthcoming five chapters. Figure 6.1 highlights stage 3 and its major components within the Sport Marketing Framework.

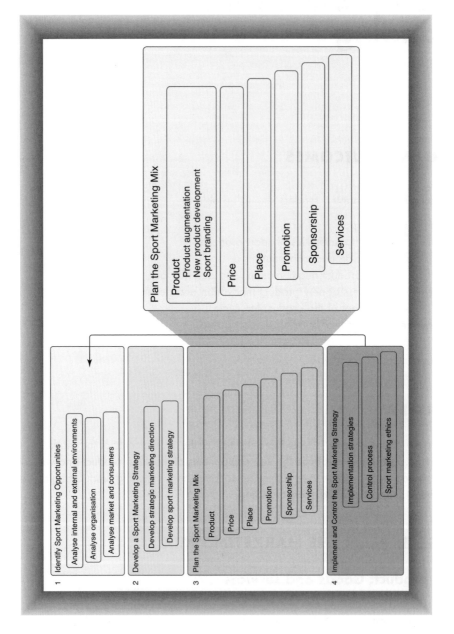

FIGURE 6.1 Plan the marketing mix

1 Identify Sport Marketing Opportunities
- Analyse internal and external environments
- Analyse organisation
- Analyse market and consumers

2 Develop a Sport Marketing Strategy
- Develop strategic marketing direction
- Develop sport marketing strategy

3 Plan the Sport Marketing Mix
- Product
- Price
- Place
- Promotion
- Sponsorship
- Services

4 Implement and Control the Sport Marketing Strategy
- Implementation strategies
- Control process
- Sport marketing ethics

Plan the Sport Marketing Mix
- Product
  - Product augmentation
  - New product development
  - Sport branding
- Price
- Place
- Promotion
- Sponsorship
- Services

What is a sport product?

A product is usually conceived as a physical good that has been manufactured; something that can be held and touched, such as a sporting shoe, football or baseball cap. However, the term product can also refer to services and ideas. In fact, the word product is used in sport marketing in several ways including (1) a good (physical item), (2) a service, (3) an idea and/or (4) a combination of these. Each is explained next.

Sporting goods

In the sport industry, examples of physical products include sport shoes, tennis rackets, memorabilia, golf balls and skateboards. There are also goods that are not only used exclusively for sport, but can be used along with sport or as part of the sport experience. These include sunglasses, caps, T-shirts, watches, iPods, gym bags, sporting apparel and sunscreen. These items are all tangible, which means that they can be experienced physically by the senses of sight, touch, taste, smell and hearing.

Sporting services

Sport services, on the other hand, are not tangible. Patrons of sport services receive benefits in the form of an intangible experience. For example, services are offered in the form of fitness and recreation opportunities, entertainment through live or televised matches, physiotherapy or coaching. These services are not physical objects that can be purchased and removed. Sport organisations cannot make extra services and store them away for consumers who may wish to buy them later. There are four important differences between sport goods and services that are highly relevant to sport marketing. These are tangibility, consistency, perishability and separability.

Tangibility

Sporting goods are tangible when they are physical and are experienced by the senses. From a practical viewpoint, sport product tangibility means that a consumer can take the product away with them for use later, and most often, for repeated use. Services are intangible because they are not physical and cannot be taken home to keep. Services are experienced for a period rather than owned.

Consistency

Consistency is another way by which sport goods and services can be separated. Consistency refers to how reliable the quality of the product is from one time that it is purchased and used to the next. Sporting goods usually have a high degree of reliability. There is not much change in the quality of a sporting shoe or a football of the same brand and model from one version to the next. On the other hand, sport services are likely to have more variable quality. The service quality of a sport experience may change depending on who is providing the service as well as the special conditions of its offering (e.g. weather). The fact that the quality of a sporting match will change from one time to the next has already been addressed in Chapter 2. Of course, an athlete may perform brilliantly in one competition or game, then fail miserably at the next. When this issue of variability in the sport product was discussed, it was emphasised that sport marketers should focus their attention on the quality of those parts of the service or product that they have some control over, such as service quality, prices, food and beverages, and the venue.

Perishability

Perishability refers to whether a sport product can be stored and used at another time. Sporting goods (such as clothing and equipment) are not perishable. Basketballs, cricket bats and bicycles can be stored if they are not bought by a consumer without any damage to the product. Services cannot be stored. For example, it is not possible to hold on to unsold tickets to a sport contest to sell them at another time. Once the game has been played any seats that were not filled are lost forever.

Separability

Separability is a term that is used to describe whether the creation or manufacture of a sport product happens at the same time as when it is consumed. Naturally, sporting goods are made prior to their use. For example, a hockey stick is made, delivered to a wholesaler and/or retailer, placed on the shelf or online and ultimately bought by a consumer. The quality of the good (the hockey stick) is separated from the quality of service at the sport store where it is bought. It is also possible to separate the item from the person selling it, although sometimes one can affect the other. Sport services, in contrast, are made and consumed at the same time. At a live sport event, the entertainment benefits are created at the same time that it is consumed by fans. It is also more difficult to separate the service from the person providing the service.

> *Chapter principle 6.1*: Sport goods may be differentiated from services on the basis of four factors: tangibility, consistency, perishability and separability

Ideas

Although it might sound strange, ideas can form the core of some sport products. One example is when a consumer buys a gymnasium membership with the idea of being thinner or more muscular. Another example is the power of sport in providing a sense of identity and vicarious achievement for fans. From this viewpoint, sport stimulates consumers to feel (emotional response) and to believe certain things (thinking response). At sport events it is not just goods and services that are offered to consumers. There may also be ideas that are sold to consumers, such as those relating to belonging and success.

A combination of goods, services and ideas

In practice, most sport products and services are a mixture of tangible and intangible elements. Many physical products have a service or idea element. In fact, sport consumers frequently buy products because of the intangible benefits they deliver. Equally, many services are sold together with something tangible to take away. For example, a membership to a football club may come with a package including club stickers, badges and regular newsletters. In many instances, a sport consumer buys a mixture of goods, services, benefits and ideas. There are also examples of sport services being transformed into sport products, such as live games that have been recorded for later sale, online streaming, or YouTube content. In sport marketing it is common to combine products and services, and the tangible and intangible, to provide a more flexible, textured and appealing set of materials to sell to sport consumers.

> *Chapter principle 6.2*: A sport product is the complete package of benefits presented to a sport consumer in the form of physical goods, services and ideas, or a combination of these to produce a sport experience.

THE SPORT PRODUCT CONTINUUM

Although sport products may feature a mixture of tangible and intangible elements, some sport products are mainly tangible and some are mainly intangible. The sport product continuum is a useful tool to help show that products can be defined along a continuum (or a scale) with *mainly tangible* products on one end, *mainly intangible* products on the other end and a mixture of the two in the middle.

As Figure 6.2 demonstrates, some products are mainly tangible, such as tennis balls and fitness equipment. Although they might provide intangible benefits that consumers want, these products depend on their tangible or physical elements. Take away the physical object and the product is essentially gone as well. In contrast, a suburban tennis competition or surfing lessons are examples of products that are mainly intangible. Even if there is a physical good supplied as part of the service (such as a racquet or surfboard), the product depends on its intangible service element. Take away the service, such as all the volunteers and administrators and the product is untenable. Finally, a sport event provides a good example of a product that is a mixture of tangible and intangible elements.

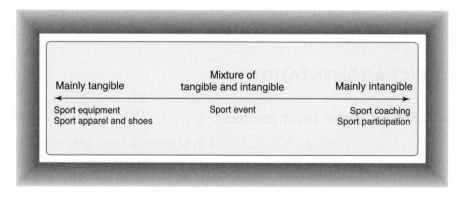

FIGURE 6.2 The sport product continuum

The intangible elements of a baseball game include what happens on the diamond, while the tangible elements include the food, beverages and merchandise that are offered as part of the experience. Fans are usually looking for all these elements in a sport event, not just one or another. For sport marketers, it is a useful exercise to locate all their products on the sport product continuum.

Mainly tangible and mainly intangible products

Products that sit exclusively at either end of the continuum can present sport marketers with unique challenges. Imagine, for example, the difficulties associated with marketing a tennis ball. There is little to make one brand of tennis ball stand out from others. One common approach is to use pricing to form a point of differentiation that can make the product more appealing for economic reasons, but it is also easy for competitors to copy this tactic. As a result, sport marketers try hard to add intangible value to their tangible products, such as the use of a famous tennis player to endorse a brand of tennis balls, or by emphasising that the product has a unique feature or quality.

Similarly, mainly intangible products are challenging to market. Consider, for example, golf lessons. When the consumer has nothing tangible to take away with them, there is no definitive reminder of what they have bought. It may be difficult for them to judge or remember what the quality of the lesson was because the advice given was essentially intangible and easily forgotten. One way to overcome these difficulties is to include some tangible elements such as brochures on certain golf skills or rules, or even bonus golf balls with the service name or logo. One pivotal tactic in sport marketing is to try to move products away from either of the extremes of the continuum, and to create a mixture of tangible and intangible elements. Sport events, for example, may emphasise the physical qualities of the venue, as well as opportunities to purchase memorabilia and merchandise. Many sport events make more profit from these tangible value add-ons than they do from the core entertainment product of the game itself. For example, it is common at sport events for consumers to spend more money on merchandise and food and beverages than they do on the actual ticket.

> *Chapter tool 6.1 Sport product continuum*: The sport product continuum is a useful tool to help show that products can be defined along a continuum (or a scale) with mainly tangible products on one end, mainly intangible products on the other end and a mixture of the two in the middle.

PRODUCT AUGMENTATION

Key variables of the sport product

Sport products possess a range a benefits as well as tangible and intangible elements. In addition, if the sport product is lacking in either tangible or intangible elements, it can be more difficult to market. It is therefore important to think of the sport product as being a complete package or a 'bundle' of elements, consisting of core benefits, product features and the augmented product, as illustrated in Figure 6.3.

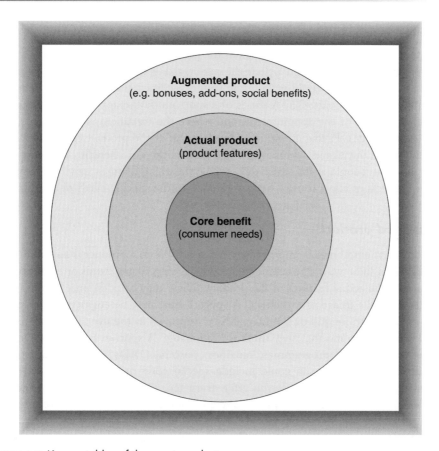

FIGURE 6.3 Key variables of the sport product

Core benefit

The core benefit represents the principal advantage that the consumer receives from buying and using a product. For example, if a consumer buys a sports car, the main benefit is transportation. If a consumer buys a T-shirt, the main benefit is a covering for the body. If a consumer buys a ticket to a sport event, the main benefit is the entertainment value or experience the consumer receives as a consequence of attendance. Finally, if the consumer buys a service, such as a sport physiotherapy session or a sport skills lesson, the core benefits are physical treatment of an injury, or instruction on how to play a sport, respectively.

It is easy to underestimate the importance of the core benefit of a product, and focus on the other variables such as features (actual product) or add-ons (augmented product). But the core benefit is the most *fundamental* benefit of the product; if it does not meet the needs of sport customers, then it is unlikely to be successful. It is always important to understand the main need that the consumer has, or the primary benefit that they get from using the product. It is no use adding frills to a product if it does not meet the basic needs of consumers in the first place.

Actual product

The actual product refers to the features of the product. The features of a merchandised sport T-shirt, for example, could include the colour, sizing, fabric and pattern. The product features of a sport event could include the venue, facilities, the participating athletes or players and the scoreboard. The features of a sport physiotherapy service could include the length of time of the appointment, and where the treatment is performed (e.g. at home or at a clinic). Paying attention to the features of the product can be one way of making it stand out against competition. As long as the core benefit of the product is something that people want, then developing the right features can help amplify a product's effects or allow it to be better moulded to the specific needs of consumers.

Augmented product

The word augmented means improved or increased. When a product is augmented, it is made better in some way. The augmented product refers to any extras or extensions that are added to the actual features of the product. These may be additional benefits, bonus extras or even the image of a product. A sport T-shirt may be augmented by adding a bonus cap (an extra or add-on); it may also be improved in the eye of the consumer by being a particular brand that they think is fashionable. A sport event could offer extras such as merchandise, programmes, fanzines, posters, DVDs and autograph signing opportunities. A sport lesson could include special guest appearances by well-known players or the bonus of a free lesson after every ten. Finally, in the case of the sport physiotherapy session, the therapist could offer information brochures, or provide a reminder call the day before the appointment. It is important to remember that aspects such as the status, image or social appeal of a product are all examples of augmentation.

Understanding how sport products can be augmented is particularly useful in markets where there is substantial competition, or where different products have similar core benefits and product features. The market for sports shoes provides a prominent example. The core benefit of shoes (a covering protection for feet) is the same no matter who makes them. Different manufacturers try to create different product features, such as colour schemes, air pockets for shock absorption or Velcro straps. However, these features are often quickly copied by competitors. One of the most effective ways of making sport shoes stand out is through the image of the product. Many manufacturers such as Nike and adidas use athlete sponsorship to give the product an association with success, exclusivity or style.

It is not as easy as it might appear to differentiate between the three variables of the sport product. Sport consumers might have different motivations for their consumption decisions. For example, although the core benefit of a sports car is transportation, it is probably reasonable to conclude that it is not actually the benefit of transport that is compelling in such a purchase. Rather, the features of a sports car make its transportation benefit much more appealing. In addition, augmented product add-ons such as belonging to a sports car club might provide a further set of advantages that add to the satisfaction of a consumer.

> *Chapter principle 6.3*: Sport products should be seen as a bundle of benefits comprising the core benefits, actual product features and the augmented product.

These three variables of the product are interrelated and should be manipulated as a group.

INTERACTIVE CASE

Consider the prototype technology developed by US start-up firm, Electrozyme (http://electrozyme.com). They have prototyped a state-of-the-art sensor technology worn like a temporary tattoo or a Band-Aid, that can record information about the wearer's sweat in order to provide detailed information about key physiological biomarkers from electrolyte balances to lactate levels.

Questions

Before long, every coach and performance manager in elite sport will know when their players need sustenance, and exactly what kind, well before the player will realise themselves. Visit the Electrozyme site to see what they have to offer. What are some future products that we might anticipate seeing soon? Then, comment on how sport marketers can employ these cutting edge devices to enhance the viewing experience for sport fans.

Points of interest

The trend towards wearable devices for both sport participants and viewers has gained in popularity to the extent that we can expect a proliferation in new product innovations in this area. Part of the massive opportunity comes from the amazing range of opportunities that wearable devices offer for sport. For example, first, participants can wear them with benefits at all levels in order to track performance and activity. A classic example is the simple heart-rate monitor. Second, elite athletes and players can wear devices as part of the viewer's entertainment experience. The performance and physiological data can be made available to (potentially) select viewers, offering a unique insight into the athletic experience. Currently, in T20 cricket, for example, players can wear microphones to discuss the game on air with television commentators, heart-rate monitors, or tracking devices that summarise their movements over time. However, newer devices such as versions of Google Glasses are likely to debut in professional sport shortly, delivering a unique first person insight into an athlete's personal perspective. Finally, sport product and technology companies are also furiously working to develop wearable technology to relay hands-free event imagery. Versions of glasses or contacts with in-built visual displays and television screens will provide a new form of interface with existing tools such as smartphones, tablets and smart watches. Such developments promise new levels of connectivity where sporting content and data are automatically collected, transferred, ordered, filtered, stored and delivered at the user's whim.

SPORT PRODUCT INNOVATION

Sport marketers may consider the possibility of new product development through a process of innovation. Developing a new product can be expensive and risky. Every year there is a proliferation of new sport products introduced to the market, but only a small fraction of these are successful. If a new product is a failure, the sport organisation has lost time and money, and perhaps even some of its reputation. But what does it mean to develop a new product? A new product does not have to mean a brand new product. In sport marketing, a new product can take many forms, such as the improved performance of an existing product, new functions added to an existing product, a new way to use an existing product, combining existing products, or a new look or design for a product. Whatever form the new or revised product takes, it arises through a successful process of innovation.

Innovation has come to mean a multiplicity of things from simple creativity to complex manufacturing. For us, from a sport product perspective, innovation refers to the translation of a new idea into a tangible deliverable via a technology, physical product, or process-based service. Unlike an invention or a discovery, an innovation actually takes a place on the real-world stage, either as a novel solution to an existing consumer problem, an improvement to a consumer experience, or even a completely new offering for a consumer to try that they had never contemplated before. Because innovation tends to be synonymous with inspiration, considerable mystery surrounds its cultivation. Here we explore the basics of the sport product innovation process and offer numerous examples of cutting-edge developments.

In sport, product innovations can be found in several forms. First, mobile technology is changing the way consumers and participants connect with sport. For example, smart devices allow consumers to watch and experience sport from anywhere and at any time. Participants, and especially elite athletes, can collect, store and analyse a vast amount of training and performance data that offer vital clues for subsequent improvement. Second, sport product innovations have made a serious impact on the support systems for sport performance, such as sports medicine, rehabilitation, pharmaceuticals, nutrition and supplements. Also, of course, sport managers and marketers can benefit from new innovations that augment audience size, consumer viewing experiences, broadcasting coverage and quality, media channels, regulation, rule enforcement and officiating, and general spectator safety and comfort.

As a result of these major opportunities arising from the application of innovations, sport marketers would be well advised to become conversant with the processes surrounding innovation. But this does not mean that sport marketers must await the development of new technologies. Instead they can aggressively pursue new product innovations through the application of available ideas and tools in new ways. Many sports, for example, have founded modified versions of their games in order to attract new audiences, including formats specifically designed for children, and those exclusively conceived for maximum entertainment. For our purposes, innovation relates to product outcomes that are more attractive to a targeted audience. An innovation can be incremental in that it shifts the existing product in modest but important ways, or radical, where a product can be completely redesigned or even replaced by something consumers never expected.

Chapter principle 6.4: In sport marketing, a new product can take many forms such as the improved performance of an existing product, new functions added to an existing product, a new way to use an existing product, combining existing products, or a new look or design for a product.

The process of new product development is usually coordinated by high-level managers in large sport organisations. However, irrespective of the level, it is important for sport marketers to understand the process to which they are expected to contribute. The process of new product innovation has five stages, which are shown in Figure 6.4.

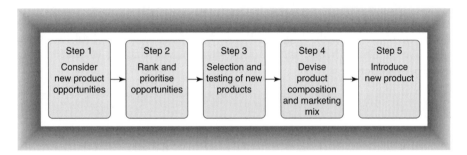

FIGURE 6.4 Steps of new product development

INTERACTIVE CASE

If we describe sports in four broad categories – outdoor, indoor, underwater or in the air, then there are innumerable possibilities for participating in sport. Many sports belong to corporate or government management organisations and some have even existed for centuries. Other sports are relatively new and innovative, attracting great interest for the twenty-first century participant. Creating the next 'big thing' in sport does require some inventiveness.

Hockey is an excellent example of a sport that has evolved and developed new sport products. Changes to the hockey product have included hockey on ice, on blades, on streets, in sledges, underwater, with unicycles and many other ways in which the principles of hockey can be applied in unique and novel packages. Creating a new sport product can be an exciting prospect for a sport marketer. The ability to attract new target markets or extend the experience for existing participants is a motivating challenge worth considering. Other sports have combined the characteristics of two or more sports to develop a hybrid version.

Questions

What are some existing hybrid sports? Propose some new versions that do not yet exist but could occupy a gap in the market. Highlight the ways in which the new hybrid sports could be marketed.

Points of interest

Hybrid sports usually start out as a novel way of exposing existing sports. Arguably, they may not be as popular as the original product but if successful they can create a new dedicated supporter base and expand their service into more formalised competitions. For example, the Biathlon is a combination of cross-country skiing and rifle shooting. Its success has been so great that it has participated at the Winter Olympics consistently since 1960. Another relatively new hybrid sport is International Rules Football. A hybrid of Australian Rules and Gaelic football has had limited success since regular international games were played from 1998. The difficulty in creating a sport product in the fragmented markets of today comes with understanding the target audience's interests and desires and fulfilling their needs in a unique and interesting way. Tazerball, Joggling, Baseketball, Polocrosse and Frisbee Golf all sound like interesting hybrid sports to investigate when it comes to understanding new sport product ideas.

Consider new product opportunities

This first step of product innovation involves creating and collecting new product possibilities and ideas. While the product innovation process can occur either spontaneously, or evolve almost unnoticed over a long period of incremental improvements, sport marketers can benefit from noting a series of steps typically present in any innovation outcome. Although beginning with a problem to be solved is a conventional and quite obviously sensible approach, innovation does not necessarily need something wrong to get it going. If we consider, for example, some of the most significant sport product innovations of the last few decades, we would have to concede that many were not responses to problems. Rather, many came about through ingenuity, market testing, examining what competitors are doing, studying what is being done overseas, consulting with other staff and current customers, and starting with a strong pool of potential ideas. Or, to put it another way, product developers and marketers imagined new products and services impelled by thoughts on new opportunities. For example, some new product options are likely to have emerged in stage 1 of the Sport Marketing Framework. Consider the recently banned, full body 'sleeksuits' used in swimming to set a gamut of new world records, or the Ultimate Fighting Championship League, which redefined the sport combat entertainment experience. Both emerged in a cluttered product market, were anticipated, or were created as solutions to problem products or services. Opportunities are the engine of innovation. For this reason, product innovation begins with the desire for new value. Step one in the sport product innovation process therefore seeks to cultivate an abundant, diverse and rich platform of potential concepts from which to conceive new value. It is important that the ideas remain unconstrained from the usual practicalities associated with convention, resources and preconceived assumptions about what sport consumers want.

Rank and prioritise opportunities

The second step in new product innovation involves sifting through all the ideas that have been collected and only keeping the ones that fit with the marketing objectives of the sport organisation. It is also helpful to consider how well the new product ideas fit with existing products, and how they relate to current trends. This is not the stage to be concerned about financial realism. However, by the end of this step, new product opportunities should be ranked according to priorities determined by marketing objectives. In short, the lengthy set of ideas from step one need to be reduced to a workable handful. A range of methods can be employed, including voting and weighting systems, pre-determined priority areas, expert advice, panels and workshops, and the capability product champions have to quickly develop their ideas into testable prototypes. Subsequently, new product and service innovations should be tested as quickly and inexpensively as possible, in step three, rapid prototyping and testing of new products.

Rapid prototyping and testing of new products

Step three of the process involves a more careful assessment of the ideas that were retained following step two. In fact, the highest ranking options should be identified and piloted to determine their potential in the market. This is the time to check feasibility by undertaking cost and financial estimates, and to conduct additional market research, or concept testing. Concept testing involves giving potential customers a description of the new product, and asking them if they would be likely to buy it. It may also mean providing a prototype of the new product for customers to try. One powerful option at this stage involves creating a 'rapid prototype'.

Recently popularised and infused into marketing and business circles, rapid prototyping is a method of quickly testing an idea to see whether it could work before significant resources are expended in creating it for the market. Because rapid prototyping has been appropriated from designers, the process reflects the fluid and iterative methods they use in testing their nascent ideas. A prototype can range from a basic sketch or flowchart to a mock-up product or an unrefined but fully functional technology. The key is not in the finish but rather in the start. Most innovations never make it to the market because they take too long to develop or require too much investment without really knowing whether it will pay off or not. Rapid prototyping attempts to sidestep the development lag that most product innovations face. By quickly converting an idea into something tangible that can be tested – preferably by the same kinds of sport users and consumers who might buy it in the end – and subsequently refined and retested, the innovation process can be radically shortened. Often, the result is the choice to abandon the new innovation. This is sometimes referred to as 'fast failure' or 'cheap failure', but reflects a positive outcome where resources have been protected from wastage in the light of early trials. In rapid prototyping, experimentation remains central, which leads to better design, faster.

It is important to understand that the rapid prototyping method does not seek to create fully functional products or services. But, they do need to evoke an experience in users that will provide them with a first-hand insight into what it is like to try the new product. For example, a marketer might conceive a new process for sport consumers to purchase tickets to events through a mobile application. Instead of spending months and thousands of dollars on development, the marketer might simply construct some cards or offline screens reflecting the steps through which a consumer would use the application. By working with users to test the idea, the marketer can quickly ascertain whether their consumers have an appetite for the actual product. A prototype could range from the low fidelity, such as a series of sketches on paper, to high fidelity, such as a working application with limited functionality. The important issue is that users can be exposed to the kind of experience that the ultimate product seeks to elicit. Better prototypes duplicate the final product experience with greater precision than lesser prototypes. But even a poor prototype can be enough to provide sufficient feedback for a successive, refined version.

Most consumers find it difficult to imagine their responses to new product innovations in the absence of any tangible experience in which to base their expectations. Prototypes vastly amplify the productivity of market testing, and have therefore become a pivotal tool in the sport product development arsenal.

INTERACTIVE CASE

Where business plans need to have a positive impact quickly, especially in highly competitive spaces, a lean start-up model of strategy implementation offers a powerful option. Adopting a lean start-up style ensures ideas are tried out quickly and cheaply. The aim is to minimise the time of delivery from idea formation to sport product implementation. Capitalising on a minimum cost (time and money)/maximum access or opportunity approach eliminates the uncertainty that consumes a new product development process. The constantly changing competitive environment is the trigger to a lean start-up concept. By adopting the 'just do it' slogan of the Nike Sports Company, lean start up avoids the complications and missed opportunities that go with protracted testing and retesting ideas. It means working smarter by challenging not whether the product can work, but whether the product should work.

Four elements make for a successful start up – money, traction, team and vision. If there are significant resources for three of these four attributes then start-up success is likely. Start from there and build a plan. Learning is a vital outcome of developing new products in a lean start-up environment. The marketer needs to learn how to build a sustainable business quickly from new products.

Questions

Learning and failing fast is the key to a lean start-up model for marketing strategy. That is, knowing when to jump in, and equally, when to jump out. You need to pivot fast and 'love it' more than anyone else so that rapid execution is effective. What do you think about shutting down programmes early in their life cycle – a so-called 'fast-failure' model? Can anything be done in the preliminary stages of product development to induce failure? How can you inspire management to support you to press the 'restart' button again?

Points of interest

For sport organisations competing for membership, sponsorship, fans and participants, the temptation to establish a 'spin-off' league as a start-up opportunity is appealing, given the success of many adapted sport leagues around the world. However, not all new or modified sport products invigorate interest. Two women's soccer leagues in the United States have failed to capture the support expected, given the success of the national team at the World Cup. The Canadian Soccer League enjoyed an inglorious lifespan of five years. Again, enthusiasm for creating a League was generated from unexpected World Cup success. This spark of enthusiasm to grow the sport of soccer in Canada was soon dampened when a lack of talent and attendances created huge financial losses, resulting in the abandonment of the League after five years.

In another example, Youcastr, a personalised, interactive and entertaining sports network was launched in 2007 but gone by 2010. YouCastr aimed to make it easier for sport fans to keep in touch and interact with each other via live, online streaming audio and video sportscasts. What started as a virtual 'sports bar' with sports fans providing 'live' commentary to games became a stage for a 'do it yourself pay per view video'. Fans controlled the content of delivery with live sports video or audio as well as uploading pictures of their favourite teams in action. Failure of the company was attributed to a few key factors including market shifts, that Youcastr team members had moved on, and the company had simply run out of cash. 'Sometimes you've simply gotta know when to move on; there's no harm in that. What matters is how and when you bounce back', said part owner Ariel Diaz.

Devise product composition and marketing mix

With the results of the new product's feasibility and market testing available, it is time to make a final decision about how to proceed. It is possible that the best decision is not to proceed and to choose the next highest ranked new product opportunity to investigate. If the feasibility and testing results are promising, the final product composition should be determined. This involves specifying the core product benefits, actual product features and augmented product composition. The other elements of the marketing mix will also need to be determined to provide the appropriate positioning strategy.

Introduce new product

Finally, if a sport product has successfully made it through all these stages, it is ready to be released onto the market. With this decision, an implementation plan will need to be created to support the deployment of all the variables in the marketing mix. The details of implementation are provided in Chapter 13.

Chapter tool 6.2 New product development: The process of new product development involves five stages: (1) consider new product opportunities, (2) rank and prioritise opportunities, (3) rapid prototyping and testing of new products, (4) devise product composition and marketing mix and (5) introduce new product.

INTERACTIVE CASE

Crowdsourcing through public funding platforms such as Kickstarter (http://kickstarter.com) and Indiegogo (http://indiegogo.com) have helped entrepreneurs all over the world to get a start by accessing small pools of capital committed by interested site visitors.

Questions

Review the websites of Kickstarter and Indiegogo. What kinds of sports-related products are being proposed? Choose one that you think has high potential and discuss how it could be marketed.

Points of interest

Today increasing numbers of sport product innovations are making their way onto crowdsourcing sites. Among the most common innovations for sport are wearable activity tracking devices, sport injury remediation products, smartphone integrated sensors, and a wide range of sport-specific equipment from swimming 3D cameras to analyse technique biomechanics to cricket balls that can record speed and spin. One thing is clear: new sport product innovations are not about accessories for sport equipment anymore. The key innovations become the new, essential sport equipment, characterised by their connectivity to everything else.

PRODUCT LIFE CYCLE

Sport products come and go. At first they seem like the latest fashion, then consumers lose interest and a new product takes its place. After a product has been on the market for a while, sometimes sport organisations change it in some way, creating a 'new and improved' version. These changes reflect the fact that every product has a life cycle. A product is 'born', introduced to the market, people learn about it and buy it, then they lose interest and the product may 'die' or be changed or upgraded. The term *product life cycle* refers to the stages that a product goes through from first being introduced onto the market to its decline. There are four stages of the product life cycle as depicted in Figure 6.5: introduction, growth, maturity and decline.

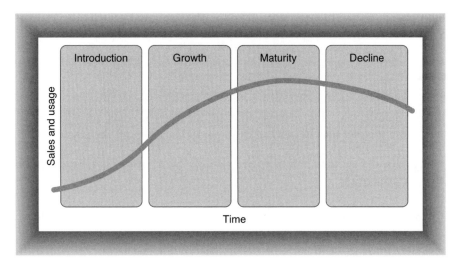

FIGURE 6.5 Product life cycle stages

Chapter principle 6.5: The term *product life cycle* refers to the stages that a product goes through from first being introduced onto the market to its decline. There are four stages of the product life cycle: introduction, growth, maturity and decline.

Introduction

The introduction phase refers to the period when a product first enters the market. Many sport products fail at this stage, and/or they are changed as problems become apparent. Sales and usage usually increase slowly, and there may not actually be a profit for the organisation once the costs of product development and marketing are taken into account. Marketing costs are usually high because of advertising needs (the need to inform consumers about the new product and its benefits), the need to give consumers incentives to try the product and the need to encourage distributors to sell the product by giving them attractive profit margins. The length of time that a sport product stays in this stage will vary greatly. For example, there may be a long introduction time if there are already plenty of other substitute products on the market.

Growth

Growth is the stage when the product has already attracted the awareness of the target consumers, and there is a rush or increase in sales. Profits usually rise quickly at this stage, however, so does the amount of competition.

Maturity

Once the product has been on the market for a long period it is in the maturity phase. There are likely to be more competitors in the marketplace for the product and the producer may be forced to make some changes. This is normally the longest stage of the product life cycle. Gradually, profits or usage will decrease during this stage.

Decline

A product is in the decline stage when it experiences a drop in sales or usage as an enduring trend; how quickly sales drop will be different for every product and every situation. Eventually the product may be substantially changed or taken off the market.

Understanding the product life cycle is pivotal in sport marketing because different marketing strategies should be used during different stages of the cycle. Some examples are reproduced in Table 6.1.

> *Chapter tool 6.3 Product life cycle stages*: Different marketing strategies should be employed at each stage of a product's life cycle using variations to the mix including price, promotions, sponsorship, distribution and services.

SPORT BRANDING

The idea of branding is closely linked with positioning. A brand is like an identifying badge, often reinforced by a name or a logo that helps consumers recognise a product or an organisation. A brand becomes linked with consumers' opinions and perceptions of a sport product and organisation. A brand serves to remind consumers of its positioning compared to other products. Because branding and positioning are associated, it is important to keep branding, segmentation and positioning strategies closely related. It is no use having a branding concept that emphasises luxury and quality, choosing a segment that is interested in value for money and positioning the product as belonging to the 'x-treme' class of sports. In this example, the branding, segmentation and positioning strategies do not match or complement one another. The result would be confusing and off-putting to consumers.

In a competitive industry such as sport, product sales can be affected by how easily a consumer can tell different products apart. Branding is one of the key strategies that sport marketers use to help their product stand out from the crowd. The way a consumer thinks about a product becomes a powerful form of reinforcement. Branding is therefore a way of augmenting a product by helping to create associated ideas that make it different. The added value that a product possesses because of its brand name and identity is called brand equity.

Brands can help consumers to remember products, and can set off images in their minds. A powerful brand is one that has both a high level of recognition in the market, and strong associated imagery. Manchester United, Ferrari, Dallas Cowboys, Los Angeles Lakers, IOC, FIFA and Nike are all examples of very powerful sport brands.

> *Chapter principle 6.6*: A sport brand is the symbolic representation of everything that a sport organisation seeks to stand for, leading to expectations about its value and performance. A brand can be portrayed as an identifying badge that triggers consumers to remember a product or an organisation. It can be a name, a design, a symbol (or logo), an image or a combination of these things. Branding is one

TABLE 6.1 Marketing strategies at each stage of the product life cycle

Stage of the product life cycle

Marketing mix	Introduction	Growth	Maturity	Decline
Product strategies	Narrow or single product option with ongoing changes to adapt to initial market feedback	More changes to product and more options to the range and variety	Introduce new variations of product to appeal to new segments	Products that are no longer popular are removed
Pricing strategies	High prices to cover high costs or low prices and discounts to encourage people to 'try and buy'	Reduce prices, especially if there are lots of competitors	Continue to reduce prices if number of competitors has increased	Continue to reduce price, unless there is not much competition
		If a low-price strategy was used in introduction, the price may be increased once some customer loyalty has been developed	Stabilise price if there is strong customer loyalty	
Promotional strategies	Advertising to develop awareness of product and its benefits	Emphasise the difference between the product and competitor's product	Increased promotion to distributors to continue to encourage them to sell product	Reduce or eliminate promotion and the costs associated with it
	Personal selling to distributors		Promote to new market segments	
	Incentives to encourage people to 'try and buy', such as offering samples			
Sponsorship strategies	High-profile athlete or team sponsorship for new product	Increase the range of sponsorship categories covered by introducing a greater range of endorsements	Reduce endorsements	No sponsorships
Distribution strategies	Offer good profit margins to distributors to encourage them to try selling the product, or use a short supply chain strategy such as the Internet	Build long-term relationships with distributors	May reduce the profit margins that are given to distributors	Stop using unprofitable distribution outlets and/or methods
		Increase number of distributors and/or different methods of distribution	May give incentives to distributors to encourage them to keep stocking product	
Services strategies	Introductory offers to build regular users	Heavy focus on service processes, quality and customer satisfaction	Develop new aspects of services to renew point of differentiation	Retrain service deliverers to prepare for end of service delivery

of the key strategies that marketers use to help their product to stand out from the crowd by positioning it through associated ideas and concepts.

INTERACTIVE CASE

Some of the most influential and valuable sport brands in the world are individual athletes. One exemplar is Usain Bolt, the multiple Olympic and world champion, and the fastest human ever. Bolt has proven remarkably adept at personal branding, or the creation of a symbolic and economic asset associated with a single person. Like all powerful brands, sport superstars have cultivated a strong identity that is differentiated from others, instantly recognisable, unique, difficult to duplicate, and delivers a lasting and positive impression.

Questions

Review Usain Bolt's website: http://usainbolt.com
How has Bolt employed symbology and imagery to create an association that he uses to represent himself and his marketing persona? How has he connected his physical performances and actions to a digital presence?

Points of interest

For individual players and athletes to generate an independent status as a brand in their own right, they have typically managed to combine their on- and off-field personas in such a way that their physical characteristics, clothing, general appearance, disposition, attitude, playing style, and fan/media interaction showcase a rare combination of talent, audacity and iconography. Of course, for athletes such as Bolt, this means that their traits can be easily converted into signature imagery, perfect for product endorsements and sponsorships. For example, Bolt's trademark lightning emblem appears prominently as a powerful visual representation of his brand and everything that it symbolises. He even uses the lightning bolt pose as a culminating cue for media attention at the conclusion of a successful race. As one of the world's most successful individual social media contributors, Bolt's digital presence stands as a benchmark for all sport brands to emulate.

Brand names and logos

To recap, a brand can be many things, including a name, a design, a symbol, an image or even a combination of these. A brand name and a brand mark (or logo) are two of the most common representations of a brand. A brand name is a word, a written label or even a group of letters and/or numbers; it is usually something that can be verbalised rather than merely an image. The choice of brand name will put across (or symbolise) a unique idea. For example, some brand names might suggest strength and confidence, such as the All Blacks New Zealand Rugby Union team, while others might suggest boldness, such as Nike. If you do not agree with these connotations it means that you hold a different brand identity in your mind.

There are a number of issues to keep in mind when choosing a brand name. It is important that it communicates ideas that an organisation would like its consumers to possess. It should be related to the kinds of benefits that consumers will get from the product. It is also useful if it is memorable and unique enough to be registered and trademarked. A brand name should be easy to say, and easily translatable into another language. The Olympic rings and the Ferrari prancing horse are two well-known logos associated with sport. Some suggestions for a good brand name follow.

What makes a good brand name?

- short
- positive
- easy to remember
- easy to say
- easy to recognise
- unique
- describes the product/product use/benefits
- able to be registered or trademarked
- translates into other languages.

Building a sport brand

Sport branding is more than choosing a memorable name, or having an appealing logo designed. A brand has to be sold to consumers if it is going to elicit the desired reaction. Brands have to be built. There are four steps to brand building as outlined in Figure 6.6.

Chapter principle 6.7: Building a brand is a process made up of four steps including (1) establish brand awareness, (2) develop and manage a brand image, (3) develop brand equity and (4) develop brand loyalty.

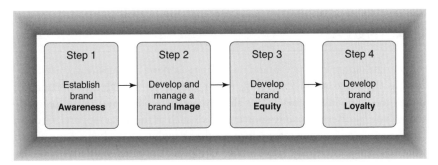

FIGURE 6.6 Building a sport brand

Step 1: Establish brand awareness

Brand awareness refers to the extent to which consumers recognise and remember a brand name. It is the first step of building a sport brand because consumers must be aware of a brand to understand its identity or image. The process of improving consumer awareness of a brand is one of the key roles of promotion, which is addressed in Chapter 9.

Step 2: Develop and manage a brand image

A brand's image is the way it is represented in the minds of consumers. For example, do consumers believe that it stands for reliability, luxury, adventure or excitement? Once consumers are aware of a brand, it is essential to mould and manage their perceptions of it. Managing a brand also means that continual effort needs to be made to remind consumers of the brand image. There are numerous variables that can be manipulated to affect consumers' perceptions of brand image. These are summarised in Table 6.2 along with the corresponding aspect of the marketing mix needed to introduce an effect.

TABLE 6.2 Image variables and the marketing mix

Image variables	Relationship to marketing mix
Brand name	Product and promotion
Product features	Product
Product quality or performance	Product
Packaging	Product
Price point	Price
Advertising	Promotion
Promotion	Promotion
Sponsorship associations	Sponsorship (promotion)
Customer service	Place and services
Distribution channels	Place

INTERACTIVE CASE

The dominant sport product brand in China, Li-Ning Company Limited, is fast occupying the stage as an emerging, major player on the global sporting scene. Although the company established its already vast high performance and recreational customer base by offering mainly sporting goods such as footwear, apparel, equipment and accessories, the Li-Ning Group is expanding rapidly, diversifying its product mix in order to compete with the other major equipment brands. Similarly, while based in Beijing, the Group is aggressively placing its research and development, design, manufacturing, distribution, retail and branding capabilities in strategic locations throughout the world. Infamously, the company has founded a major retail outlet in Nike's heartland of Portland, Oregon. It also uses a controversially similar logo to the Nike 'Swoosh'.

Questions

Examine the Li-Ning web presence: www.li-ning.com
How would you describe the company's approach to branding? What does the brand represent? How has the company managed its brand image to secure success in both the Eastern and Western markets?

Points of interest

Part of Li-Ning's astonishingly swift rise to success reflects its unusual infusion of Western approaches to branding at the same time as reaping the benefits of a dominant market position in China. In short, Li-Ning has captured the best of both worlds: the loyalty of an immense local population combined with the nascent curiosity of an over-stimulated Western market of sport equipment consumers. For example, the Li-Ning sponsorship model has been aggressive in targeting the strongholds of professional sport and its long-standing brand icons, especially footwear. From 2006, Li-Ning secured sponsorship arrangements with high-profile sports and leagues such as the US National Basketball League, the Association of Tennis Professionals, along with a suite of Chinese associations, leagues, national teams, athletes and celebrities. It provided apparel to several national squads for the 2008 and 2012 Summer Olympic Games, not to mention some astute ambush marketing by outfitting 2008 Olympic's broadcasters without ever being an official sponsor. Having determined that the NBA represented a pivotal communications channel, Li-Ning has gradually escalated its relationship, including athlete sponsorship deals with high influence players, most notably Shaquille O'Neal until he retired. In 2012, Dwyane Wade left the Jordan Brand for Li-Ning.

Step 3: Develop brand equity

Brand equity is the added value that a sport product holds because of its brand name. Consumers are more likely to be loyal to a product if it develops high levels of brand equity. Brand equity can be influenced by several factors including consumer awareness, price, concepts and ideas that consumers connect to the brand, the prominence of competitor's brands and their respective images, the nature of the products offered under the brand, and consumer loyalty. However, the most influential factor is perceived quality. This means that the most productive avenue to develop brand equity is by increasing awareness while controlling the quality of the products offered. Because of the differences between goods and services, there are additional issues to consider when it comes to service quality compared to goods quality. In fact, there are five areas that are commonly used to describe the specific aspects of service quality. These five areas were originally developed by Parasuraman *et al.* (1985). They are reliability, assurance, empathy, responsiveness and tangibles. Each is briefly described in Table 6.3 and explained in detail in Chapter 11.

There are also several important considerations when it comes to the quality of goods in comparison to services. There are eight elements of quality when it comes to physical goods (Garvin, 1987). These are features, performance, reliability, conformity to specifications, durability, serviceability, aesthetic design and product warranties. Each is summarised in Table 6.4.

Chapter principle 6.8: Brand equity increases when consumers rate products as high quality. There are different elements of product quality for goods compared

TABLE 6.3 Five elements of sport service quality

Service quality element	Explanation
Reliability	The ability to provide a service in a consistent and dependable way
	How reliable a customer believes a service is depends on how strongly they believe their expectations of the service will be met every time
Responsiveness	The willingness to help customers and to provide them with the service on time
Assurance	The level of confidence and trust that a customer has in the service
Empathy	The ability to get to know customers and their needs, and to deliver a personalised service
Tangibles	Physical features of the service (e.g. information booklets, equipment, appearance of staff, facilities, sport venue)

TABLE 6.4 Eight elements of sporting goods quality

Service quality element	Explanation
Conformity to specifications	Whether the goods meet the design standards of the manufacturer
Features	Whether the features of the product are high quality
Performance	How well the product carries out its main function (core product)
Reliability	How consistently the product performs
Durability	How long the product will last
Serviceability	How quickly and conveniently the product can be serviced if there are problems
Aesthetic design	Whether the design of the product looks to be of high quality
Product warranty	The guarantee of support if something goes wrong with the product

with services. There are five elements of *service* quality: (1) reliability, (2) assurance, (3) empathy, (4) responsiveness and (5) tangibles. There are eight elements of *goods* quality; these are (1) features, (2) performance, (3) reliability, (4) conformity to specifications, (5) durability, (6) serviceability, (7) aesthetic design and (8) product warranty.

Step 4: Develop brand loyalty

When a customer is loyal to a brand it means that they will choose it repeatedly in preference over alternatives offered by competitors. As explained in the previous section, the quality of a sport good or service will play a role in encouraging loyalty, and it therefore needs to be continually addressed. It is also useful to look at how easy it is for consumers to buy the product on an ongoing basis. For example, is the product distributed in a way that is convenient for consumers to access? Sport organisations sometimes try to encourage loyalty by offering rewards to consumers for buying their product more than once.

BRANDING AND LICENSING

Licensing is an arrangement where a sport organisation allows another party to use their brand for a fee. The organisation that purchases the right to use the brand (called the licensee) will then produce a good, service or promotion, and will give a percentage of the money they make, or pay a fixed fee to the real owner of the brand (called the licensor).

Licensing is particularly common in the area of sporting merchandise and apparel. Sport merchandise can include toys, collectible cards, board games, school supplies, videos, DVDs, magazines, and computer and console games. Sport clubs and leagues do not have the resources to make all of these kinds of products by themselves. Instead, they may make an agreement with another company to make the merchandise for them, and of

TABLE 6.5 Licensing sport brands

	Opportunities	Risks
For the licensee	• An association with a prominent sport brand with an automatic level of brand awareness and equity	• Reliant on the continued (sporting) performance of the brand
	• After heavy investment, the licensor can terminate the agreement	
For the licensor	• New markets become accessible through broader distribution network	• Out of control of the way their brand is portrayed and marketed
	• More volume of the product can be made available	• More difficult to manage quality of the product
	• Increase brand awareness and equity through greater exposure of the brand to new consumers	
	• No capital investment	

course they will want their sport brand or logo to be used. As a result, sport brands offer specific companies the right to use their brand. Also, both organisations will want to make money out of the agreement, so each of them will agree on a percentage of profits that they will receive.

Licensing is a very common product strategy in sport, and each year it generates billions of dollars in sales internationally. As with all strategies there are opportunities and risks associated with licensing for both parties. These are outlined in Table 6.5.

INTERACTIVE CASE

Companies such as the Anschutz Entertainment Group (AEG) are in the business of marketing sports entertainment. It began at the start of the century and owns various stadiums as well as numerous sports team franchises around the globe (www.aegworldwide.com). Sporting franchises are not a new marketing strategy. In 2014 Manchester City Club (MCFC) purchased Melbourne Heart Football Club for just over AU$11 million. The club already owns New York FC and its management believe that the Australian Soccer League provides a sound platform to extend their global strategy. The Australian Soccer League is recognised as one of the more corruption-free football leagues in the world and MCFC penetration into the Oceania region is seen as an opportunity to build support in a developing competition. However, can any city in Australia sustain a global sports team at full scale?

Questions

Can Australia sustain more than one global sporting franchise? Is it feasible to attract international sporting franchises to Australia? Which franchises would have the best chance of success? What impact would a foreign franchise have on the traditional sporting culture of the country?

Points of interest

Other successful sporting franchises such as Manchester United Football Club and the Dallas Cowboys not only have successful on-field performances, they have phenomenal global supporter bases. Australia may be viewed as an opportunity to expand a franchise because of its ability to access global sports readily through television and the Internet. Although the population is rising, it is only 56th in the world rankings (www.cia.gov). While the country has a strong sports culture, many successful international Australian athletes relocate overseas to larger, more lucrative competitions. Fans may enjoy attending a sport competition but being easily connected from any place in the world lessens the need to be 'at the game'.

PRINCIPLES SUMMARY

- Chapter principle 6.1: Sport goods may be differentiated from services on the basis of four factors: tangibility, consistency, perishability and separability.

- Chapter principle 6.2: A sport product is the complete package of benefits presented to a sport consumer in the form of physical goods, services and ideas, or a combination of these to produce a sport experience.

- Chapter principle 6.3: Sport products should be seen as a bundle of benefits comprising the core benefits, actual product features and the augmented product. These three variables of the product are interrelated and should be manipulated as a group.

- Chapter principle 6.4: In sport marketing, a new product can take many forms such as the improved performance of an existing product, new functions added to an existing product, a new way to use an existing product, combining existing products or a new look or design for a product.

- Chapter principle 6.5: The term *product life cycle* refers to the stages that a product goes through from first being introduced onto the market to its decline. There are four stages of the product life cycle: introduction, growth, maturity and decline.

- Chapter principle 6.6: A sport brand is the symbolic representation of everything that a sport organisation seeks to stand for, leading to expectations about its value and performance. A brand can be portrayed as an identifying badge that triggers consumers to remember a product or an organisation. It can be a name, a design, a symbol (or logo), an image or a combination of these things. Branding is one of the key strategies that marketers use to help their product to stand out from the crowd by positioning it through associated ideas and concepts.

- Chapter principle 6.7: Building a brand is a process made up of four steps including (1) establish brand awareness, (2) develop and manage a brand image, (3) develop brand equity and (4) develop brand loyalty.

- Chapter principle 6.8: Brand equity increases when consumers rate products as high quality. There are different elements of product quality for goods compared with services. There are five elements of *service* quality: (1) reliability, (2) assurance, (3) empathy, (4) responsiveness and (5) tangibles. There are eight elements of *goods* quality, these are (1) features, (2) performance, (3) reliability, (4) conformity to specifications, (5) durability, (6) serviceability, (7) aesthetic design and (8) product warranty.

TOOLS SUMMARY

- Chapter tool 6.1 Sport product continuum
- Chapter tool 6.2 New product development
- Chapter tool 6.3 Product life cycle stages

REVIEW QUESTIONS

1   What is the difference between a sport product and a sport service?

2   Provide a simple definition of a sport product.

3   Sport products can provide both tangible and intangible benefits. Why does this present challenges for sport marketers?

4   What are the three variables of a sport product and provide an example of each for a sport product of your choice?

5   Identify the four stages of the product life cycle. Provide a brief description of the best marketing strategy to employ at each stage.

6   How does product innovation come about? Provide an example of a new innovation in a sporting product.

7   What is product prototyping and how does it apply to sporting products?

8   What is the relationship between branding and positioning?

RELEVANT WEBSITES

http://electrozyme.com   Electrozyme
http://kickstarter.com   Kickstarter
http://indiegogo.com   Indiegogo
http://usainbolt.com   Usain Bolt
www.li-ning.com   Li-Ning Company Limited

FURTHER READING

Chiu, L.K., Radzuwan, R.B. and Ting, C.S. (2014). Assessing sport and recreation programmes' service quality at hotels and resorts: Towards enhancing customer participation. *Journal of Tourism and Hospitality Management*, 2(1): 6–17.

Garvin, D.A. (1987). Competing on the 8 dimensions of quality. *Harvard Business Review*, 65(6): 101–109.

Lee, J.W. (2010). *Branded: Branding in Sport Business*. Durham, NC: Carolina Academic Press.

Parasuraman, A., Zeithaml, V.A. and Berry, L.L. (1985). A conceptual model of service quality and its implications for future research. *Journal of Marketing*, 49(4): 41–50.

CHAPTER 7

Sport pricing

LEARNING OUTCOMES

At the end of this chapter, readers should be able to:

- describe the strategic pricing process
- outline the different pricing goals available to sport marketing managers
- outline the factors that influence price sensitivity
- explain what a break-even analysis is, and how to perform it
- discuss other factors that influence pricing decisions
- outline the different pricing strategies used in the sport industry.

OVERVIEW

The purpose of this chapter is to explore the second of the six elements in the marketing mix – price. The chapter is structured around a multi-step pricing process. Steps 1 and 2 provide guidance on setting pricing goals and analysing market sensitivity. The remaining steps include break-even analysis, the consideration of other variables that affect pricing, and the choice of pricing strategies for specific sporting goods or services.

PRICING: A MULTIFACETED ISSUE

Chapter 6 explained the first element of the marketing mix – the product – and this chapter expands the discussion to consider the second element of the marketing mix – price. Price and its components can be located in Figure 7.1 within the Sport Marketing Framework. In order to set the groundwork, there are four important terms to understand: price, value, revenue, and profit, which are reviewed in the following sections.

It is easy to imagine that pricing a sport product (or service) simply involves working out what it costs to produce, then adding on a margin for profit. This is a useful beginning point, since price setting is crucially important when working out budgets, and establishing the minimum price necessary to cover the costs of producing the product, getting it onto the market, advertising it, and finally selling it. Take, for example, a tennis coaching business, where the proprietor of the business and the senior instructor happen to be the same person. This multitasking requirement is a common feature of most small businesses. Setting the right price is crucial for this business, since it may be the difference between making profits and incurring losses.

The example tennis coaching business has a few options to consider. A coaching fee that will undercut competitors' fees is likely to secure a few more tennis beginners, but if it does not cover the coach's costs of delivering the group instruction, it will make the business unviable. On the other hand, a premium fee that provides a handy surplus may look good on paper, but may be so uncompetitive that no one takes up the service offer because it is too expensive. In this instance the business has priced itself out of the market. The business is on the horns of a dilemma. However, there is a way out. The solution to this vexing issue is to design a product – in this case a tennis coaching programme – that offers a scale of value (with an accompanying fee, or price) that can be delivered within a cost structure that accommodates an operating surplus. This means there are at least two options to consider. The first is to run a low-cost business that delivers a basic no-frills discount programme to families on limited budgets, but who are committed to improving their tennis playing abilities. So, this programme is about learning the basics in a larger group in a low-rent, public court setting with little one-on-one instruction. Families with constrained budgets become the target market. Alternatively, the business could take on a more selective image, and thus charge a much higher fee, but offer a premium service at well-maintained clubs, and with smaller classes and the occasional personalised instruction. In this case the target market is families with a bit more discretionary income, and who feel more comfortable in settings commensurate with their social aspirations.

As the above case shows, pricing sport products is a complicated process. In fact, the way that a sport product is priced will have a dramatic influence on the way that consumers perceive it. In addition, pricing tends to change continually, depending on a range of variables including a product's position in its life cycle. This tennis coaching case shows that pricing not only influences a sport product's profitability, but also communicates a powerful message to consumers about the brand and its image. A simple example can be found in the contrasting prices of general admission tickets (low price) versus corporate box tickets (very high price) to sport events. The variable ticket prices will immediately communicate different messages about the sort of experiences that a consumer might expect. The higher the price of the corporate box tickets, the more consumers would expect quality service, networking opportunities, lounge room style seating, weather protection, and quality food and alcohol. On the other hand, the cheaper general admission tickets will imply poor seating arrangements, exposure to the weather, the likelihood of mixing with unruly fans, and long queues for cafeteria service. The difference in price is a key symbol that immediately signifies what consumers should expect. It also signals the social setting in which the experience will take place. This is very important to many people. However, when there is little difference in price, consumers expect little difference in the quality of the experience.

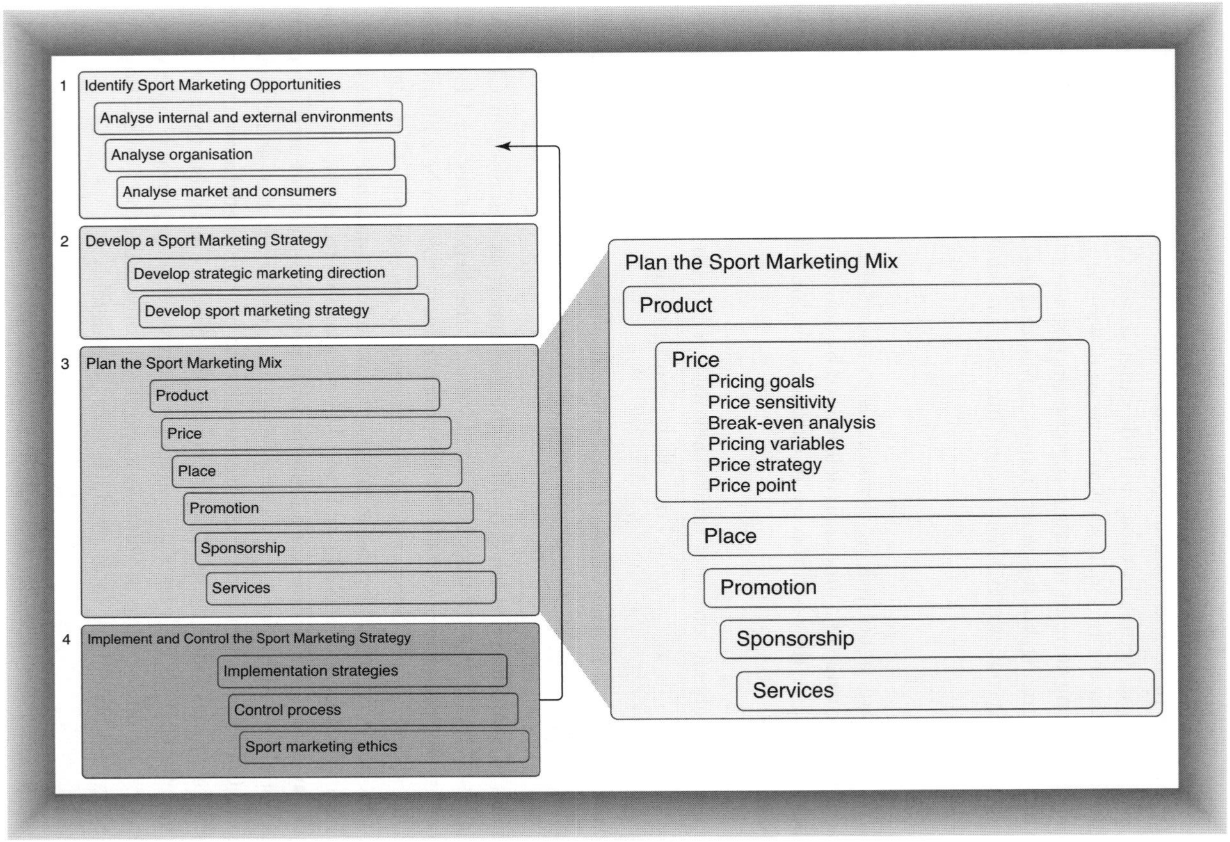

1
Identify Sport Marketing Opportunities
Analyse internal and external environments
Analyse organisation
Analyse market and consumers
2
Develop a Sport Marketing Strategy
Develop strategic marketing direction
Develop sport marketing strategy
3
Plan the Sport Marketing Mix
Product
Price
Place
Promotion
Sponsorship
Services
4
Implement and Control the Sport Marketing Strategy
Implementation strategies
Control process
Sport marketing ethics
Plan the Sport Marketing Mix
Product
Price
Pricing goals
Price sensitivity
Break-even analysis
Pricing variables
Price strategy
Price point
Place
Promotion
Sponsorship
Services

FIGURE 7.1 The Sport Marketing Framework

Chapter principle 7.1: Pricing communicates an important symbolic positioning message to consumers about a sport product.

Price

The price of a sport-related product represents what a consumer relinquishes in exchange for the product. A price should also reflect the value of a product. Generally, price is thought of in financial terms, but may include other things that a customer has to give up in order to obtain the product, such as time (e.g. waiting in a queue) or social costs (e.g. no longer having time to maintain membership of a book club). This chapter will focus on monetary pricing, but it is worth remembering that the other sacrifices a consumer makes to acquire a product may also have an influence on whether they buy it.

Value

A useful way to think about pricing decisions is to consider them in terms of value. In sport marketing, the value of a product is determined by how its price relates to the benefits that consumers believe they will receive in exchange. Value is expressed in terms of the following equation.

$$\text{Value} = \frac{\text{Benefits a consumer thinks they will receive from the sport product}}{\text{Price of the sport product}}$$

Chapter principle 7.2: The value of a sport product is the relationship between its price and the benefits a consumer believes they will receive from it.

The benefits of a product are what it offers the consumer, as described in Chapter 6. Consumers will feel that a product is of good value if the benefits received from it are equal to or greater than the price paid. With sport products, this can be a highly variable and individual assessment. Sport memorabilia provides an example. Consider a sport uniform that has been signed by the members of a prominent national cricket team. An unsigned uniform may sell for $200, so it would be reasonable to assume that a dedicated fan would pay considerably more for a uniform with players' signatures on it. Depending upon the popularity of this type of sport memorabilia, it is likely that some fans would pay up to $2,000. Many sport consumers are prepared to pay substantial amounts of money for unusual or special sports items. This is because the product has value to them. Value, and the benefits that go with it, is thus a very subjective concept, since people who are not sport fans would see little of value in a sports uniform soiled by graffiti. Both value and the perceived benefits of sport products vary considerably.

Chapter principle 7.3: The price of a product is the amount of money a consumer must give up in exchange for a good or service. However, price is not the same as value, since value is the difference between price and the anticipated benefit. Although price is usually viewed in monetary terms, it may also include other consumer sacrifices in order to acquire a sport product, such as time or social cost. Additionally, in some instances the value secured from a sports product can be well in excess of its purchase price. This is a good position for a product to be in, since the expectation of getting more value for money will be an incentive to purchase the product.

Revenue and profit

Two further relevant pricing terms are revenue and profit. For product suppliers revenue is the price that consumers pay for a product, multiplied by the number of product units sold. For example, if a sport venue sells tickets to an event for $38.00 each, and 45,000 tickets are sold, then revenue is $133,000. When the supplier's costs are removed from this revenue figure the remainder is considered profit. In other words, profit equals revenue minus expenses.

On the surface, it is logical to assume that the higher the price, the more revenue earned, and the larger the resulting profit. However, in order to make a sale, the price of a product should not be higher than its perceived value to consumers. Problems emerge when the price of a product exceeds its perceived value. There is always a risk that an increase in price will force some customers to shift their spending somewhere else since the perceived value of the product may now be lower than the cost of securing it.

> *Chapter principle 7.4*: *Revenue* is the price that consumers pay for a product, multiplied by the number of units sold. *Profit* is revenue minus the costs of producing and selling the product.

STRATEGIC PRICING PROCESS

By calling the pricing process 'strategic', it is meant that setting a product's price should be planned with careful analysis and a consistent aim. The steps of the strategic pricing process are outlined in Figure 7.2. The remainder of the chapter will examine each of these steps in turn.

> *Chapter principle 7.5*: The strategic pricing process provides a structure for setting price. The process involves: (1) setting a pricing goal, (2) determining price sensitivity, (3) conducting a break-even analysis, (4) assessing pricing variables, (5) selecting price tactics and (6) setting a price point.

Pricing goals

Because different pricing strategies will achieve different outcomes, it is important to begin by determining what goals are being sought. It is essential to remember that pricing goals should support a broader product and brand positioning strategy, which in turn should underpin marketing objectives and the achievement of organisational objectives.

There are two main types of pricing goals: (1) profit-based pricing goals, and (2) sales-based pricing goals. Profit-based goals are focused on how much money a sport organisation earns after it has paid all of its costs. Sales-based pricing goals are focused on the amount of sales an organisation makes. Both of these goals have a number of sub-goals, which are described next.

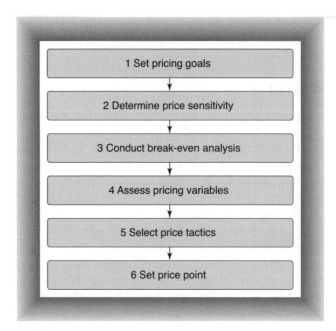

FIGURE 7.2 The strategic pricing process

INTERACTIVE CASE

A significant part of the sport industry comprises sport footwear and apparel suppliers. They are useful barometers of the state of sport since the more people there are engaging with sport, the more sales will expand. The most successful sport footwear and apparel suppliers have become household names, and have created some of the commercial world's strongest global brands. Four of the world's most popular brands are listed below, together with their website addresses.

www.rbk.com (Reebok website)
www.nike.com (Nike website)
www.fila.com (FILA website)
www.adidas.com (adidas website)

Choose one brand of athletic footwear from Nike, Reebok, FILA and adidas.

Questions

1   How might you go about creating a list of shoe products from the least expensive to the most expensive?
2   Having created a list, how wide is the range of pricing?
3   Can you identify a particular positioning strategy that drives these pricing arrangements?

4 How many distinctive price 'points' are there? In other words, at what levels are the prices set (e.g. $80, $100, $130, $160 and so on)?
5 To what extent are these different price points indicative of differences in manufacturing costs?
6 Is there a close correlation between price and quality?
7 Apart from cost and quality, is there any other factor that might explain the price differentials for these shoe products?

Points of interest

Sport footwear and apparel suppliers have made a significant contribution to sport around the world. They have made many innovations, and have delivered their customers a diverse range of high quality running shoes and outdoor adventure footwear. At the same time they have used low cost manufacturing sites to spread the gap between costs and prices. In some instances the mark-ups have been obscenely high, and as a result these suppliers have been pressured into ensuring good pay and safe employment conditions for the workers who actually make the shoes and related apparel. Despite their concerted efforts to become socially responsible, and despite their generous funding of international aid programmes, the mark-ups on their products are still high. The high mark ups are possible because the suppliers have convinced the public – that is, sport consumers – that their products are of the highest quality, having gone through an intensive research and design process that delivers high levels of both functionality and reliability, while also enabling its wearers to make a fashion statement. How good is that in view of the fact that they were produced within the lowest possible cost structures?

Profit-based pricing goals

Profit maximisation means setting a price that will maximise the margin or difference between revenue and expenses. It does not automatically mean that prices should be set as high as possible. It is unwise for an organisation to set a price above the *perceived value* of the product. One of the potential problems with a profit maximisation goal is that it can encourage sport organisations to think in the short term rather than the long term. For example, it could lead a sport organisation to cut costs and wages as much as possible, and as a result lead to a lower quality product delivered by unhappy staff.

Satisfactory profit means a reasonable or realistic profit. What is reasonable and realistic will vary for different organisations and different product markets. It can be difficult to set a specific goal corresponding to how much profit is reasonable because it requires research into the market and competitors.

Target return on investment is the most common profit-based pricing goal. In principle, target return on investment means an earnings target for a predefined target market. Using this approach, a sport organisation would consider the amount of money it intends to make from selling a product, taking into account the amount they had to invest to develop and bring it to the market. Based on this calculation, a price can be determined. Naturally, a higher return on investment is better, but of course, many sport organisations are not profit seeking and therefore choose a price that is sustainable rather than profitable.

Sales-based pricing goals

Market share is a measure of the percentage one product or brand has acquired of the total sales in a sector or part of the sport industry. Market share can be calculated in terms of dollars, or in terms of how many units of the product are sold. It is not automatic that sport organisations with the largest market share make the biggest profits. While it is true that increasing market share can increase profit, some organisations with a low market share can survive and do very well. Market share tends to be a better measure for the sporting goods sector as sport teams and sport organising bodies are not oriented towards profit. Indeed, sport organisations participating in competitions will never hold the allegiance of all fans, and were they to, it would mean the end of the competition. However, it is reasonable that sport organisations oriented towards participation may find market share useful to gauge whether they are attracting more or fewer participants.

Sales maximisation refers to the goal of acquiring as many sales as possible. Sport organisations that pursue this goal are less concerned with profit, and are more focused on increasing the number of sales. For profit-oriented sport organisations, this goal is generally not a good long-term goal because it does not pay enough attention to whether the organisation is earning enough money to survive. It can be a short-term goal, however, if an organisation needs to generate some quick cash, or if it wants to sell off some old stock to make way for new products. For participant-based sport, sales can translate into participant numbers. For these organisations, as long as they can cover their costs, an increase in participation represents improved performance.

Chapter tool 7.1 Pricing goals:

- profit maximisation: setting a price that aims to maximise profit, but also making sure that it is not above the *perceived value* of the product;
- satisfactory profits: a reasonable or realistic profit;
- return on investment: a mathematical sum where net profit is considered in light of the investment in the product;
- market share: how many sales or how much money an organisation makes as a percentage of the total sales/revenue in the market or a segment of the market;
- sales maximisation: trying to achieve as many sales as possible.

Price sensitivity

The second step of the strategic pricing process involves determining how sensitive consumers are to the price of the product. Price sensitivity is sometimes called *market sensitivity* because it refers to how sensitive consumers are (in other words how sensitive the market is) to changes in the price of a product. For example, if prices for a product rise, will customers be very sensitive and stop buying it, or will they ignore the price rise and keep spending their money? Price sensitivity is influenced by demand, supply, price elasticity and the perceived value of the product.

Demand

Demand represents how many units of a sport product the market will want (the sum total of consumers) at a certain price. Usually the higher the price for a product, the fewer goods or services consumers will want. Equally, the lower the price, the more goods and services customers will want. This relationship is shown in Figure 7.3.

Product demand is also influenced by product *substitutes* and *complements*. Product substitutes are products that can be used in place of another product. For example, if the price of a family ticket to the tennis increased dramatically, other products such as movie or theme-park tickets could be used as a substitute for a cheaper family outing. Product complements are those that are used together. For example, membership to a rock-climbing gymnasium and sales of climbing harnesses are complementary products. If the cost of a membership rises, the quantity of both products (memberships and harnesses) demanded by consumers would likely fall.

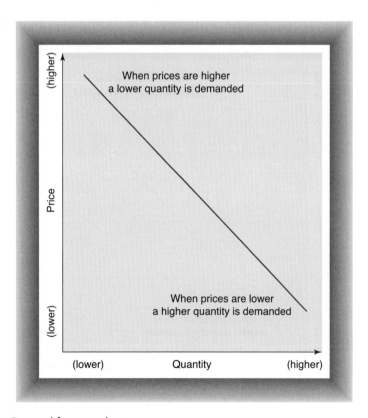

FIGURE 7.3 Demand for a product

Supply

Supply represents the quantity of a product that is available in the market at certain prices. In principle, the higher the price of a product, the greater the returns to the supplier. Also, high prices signal for other organisations to enter the market and produce a similar product themselves. In other words, a higher product price usually leads to a greater amount of the product being supplied to the market. This is illustrated in Figure 7.4.

The volume of a product supplied to the market will also be influenced by other factors, such as the prices of raw materials and resources, the number of competitors, and consumers' expectations about future prices and technology. For example, if the cost of cotton (a raw material) to make a sport branded T-shirt dramatically increased, then the number of T-shirts supplied in the sporting apparel industry would fall. Another example is that the volume of a product supplied to the market increases with growth in the number of competitors (suppliers) offering it.

The graph shown in Figure 7.5 illustrates the theoretical conditions when demand equals supply, also known as market equilibrium. At market equilibrium price, the quantity of the product that is produced by suppliers is the same as the quantity demanded by consumers. There is no excess product left unsold, and there are no consumers who want to buy the product but miss out. Of course, this is merely a theoretical possibility that is almost impossible to predict or achieve in practice. However, the concept of market

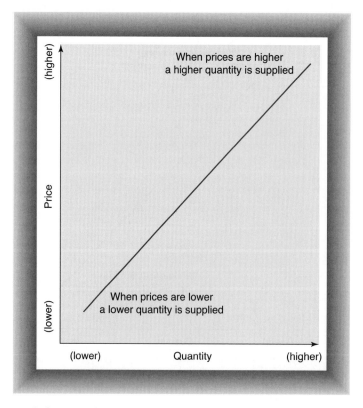

FIGURE 7.4 Supply for a product

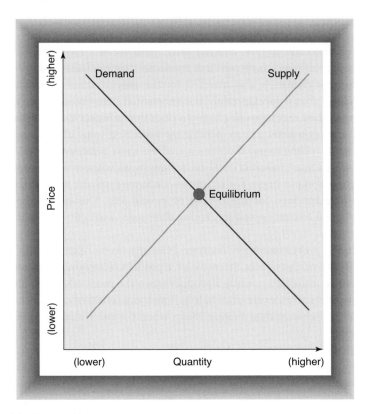

FIGURE 7.5 Market equilibrium

equilibrium helps to explain why sport organisations review the relationship between the volume of their product or service offerings and demand. Equally, sport organisations can deliberately influence demand by changing their pricing structure.

Price elasticity

Price elasticity refers to how easily consumer demand for a product changes when there is a change in price. There are two different types of price elasticity: inelastic demand and elastic demand. In most competitive sport, inelastic demand is more prominent. This means that it is difficult to substitute (or replace) one sport league, team or competition for another. Many sport fans are fiercely loyal to their team or their sport. Even if the price of tickets to games increases, loyal fans are unlikely to stop attending. They are thus insensitive to price changes. The other type of elasticity is elastic demand. This means that demand for the product will change dramatically, even when the price change is small. In this case, if the price of a product increases, consumers will buy less of it, but if the price falls, a higher quantity will be demanded. Demand for the product is like an elastic band. Being elastic means demand is sensitive and therefore responsive to price changes. On the other hand, being inelastic means that demand is insensitive, and therefore unresponsive to price changes.

Perceived value

The level of demand and supply, and the price elasticity of a sport product are not the only variables that influence how sensitive consumers are to changes in price. Consumer sensitivity to price change is also affected by the perceived value of the product. If consumers believe that a sport product has substantial benefits, or provides them with social status, then they may be willing to pay a price that is higher than the market average. Furthermore, if sport marketers can increase the perceived value of a sport product, then consumers may be willing to pay more for it, and the sport organisation may receive more revenue. Equally, some consumers will be willing to go without some product benefits in exchange for a cheaper price. For example, consumers may be willing to buy a T-shirt without a fashionable logo for the benefit of paying less. This means that the T-shirt producer can spend less money on marketing their logo, and sell the product for less.

> *Chapter tool 7.2 Price sensitivity analysis*: Price sensitivity refers to how sensitive consumers are to changes in the price of a product. Consumers are considered price sensitive if they do not buy a product when the price is high, or if they buy more of a product when the price is low. The more sensitive consumers are, the more they will change their buying habits when the price changes. The process involves:
>
> 1   examining how much of the same or a similar product is supplied and demanded at each price level. This may provide a guide in order to determine a realistic price that consumers are willing to pay. This is an assessment of supply and demand;
> 2   considering how many product substitutes exist in the market. The more product substitutes, the more sensitive consumers will be to higher prices. This is an assessment of price elasticity;
> 3   determining whether there are any product complements. It can be revealing to discover that sales of complementary products change corresponding to price changes of a sport product. This is an assessment of the price elasticity of the product;
> 4   assessing the degree of perceived product value held by consumers. This is undertaken through market research.

INTERACTIVE CASE

Over the last few years a number of professional sports leagues – with America's Major League Baseball (MLB) in the vanguard – have begun experimenting with flexible ticket pricing. Under this arrangement (which also goes under the banner of dynamic pricing), ticket prices to games are changed over time in accordance with supply and demand conditions. That is, some admission tickets will no longer have a fixed price attached to them. More information on these types of ticketing arrangements is available in the following websites.

www.forbes.com/sites/prishe/2012/01/06/dynamic-pricing-the-future-of-ticket-pricing-in-sports
www.economist.com/blogs/gametheory/2012/01/sports-ticketing
www.cnbc.com/id/48194739

Questions

1 What types of economic activity use dynamic pricing as a 'matter of course'? Think of travel and tourism when formulating your answer.
2 Why has it taken so long for professional sports leagues to adopt dynamic pricing principles for their schedules of games and tournaments?
3 Can you give examples of how dynamic pricing would work in professional sports leagues?
4 What are the benefits of dynamic pricing in sport?
5 What are the weaknesses of dynamic pricing in sport?

Points of interest

The use of dynamic pricing strategies in sport appears to have happened in response to arguments that fixed pricing is too rigid. This really means that fixed pricing arrangements for sport competitions will fail to maximise revenues. This is because in situations where seats are limited, and demand is high, fixed prices will undervalue many of the tickets. The customer's willingness to pay more than the price listed on the ticket is called the 'consumer surplus'. With a fixed ticket price arrangement the surplus stays with the customer, while in a flexible or dynamic ticketing arrangement, the higher price will deliver the consumer surplus to the supplier.

Break-even analysis

The third step of the pricing process requires a break-even analysis to be conducted. Break-even analysis is used to determine how many product sales are needed in order to ensure that revenue is equal to the costs of producing the product. When a product reaches break-even point, its revenue is equal to its costs; there is no extra money left over (this would be a profit), and costs are not greater than revenue (this would be a loss).

The costs of delivering a product are usually divided into fixed costs and variable costs. Fixed costs are the expenses an organisation incurs in producing and delivering a product that will not change, no matter how much of the product is sold. For example, the cost of rent, equipment and insurance are often constant for a sport organisation, no matter how many products are made or services delivered.

Variable costs are the expenses that change (either up or down) depending on how much of the product or service is made or delivered. For example, the cost of fabric for a sport apparel producer would increase if it had to buy more fabric to make additional

T-shirts. Another example is the cost of staff in a service business; more staff are needed to deliver more services, which in turn costs the sport organisation more. Usually, an organisation will calculate how much it spends on variable costs per unit. For example, a sport shoe company might calculate that for every pair of shoes they make (one unit each), they spend $15 on variable costs (such as leather and shoelaces). Similar calculations can be performed as extra participants are added to sport events.

To calculate a break-even point, the following formula can be used:

$$\text{Break-even point} = \frac{\text{Total fixed costs}}{\text{Price per unit} - \text{variable costs per unit}}$$

For example, imagine the situation of a company that produces collectible sports cards. Its fixed costs (such as factory rental, printing equipment and insurance) equal $450,000. The variable cost for each packet of cards (such as paper, ink and packaging) is $1.50. It sells each packet for $10.00.

Step 1   Put the amounts for total fixed costs, price per unit and variable costs per unit into the formula.

$$\text{Break-even point} = \frac{450,000}{\$10 - \$1.50 \text{ per unit}}$$

Step 2   Take the variable costs per unit away from the price per unit ($10.00 minus $1.50 equals $8.50). This is called the contribution margin.

$$\text{Break-even point} = \frac{450,000}{\$8.50 \text{ per unit}}$$

Step 3   Divide the total costs by the figure on the bottom (remember, the figure on the bottom is the price per unit minus the variable costs per unit).

$$\text{Break-even point} = \frac{450,000}{\$8.50 \text{ per unit}}$$

Step 4   The outcome represents the number of units needed to break even.

Break-even point 52941 units

The company in the example needs to sell 52,941 packets of sports collector cards in order to break even. Determining the break-even point is advantageous in setting a price for a product because it means that the financial implications of various alternative pricing strategies can be explored. When these are considered in light of other factors that influence pricing, then a final price can be set.

> *Chapter tool 7.3 Break-even analysis*: A *break-even analysis* calculates the quantity of sales needed to ensure that revenue earned is equal to the costs of producing the product or service. At *break-even*, revenue is equal to costs.

The costs of producing a product are divided into *fixed* costs and *variable* costs. Fixed costs are the expenses an organisation has that do not change no matter how much they sell of their product. Variable costs are the expenses that change (either up or down) depending on how much of the product is made.

Break even: Total fixed costs/Price per unit less variable costs per unit.

Pricing variables

Armed with an appreciation of a price point required in order to break even, the next stage is to consider any other variables that could affect the price set. These other factors include the pricing strategies of competitors, any legal or technical boundaries that may be relevant to the pricing of the product and the impact of choices associated with other marketing mix variables.

Competitor pricing

The price that competitors charge for the same or similar products will offer an insight into consumer expectations. When considering the pricing approach of competitors, it is important to keep positioning and quality in mind. For example, some competitors will offer a product or service at the upper end of the quality scale, and will position the product with supportive marketing accordingly. It is helpful to determine which competitors' pricing strategies are most successful. In some cases, competitors' pricing levels will be unsustainable to match, and an alternative positioning approach will be essential in order to compete with a higher price.

Legal and technical boundaries

A pricing boundary is an encumbrance that restricts or limits the price that can be set. One prominent boundary placed upon pricing comes in the form of laws or regulations established by government or governing sport bodies that restrict or modulate the prices that can be set. For example, clubs in a sport league may be told by the league what prices they can charge for tickets. Alternatively, a local council may control the range of fees that a club passes on to its customers for using council facilities (such as a council-owned gymnasium or tennis court). In addition, in most countries there are laws that affect the way price can be structured. For example, price fixing (agreeing with competitors to each charge the same price) is illegal in many industries, although as noted in Chapter 2, many sport leagues are allowed to collude on prices. There are frequently laws preventing prices being set so low that they drive competitors out of business. This practice is known as predatory pricing. Further boundaries can be technical in nature, such as production methods, which limit supply, and environmental sustainability, which adds to costs.

Marketing mix

All of the marketing mix variables should reflect the positioning strategy a sport brand selects. As a result, it is important to consider how the other marketing mix variables influence price setting. The approaches chosen with the other variables (product, promotion, place, sponsorship and services) will have an effect on the choice of the best pricing strategy. For example, the way that a product is distributed to consumers may affect the price that they are willing to pay. If a product is convenient to buy, consumers may be willing to pay a little more than normal for it. This is why food, beverages and merchandise always cost more at a sporting venue than they do in other outlets. Also, sport services can be priced higher if a tangible product, such as a junior football programme, comes with a backpack, stickers and a football. Finally, if a product is positioned at the top end of the market, it is advantageous to bolster the brand with a prominent sponsorship.

> *Chapter tool 7.4 Assess pricing variables*: Several environmental factors can influence the price set for a product, including the pricing strategies of competitors, any legal or technical boundaries, and the impact of the other marketing mix variables in the marketing plan.

INTERACTIVE CASE

Mega sport events are often quite expensive to attend. There are two main reasons for this. First, they are costly to organise, and second, they deliver a quality experience to customers. At the same time, there will be differences in pricing for events that are both costly to run and are of premium quality. For instance, the websites for the Wimbledon All England Tennis Championships and the Indianapolis 500 provide many similarities, but they also show many differences. Visit the home page for each of the events and then click on 'tickets'.

www.wimbledon.org
www.indy500.com

Questions

1 What initially strikes you about the ticketing arrangements and the prices charged?
2 Is there any logic to the ticket pricing?
3 How do you explain the differences in ticket prices for different event days?
4 Which event offers the best value for money?
5 Or, is this question of little relevance to tennis fans and motor sports fans?

Points of interest

The first thing that strikes one about ticket prices for mega-sport events is that the prices for the best seats at the best times are always going to be high. For most fans they are prohibitively high. Some seats are deliberately priced beyond the financial reach of most people. Highly sought-after seats are highly priced because they are relatively scarce and only available to a select few. They are known as 'positional goods'. Positional goods, such as a prime seat at a Wimbledon tennis final, are highly valued because they are in extremely short supply and thus offer the purchaser not only a great viewing experience, but also prestige and status because, by securing the ticket, they have signalled their superior class and social position.

Pricing tactics

The fifth step in setting a price is to select a pricing tactic. The pricing tactic should be directly related to the positioning strategy that is chosen for the product. As a reminder, market positioning refers to how consumers think and feel about a brand or product when they compare it with others. It is the image or perception of a sport brand or product. For example, consumers might perceive a brand or product as luxury and high quality, or as basic and value for money. Consumers might see a brand or product as conservative and reliable or exciting and changeable. Positioning takes into account the fact that consumers will place a brand or product into a position in their minds that is relative to others. The positioning strategy that is chosen will have an influence on the best choice of pricing strategy. For example, if a sport organisation has decided to position one of its products as high quality, it would be appropriate to set a premium price goal. A high price can help to give consumers the idea that the quality of the product is correspondingly high. There are a number of common pricing strategies that sport marketers should consider, which are outlined in the following subsections.

Prestige pricing

In some situations the quality or benefits of a product may be more important to consumers than price. The product may be so excellent, fashionable or even essential that the price is not important. In the sport industry, examples of prestige pricing include exclusive memberships, special events, prestige seating, celebrity seating or special services. Because price is not the most important variable in the decision to purchase a product, prestige pricing involves setting a high price. It must be remembered that by setting a high price, a product appears to be exclusive and of high quality. Sometimes it can be effective to produce only a limited number of goods or provide a limited service in order to enhance the image of a product or service. For example, a gymnasium may decide to offer only premium-priced memberships, and give consumers higher quality service, state-of-the-art equipment and less crowding than competitors. One of the drawbacks of prestige pricing is that it will only appeal to a relatively small number of consumers. The power of prestige pricing is that it confers a psychological benefit by encouraging consumers to believe they are special because they have access to such an exclusive product. This is why a variation of prestige pricing is called psychological pricing, which emphasises the intangible quality of a special product.

Status quo pricing

Maintaining the status quo means keeping things the way they are. Status quo pricing aims to either keep prices at the same level or to meet competitors' prices. One advantage of this strategy is that it does not require much planning. It can be a useful approach against a competitor that is an established price leader. However, it is also worth noting that offering a lower price (and therefore better value) and a higher price (for a better product) are two ways of setting a product apart from competitors.

Price skimming

Price skimming involves setting the highest price possible that consumers will pay for a new product. This can help an organisation to quickly cover the costs of product development and promotion. Price skimming will not work in all situations or for all products. It is best used when new equipment or technology is introduced, such as a brand-new golf club or a new exclusive service. Because price skimming is likely to reduce the total number of consumers who buy the product, it is not suitable for all products. Some sport products need a large volume of consumers in order to be successful (like ticket sales to a sport event). However, there are examples in sport where demand is so high for a prestige event that price skimming can be combined profitably with high volume. Good examples are the finals of major sport competitions and hallmark events, such as the Olympic Games opening and closing ceremonies.

Penetration pricing

Penetration pricing is the opposite of price skimming because it involves setting a low introductory price for the product in the hopes of encouraging people to give it a first try. The word penetration is used to mean entry or access to the market. Penetration pricing can be effective in parts of the sport industry where there is a high level of competition, or where consumers already have strong loyalties to products. It is one way of developing some interest in a new product, or trying to increase its market share. After a certain amount of time, penetration pricing is usually replaced with a more standard price that can be realistically maintained. It is hoped that by this time sufficient numbers of consumers will continue to use the product.

Cost-plus pricing

The cost-plus pricing method is common in the sport industry. Using this method, the price is set by calculating the costs of the product, then adding a flat fee or a percentage (e.g. cost plus 10 per cent). If this method is selected, it is essential to have accurate information about fixed and variable costs.

Break-even pricing

A break-even price is one that generates just enough money to cover the costs of the product. This may be a pricing tactic that is useful to non-profit or community sport organisations. It has the advantage of being a simple, consumer-friendly strategy. However, the danger is that consumers will become used to the 'cheap' price, leaving the organisation with little opportunity to change prices in the future, even if costs rise unexpectedly.

Competition pricing

This means setting prices that copy those of competitors. In a highly competitive market, this may prove a useful strategy. It has the advantage of reducing the possibility of being undercut, but it does require a reactive rather than proactive approach. As such it is best employed selectively.

Market demand pricing

Market demand pricing involves setting a price according to the level consumers are willing to pay at a given time. It has the potential of generating high profits for a sport organisation, but it may need to be changed over time because the price consumers are willing to pay changes. It is possible that consumers could feel exploited if they believe they are being charged high prices just because they will pay them. It may also leave an organisation vulnerable to the penetration pricing of competitors.

Discount pricing

Discounting involves reducing or cutting a price in special situations. In the sport industry, discounts may be offered for long-term memberships, group or family concessions, frequent use or bulk purchases. It is used as a way of encouraging consumers to buy more than they otherwise would. Discount pricing can increase overall sales, and by selling more, an organisation can still earn a good profit even though the price per product is reduced. Of course, discounts can only be used occasionally if they are to be successful. Variations of discount pricing include sales and two-for-one offers.

Seasonal pricing

Sometimes it is possible to price a product based on changes in demand that occur over a time period. In competitive sport, leagues often charge different prices at different times in the playing season; they may have different prices for off-season, pre-season, regular season and finals. This is one way that sport leagues can stimulate sales when they are not in the main playing season. Seasonal pricing can cause difficulty if the price needs to be set below cost to stimulate demand.

Off-peak pricing

Like seasonal pricing, off-peak pricing involves setting different prices for different periods. Where seasonal pricing takes advantage of changes over the course of a year, off-peak pricing focuses on changes over the course of one day. Off-peak pricing is commonly employed in sport services where demand is centred on a particular period. For example, gymnasiums and leisure centres often provide discounted memberships for consumers prepared to use the facilities at low-demand times. One of the problems with this kind of pricing is that it can be difficult to control and manage.

Price bundling

A more sophisticated but common pricing tactic is known as bundling, where numerous product benefits are included in one price. Bundling has been popularised through television advertising promising 'steak knives' and other extras when a product is ordered. In a sport context, bundling may include free merchandise with a product purchase, such as a sports watch with a sporting magazine subscription. Bundling is most common in memberships where consumers are offered a range of services and products in one package, such as access to a pool, social club, gymnasium, spa and sauna for one price in a health club. Bundling is effective because it gives consumers the experience of receiving something extra for nothing. For sport marketers, bundling is popular because the extras offered are rarely expensive to include.

Discriminatory pricing

Sometimes known as differential pricing, discriminatory pricing involves making changes to prices according to the category or segment of consumer to whom it is offered. As a result, this tactic is particularly useful for sport organisations that deal with a range of target segments. For example, a sport organisation might offer a less expensive membership to students, pensioners or the unemployed even though the service and benefits are the same.

Exchange pricing

Exchange pricing is a form of reciprocal trade where exchanges are made, such as corporate boxes, signage, tickets to events, and access to players and athletes, for 'everyday' items, including furniture and paper, as well as other necessities such as travel, accommodation and advertising. This is a useful tactic for sport organisations because exchange pricing is effectively bartering, allowing asset-rich, cash-poor sporting organisations to 'save' their liquid finances. It is worth noting that in most countries, while legal, exchange pricing does incur tax. Table 7.1 provides a summary of pricing tactics.

> *Chapter tool 7.5 Select pricing tactics*: A pricing strategy should be related to the positioning strategy that an organisation selects for its product. There are at least 14 types of pricing strategies that sport organisations might employ: prestige pricing, status quo pricing, price skimming, penetration pricing, cost-plus pricing, break-even pricing, competition pricing, market demand pricing, discount pricing, seasonal pricing, off-peak pricing, price bundling, discriminatory pricing and exchange pricing.

Price point

The final step of the pricing process is to set the final price point for each product. A price point is a deliberately selected level of price that reflects the positioning approach underpinning the product's marketing strategy. In general, it is advisable to select a final price point that makes positioning as clear as possible. For example, if the positioning strategy calls for differentiation from a competitor's product, then it is critical to set a

TABLE 7.1 Summary of pricing tactics

Tactic	Summary
1 *Prestige (psychological)*	Setting a high price for a product that has a high perceived value.
	Pricing where quality is more important than price because of 'special' circumstances.
2 *Status quo*	Keeping the price the way it is, or following competitors' prices.
3 *Skimming*	Setting the highest price possible that consumers will pay.
4 *Penetration*	Setting a low, introductory price for a product. The opposite of skimming is to introduce the product at such a low price that it will attract a large market share.
5 *Cost plus*	Pricing calculated by adding the costs of delivering the product, then adding a flat fee or percentage (e.g. cost + 10 per cent).
6 *Break even*	Pricing products at 'cost'.
7 *Competition*	Pricing copies competitors.
8 *Market demand*	Setting pricing according to market demand at the time, taking into account elasticity and growth/shrinkage rates.
9 *Discount*	Decreasing the price of a service or a product in special circumstances.
10 *Seasonal*	Pricing according to seasonal demand.
	Useful for extra stock or downturns due to the season (e.g. winter competitions).
11 *Off-peak*	Pricing according to daily demand.
	Useful for maintaining turnover during normally lower daily usage times.
12 *Bundling*	Offering additional products, services or benefits at the same price.
13 *Discriminatory*	Prices change according to categories of customers (differential).
14 *Exchange*	Reciprocal trade where exchanges are made.

price that is distinctly different from that of competitors. If one were to study the price points of most major sport products, it would become clear that pricing tends to operate at different levels. An obvious example is that it is easy to find tennis racquets and cricket bats at around $150, $250 and $400 for each of the dominant brands. Consumers will tend to select between products that cost approximately the same. This is not the end of the work, however, as pricing strategies need to be reviewed and their success evaluated. Like all stages of the Sport Marketing Framework, pricing requires research and should be managed and controlled over time.

> *Chapter tool 7.6 Select price point*: A price point is a deliberately selected level of price that reflects the positioning approach underpinning the product's marketing strategy.

INTERACTIVE CASE

What price for an Olympic Games? This age-old question rears its ugly head every two years for both summer and winter Olympic events. Montreal (1976) bankrupted the city. Sydney (2000) had approximately a 90 per cent cost overrun, and Athens (2004) a 60 per cent overrun. Beijing (2008) has seen its extravagant 'Bird's Nest' stadium erode into a second-rate tourist attraction. Pre-Games angst centres on the financial costs of staging an Olympic event to improve the social benefits of the chosen city. For London it was the intended development and regeneration of East London.

Questions

Consider the case of Sochi 2014. Do some 'Google' digging on the event and its costs. Did it really cost $50 billion dollars to stage? What legacy is inherited for that price?

Points of interest

Pricing decisions for any product or service is dependent on internal influences such as organisational objectives, the marketing objectives and the costs incurred. The economic climate, regulatory systems and prudent government controls influence the management of the organisation committee's spending. Other factors, including quality of facilities and services and transparency, influence price sensitivity. The greater the outlay the more sensitive the price becomes. Measuring it against the key areas for UK public spending makes it difficult to justify the price of staging such an event. When it is all said and done and the last gold medal is handed over, the end benefit of hosting an Olympics comes under its greatest scrutiny. Next stop Rio de Janeiro, 2016. What price then?

PRINCIPLES SUMMARY

- Chapter principle 7.1: Pricing communicates an important symbolic positioning message to consumers about a sport product.

- Chapter principle 7.2: The value of a sport product is the relationship between its price and the benefits a consumer believes they will receive from it.

- Chapter principle 7.3: The price of a product is the amount of money a consumer must give up in exchange for a good or service. However, price is not the same as value, since value is the difference between price and the anticipated benefit. Although price is usually viewed in monetary terms, it may also include other consumer sacrifices in order to acquire a sport product, such as time or social cost. Additionally, in some instances the value secured from a sports product can be well in excess of its purchase price. This is a good position for a product to be in, since the expectation of getting more value for money will be an incentive to purchase the product.

- Chapter principle 7.4: *Revenue* is the price that consumers pay for a product, multiplied by the number of units sold. *Profit* is revenue minus the costs of producing and selling the product.

- Chapter principle 7.5: The strategic pricing process provides a structure for setting price. The process involves: (1) setting a pricing goal, (2) determining price sensitivity, (3) conducting a break-even analysis, (4) assessing pricing variables, (5) selecting pricing tactics and (6) setting a price point.

TOOLS SUMMARY

- Chapter tool 7.1 Pricing goals
- Chapter tool 7.2 Price sensitivity analysis
- Chapter tool 7.3 Break-even analysis
- Chapter tool 7.4 Assess pricing variables
- Chapter tool 7.5 Select pricing tactics
- Chapter tool 7.6 Select price point

REVIEW QUESTIONS

1   What effect does pricing have on positioning? Provide an example of how price can influence a consumer's perception of a product.

2   What is the difference between value and price?

3   Outline the steps of the strategic pricing process.

4   Using examples to illustrate, describe some conditions that make sport consumers more price sensitive.

5   Why is price bundling so popular? Why do you think it works for both consumers and sport marketers?

6   Explain what a price point is and why it is so important to think of pricing in levels.

RELEVANT WEBSITES

www.rbk.com	Reebok
www.nike.com	Nike
www.fila.com	FILA
www.adidas.com	adidas
www.wimbledon.org	Wimbledon All England Tennis Championships
www.indy500.com	Indianapolis 500

FURTHER READING

Stewart, B. (2014). *Sport Funding and Finance* (2nd edn). London: Routledge.

CHAPTER 8

Sport distribution

LEARNING OUTCOMES

At the end of this chapter, readers should be able to:

- understand the importance of distribution to successful sport marketing
- discuss the basic concepts of sport distribution
- identify the different types of sport distribution channels
- specify the importance of the sport facility as 'place'
- explain the main issues in ticket distribution.

OVERVIEW

The purpose of this chapter is to explore the third of the six elements of the marketing mix, which is place. The place can also be alternatively described as distribution, which focuses on the ways in which products might be best delivered to customers. The chapter begins by introducing the basic concepts underpinning sport distribution, and then moves on to examine three central issues. They are first, the different types of distribution channels, second, the sport facility as a 'place' for distributing sport products, and finally the ticket distribution process.

INTRODUCTION

Distribution is a crucially important part of the marketing mix. However, before proceeding, it is essential to clarify the concept, since it is often interchanged with the term 'place'. When the term 'place' is employed in marketing it can have multiple meanings. It might, for example, refer to the location where goods and services are exchanged for the customer's money payment. Attending a dental surgery for an annual check-up service is a case in point. It can also refer to a method for distributing products along a specific pathway or channel. In this instance it might refer to the process by which motor vehicle parts are produced, the vehicles are assembled, the vehicles are shipped to dealers, and finally the process by which the vehicles are sold to customers via the dealer's showrooms and sales staff. Similarly, distribution means transporting products from the producers to the final consumers. Either way, the sale takes place, and the good or service is delivered in a designated space. In a product marketing context, this space is identified as the 'place'. To avoid any confusion over definitions and nomenclature, for the purposes of this chapter, the words *distribution* and *place* should be considered interchangeable. The concept of distribution/place, and where it fits within the Sport Marketing Framework, is illustrated in Figure 8.1.

THE SPORT DISTRIBUTION PROBLEM

In sport, like any other industry, decisions have to be made about how to get products to customers. Sport distribution concerns how and where consumers access sport products in order to use them. There is little use in having a great product available for a value-for-money price if consumers cannot easily acquire it.

There are several quite different ways in which sport products are distributed in the sport industry, largely due to its fragmented structure and the diverse array of products it supplies to various markets. The first point to note is that the sport industry not only produces highly tangible goods, but also produces many highly intangible services. And, it is easy to see that sporting goods are distributed differently to sporting services.

The transportation of sporting goods from producers to consumers can involve a number of stages. For example, golf equipment – including clubs, balls, bags, and for the wealthy and physically disabled, golf buggies – are, in the first instance, made by a range of manufacturers. These manufacturers will not normally sell direct to the final users – the golf players – but will instead distribute their golf equipment to wholesalers, who will store their products in warehouses together with other golf equipment brands. The wholesalers will then forward these different brands to retailers who will display and advertise them with a view to attracting customers. Sales are made in these retail outlets. This series of connections and transactions reflects the conventional way of getting products to customers efficiently. First, it means that manufacturers do not have to bear the cost of warehousing, and second, customers have the convenience of comparing and contrasting competing golf brands in the same place under the same roof.

In contrast, sport services tend to be distributed through entirely different methods. For example, a professional sporting match could be 'produced' by two competing teams, filmed by a television network, broadcast to viewers, and deposited in modified form on the Internet. For a spectator watching the game live at the sport venue, the stadium itself provides the 'place' where the sport product is distributed. One final example is a sports masseuse, who produces the service and delivers it directly to the customer; there are no people or organisations in the middle at all.

As can be seen from these simple examples, there are many different means and methods through which sport products are distributed. This chapter will introduce the variety of places pivotal to the distribution of sport products. First, some of the important concepts used in distribution will be introduced, at the core of which is the notion of a

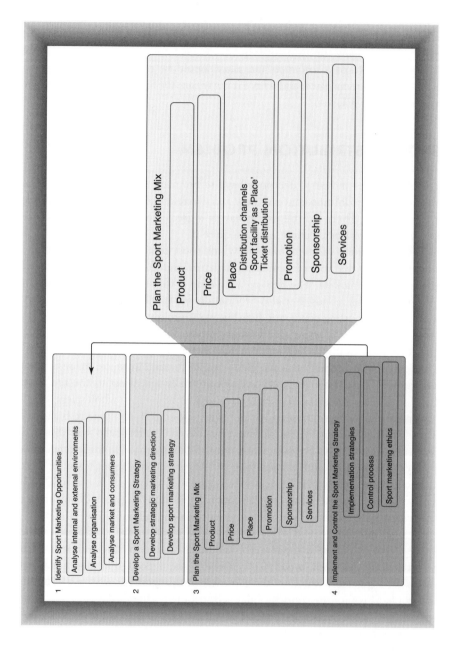

FIGURE 8.1 The Sport Marketing Framework

distribution channel. Second, the centrality of the sport facility or venue as a place where consumers buy and experience sport products will be considered, followed finally by a review of sport ticket distribution.

DISTRIBUTION CHANNELS

As noted earlier, sporting goods or products undergo numerous steps in their distribution from the producer to the sport consumer. Take, for instance, the case of basketballs. To begin with, there is the manufacturer who physically makes the ball, but who usually does not sell it directly to the public. Often manufacturers sell their goods to a wholesaler, who in turn sells it to a retailer. Finally, the retailer operating out of a store in a shopping mall sells the balls to sport consumers. In other words, there is a chain of businesses that are involved in getting the basketball to the consumer; it gets passed from one to the next down a path or a channel.

The sequence described above is all well and good, but what if the sport product comes in the form of a professional basketball game on television, and what if a sport consumer watches in a bar with friends? There is no 'manufacturer' or 'retailer' in the same way as there is for basketballs. Rather, two competing teams produce the product. They sell this product via the league they compete in to the television network, which puts the contest on air. In this example, the bar accesses the television broadcast and shows it to the consumers present. This is another example of a distribution channel because the product has been moved from the producer of the product (the two professional basketball teams) to the consumers of the product (the people watching the game).

When considering the two examples of distribution channels just described, it is obvious that they both involve the circulation of a product from the producer to the consumer through a sequence of operational steps. This sequence of operational steps is known as a distribution channel.

> *Chapter principle 8.1*: A sport distribution channel is an organised series of organisations, suppliers and individuals that move products from the producer to the final consumer.

Distribution systems

Two different kinds of sport distribution channels have been used as examples. They both described the movement of products from producers to consumers, but they do it in different ways, or with different *sport distribution systems*. A distribution *system* is the way that a distribution channel is organised or arranged. There are different ways of structuring distribution, explained in the following subsections.

Types of distribution channels

Distribution channels have different lengths, and as a consequence they may be characterised as *direct* or *indirect*. A direct distribution channel is short where the producer sells the product directly to the consumer. For example, a sports physiotherapist produces the service and sells it directly to the consumer. Direct distribution also occurs when a sporting good producer sells products on the Internet, or by direct mail. Many manufacturers of sport products do this in addition to the use of normal retail stores. The process is illustrated in Figure 8.2.

An indirect distribution channel is long because there are numerous organisations or people involved along the way. Those in the middle are usually called *intermediaries*, because they mediate between producers and consumers. When it comes to sporting goods, wholesalers and/or retailers are added into the channel. The following diagrams show two different kinds of indirect distribution channels. Figure 8.3 shows both a retailer and a wholesaler in the channel, while Figure 8.4 excludes the wholesaler step.

> *Chapter principle 8.2*: There are both direct and indirect distribution channels that vary in length. A direct distribution channel is short where the producer sells the product directly to the consumer. An indirect distribution channel is a long channel where there are a number of intermediaries involved along the way.

Channel members

A channel member is any organisation or individual involved as part of a distribution channel. When it comes to sporting goods, in addition to the producers (manufacturers), the most common channel members are wholesalers and retailers.

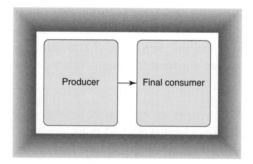

FIGURE 8.2 Direct distribution channel

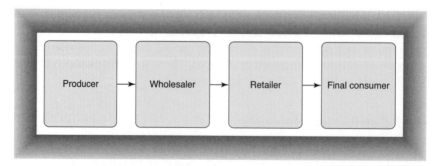

FIGURE 8.3 Indirect distribution channel A

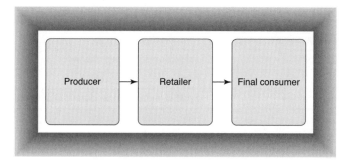

FIGURE 8.4 Indirect distribution channel B

Wholesalers

A wholesaler is an organisation or individual acting as the middle step between a producer and a retailer. It is reasonable to ask what the point might be of having a wholesaler in the distribution channel. Why would the manufacturer not simply pass the sporting goods straight on to the retailer? However, a wholesaler can be important in helping other channel members. First, they usually buy goods in bulk from the manufacturer and then store them. When the retailer is ready to order some goods, the wholesaler transports the sporting goods to them. A wholesaler can also stock a large range of goods from a variety of different manufacturers. As a result, instead of having to contact all of these producers, the retailer only has to talk to the one wholesaler to gain access to a range of different sporting goods.

Of course wholesalers are not always involved in a distribution channel. If a retailer does not want to use a wholesaler (e.g. they may not want to pay extra for the product), then they have to undertake for themselves all the tasks performed by the wholesaler. They may have to store and transport the sporting goods, and may have to keep in contact with a diverse number of producers.

Retailers

Retailers are the organisations and individuals involved in the final sale of a sporting good or service to a consumer. There are many different kinds of retailers, and choosing the right retail outlet can be an important decision for a sport marketer. Most importantly, the retail outlet that is selected should be convenient for consumers and suitable for the kind of products being sold. For example, it might seem convenient to be able to buy a tennis racket from the corner store, but a specialised retail sports outlet would be more appropriate for the range and advice required to make a fitting selection.

There are several different kinds of retail outlets. To begin with there are physical locations housed in buildings such as department stores and shopping centres. These retailers are sometimes called 'bricks and mortar' retailers. There are also 'virtual' stores such as Internet sites, television home shopping and mail order catalogues. These retailers can be called virtual retailers. Some examples of both are provided in Table 8.1.

TABLE 8.1 Types of sport retailers

Bricks and mortar retailers	Virtual retailers
Supermarkets	Television shopping channels
Shopping centres	Mail order catalogues
Speciality sporting shops	Special merchandise during televised sport
Sport clubs	Internet sites and downloads
Recreation and leisure centres	Infomercials
Gymnasiums	Mobile or cellular phone offers
Factory direct outlets	
Sport stadiums and venues	

Chapter principle 8.3: A channel member is any organisation or individual that is involved in the sport distribution channel. Channel members may include wholesalers and retailers, as well as producers and consumers.

Distribution issues for sport products

Table 8.2 highlights the main distribution issues that different sport products, such as sporting goods, sport-consulting services and facility-dependent sport services, are faced with. Sport-consulting services include market researchers, sport management consultants and even sport psychology experts. Facility-dependent sport services are those that need

TABLE 8.2 Distribution issues for sporting products

Distribution variables	Sporting goods	Sport-consulting services	Facility-dependent sport services
Length of distribution channel	Long, often many channel members	Short, often just the producer (service provider) and consumer	Short, often just the producer (service provider) and consumer
Location of distribution	Many locations (potentially unlimited)	Many locations (potentially unlimited)	The sport facility
How customer accesses distribution	Consumer goes to distribution point	Service provider usually goes to consumer	Consumer goes to distribution point
Interaction between producer and customer	Indirect	Direct	Direct
Use of technology	Limited but increasing	Technology usually used for initial contact (e.g. website, email contact etc.)	Heavy for the sale of tickets

a sport facility to run, like a community netball competition, a recreation centre or a professional league. Table 8.2 shows that sport products can have different distribution channel lengths, different kinds of distribution locations, different kinds of consumer interaction, and various levels of dependent technology and consumer access.

> *Chapter tool 8.1 Distribution issues analysis*: Different sport products have different distribution issues to deal with. Sport marketers can employ various distribution channel lengths, kinds of distribution locations, consumer interaction, dependent technology and consumer access. These can be examined against the type of sporting product offered, whether sporting goods, consulting services or facility-dependent sport services.

INTERACTIVE CASE

Some interesting figures on the distribution channels for sporting goods in the US are provided in the following website.

www.statista.com
(www.statista.com/statistics/201225/sport-eqipment-sales-by-channels-of-distribution)

Questions

1   What are the six most important retail outlets for sporting goods?
2   How important are department stores and mail-order arrangements?
3   What is the difference between a sporting goods store and a speciality sports shop?
4   Are these stores and shops more or less popular sales outlets now than they were ten years earlier?
5   How important are Internet sales?
6   Are Internet sales increasing or decreasing?

Points of interest

The Internet has totally transformed the ways in which products are sold and purchased. Sporting goods are no exception. There are now thousands of websites around the world where both new and used sporting goods are put up for sale. However, it is unlikely that online distribution will lead to the demise of speciality sporting goods shops. This is because many sport products need to be customised to fit special needs and satisfy the idiosyncratic requirements of individuals. In many instances it can never be a case of 'one size fits all'. Two good examples of the critical importance of product–user 'fit' are running shoes and tennis rackets.

SPORT FACILITY AS 'PLACE'

Sporting goods are delivered to consumers in quite conventional ways, and most sales end up in retail stores somewhere along a shopping strip or shopping mall. Sports services are something else, since they are both delivered and experienced in a specialist 'sport facility'. A sport facility is a place where sport competitions are delivered as entertainment to sport spectators on one hand, and as an activity to sport participants on the other. Thus, the sport facility is the most important distribution channel for two types of sport products: (1) sport activity services and (2) professional sport events. Sport activity services are those offering participation or a personal service in sport including physical education lessons, coaching, community competitions, health and rehabilitation consultations, and local or recreational sport practice and events. Professional sport events offer a forum for elite athletes to compete, and entertainment for spectators. They include state, national or international competitions, covering all sports from football, swimming and motor racing, to gymnastics, surfing and rock-climbing. All of these sport activities and events need a sport facility. Without a sport facility these products cannot be made, and there is nothing to market.

Designing a sport facility to fit in with the local area can help to make it an attractive distribution point, which is also useful for media attention. For example, many sport facilities possess a special design element that reflects the character of the city or country. However, marketers have little control over the design of sport facilities and even less over their composition once built. This part of the chapter therefore focuses on the aspects of the sport place that can be manipulated by facility and event marketers. For sport activity services and professional sport events, the sport facility represents the 'place' dimension of the marketing mix. A fundamental point to remember is that the sport product (the competition or activity) is both produced and consumed at the same location and at the same time. There are a range of sport facility features that a sport marketer must manage, which are considered next.

> *Chapter principle 8.4*: The sport facility is the most important distribution channel for sport activity services and professional sport events.

Features of sport facilities

The features of sport facilities have a powerful influence on a sport consumer's experience of an event. These features include seating, layout, accessibility (how easy it is to get to, and to get around in), the overall 'look' or design of the venue, its cleanliness, and even the technical capabilities of the scoreboard. When consumers perceive that a venue is of high quality, they are more likely to be satisfied and return for a similar experience. The sport facility is most effective as a distribution channel when its features are designed and handled carefully as part of a well-considered marketing plan.

Sport stadia and venues that have a good location, an attractive atmosphere, luxury seating, excellent eateries and other entertainment services such as nightclubs, bars, theatres and shopping areas, attract larger crowds. As a consequence, sport marketers are compelled to consider four main areas in which they can maximise the sport consumer experience. These pivotal marketing features of a sport facility are: (1) location and accessibility, (2) design and layout, (3) facility infrastructure and (4) customer service. The core characteristics of each feature are provided in Table 8.3, and are discussed in more detail in the following sections of this chapter.

> *Chapter principle 8.5*: Sport marketers must consider four main aspects of sport facilities in which they can maximise the sport consumer experience: (1) location and accessibility, (2) design and layout, (3) facility infrastructure and (4) customer service.

INTERACTIVE CASE

Log in to YouTube and enter the word 'tailgating' in the search engine.

www.youtube.com

Questions

1 What is tailgating?
2 What events and facilities are especially suitable for tailgating?
3 Why would a sport event organiser want to encourage tailgating?
4 What marketing activities could be implemented to support and surround tailgaters?
5 How could a sport facility be reconfigured to make tailgating easier to operate and manage?
6 Are there tailgating equivalent designs that could be built into sport facilities in countries outside the US?

Points of interest

'Tailgating' is a practice where sport fans gather in the parking lot of a sport stadium or venue, and have a party, barbeque, or drinking session prior to a big game. It is especially popular in the United States. The practice has a rich tradition in Europe and Australia as well, particularly for motor and horse racing enthusiasts. Tailgating is not for everyone, though. The opportunity to tailgate is constrained by first the space available for car parking, and second the ownership of motor vehicles that are suitable for tailgating activities.

Tailgating is often problematic. In the US sport fans arrive at stadia parking lots well prepared. In some instances fans come too well prepared, and as a result there have been mixed feelings about the appropriateness of tailgating given its tendency to encourage excessive alcohol consumption. However, given its popularity, sport marketers found ways of supporting the practice while regulating some of its more antisocial and offensive practices. While tailgating has its critics, it provides a good case study of how sport experiences outside of the venue 'space' can be used as an additional marketing strategy.

TABLE 8.3 Features and characteristics of sport facilities

Location and accessibility
Attractive location
Convenient to get to
Good signage and directions
Enough parking
Accessible by public transport
Accessible by different forms of public transport
Easy to enter and exit facility
Disabled access (ramps, lifts, washroom facilities)

Design and layout
Fits in with local area
Attractive design (size, colour, shape and light)
Ambience and atmosphere
Easy to get from one area to another
Good direction signs
Seating arrangements with good viewing
Weather protection
Control of noise levels
Areas for non-smokers and non-drinkers
Lighting of playing area
Protection from heat and cold
Air circulation
Adequate storage
Safety issues (emergency procedures, fire detection, standby power, emergency communication, exits)
Security (surveillance, control room, entrance security)
Spectator control (zones, safe barriers, security, police)

Facility infrastructure
Variety of food and drink outlets
Overall seating quality
Premium seating available
Corporate boxes and special services
Toilets: number and location for convenient access
Childcare facilities
Scoreboards and screens
Message centres and sound systems
Emergency medical services
Merchandise areas
Broadcasting and media requirements

Customer service
Queuing and waiting times
Prominent information stands/booths
Efficient, friendly and helpful staff
Sufficient security and emergency staff
Entrance staff, ushers
Services for elderly, disabled and children
Telephone enquiry service

Tools for marketing sport facilities

In an ideal sports marketing world every sport facility would be located in a central location, have quick and easy access to public transport, include the latest design features, provide unimpeded sight lines, have a perfect playing surface, include a retractable roof, have a raft of impeccably appointed dining rooms, provide player-friendly training facilities, contain various safety features, have state of the art surveillance, deliver long-life infrastructure, include the highest quality night-lighting, and have well-trained attendants and security staff, and friendly and efficient catering staff.

In reality, there are many constraints on what sports facilities can deliver fans and participants. As a result, sport marketers have limited control over the features, and may be able to do little to enact change because to do so would require substantial expenditure on a venue's infrastructure. While sport marketers are frequently unable to make many changes to a facility's features, they need to be aware of the impact that facility features have on the consumer experience. In some cases it may be possible to take action in one area to compensate for poor features elsewhere that cannot be modified. For example, it may be appropriate to reduce the price of seats with sight line obstructions, and thus minimise the likelihood of receiving additional complaints. Additionally, the lack of easy access to public transport may be alleviated by providing high-speed shuttle bus services to surrounding railway stations.

Smart sport marketers are thus not only aware of the limitations imposed by the location, design and operation of sport facilities, but also understand that adjustments around the edges are always possible. In the following section eight practical marketing tools for managing distribution channels in sport are discussed. Customer service is identified as a crucially important contributor to the quality of the experience, but is not discussed in detail here. However, it forms a central part of Chapter 11.

Seating

The most important marketing aspects of seating selection include cost, look, comfort, durability and ease of maintenance. Their purpose is also relevant, such as whether the seats are to be used for a corporate box or for public access. Some sport facilities include ventilation holes and a full back support to prevent spectators from pushing their feet into the person sitting in front of them. It is also useful in most instances to have seats that can be easily removed, so that damaged seats can be replaced or new sponsorship logos attached. The most versatile seating options in recent venues are moveable seats that can be relocated in sections to different parts of the venue. This is advantageous because it allows more flexibility in the types of sport that can be played and watched at a venue. Some venues use their seating selection as part of their positioning strategy. For example, most contemporary stadia have employed a material and design that increases the sound of the stomping noise spectators make during games, thereby amplifying the atmosphere for fans. In addition, seats can be used to differentiate the level of consumer spending. Most new venues use some form of personal viewing screen for corporate sections or for special kinds of memberships. From a marketing perspective this means that there is greater opportunity to enhance consumers' interaction with the sport product, other entertainment options such as gaming, statistics and alternative camera angles, as well as with all marketing messages.

Chapter tool 8.2 Seating: Seating selection influences sport consumers' experience and can be used to enhance their viewing comfort as well as the marketing messages they are exposed to.

Scoreboards and signage

The scoreboard requirements of a small, recreational basketball venue will obviously be quite different to those demanded by an international multipurpose stadium, which will need to broadcast video replays and advertisements. However, for all sport facilities the scoreboard is one of the main spaces to promote sponsors. After all, it is guaranteed that spectators will be looking at the scoreboard. Similarly, even a small facility can use signage to promote sponsors, other events or even further products that are available.

Chapter tool 8.3 Scoreboards and signage: Scoreboards and signage are an essential method of communicating marketing messages irrespective of the size of a venue.

Lighting and sound system

Strong lighting on a sport field is ideal for both large and modest grounds. In fact, smaller-sized outdoor sport venues can attract larger crowds if they employ flood lighting. For example, local recreational and school sport fields can benefit from installing night-time illumination because but they can radically increase participation and crowds by allowing activity after working hours. This approach is extremely successful for outdoor tennis courts and athletics tracks. Lighting is also important in car parking areas for both safety and security. For a limited cost it is possible for indoor venues to install lighting and sound systems that have a significant effect on the atmosphere of the event as well as improving general communication about the activities and opportunities in the venue.

Chapter tool 8.4 Lighting and sound systems: Lighting and sound systems can be used to attract sport consumers at attractive times and can also improve the atmosphere of a venue and event.

Transport

It is often important for consumers to be able to easily access a sport facility by public transport or by other services offered by the venue. If a facility is easy to get to, then consumers are more likely to make return visits. Public transport is particularly important for large national or international events when thousands of people need to get to an event. Modest events and venues may consider using buses or minibuses to help move crowds from parking areas to the main doors. It is especially important to provide some transportation services to assist those with restricted mobility. These services may also be branded with marketing signage. They do not necessarily have to be complementary services either.

Chapter tool 8.5 Transport: Transport can be used to assist consumers in accessing a facility and can be marketed as a special customer service.

Media and broadcasting

Sport facilities need to consider how they can facilitate media involvement with their sport events. Most large sport and entertainment facilities have recently installed wireless technology so that media representatives can use a high-speed connection from any 'hot-spot'. Display screens for spectators and VIPs can also be important in some venues and events. Almost every sport facility can benefit from a dedicated area for sport broadcasting and media commentary. The most recent sport stadia are built as immense television studios with the infrastructure for broadcasting embedded underground.

> *Chapter tool 8.6 Media and broadcasting*: Providing media facilities can encourage broadcasting and general media interest in events that occur in a sport facility.

Childcare facilities

While a suburban football ground is unlikely to offer childcare facilities, it has become an increasingly important service for community recreational facilities. Sport facilities, especially where they offer mixed gender activities need to consider the childcare needs of their staff and patrons. For example, a facility that wants to attract 30- to 40-year-old women to a fitness programme must look at how they can facilitate their potential customers' involvement. It is complex and expensive to set up a childcare centre in a sport facility, but in some cases it might be possible to work out a deal with a local childcare centre to provide casual care to the children at certain times of the day, or during particular events.

> *Chapter tool 8.7 Childcare facilities*: The provision of childcare facilities can be important in attracting consumers during non-peak periods or to special events.

Merchandising

The price of a ticket to a sport competition may not be the only thing that a customer is willing to spend money on at a sport event. In fact, sales from merchandise can be more profitable than gate receipts. Small community facilities can usually accommodate merchandise in the front reception, which takes up less space and staff time. Medium-to larger-sized sport facilities can sell merchandise in a number of different ways, such as having a temporary sales tent, roaming sales staff, a special merchandise shop or an online outlet.

> *Chapter tool 8.8 Merchandise*: Selling merchandise in sport facilities is a powerful marketing tool because it provides consumers with a convenient way of spending more money on items that emphasise the sport product's brand image.

Food and beverages

The supply of food and beverages is among the most lucrative of all services that can be offered at a sport facility. The type of food and beverages sold should reflect consumer preferences. This means, of course, that some market research is required before food and beverage outlets are planned and built. This is especially important in regards to where the outlets are positioned within a facility. For example, if sport consumers cannot get to a food and beverage outlet within 60 seconds of leaving their seats from anywhere in a stadium, then there are probably too few outlets available. Equally, it is unsatisfying for consumers to have to stand in a queue for lengthy periods. It is critical to examine not only what consumers like to eat and drink but also when, how often and why they leave their seat to buy food or drinks. Spectators will eat and drink more or less, and at different times, depending on the sport they are watching. It is particularly annoying to spectators when they miss pivotal moments of play because they were standing in a queue. As a result, many venues are beginning to build food and beverage stands facing the field of play so that spectators can continue to watch the action.

> *Chapter tool 8.9 Food and beverages*: The supply of food and beverages is among the most lucrative of all services that can be offered at a sport facility, which means that they demand careful planning.

TICKET DISTRIBUTION

Ticket sales are still one of the most important sources of revenue for sport organisations that conduct competitions or events. It follows then that ticket distribution is an extremely important issue for sport marketers. For large sport organisations, most tickets are purchased from a ticket distributor, either in person, over the phone or on the Internet. For smaller sport organisations, tickets might be bought directly from a sporting club or event organiser. In general, like other sport products, sport tickets get passed down a distribution channel from the producer to the consumer. The ticket distributor is one of the channel members. In this model, ticket distributors do more than just provide tickets, they also show advertisements, offer sales promotions, provide customer service, conduct personal selling and physically send out the tickets to consumers.

When consumers contact a ticket distributor to purchase a ticket for a sport event, they are often looking for more than just a ticket. They want convenience, easy accessibility and a fast, user-friendly service. Some consumers may want to have questions about the event or the sport facility answered, and they certainly want a reasonable price that has not been increased too much because the ticket distributor is taking a large percentage. If a consumer becomes unhappy with the service or price they receive from a ticket distributor, they can feel dissatisfied about the sport event or club as well. It is therefore important that the sport organisation carefully discusses the features of a contract with the ticket distributor. Furthermore, sport organisations should maintain communications with the ticket distributor's customer service staff, which should include regular training and information updates.

One of the trends in ticket distribution is to sell tickets online. Ticketmaster in the United States and Ticketek in Australia are examples of online ticket distributors. These companies usually sell tickets for a wide variety of events, including music concerts, comedy, theatre and sport events. Even though they are not specialist sport ticket distributors, the general public know that they sell tickets to almost any entertainment event in their city. As a result, it is easy and convenient for consumers to remember the website and log on. One of the drawbacks is that consumers are able to easily compare the different entertainment events that are available, and could choose another activity. The use of a distribution agent also increases the cost of a ticket as they charge a percentage of the ticket price to manage the booking and distribution process.

> *Chapter principle 8.6*: Ticket sales are one of the most important sources of revenue for sport organisations that conduct competitions or events. The smooth distribution of tickets is essential to the satisfaction of consumers and the maximisation of sales.

INTERACTIVE CASE

In 2006 the FIFA World Cup organisers developed an innovative idea for bringing fans together in a physical space. The organisers recognised that sport fans, who were unable to get match tickets to support their team, could experience the atmosphere by creating fan venues. FanZones became the place where team supporters congregated to watch the game on big screens for free, drank the team sponsor product, and embraced the World Cup atmosphere. For the organisers it was an opportunity to generate revenue from official partners and other organisations that wanted to feature their brands to a specific target market. It was an innovative idea and its success started a trend in managing fans at international events. The 2015 World Cup Rugby organisers issued formal guidelines for managing FanZones, indicating the significance these physical spaces have for marketing an event. The challenge of marketing 'place' for sport fans is to devise strategies that strengthen the capacity of the fan community to unite, engage and to sustain a vitality of the space.

Questions

Establishing a productive physical or virtual FanZone depends on traditional marketing rationale. That is, the basic service provided must satisfy the needs of its fans, other businesses and visitors in the right place at the right time. Place objectives must build a realistic vision where the strategies devised complement that vision. If it doesn't have authenticity it will be worthless to the sport fan. How can sport marketers establish a sense of authenticity in their FanZones? Consider key attributes such as image marketing, site attraction, infrastructure and people as critical to a successful FanZone place strategy.

Points of interest

An online FanZone is all about uniting fans in a virtual space. Online place marketing must have the right mix of 'community' features to encourage a sport's scattered community to come together. Online FanZones are particularly appealing to global sport franchises because their fan base is spread far and wide. Hong Kong Sevens Fanzone (www.hksevens.com) creates an opportunity for rugby fans around the world to engage with each other, and at the same time, promote the Rugby Sevens image and services. Online FanZones are not exclusive to global franchises. Forums can be created by the fans or for the fans, for events (Rugby Sevens), media (www.skysports.com/fanzone-holding) individual players, clubs and associations (fanzone.netball.asn.au), and supporter groups such as the 'Barmy Army'.

PRINCIPLES SUMMARY

- Chapter principle 8.1: A sport distribution channel is an organised series of organisations, suppliers and individuals that move products from the producer to the final consumer.

- Chapter principle 8.2: There are both direct and indirect distribution channels that vary in length. A direct distribution channel is short where the producer sells the product directly to the consumer. An indirect distribution channel is a long channel where there are a number of intermediaries involved along the way.

- Chapter principle 8.3: A channel member is any organisation or individual that is involved in the sport distribution channel. Channel members may include wholesalers and retailers, as well as producers and consumers.

- Chapter principle 8.4: The sport facility is the most important distribution channel for sport activity services and professional sport events.

- Chapter principle 8.5: Sport marketers must consider four main aspects of sport facilities in which they can maximise the sport consumer experience: (1) location and accessibility, (2) design and layout, (3) facility infrastructure and (4) customer service.

- Chapter principle 8.6: Ticket sales are one of the most important sources of revenue for sport organisations that conduct competitions or events. The smooth distribution of tickets is essential to the satisfaction of consumers and the maximisation of sales.

TOOLS SUMMARY

- Chapter tool 8.1   Distribution issues analysis
- Chapter tool 8.2   Seating
- Chapter tool 8.3   Scoreboards and signage
- Chapter tool 8.4   Lighting and sound systems

- Chapter tool 8.5   Transport
- Chapter tool 8.6   Media and broadcasting
- Chapter tool 8.7   Childcare facilities
- Chapter tool 8.8   Merchandise
- Chapter tool 8.9   Food and beverages

REVIEW QUESTIONS

1 What is a sport distribution channel? Provide an example.

2 What is the difference between a direct and an indirect distribution channel?

3 What kinds of sport products might pass through wholesaler and retailer intermediaries?

4 Provide five examples of sport activity services and five examples of professional sport events.

5 Of the eight tools for marketing facility features, which three do you think are the most practical for a sport marketer to manipulate?

6 What are the advantages and disadvantages to using a ticket distributor?

7 In what ways is the distribution of sport and its 'place' marketing changing as a consequence of mobile technologies?

RELEVANT WEBSITES

www.statista.com	The Statistics Portal
www.youtube.com	YouTube
www.hksevens.com	Hong Kong Sevens
www.skysports.com	Sky Sports
http://netball.asn.au	Australian Netball individual players, clubs and associations

FURTHER READING

Fried, G. (2010). *Managing Sports Facilities*. Leeds: Human Kinetics.
Schwarz, E. (2009). *Sport Facility Operations Management: A Global Perspective*. Oxford: Butterworth Heinemann.

CHAPTER 9

Sport promotion

LEARNING OUTCOMES

At the end of this chapter, readers should be able to:

- define the term promotion
- outline the elements of the promotions mix
- describe the strengths and weaknesses of each element of the promotions mix
- identify the three main goals of promotions
- explain the steps involved in planning a promotions approach.

OVERVIEW

The purpose of this chapter is to explain the role of the fourth element of the marketing mix – promotion. It begins by examining what promotion means in the context of sport marketing, as well as its range of uses. The chapter also highlights the application of four promotional tools, known as the promotions mix, which includes advertising, personal selling, sales promotions and public relations. Promotional goals are examined and the process of promotions planning is outlined.

ADVERTISING TO PROMOTIONS

It is common for people to think of promotion as being nothing but advertising in the form of commercials on the television, radio, Internet and in the print media. However, other common applications of promotional activities include face-to-face personal selling, free samples, trade shows, contests and give-aways. The first step is therefore to clearly define the scope of promotion in sport marketing. Its position in the Sport Marketing Framework is shown in Figure 9.1.

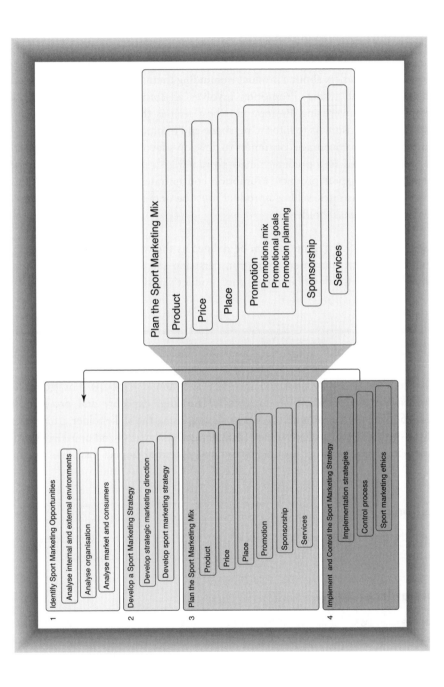

FIGURE 9.1 The Sport Marketing Framework

1 Identify Sport Marketing Opportunities
- Analyse internal and external environments
- Analyse organisation
- Analyse market and consumers

2 Develop a Sport Marketing Strategy
- Develop strategic marketing direction
- Develop sport marketing strategy

3 Plan the Sport Marketing Mix
- Product
- Price
- Place
- Promotion
- Sponsorship
- Services

4 Implement and Control the Sport Marketing Strategy
- Implementation strategies
- Control process
- Sport marketing ethics

Plan the Sport Marketing Mix
- Product
- Price
- Place
- Promotion
  Promotions mix
  Promotional goals
  Promotion planning
- Sponsorship
- Services

PROMOTION

In sport marketing the word promotion covers a range of interrelated activities. All of these activities are designed to attract attention, stimulate the interest and awareness of consumers, and of course, encourage them to purchase a sport product. Promotion is about communicating with and educating consumers. For example, promotion might involve telling potential consumers about a product, reminding them of its benefits, or persuading them that it is worth trying. Promotion involves all forms of communication with consumers, not just advertising. Promotion is best seen as the way that sport marketers communicate with consumers to inform, persuade and remind them about a product. The aim of promotion is to encourage consumers to develop a favourable opinion about a sport product that is aligned to a predetermined positioning strategy, and then to stimulate consumers to try the sport product. Promotion concentrates on *selling* the product. As the following case illustrates, selling a product must be undertaken within the context of a group of interested stakeholders.

> *Chapter principle 9.1*: Promotion can be defined as the way that sport marketers communicate with consumers to inform, persuade and remind them about the features and benefits described by a sport product's positioning.

INTERACTIVE CASE

Stakeholders are generally classified into key and non-key groups. For example, Grassrootsoccer is dependent on support for funding, exposure and programme delivery to many regions around the world. Categorising the stakeholder groups and individuals of Grassrootsoccer into key (primary and secondary) and non-key groups is worth examining in order to understand the potential impact each has on the project.

Questions

Who are the stakeholders and how difficult is it for the organisers of Grassrootsoccer to maintain relationships evenly and regularly with all stakeholder groups?

Points of interest

Grassrootsoccer (www.grassrootsoccer.org) is a charitable organisation formed in 2002 that has combined the delivery of a health promotions message with the goal of promoting sport in Africa. Its mission aims 'to educate, inspire and mobilise communities to stop the spread of HIV'. A key task of pursuing a strategic intention is to identify all stakeholders without which organisations such as Grassrootsoccer would not be able to achieve its aims. Financial support for the organisation is solicited from three broad groups: individuals, corporations and foundations. Additional to this, the organisation has over 70 employees and interns and more than 500 volunteers across 20 countries worldwide. The overarching management structure includes a Global Board of Directors, Ambassadors, Research Council and Affiliated Boards in various countries. Among the key sponsors are USAID, Nike, Barclays Bank, ExxonMobil, Elton John Aids Foundation, the Bill & Melinda Gates Foundation, as well as over 50 supporter organisations globally.

The promotions mix

It is common for sport organisations to use a number of different promotional activities simultaneously, rather than to just focus on one. Because different promotional activities can be combined together, they are collectively known as the promotions mix. In other words, it is advantageous to combine a number of promotional activities together into one promotional plan or strategy. A promotional strategy is a plan that aims to use the four main elements of the promotions mix for the best results. The promotions mix elements are: (1) advertising, (2) personal selling, (3) sales promotions and (4) public relations.

> *Chapter principle 9.2*: The promotions mix consists of four marketing tools: (1) advertising, (2) personal selling, (3) sales promotions and (4) public relations.

Advertising

It is easy to think of advertising examples: television commercials, magazine and newspaper advertisements, radio spots, posters, billboards, Internet pop-ups and advertisements on public transport. In all of these examples, a sport organisation would pay someone else (such as a radio station or magazine) to present the advertisement. Even though intermediaries present advertisements, they are always produced from the perspective of the organisation or brand that is paying for it. A first important point about advertising is that it is a one-way communication from marketers to consumers. Advertising is a form of one-way communication where a marketer pays someone else to have a product, brand or organisation identified. One of the advantages of advertising is that it can reach a large number of people at once. However, it is often an expensive form of promotion that few sport organisations can afford.

> *Chapter tool 9.1 Advertising*: Advertising is a form of one-way communication where a marketer pays someone else to have a product, brand or organisation identified. Common examples include television commercials, magazine and newspaper advertisements, radio spots, posters, billboards, Internet pop-ups and advertisements on public transport.

Personal selling

Personal selling involves one-to-one communication between a consumer and a salesperson. Personal selling might involve talking to a consumer on the phone, talking face-to-face, communication through text messaging on a mobile cellular phone or through an Internet portal. The aim of personal selling is to build relationships with consumers in order to convince them to accept a point of view about the brand or product in question, and ultimately to convince them to take some action and try the product. Endorsements and sponsorships are two forms of personal selling that are common in the sport industry, each of which will be explained further shortly.

> *Chapter tool 9.2 Personal selling*: Personal selling involves one-to-one communication between a consumer and a salesperson. Common examples include talking to a consumer on the phone, talking face-to-face, communication through text messaging on a mobile cellular phone or through an Internet portal. Endorsements and sponsorships are two forms of personal selling that are common in the sport industry.

Sponsorship

Endorsements and sponsorships are two forms of personal selling that are prevalent in the sport industry. *Sport sponsorship* occurs when a sporting organisation or an individual athlete is supported by a separate company (or person). The sponsorship is designed to benefit both parties: the sport organisation (or sponsee) receives money or products, and the sponsor receives the benefits of positive associations with prominent sporting teams or athletes. It can sometimes be unclear what these other benefits are for the sponsor. For this reason, the sporting organisation is nearly always the one approaching a company for a sponsorship. Sport organisations therefore must have a clear idea of what they have to offer or 'sell' to the potential sponsor. Common benefits that are offered to sponsors include:

- naming rights;
- signage;
- media coverage/indirect advertising;
- goodwill (reputation) for being involved with sporting heroes;
- direct advertising opportunities;
- access to a new consumer market;
- opportunity for new sales (e.g. special offers to members);
- demonstration of products (e.g. use of product at a sporting event);
- political benefits.

Because the sporting organisation is nearly always the one asking a company for sponsorship, they must undertake substantial preparatory planning. This involves conducting some research to ensure that they are choosing the right company to approach with a formal proposal. Sponsorship is such an important part of sport marketing that Chapter 10 is exclusively dedicated to it.

INTERACTIVE CASE

The UN Millennium Declaration of 2000 was written in support of an international commitment to peace. When conflict rages and wars drag on, a country's infrastructure is severely damaged. In the past few years there have been over 25 countries involved in conflict or tension where critical resources are drawn away from civil activity towards military activity. Recovering from political turmoil can be a slow and disheartening process. Sport participation is often a means of drawing attention away from tensions that exist in society. A sport agenda offers a powerful platform for promoting social responsibility. At the same time, the evidence that sport improves communication between rival ethnic groups is more anecdotal than substantial. However, sport at all levels can profit from social engagement activities.

Questions

How can sport organisations exercise their influence to promote social responsibility? What political, social and economic challenges would they face if they were to promote a social responsibility strategy?

Points of interest

The British Council in Sudan has actively set up peace-building programmes aimed at developing local coaches and encouraging the integration of children through sport. Sport has often been used as a means of breaking down barriers between social groups.

The Afghan Civil War began in 2001 but the country was able to resume international football competition recently for the first time in over a decade, winning respect and support from the governing body FIFA resulting in being awarded the Fair Play Award in 2013.

Recently, North Korea opened the 2014 Pyongyang Marathon to international competitors for the first time in its 27-year history. Sport can be the mechanism to connect people to a wide range of support services and a more positive environment. The significance of sport as a promotional mechanism for social inclusion has not gone unnoticed.

Endorsements

An *endorsement* occurs when a well-known celebrity or athlete uses their fame to help a company sell its products. They may also use their reputation to help enhance the image of the company, its products or brand. A celebrity athlete may appear in an advertisement or other public forum using a product, saying that they endorse it, and recommending that everyone use it. Because sport fans can have a strong psychological connection to celebrity sport stars, endorsements can be an effective method of persuading fans to buy particular products. If the sports star is seen as trustworthy, this can help fans to believe that the product is reliable. This is why superstars such as Kobe Bryant in the National Basketball League in the United States can be so effective when they endorse a product.

Sales promotions

A sales promotion is usually a short-term programme that aims to stimulate an increase in sales. Examples of sales promotions include 'two-for-one' offers, prize give-aways, competitions and free trials or samples. Sales promotions can be useful supplements to other promotional activities, as they tend to draw attention thereby providing the other activities with more exposure. Typically, sales promotions provide consumers with an incentive (or a bonus) to buy the sport product.

A sport organisation may target a sales promotion towards the general public or sometimes to wholesalers and retailers. One of the advantages of sales promotions is that it is relatively easy to keep track of how many consumers were enticed to use a product because of a special deal. For example, if a 'two-for-one' coupon is part of the sales promotion, it is possible to count the number redeemed. Sales promotions can help to achieve a variety of promotional goals, such as encouraging loyal customers to buy more often, encouraging consumers to change when they buy a particular product or persuading consumers to switch to the brand being offered.

> *Chapter tool 9.3 Sales promotions*: A sales promotion is a short-term programme that aims to stimulate an increase in sales. They offer consumers an *incentive* (or a bonus) to buy the sport product. Common examples include 'two-for-one' offers, prize give-aways, competitions and free trials or samples.

Public relations

Public relations is concerned with building a good 'image' for sport organisations. It is important for sport organisations to have a good relationship with different groups in the community, including the media, government sport departments, local councils and even fan clubs. To have a good relationship with these groups, sport organisations need to communicate with them on a regular basis. It is therefore essential that sport organisations identify what sort of information about their products public groups will be interested in. Once determined, it is a matter of working out how to communicate this information in a way that will enhance the sport organisation's reputation and cultivate improved relationships.

Public relations is different to other forms of promotion in that it is free to a sport organisation. It usually involves getting some information into the mass media as a news item. For this reason, *public relations* is often called *publicity*. For example, a surfing manufacturer might provide a 'press release' about a new product in the hope that the media will want to make a story out of it. Another example could be a sport club that publishes result lists on the Internet, or submits an article about the club or a prominent player to a magazine. In these examples the sport organisation does not have to pay to have their information presented as they would with advertising. However, one problem is that they do not have control over how their organisation or product is presented; it is just as easy to get bad publicity as it is to get good publicity.

Chapter tool 9.4 Public relations: Public relations is concerned with building a good 'image' for a sport organisation. Public relations is different to other forms of promotion because it is free. It usually involves getting some information into the mass media as a news item, and for this reason it is often called *publicity*.

Each of the four elements of the promotions mix represents a tool that can be used to promote a sport product. Table 9.1 summarises the key strengths and weaknesses of each of the four promotion tools, and provides examples helpful to their application.

Chapter principle 9.3: Promotional elements should be combined in order to complement one another in order to achieve a promotional goal that is consistent with the overall marketing and positioning strategy.

INTERACTIVE CASE

Publicity is one of the creative tools used in public relations to achieve an organisation's overall PR objectives. Sporting events and activities are socially acceptable platforms for generating positive publicity. MSMudRun (www.msmudrun.com.au) or the Tough Mudder mud run (www.toughmudder.com) are popular public relations stunts staged in order to generate media exposure and mass participation. Tough Mudder, for example, has attracted over one million participants around the world, testing participants' strength, stamina and fellowship skills in a physically and mentally challenging obstacle course.

Question

Gone are the days of Telethons, Walkathons, or Ride-a-thons for credibility and exposure. Organisations are continually on the lookout for novel and innovative activities to appeal. What makes a successful sport public relations event? Why do you think Tough Mudder has been so successful?

Points of interest

According to Tough Mudder organisers, participants will endure pain, meet new people, receive 'a medal you'll never wear again' and more importantly score a trademark orange headband for completing the course and 'earn a pint and bragging rights'. Such events are designed to appeal to participants' competitive spirit as well as to their social consciences. Coming up with creative ways of capturing publicity to feed the voracious appetite of the media and to reach and engage with the widest possible audience is the key to a public relations strategy.

TABLE 9.1 Promotional techniques

Tools	Advantages	Disadvantages	Methods
Advertising	Wide reach	High initial outlay	Press
			Radio
	Dramatic images	Impersonal	Television
			Magazines
	Reaches consumers fast	Very little feedback from consumers	Direct mail
			Ticketing agents
			Scoreboard displays
	High exposure	Delayed feedback	Bus and taxi posters
			Billboards and posters
		Unable to customise message to individual consumers	Brochures
			Ticket stubs
			Internet
			Text messages
		Difficult to tell how many consumers buy the product as a result of viewing or hearing the advertisement	Multimedia messages
Sales promotion	Attention-grabbing	Minimum reach	In-store promotions
			Point of purchase sales
	Informative	Medium cost per exposure	Exhibitions
	Fast in reaching consumers	Usually impersonal	Product give-aways, stickers, shirts, admission give-aways
	Moderate control over the communication	Unable to customise message to individual consumers	Two-for-one offers
			Free admission with purchase
	Relatively easy to track how many consumers buy the product because of the promotion		Prizes tied to tickets
			Frequent purchaser of cards (loyalty cards)
			'Selling' of heroes
			Competitions
			Free trials or samples
			Bonus packs
			Trade deals

TABLE 9.1 continued

Tools	Advantages	Disadvantages	Methods
Personal selling	Direct communication	Narrow reach	Telemarketing
			Door-to-door sales
	Informative	Variable cost per exposure	Endorsements
			Referrals
			Party plans
	Immediate feedback from consumers	Slow to reach target customers	Sponsorship
	High control over promotional message		
	Able to customise message to individual consumers		
Public relations	Wide reach	Variable image	Press releases
			Result lists
	Informative	Very little feedback from consumers	Photographs
			Commentary and reviews
	Low cost per exposure	Delayed feedback	Feature articles
	Fast in reaching consumers	Impersonal	

Promotional objectives

To review, promotion is the way that sport marketers communicate with potential consumers in order to inform, persuade and remind them about a product or brand. The aim of promotion is to encourage consumers to develop a favourable opinion about a product or brand with the intention of stimulating them to try it. There are four main kinds of promotional activities that are collectively known as the promotions mix, because the different activities can be effectively combined. With this background in place, it is now time to consider the goals of promotion, or what it aims to achieve. There are three main objectives of promotion: (1) to inform, (2) to persuade and (3) to remind.

> *Chapter principle 9.4*: There are three main objectives of promotion: (1) to inform, (2) to persuade and (3) to remind.

Informing

Until a new product is promoted, consumers are unlikely to be aware that it exists. Naturally, it is important for potential consumers to be aware of a sport product, to understand its benefits, to respond to how it is positioned in the marketplace, and to know how to acquire it. Promotions that aim to *inform* consumers of these aspects of a product are usually done during the early stages of the product life cycle. Informative promotions are also helpful if the product is complex or technical, such as a range of sports equipment with sophisticated electronic components.

> *Chapter principle* 9.5: Promotions that *inform* aim to communicate the product's existence, its benefits, its positioning and how it can be obtained. Promotions that aim to inform consumers are usually undertaken during the early stages of the product life cycle.

Persuading

Once consumers are aware of a product and its benefits, it may be necessary to persuade them to try it. *Persuading* consumers means convincing them, or influencing them, to buy a sport product. In order to achieve this aim, it is essential to give consumers a good reason to buy the product. It is important that sport marketers do not deceive consumers in order to persuade them to buy it. Aside from being illegal, it is counterproductive, as the product will not reach expectations, leading to consumer dissatisfaction.

Persuasive promotions are more common when a product enters the growth stage of the product life cycle. By this time consumers should have a general awareness of the kind of product that is being offered, as well as the benefits that it can give them. At this point it is unnecessary for sport organisations to utilise promotional activities that inform, but it remains important to convince consumers to purchase the product on offer and not one offered by competition.

Persuasive promotions are used when the aim is to change the ideas that consumers hold about a product. For example, it might be desirable to change consumers' ideas about a product's features, or a brand's image. Persuasion is also a common strategy that sport organisations employ when they want consumers to switch from a competitor's brand to their own.

> *Chapter principle* 9.6: Persuasive promotions are utilised when trying to give consumers good reasons to buy a sport product. Persuasive promotions are more common when a product enters the growth stage of the product life cycle.

Reminding

Reminder promotions aim to keep a product or brand name prominent in consumers' minds. Once consumers have been informed about a product and have been persuaded to buy it at least once, it is sensible to remind them to continue buying it in the future. Reminder promotions are most common during the maturity stage of the product life cycle.

> *Chapter principle* 9.7: Reminder promotions aim to keep a product or brand name prominent in consumers' minds. Reminder promotions are most common during the maturity stage of the product life cycle.

The three types of promotional goals are summarised in Table 9.2 along with advice on their best timing and some typical examples.

Promotion planning

A common theme in excellent sport marketing is careful planning. Designing a promotional strategy is no exception. A promotions mix needs to be supported by market research and a well-structured plan in order to ensure that it remains aligned with other marketing initiatives and stays on track once it has begun. The promotions planning process is also essential to determining whether the deployed promotional strategy has been effective. Figure 9.2 outlines the stages of the promotion planning process.

Chapter principle 9.8: A promotional strategy is a plan that aims to use the elements of the promotions mix for the best results. The promotions planning process involves five steps: (1) align with marketing objectives, (2) consider target market, (3) set promotional objectives, (4) set promotional budget and (5) develop promotional mix.

TABLE 9.2 Promotional goals

Goal of promotion	Timing	Examples
To inform	Commonly used during the introduction stage of the product life cycle	Make consumers aware of a new brand
		Make consumers aware of new product
		Inform consumers of product features
		Inform consumers of price and where to buy
		Explain how a product works, especially a complex or technical one
		Build a positive image for the organisation
		Suggest new ways to use a product
To persuade	Commonly used during the *growth* stage of the product life cycle	Encourage brand switching
		Convince consumers to buy a product
		Change consumers' ideas about the product
To remind	Used in highly competitive marketplaces	Remind consumers they need a product
		Remind consumers where to buy it
	Commonly used during the *maturity* stage of the product	Keep consumers aware of the product life cycle

FIGURE 9.2 Promotion planning process

Align with marketing objectives

The first step in planning a promotional strategy is to use general marketing objectives as a guide to formulating a promotional plan. As a reminder, a marketing objective is a goal to be achieved as the result of a selected marketing strategy. Any choices made for the promotion plan need to align with marketing objectives and further their achievement.

> *Chapter tool 9.5 Align with marketing objectives*: Any choices made for the promotion plan need to align with marketing objectives and further their achievement.

Consider the target market

The second step of the promotion planning process is to examine the intended target market. The promotional strategies selected should be specific to the target market. There are two ways of promoting a sport product, depending on whether the target market is the final consumer of the product, or whether it is an intermediary (an 'in-between' company such as a wholesaler). The two types are known as a push strategy and a pull strategy.

Push strategy

A push strategy involves promoting a sport product to a wholesaler with the ambition of convincing them to carry the product. If successful then the wholesaler must also push the product towards a retailer. In turn, the retailer promotes the product to the eventual consumer and may use advertising or other forms of promotion in the process. This is called a push strategy because the sport product gets *pushed*, step-by-step, down the line of distribution to the final consumer. With a push strategy it is common to rely strongly on personal selling strategies, although other promotional techniques can also be used. A push strategy is appropriate when specific wholesalers or retailers have been identified as the primary target market.

Pull strategy

A pull strategy involves promoting a sport product directly to the final consumer. A pull strategy requires that demand for the sport product must first be developed. The assumption behind the pull strategy is that as consumers become aware of the product they will ask retailers to stock it. Retailers will then have to ask wholesalers to sell them the product, and in turn these wholesalers will have to order it from the manufacturer. When using a pull strategy, it is common to use advertising, as well as sales promotion techniques such as sampling, discounts and coupons. A pull strategy is appropriate when a group of final consumers has been identified as the primary target market.

Since the goals of sport organisations vary considerably, there are different ways in which a push or pull strategy can be used. For example, a large national governing sport organisation might have the objective of winning more medals at the international level. A push strategy would involve bolstering the grassroots levels of the sport to encourage more participation with the intention that a larger participation base will push a higher range and quality of athletes to the elite level. In contrast, a pull strategy would involve offering more support directly to the elite level through coaching or training academies in order to pull the best athletes through to the highest level. It is important to realise that it is unusual for sport organisations to use exclusively a push strategy or a pull strategy. Rather, most use a combination. For example, sporting equipment and apparel manufacturers work hard to convince wholesalers and retailers to stock their brand (push), while also marketing heavily to consumers about the value of the brand itself (pull).

> *Chapter tool 9.6 Consider the target market*: Promotional strategies should be selected with the target market in mind. There are two strategies behind promotion depending on whether the target market is the final consumer of the product or an intermediary. The two are a push strategy and a pull strategy.

A push strategy involves promoting a sport product to a wholesaler with the ambition of convincing them to carry the product. If successful then the wholesaler must also push the product towards a retailer. In turn, the retailer promotes the product to the eventual consumer, and may use advertising or other forms of promotion in the process. A pull strategy involves promoting a sport product directly to the final consumer.

Public relations events are devised to be memorable occasions. Securing financial support, sponsorship, participants and a safe and identifiable location are only the backdrop factors for successful PR exposure. A unique idea such as the Color Run (www.thecolorrun.com.au), shows how a simple combination of getting together, exercising and getting dirty with colour can spread. The aim of a colour run is for participants to begin the event in white while being bombarded by spectators with various colours of powdered paint as they complete a 5km run.

Questions

How is public relations different from other elements of the promotions mix, when presented this way? How can sport leverage its unique attributes to amplify the effects of a public relations strategy?

Points of interest

The Color Run began in 2012 and is now a frequent event on the calendar in over 30 counties. By 2013 The Color Run LLC formalised an arrangement with IMG Worldwide to deliver the event across the globe. The event venue is generally close to, or accessible via a city's CBD, maximising the exposure to a wider audience as participants and paint 'bombers' proudly traipse around like rainbow warriors. Added publicity is gained via personal social media networks such as Instagram, Tumblr, Facebook or Retrica.

Set promotional objectives

The third step in the promotion planning process is to set promotional objectives. The three main goals of promotion – to inform, persuade and remind – have already been introduced. These represent the broad objectives of promotion. It is therefore important to pinpoint which of these goals will be the focus of the promotion plan. However, when setting promotional objectives, it is possible to be even more specific. The ultimate promotional objective is to stimulate consumers to act. For example, it may be desirable for consumers to buy the product, volunteer their time, donate money to fundraising or just attend an event. It is easy to understand how to inform, persuade or remind consumers, but it is more difficult to get them to take action. Sport marketers can encourage consumers to act by guiding them through a series of steps known as *a hierarchy of effects*. The word *hierarchy* means that there are stepped levels, and that one step builds on another to reach an ultimate goal. The hierarchy of effects is displayed in Figure 9.3.

The idea behind the hierarchy of effects is that all consumers must pass through each stage (starting at the bottom) before they consume a product. Consumers are unaware,

aware, informed, attracted, inclined, and convinced before they actually consume. It is worth remembering that there are some common situations where consumers might not pass through every stage of the hierarchy. For example, when someone makes a split-second decision to buy a product (called an impulse purchase), they may not know much about the product benefits. Also, sometimes consumers purchase a product for someone else as a gift, and may not even like it themselves.

Even though the hierarchy of effects is not useful in every situation, sport marketers may employ it to give them a general guide for developing promotional goals. If a group of consumers can be located on the hierarchy, then it is easier to select a matching promotional objective.

The hierarchy of effects starts at the bottom of the pyramid when consumers are *unaware* that a product exists. At this stage the promotional objective is to make consumers *aware* of the product. When consumers are aware of the product they know it exists but may not know much else about it. Thus, consumers need to be educated about the product's tangible and intangible benefits. At this stage the central promotional objective is to give consumers product information so that they become *informed*. Just because a consumer is aware of a product and knows about its benefits does not mean that they will necessarily like it. The main promotional objective at this stage is to encourage consumers to be *attracted* to the product, and to create positive feelings towards it. Once consumers are attracted to the product it is important to convince them to prefer it, or become *inclined* towards it over all alternatives. The corresponding promotional objective is to establish that the product on offer is the best available for the target market. With consumers' interest in the product, they must next become *convinced* that the product is right for them, leading to a definitive intention to make a purchase. Therefore, the main promotional objective at this stage is to create a strong desire to act. Desire does not automatically mean that a consumer will act, as they may not have enough money or time, or new and superior alternatives may become available instead. However, desire is a powerful precursor to *consumption*. There are circumstances where consumers have become convinced about a product and do genuinely intend to purchase it, but still do not act. Dealing with this problem requires a good understanding of what is stopping consumers from buying a product when they desire it. In some cases, the obstacle might simply be price. A Ferrari is desired by many but purchased by few. In the case of sport services, availability might be an issue, such as with tickets to hallmark events or the final series of a league.

> *Chapter tool 9.7 Set promotional objectives*: The hierarchy of effects shows how consumers may pass through a number of stages before they actually consume, and represents a tool for connecting promotional objectives with the promotions mix. The stages of the hierarchy of effects are: (1) unaware, (2) aware, (3) informed, (4) attracted, (5) inclined, (6) convinced and (7) consumption. These stages illustrate how consumers first become aware of a product (from unaware to aware), learn about its benefits (informed), (3) become interested in it (attracted), (4) develop a preference for one product or brand over others (inclined), (5) experience a desire to do something about it (convinced) and (6) then act (consumption).

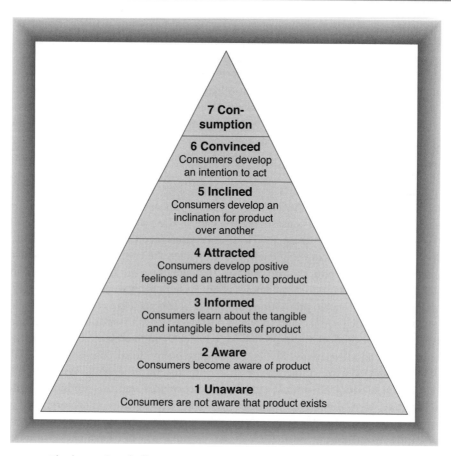

FIGURE 9.3 The hierarchy of effects

Set a promotional budget

The next step in a promotional plan involves setting a promotional budget. A budget determines how much money will be spent on promotion. Not only do sport organisations typically have limited resources available to spend on promotion, it is possible for them to choose different methods for deciding on how much is appropriate. Some of the common methods used for deciding on a budget include: (1) arbitrary allocation (randomly choosing an amount), (2) competitive parity (matching competitors), (3) competitive disparity (being deliberately different to competitors), (4) percentage of sales and (5) the objective and task method (the amount is determined by promotional objectives and tasks). Each is overviewed next.

Arbitrary allocation

If an amount to spend on promotion is determined *arbitrarily*, then it is done subjectively, or without an obvious reason. Often this means that the sport organisation will allocate as much money as it can afford to promotion (after all the other business costs are considered). If a sport marketer chooses this method, then they are not paying any attention to what their competitors are doing, what the economic climate is, or how effective their promotional budget was last year. In other words, this is not a very sensible or well thought out way to allocate a budget.

Competitive parity

Competitive parity (or equality) means deciding to spend a similar amount to that of competitors. Competitive parity is more common in highly competitive marketplaces, where a number of businesses are trying to attract the attention of consumers. However, this may be a difficult (and even impossible) method for some organisations if they do not have the same revenue to spend.

Competitive disparity

It is also possible to estimate what competitors are spending on promotion, and deliberately decide to spend a different amount. This is known as competitive disparity. Disparity means difference or inequality. It can be a way of standing apart from competitors, and differentiating the product or brand. Competitive disparity is also common with sporting goods that are designed with a low cost in mind and that are successful when sold in large volumes with few costs allocated to promotions.

Percentage of sales

It is possible to calculate a promotional budget as a percentage of total sales. To do this it is first essential to determine a standard percentage of sales that will be allocated to promotions. Sometimes sport organisations will choose a percentage based on what their competitors are doing, while at other times it may be an arbitrary choice. Once the standard percentage has been determined, the previous year's sales figure is used as a guide to next year's sales. From here it is possible to calculate a percentage of the predicted amount of sales. For example, if 5 per cent of sales is set as a guideline, and five million dollars in sales is expected in the forthcoming year (5 per cent of five million), then the promotional budget is $250,000.

There are several limitations to the percentage of sales approach. First, it may be difficult to calculate what level of standard percentage should be used in the first place. Second, it may not be accurate to use last year's sales as a guide to estimating the forthcoming year. Finally, if sales are declining, it may be more important to spend additional money on promotion rather than less.

Objective and task method

The objective and task method demands that the promotional *objectives* that have been set, and the promotional *tasks* needed in order to carry out those objectives, should guide the budget that is allocated. It is simply a matter of calculating what it will cost to actually carry out the tasks. This method is logical, but it can run into difficulty if the promotional objectives and tasks that were planned were actually inappropriate, leading to substantial spending on a promotional plan that is not going to be effective.

Chapter tool 9.8 Set promotional budget: Setting a promotional budget means deciding how much money to spend on promotion. Some of the common methods used for deciding on a budget are: (1) arbitrary allocation (subjectively choosing an amount), (2) competitive parity (matching competitors), (3) competitive disparity (being deliberately different to competitors), (4) percentage of sales and (5) the objective and task method (the amount is determined by promotional objectives and tasks).

Develop a promotional mix

The final step of the promotion planning process is to develop a promotions mix. To recap, the elements of the promotions mix are: (1) advertising, (2) personal selling, (3) sales promotion and (4) public relations. These elements are called a *mix* because they are combined together. Sport organisations do not just use one promotions element but rather use a mixture of some or all of them in their promotional strategy. It is important to realise that if a number of promotional elements are used, they should be designed to complement one another. In the end, a promotions strategy should be created so that the different elements of the promotions mix are combined together to work towards the promotional goals that have been set.

Chapter tool 9.9 Develop promotions mix: In developing a promotions mix, sport marketers must choose which elements of the promotions mix will reach the desired promotional objectives and be achievable within the budget that has been set.

PRINCIPLES SUMMARY

- Chapter principle 9.1: Promotion can be defined as the way that sport marketers communicate with consumers to inform, persuade and remind them about the features and benefits described by a sport product's positioning.

- Chapter principle 9.2: The promotions mix consists of four marketing tools: (1) advertising, (2) personal selling, (3) sales promotions and (4) public relations.

- Chapter principle 9.3: Promotional elements should be combined in order to complement one another in order to achieve a promotional goal that is consistent with the overall marketing and positioning strategy.

- Chapter principle 9.4: There are three main objectives of promotion: (1) to inform, (2) to persuade and (3) to remind.

- Chapter principle 9.5: Promotions that *inform* aim to communicate the product's existence, its benefits, its positioning, and how it can be obtained. Promotions that aim to inform consumers are usually undertaken during the early stages of the product life cycle.

- Chapter principle 9.6: Persuasive promotions are utilised when trying to give consumers good reasons to buy a sport product. Persuasive promotions are more common when a product enters the growth stage of the product life cycle.

- Chapter principle 9.7: Reminder promotions aim to keep a product or brand name prominent in consumers' minds. Reminder promotions are most common during the maturity stage of the product life cycle.

- Chapter principle 9.8: A promotional strategy is a plan that aims to use the elements of the promotions mix for the best results. The promotions planning process involves five steps: (1) align with marketing objectives, (2) consider target market, (3) set promotional objectives, (4) set promotional budget and (5) develop promotional mix.

TOOLS SUMMARY

- Chapter tool 9.1 Advertising
- Chapter tool 9.2 Personal selling
- Chapter tool 9.3 Sales promotions
- Chapter tool 9.4 Public relations
- Chapter tool 9.5 Align with marketing objectives
- Chapter tool 9.6 Consider the target market
- Chapter tool 9.7 Set promotional objectives
- Chapter tool 9.8 Set promotional budget
- Chapter tool 9.9 Develop promotions mix

REVIEW QUESTIONS

1   In what ways are promotions more than just advertising?

2   What are the four tools of the promotions mix? Provide an example of each.

3   Why is public relations such a useful tool for sport organisations with constrained marketing resources?

4   Describe how a sport brand such as adidas uses push and pull strategies simultaneously.

5   Provide some examples illustrating when the hierarchy of effects is not an accurate description of a consumer's decision-making process.

6   Explain why the promotions mix should be integrated for best results.

RELEVANT WEBSITES

www.grassrootsoccer.org	Grass Roots Soccer Organisation
www.msmudrun.com.au	MSMudRun
www.toughmudder.com	Tough Mudder
www.thecolorrun.com.au	The Color Run

FURTHER READING

L'Etang, J. (2013). *Sports Public Relations*. London: Sage.

CHAPTER 10

Sport sponsorship

LEARNING OUTCOMES

At the end of this chapter, readers should be able to:

- define the term sport sponsorship
- identify potential sponsorship objectives and associated market segments
- highlight the key elements of sponsorship targeting
- outline the sections of a sponsorship proposal
- specify how sponsorship may be augmented through leveraging
- highlight the main principles of sponsorship evaluation
- explain what is meant by ambush marketing
- identify the five main tactics in preventing ambush marketing.

OVERVIEW

This chapter describes the use of sponsorship in sport marketing and explains the major principles and tools of its deployment. Although sponsorship is usually considered a subsection of promotions, it has become so pivotal to sport marketing that it is being treated here as the fifth element of the sport marketing mix. This chapter outlines five essential aspects of sport sponsorship: (1) sponsorship objectives, (2) sponsorship targeting, (3) sponsorship leveraging, (4) sponsorship evaluation and (5) ambush marketing.

SPONSORSHIP IN THE MIX

Chapter 9 examined promotions as the fourth element of the sport marketing mix. It also introduced the concept of sport sponsorship as a kind of promotional activity. Conventionally in marketing, sponsorship is viewed as a subcategory of personal selling because it involves personal contact between an organisation and a sponsor. Given that sponsorship is not a dominant form of promotions for most non-sport organisations, textbooks tend to treat it as part of personal selling. However, the prominence of sponsorship in sport marketing demands that it be treated as a variable to be managed in its own right. With this in mind, sport sponsorship is treated here as an equal part of the marketing mix. The chief components of sport sponsorship are highlighted in Figure 10.1, which locates sponsorship within the Sport Marketing Framework.

WHAT IS SPORT SPONSORSHIP?

Sport sponsorship has increased dramatically over the past two decades. For many large non-sport corporations such as Shell, Coca-Cola, Emirates and Vodafone, sponsoring sport organisations and athletes is an important part of their marketing strategies. Many different kinds of sport organisations and individuals may be sponsored, including individual athletes, clubs and teams, events, leagues, unions, federations, competitions, venues and special causes.

Sport sponsorship occurs when a sporting organisation, club, league, venue, cause or athlete is supported by a separate company (or person). The recipient of the sponsorship is known as the *sponsorship property* or the *sport property*. These legal-sounding terms are indicative of the fact that sponsorship is a business agreement between two parties. A non-legal term for the sponsorship recipient is the 'sponsee'.

> *Chapter principle 10.1*: The term sport property refers to the recipient of the sponsorship. This could be an athlete, team, event, venue, association, cause or competition.

Sponsorships are supposed to benefit both parties. Usually the sport property receives cash, goods, services or expert advice, and the sponsor receives benefits such as promotional rights and the marketing advantages of being associated with a particular sport property. Sponsors hope that by investing in a sport property, they will increase consumers' awareness of their brand, and consequently build brand equity. It is important to realise, however, that sponsorship can be a high-risk investment. This is mainly because the outcome of the agreement can be unpredictable. For example, there is no guarantee that a sponsor will achieve the increased sales, improved brand image or changed consumer perceptions that they are seeking. The risk of sponsorship may be particularly high if individuals are sponsored. Like any investment, risk decreases with diversification. Because any individual athlete can easily fall prey to ill health, injury, poor performance, or even personal circumstances that are unfavourably interpreted in the media, it is more likely that a sponsor can lose its investment. On the other hand, the right prominent athlete can be a sponsor's dream.

> *Chapter principle 10.2*: Sport sponsorship is a business agreement where one organisation provides financial or in-kind assistance to a sport property in exchange for the right to associate itself with the sport property. The sponsor does this to achieve corporate objectives (such as enhancing corporate image) or marketing objectives (such as increasing brand awareness).

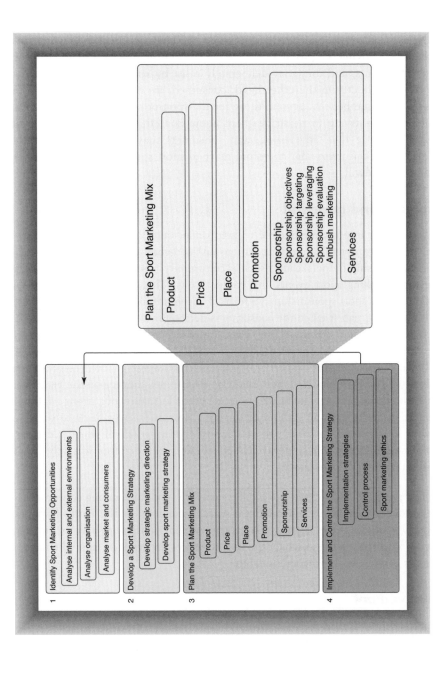

FIGURE 10.1 The Sport Marketing Framework

Sponsorship and advertising

To really understand the benefits of sponsorship, it is useful to consider the ways in which it can be distinguished from advertising. Consumers generally see advertising as a selfish activity; they believe that the company or brand being advertised is out to promote their own interests. Consumers may even suspect that the company is trying to pressure or coerce them into buying the product. This can make consumers sceptical and suspicious about advertisements, and they may deliberately resist by ignoring or wilfully disliking the advertised product. On the other hand, consumers are more likely to think that a sponsorship has some benefits beyond those for the sponsor. Although they may realise that the sponsor is trying to persuade them about something, the approach is more disguised and subtle than advertising, and consumers may be less defensive about responding to it. Consumers may therefore react to sport sponsorship communications with a general goodwill.

Sponsorship and goodwill

Goodwill offers an important principle to help understand why sport sponsorships are effective. There are several important dimensions of goodwill. First, more goodwill is created for sponsorship of social causes such as community-based sports organisations than for large profit-seeking sport events and competitions. This opportunity has led some corporations to use sport sponsorship as a form of corporate social responsibility. Second, goodwill is usually greatest when the consumer is personally involved in the sport activity being sponsored. In fact, the more that a consumer is personally involved in the sport property, the higher the level of goodwill generated. Third, the time at which a sponsor becomes involved with a sport property can influence the level of goodwill associated with it. Sponsors who become involved later might be seen to be 'jumping on the bandwagon' compared with those perceived to be instrumental in the formation of a strong relationship with a sport property early in its life, or during a downturn. This leads to the fourth observation, as there can be some risk of a sponsor losing goodwill when it decides to discontinue an agreement. Consumers might conclude that the sponsor was only involved to exploit a temporary opportunity.

> *Chapter principle 10.3*: Sport sponsorship generates goodwill among consumers. The amount of goodwill generated can vary depending on the kind of sport property sponsored, the degree of involvement that consumers have with the sport property, the time at which the sponsor becomes involved, and when and how the sponsor ceases the sponsorship.

Fan involvement

One important implication leading from the previous section is that a sponsor will generate more goodwill among consumers who are personally involved with the sport property compared with those who are more casually involved. The idea of fan involvement was introduced in Chapter 3, and is a term that describes the degree to which fans personally identify with a particular sport, competition or athlete, or the level of personal affiliation and engagement they possess in regard to the sport property.

Fan involvement is an important consideration in sponsorship because a sport consumer's response to a sponsorship is driven by his/her level of involvement in the sport property. For example, strongly involved sport consumers show higher levels of sponsorship awareness, a more substantial sense of goodwill towards the sponsor, a greater brand preference for the sponsor and a stronger intention to purchase a sponsor's products. Consumers are also more likely to change brands as a result of sponsorship, and because they are knowledgeable about the sport property, they are better able to judge whether there is a logical connection or congruence between the sport property and the sponsor.

Positive responses from highly involved sport consumers are more likely to occur in certain situations. In general, sport consumers tend to be more personally involved in events, teams or individual athletes, and will respond better to the sponsors of these kinds of sport properties, compared with the sponsorship of competitions or a sporting broadcast. In addition, involved fans are more likely to respond positively when there is one clear sponsor of an activity instead of several sponsors competing for attention. All of these points teach us that fan involvement is an important element to consider when looking at sponsorship.

Chapter principle 10.4: Fan involvement is an important consideration in sponsorship because a consumer's response to a sponsorship is driven by the level of involvement that he/she has with the sport property.

INTERACTIVE CASE

Sponsorship through sport is a reciprocal relationship. Companies persistently use sponsorship to leverage their brand value, but not necessarily through the traditional 'tell and sell' method. Sport is ideal for engaging consumers to participate with the sponsor's product or service.

Questions

As a sponsorship manager for a sporting event, how could you exploit a co-sponsor relationship that meets the marketing objectives for each sponsor as well as engage the sport consumer with sponsor products and services? Look at the case of the 2014 Australian Tennis Open, in partnership with event sponsor Kia Australia: www.kia.com.au/game-on

Points of interest

The 2014 Australian Tennis Open, in partnership with event sponsor Kia Australia and Mnet Mobile App, was able to leverage its sponsorship when spectators challenged the world's fastest server. Kia Game On was launched with great success. Spectators armed with smartphones and the downloaded app could face a Sam Groth serve of 260kph. At least 135,000 spectators participated in the challenge at the event.

In this instance a cooperative engagement benefitted both the maker of the app, Mnet, and the Grand Slam event sponsor, Kia. Sponsorship value for Kia was generated not by saying how good their cars are, but by doing something at the event that had meaning for the sports fans. For Mnet it was able to showcase its product through an interactive activity.

SPONSORSHIP OBJECTIVES

The sponsors and sport property will have different objectives they want to achieve as a result of a successful sponsorship. The two most common objectives for sponsors are enhancing brand image and increasing brand awareness. For the sport property, the most common objective is to attract financial support, which in turn helps to meet other administrative and developmental goals. While these may be the most common, the objectives of sponsorship can vary greatly, depending on the size of the partners, the nature of the sponsorship relationship, and the type of sport property being supported. For this reason, it is essential that both the owner of the sport property and the sponsor have a clear understanding of the objectives behind a sponsorship agreement. By understanding the benefits a sponsor seeks, the sport property is in a better position to 'sell' the idea of the sponsorship, and to ensure that they can provide what the sponsor needs. In the next section, possible sponsorship objectives from the perspective of the sponsor, and from the perspective of the sport property, are reviewed.

Sponsor objectives

Although there are some non-marketing goals that will be mentioned shortly, for a sponsor, the objectives of a sport sponsorship programme align to general marketing goals. This means that most sponsorship objectives can be related to a specific market segment (or segments) that a sponsor aims to reach with the sponsorship programme. Some potential objectives are outlined in Table 10.1 where each has been related to a market segment. The table highlights the fact that sponsorship is a versatile promotional tool because it can reach many different market segments and help to achieve a range of promotional objectives relevant to the sponsor.

At first glance it might appear that the sponsorship objectives highlighted in Table 10.1 are exclusive to the sponsor. After all, one of the main objectives for the sport property is to attract financial or in-kind support, which the owner organisation might employ in a variety of administrative, promotional or developmental projects. However, the association between the sponsor and the sport property can yield significant branding benefits to both parties. By attracting the 'right' sponsor, the owner of a sport property can influence the way that his/her target market thinks about his/her brand (brand image). A corporate sponsor can add substantial credibility to this image, in turn enhancing the sport property's brand equity, brand loyalty, and even ticket or product sales. Those employed by the sport property might even feel satisfied and proud to know that their organisation has the reputation to attract powerful or important sponsors. In fact, many of the objectives (either directly or indirectly) may be considered relevant to both the sport property owners as well as the sponsor.

> *Chapter principle 10.5*: The objectives of sponsorship can vary greatly, depending on the size of the partners, the type of sponsorship and the type of sport property being supported. Some common objectives for the sponsor are to enhance sales, to promote the public image of its brand, to increase consumer awareness, to modify its brand image, and to build business relationships.

TABLE 10.1 Major sponsorship objectives for sponsors

Market segment	Objective
General public	To promote the public image of the organisation
	To increase mass media exposure and public relations
	To increase general public awareness of organisation and/or product
	To generate goodwill
	To form a general brand perception
	To create a favourable community perception through social or cause-related sponsorship
Target market	To increase consumer awareness of a product/service/brand
	To increase sales/market share of a specific product
	To establish a brand association between the sport property and sponsor
	To create an 'image transfer', where values are transferred from the sport product or type of sponsorship to the sponsor
	To develop brand equity (the added value a product has because of the brand name)
	To develop, manage and/or change brand image (what values and ideas consumers associate with the brand)
	To promote brand loyalty (e.g. repeat purchasing)
Distribution channel members	To increase sales to channel members (e.g. wholesalers)
	To promote discounts and deals from channel members (e.g. suppliers)
	To develop new relationships/new distribution channels (e.g. pouring rights at an event)
Internal stakeholders	To improve staff morale and relations
	To increase staff satisfaction (e.g. through a sense of pride in the association or through corporate hospitality/entertainment)
	To promote satisfaction of shareholders (e.g. due to pride in association, improved brand equity/sales/market share)
	To promote positive communications with the media (e.g. through corporate hospitality, corporate social responsibility)

Sport property objectives

Table 10.2 outlines the major sponsorship objectives of sport organisations as owners of sport properties. Unlike the previous table detailing sponsor objectives, each of the following objectives is not associated with a market segment. This is because a number of the objectives relate to non-marketing areas such as corporate and operational development.

> *Chapter principle 10.6*: The objectives of sponsorship for the sport property will vary. In addition to attracting financial support, objectives include increasing credibility, increasing awareness, and managing brand image.

TABLE 10.2 Major sponsorship objectives for sport properties

Activity area	Objective
Corporate objectives	To promote the public image of the sport property through a credible association and brand match up
	To increase mass media exposure and public relations (directly through the use of new funds, or indirectly through PR undertaken by the sponsor)
	To increase general public awareness of the property and/or product (directly and indirectly)
Marketing objectives	To increase consumer awareness of a product/service/brand (directly through the use of sponsor funds/resources, and indirectly through the PR undertaken by the sponsor)
	To increase credibility among consumers (via credibility of sponsor)
	To establish a brand association between the sport organisation and sponsor to create an 'image transfer' from the sport product
	To position or re-position the sport brand in the minds of consumers
	To develop, manage and/or change brand image (what values and ideas consumers associate with the brand)
	To promote discounts and deals from channel members (e.g. from suppliers at an event through offering sponsorship rights)
	To develop new relationships/new distribution channels (e.g. granting exclusive pouring rights at an event)
Operational objectives	To obtain funding, resources and/or services to support operation and development
	To increase staff satisfaction (e.g. pride/credibility in the association/free goods and merchandise)
	To promote credibility with stakeholders (e.g. politicians, regulators, shareholders and the media)
	To promote satisfaction of shareholders (e.g. due to pride/ credibility in association)

SPONSORSHIP TARGETING

It is more common for the sport property to be the one that introduces the idea of sponsorship to a sponsor rather than the reverse. This is partly because the benefits for the sport property are easier to measure (such as the amount of money received) compared with those for the sponsor. It is difficult, for example, for a sponsor to know how much its sales have increased as a result of the sponsorship compared with how much they have increased because of other promotions and marketing. Therefore, when a sport property approaches a potential sponsor, it is important that they have a clear idea of what they have to offer or 'sell'. Usually the sport property would approach a sponsor with a written sponsorship proposal designed to highlight the potential benefits of the relationship. There are two central elements to this process: the first is choosing the right potential sponsor, and the second is writing an appropriate proposal.

Choosing the right sponsor: sponsorship affinity

Attracting the 'right' sponsor for a sport property is not just a matter of locating one willing to hand over some cash. Sponsorship relationships are more successful, and more likely to be renewed, when there is the right match between partners. Sponsorship in motor racing provides a good example. Motor racing teams need large sums of money to maintain their competitiveness in an expensive sport. In other words, they need sponsors. The sport consumers who watch motor racing are usually people interested in buying and maintaining their own cars. It stands to reason that companies such as BMW and Shell want to reach these consumers in order to influence their buying decisions. Motor racing teams need money from sponsors, and sponsors want to promote their products to the people who watch the motor racing teams.

When companies consider sponsoring a sport property, they focus on two priorities. First, they look for an affinity between the sponsor and the sport property. Second, they look for an affinity between the target markets of the sponsor and those of the sport property. It is important that the brand positioning strategies of both parties match, and that the target market the sport property reaches is the same (or partially the same) as the target market the sponsor is trying to reach. Figure 10.2 shows these two vital components for ensuring a good match between sponsorship partners.

> *Chapter principle 10.7*: Sponsorship affinity refers to whether there is a good fit or match between the sponsor and the sport property. Two factors are particularly important for ensuring a good match: (1) an overlap of target markets and (2) a match up of brand positioning strategies.

INTERACTIVE CASE

Women's tennis is one of the global leaders in professional women's sport. With over 50 events worldwide and four Grand Slam tournaments, women's tennis has the propensity to attract millions of spectators at events and through televised programming or online channels. Evaluating the potential value that sponsorship exposure brings to women's tennis is an important measure of its success. Choosing the right sponsor for women's sport is not necessarily just about identifying the products and services women use.

Questions

As an example, what is the link between Fiat cars and netball? Why would Investec support women's hockey? Log on to www.wtatennis.com and www.alpg.com.au and consider their partnership arrangements in terms of the strong affinity they have with existing partners. How suitable are they for the sport and their target audience? How creative could they be?

Points of interest

Sponsorship affinity is an important aspect of targeting sponsors but may limit the opportunity to think creatively about attracting potential sponsorship. Given that women's sport attracts less than 1 per cent of all sponsorship, sport marketers need to think outside the square. The lack of interest in the past shown by sponsors and the media towards women's sport has had a cascading effect at all levels through to grassroots. Increasingly fragmented markets, waning consumer interest and cluttered mediums for message delivery are factors impeding the existing sponsorship opportunities. Women's sport sponsorship needs a revolution.

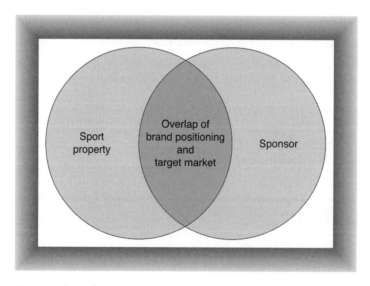

FIGURE 10.2 Sponsorship affinity

Match up of brand positioning

To recap, brand positioning or market positioning refers to how a sport organisation would like its consumers to think and feel about its brand when compared to competitors. It is the image or perception of the sport brand that consumers carry in their minds. Positioning takes into account the fact that consumers will compare a given sport brand with others in the market. When a company sponsors a sport property, the way that consumers think and feel about the sponsor and its brand(s) will be influenced by the way they think and feel about the sport property. Equally, the way that consumers think and feel about the sport property will be influenced by the way they think and feel about the sponsor. The key implication is that there must be a match between the brand positioning strategies of both parties. For example, Shell positions many of its motor oil products as being good quality and high performance. This matches the high-performance image of professional motor racing teams and means that there is a strong overlap between Shell and the sponsored teams Ducati and Ferrari.

INTERACTIVE CASE

Brand sponsorship and licensing is a multi-billion dollar industry. However, not all brands have longevity. Sports brands are generally steeped in meaning and backed up with a history of success. For example, the Puma (www.puma.com) sporting brand is a distant third in sales behind adidas and Nike after their profit crashed by a massive 70 per cent in 2012. At the same time, Nike's world revenue topped €18.7 billion in 2013 while adidas sits in second place with €14.6 billion in revenue. Added to this is the increasing exposure of new lifestyle brands such as Lululemon, or rejuvenated sport specialists Asics and Brooks.

Questions

How does a besieged brand such as Puma react to the strong competition above them and rapidly emerging competition below? By addressing its sponsorship relationships, Puma can refocus its attention on their priorities and reflect a desirable and successful brand. Puma is now 'Forever Faster'. Is this the transformation that will work for them?

Points of interest

One reason for Puma's declining sales success has been its drift from a long-standing and well-established core image. The brand's roots connect with soccer and athletics. It even has the fastest man on the planet, Usain Bolt, on its books. The brand's management strength in the past was in its ability to recruit good sales staff and in promoting high levels of sales turnover. Surviving and succeeding as a sport brand today requires a multifaceted approach.

SPONSORSHIP PROPOSALS

The sponsorship proposal should be a specific document that is targeted towards a specific sponsor. Writing a general proposal and sending it to a number of potential sponsors is ineffective because it will be obvious to the sponsors that their brand positioning and target market have not been considered. The proposal should take into account the market position as well as the resources of a potential sponsor, and should describe the return a sponsor could reasonably expect from their investment. A sponsorship proposal should generally address a number of key areas including an overview of the sport property, a description of the target audience of the sport property, the goals of the sponsorship programme, the type and period of association, sponsorship benefits and rights, the investment required, the ambush prevention strategy and an evaluation strategy. A detailed outline of the key sections of the sponsorship proposal is provided in Table 10.3.

A number of the key areas described in Table 10.3 have already been discussed in this chapter, such as the goals of sponsorship and the issue of brand/target market affinity. The remaining areas are examined in detail in the forthcoming sections of this chapter, including evaluating sponsorships and ambush prevention strategies.

> *Chapter tool 10.1 Sponsorship proposal*: A sponsorship proposal should be researched and written for a specific sponsor (rather than writing a general proposal that is sent out to various potential sponsors). This way the proposal can take into account the market position and resources of the potential sponsor, and it can address issues of sponsorship affinity between the two parties.

A sponsorship proposal should generally address a number of key areas including an overview of the sport property, a description of the target audience of the sport property, the goals of the sponsorship programme, the type and period of association, sponsorship benefits and rights, the investment required/cost, the ambush prevention strategy, and an evaluation strategy.

SPORT SPONSORSHIP RIGHTS

The rights that are given through a sponsorship are sometimes called *entitlements* or *sponsorship assets*. There is a vast array of rights that can be delivered through a sponsorship beyond the obvious ones such as naming rights and signage. Table 10.4 provides a detailed inventory of the kinds of sponsorship rights that a sport property might offer a sponsor during a negotiation.

> *Chapter tool 10.2 Sport sponsorship rights*: Sport properties can offer a range of sponsorship rights that can be negotiated with potential sponsors into a customised package of benefits. The inventory of sponsorship rights provides the starting point for a suite of rights to be considered.

TABLE 10.3 Key sections of sponsorship proposal

Covering letter
Maximum one page
Addressed to an appropriate staff member working with the potential sponsor. Usually a marketing manager, but could be a sponsorship manager in a large company

Cover page
Clear, professional and attractive presentation
Identify the potential sponsor and the sport property

Executive summary
An overview/summary of the proposal

Overview of the sport property and its owner sport property
History, context and social/community significance
List of current and past sponsors (if applicable)
References or endorsements from past sponsors (if applicable)
Media attention (frequency and type, include brief examples)
Programmes and events organised by the owner sport property (target groups, participation numbers, audience demographics, promotional activities)

Target market
Identify consumer targets reached by the sport property
Demonstration of how this consumer audience matches and/or expands the target market of the proposed sponsor
Consider internal and external audiences (e.g. existing consumers, potential consumers, local community, general public, suppliers, wholesalers, distributors, government, shareholders)

Brand affinity
Identify the brand positioning of the sport property
Demonstrate how this positioning matches or complements the brand positioning of proposed sponsor

Goals of the sponsorship programme
What can be realistically achieved for the sponsor (e.g. brand awareness among a target group, media exposure, increased sales/market share, community involvement/social responsibility, building goodwill, general public awareness, staff relations)

Sponsorship type
Event, team/individual, competition, venue

Period of association
Duration of agreement

Sponsorship benefits and rights
Detail the rights of the sponsorship agreement
Note whether these sponsorship rights are exclusive or shared with other partners
Note other benefits for the sponsor (e.g. special seating, client entertainment at events, cross-promotional activities, networking opportunities, image enhancement)
Outline different 'packages' available (if applicable)
Demonstrate how the sponsorship benefits relate to the sponsor's mission/vision and business objectives

Investment
Costs (include varying cost options if appropriate)
Could include an upfront fee and performance-based incentives
In-kind investments
Term/duration of agreement

Ambush prevention strategy
Outline exclusivity of sponsor rights and how their exclusivity will be protected

Evaluation strategy
Performance measures and targets
How these measures and targets will be assessed

TABLE 10.4 Sport sponsorship rights

General sponsorship rights

Naming rights to an event, competition or club

On-site signage rights

On-site sales rights

On-site product sampling/trials

Corporate entertainment and hospitality

VIP tickets

Merchandising and promotional give-aways

Use of venue for sponsor functions

Athlete/celebrity appearances for sponsor

Right of first refusal to new sponsorship opportunities

Use of event volunteers

Additional advertising opportunities

Product placement – use of sponsor branded equipment/product at event

Access to mailing lists/databases

Trademark/logo display on equipment, clothing, media promotions

Public-speaking opportunities

Product category exclusivity

Interactive areas, e.g. message boards, polls, quizzes, game-zones

Consumer promotion exclusivity

Non-profit/cause overlay/social responsibility option

Jumbotron/large-screen signage

Mobile phone content

Plasma or LED screens

Radio (buys or event broadcast)

Video-on-demand content

Media rights

Media rights, including photography and footage rights

Press releases, announcements and press kits

Public service announcements

Internet content/links

Newspaper (buys or special event coverage)

Pre-event and post-event promotional activities

Print media presence (programmes, guides, etc.)

Webcast (live stream or on-demand)

SPONSORSHIP LEVERAGING

Leveraging sponsorships means getting additional value out of an already existing sponsorship investment. It is concerned with getting the maximum benefit and advantage from the sponsorship through careful integration with other marketing activities. Leveraging also helps to combat ambush marketing, which will be explained shortly. In fact, one of the keys to a successful sponsorship for both parties is leveraging activities. Leveraging helps to build a more positive and long-lasting relationship between the partners because it involves investing time and resources in one another, and seeing the relationship as a strategic alignment.

For a sponsor to make the most of a sponsorship, it needs to invest resources over and above the costs of the sponsorship itself. By paying the sponsorship fee, a sponsor is really only buying the right to associate themselves with the sport property; they must invest more money in order to make the most of this right by communicating the affiliation to their target market. Many sport marketing experts believe that a sponsor will need to invest at least three times more money than the cost of the sponsorship itself in order to leverage successfully. The aim of leveraging is to promote the association between the two brands from every angle possible, and not just leave it up to the sport property.

Sponsorship is only one promotional tool. In order to leverage the value of this tool, it is recommended that sponsors also use the other elements of the promotions mix in order to complement and draw attention to the sponsorship. For example, advertising, public relations and sales promotion activities could all be used in conjunction with the sponsorship to strengthen the effect. Corporate hospitality and an online presence could tie in with sales promotions to maximise the impact of the sponsorship. In fact, all four of the traditional promotions mix elements should be used to properly leverage a sponsorship, that is advertising, public relations, sales promotions and personal selling. Sponsors need to advertise, publicise, promote and personally sell their sponsorship association to consumers in order to create greater impact. Using a suite of promotional elements in addition to the sponsorship can create a kind of synergy, where the whole of the marketing programme is greater than the sum of the individual elements of the promotions mix. This is, of course, the whole point of using a strategic framework as the basis of a sport marketing approach. Thus, it is not enough to just use the other elements of the promotions mix to leverage a sponsorship, but the four elements of the general marketing mix should also form part of an integrated sponsorship leveraging plan. For example, a sponsor may introduce a new product for the duration of the sponsorship, or use special packaging relating to the event. The price of the sponsor's goods or services may be discounted during the event, or a percentage may be donated to a prominent or related cause. Distribution channels (place) may be expanded so that the sponsor's product can be bought exclusively at the event.

It is not only important to consider how to leverage a sponsorship, but also to whom the leveraging efforts should be directed. One good recommendation is that sponsorships should be leveraged towards a choice of three different groups of stakeholders: consumers, employees and corporate stakeholders including distribution channel members. These three possibilities are outlined in the following subsections.

Leveraging sponsorship towards consumers

Many of the promotional activities that were mentioned in relation to leveraging can be aimed directly at a sponsor's target market. Advertising to promote the connection with the sport property, sales promotions that coincide with the event and public relations through high-profile media outlets can all reinforce the sponsorship relationship to consumers. The sponsorship may also give the sponsor access to content about the sport property that its consumers may be interested in. This tactic works particularly well with technology or communications category sponsors who can use their sponsorship of sport properties to provide extra content to their customers.

Leveraging sponsorship towards employees

In the earlier section on sponsorship objectives, it was highlighted that a sponsorship may help to meet internal marketing goals by improving staff morale, increasing staff satisfaction, and creating a sense of staff pride in the organisation. If a sponsor's employees have an emotional connection to the sport property being sponsored, then the sponsorship may help them to develop emotional connections to the workplace. As a result, some leveraging can be usefully directed towards the sponsor's employees, offering them the opportunity to attend games or events and receive corporate hospitality. This can create a positive brand experience and enhance loyalty among employees, which in turn is more likely to lead to quality interactions with customers.

Leveraging sponsorship towards corporate stakeholders

A sponsorship can improve the goodwill and business relationships that a sponsor has with its stakeholders. This might include distribution channel members, shareholders, the media and politicians. For example, corporate hospitality is one concrete way in which sponsors can build positive relationships with their suppliers and other distribution channel members.

> *Chapter tool 10.3 Sponsorship leveraging*: Leveraging sponsorships means getting value out of the sponsorship investment. It is concerned with getting the maximum amount of benefit and advantage from the sponsorship through careful integration with other elements of the promotions and marketing mix. For a sponsor to make the most of a sponsorship, it is recommended that it invest resources over and above the costs of the sponsorship itself.

To leverage a sponsorship, a sponsor should use all four elements of the marketing mix, including all of the promotions mix activities.

Leveraging activities should be directed towards three different groups of stakeholders: (1) consumers, (2) employees and (3) corporate stakeholders (including distribution channel members, suppliers, shareholders, the media and politicians).

CORPORATE SOCIAL RESPONSIBILITY AND CAUSE-RELATED SPORT MARKETING

Sometimes corporations or other commercial enterprises seek a beneficial brand association as a result of providing support to a specific charitable or non-profit cause. It is common in these arrangements for sport organisations to partner with corporations in order to provide a high-profile cause. The characteristics of sport tend to make it an attractive partner for social engagement. For example, sport generally enjoys a good media profile, is associated with fun and entertainment, is healthy and encourages social interaction. As a result, sport presents a powerful vehicle for corporations to demonstrate that they are meeting their social and community obligations. Cause-related sport marketing, or its more recent successor sport corporate social responsibility, is effective in heightening the brand awareness of sponsors and tends to connect their brand with a more trusting and caring image. Sport marketers should remain aware of the ways in which sport brands can be employed as platforms for corporate social activity.

SPONSORSHIP EVALUATION

Some sport marketers believe that the true effects of a sponsorship are impossible to evaluate. For example, sponsorship usually occurs in conjunction with other promotional strategies, which makes isolating its effects difficult. It is also possible that the interaction of a number of promotional strategies is what helps to make a sponsorship work, rather than any one strategy on its own. In other words, different strategies rely on one another to be successful. It is clear that sponsorships are more successful at increasing consumer awareness when they are combined with advertising and other leveraging that reinforces and highlights the sponsorship association. The problem is that this interdependence can make it difficult to evaluate sponsorship on its own.

While it is true that measuring the effect of a sponsorship independent of all other marketing activities is extremely difficult, there are ways in which the success of a sponsorship can be judged. A careful evaluation strategy is important because sponsors expect to receive some objective feedback about the effect of the money they have invested in a sponsorship. Without a clear return on their investment, it is unlikely that a sponsor will continue an association. Even small businesses that sponsor on a more modest level (such as local community clubs) need evidence that the money they commit to a sponsorship will yield benefits. After all, small businesses have far less money to spend and will tend to be discerning about such investments. To be able to demonstrate that sponsorship has a positive outcome for sponsors is the best way to legitimise it as a marketing technique, and to attract and retain sponsors.

> *Chapter principle 10.8*: To be able to demonstrate that sponsorship has a positive outcome for corporations is the best way to legitimise it as a marketing technique, and to attract and retain sponsors.

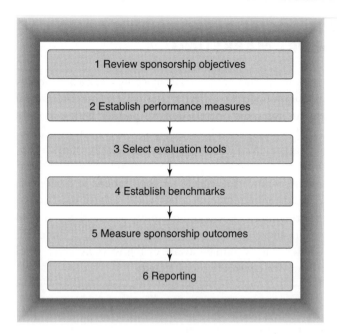

FIGURE 10.3 Sponsorship evaluation

The sponsorship evaluation process is a systematic tool for sport marketers to apply to sponsorship evaluation. The sponsorship evaluation sequence is presented in Figure 10.3, followed by guidance about each stage of the evaluation process.

Review sponsorship objectives

To evaluate the success of a sponsorship programme, there must be a clear understanding of what it was aiming to achieve in the first place. Potential objectives of a sponsorship agreement were highlighted at the beginning of this chapter. They are worth revisiting now because they provide the basis for the next step of establishing performance measures.

Establish performance measures

To evaluate whether objectives have been achieved, it is useful to attach a *performance measure* to each objective. A performance measure is a guide for determining whether the sponsorship objective has been achieved. The word *measure* means a way of estimating, calculating or assessing whether a goal has been achieved. It usually involves finding a way to *quantify* or put a number to the objective. Some important basic examples appear in Table 10.5.

Select evaluation tools

Once marketing objectives have been set, and corresponding performance measures allocated, it is possible to choose the evaluation tools that will be used. Each performance

TABLE 10.5 Examples of performance measures

Sponsorship objective	Possible performance measures
To increase mass media exposure	Number of times the sponsor logo is seen on free-to-air TV during live telecasts per game
To increase the number of people who use the product/service as a result of the sponsorship association	Number of customers who use our service as measured on a post-purchase questionnaire
To increase staff satisfaction levels through corporate hospitality	Satisfaction levels as rated by staff survey, which asks questions about the importance of corporate hospitality
To increase customer awareness of the product	Number of people who have heard of the product in a geographical area as measured by a phone survey
To increase sales	Sales during the sponsored event, compared with sales at the same event last year

measure will be suited to a particular kind of evaluation tool. The key message here is that sponsorship evaluation is best conducted using a range of evaluation tools. Choosing from a 'suite' of evaluation tools helps to overcome the limitations of each method on its own; a number or a group of tools are most useful in providing a breadth of information. Table 10.6 outlines the suite of potential evaluation tools.

Table 10.6 has two important lessons. First, the tools selected to evaluate a sponsorship programme should be directly related to its objectives and performance measures. Second, five main kinds of evaluation are used: (1) exposure, (2) consumer awareness, (3) consumer attitudes, (4) sales effects and (5) satisfaction. The most effective and informative sponsorship evaluation programme will use tools from many, if not all, of these five areas. Each is expanded and explained in the following subsections.

Exposure

Media exposure monitoring is currently the most widely used form of sponsorship evaluation, mainly because it is one of the easiest methods to use. At its most simple, exposure can be measured by documenting the type, frequency and duration of sponsor name and logo appearances in television, radio, press, print and online sources (such as number of page views or hits). For example, how many times a brand name or logo is observable in print media, or how many seconds it appears on television, may be measured. This can be a simple measure, although it can also become time-consuming if significant volumes of media need to be audited. For larger corporations with sufficient resources, there are software programs that can help with storing and analysing this kind of data. One of the limitations of collecting information about the type, frequency and duration of exposure is that it does not provide any indication of how many people, or what types of consumers were exposed. It is therefore useful to also gather information about the readership of the particular publication, the viewer statistics, and the demographic profile of viewers/readers.

TABLE 10.6 Evaluation tools

Objective area	Type of evaluation	Aim in evaluation	Types of tools
Public image	Consumer attitude	Determine what consumers in the general public think and believe about the brand/product/sport	Surveys and focus groups
Media exposure	Media exposure analysis	Determine the type, frequency and/or duration of exposure	Exposure audit
		Determine readership/viewer statistics and demographics	Numerical estimations of exposure value
Awareness (of general public or a target group)	Consumer awareness	Determine whether consumers can recognise and recall the brands involved in the sponsorship (brand awareness), and the association/link between the partners (sponsorship awareness)	Recall and recognition tests through surveys and focus groups
Sales rates or market share	Sales effects	Estimate sales made directly and indirectly as a result of the sponsorship	Tracking of actual sales
			Consumer self-report survey (claimed sales)
			Coupons and 'bounce-backs'(sales by proxy)
			Comparison with competitors' sales to determine market share
Brand association	Consumer attitude Consumer awareness	Determine whether there is a link made between the sponsor and the sport property	Surveys and focus groups
Brand equity	Consumer attitude	Determine what consumers think about the brand. What do they associate with it?	Surveys and focus groups
Brand image management	Consumer attitude	Determine the values and ideas consumers associate with the sponsor/sport property	Surveys and focus groups
		Determine how consumers 'position' the brands/products compared to competitors	
Brand loyalty	Consumer attitude Sales effects	Establish whether the sponsorship affects long-term associations with a brand	Tracking of purchases
			Loyalty programmes
			Focus groups and consumer surveys
Satisfaction and positive relationships*	Satisfaction	Determine the levels of satisfaction that are generated through the sponsorship agreement	Surveys and focus groups

* consumer, channel member, staff, stakeholder

Most sport marketers agree that this information is still insufficient on its own, and that it is necessary to put a monetary value on the media exposure that has been obtained. For example, some sponsors may calculate how much it would cost them to pay for advertising of the same frequency and duration as the sponsorship exposure. This usually involves a mathematical calculation, which considers the duration and time of exposure, estimated audience levels, television ratings, the size/location of the exposure as well as the standard cost for advertising at that time. Other methods apply different kinds of advertising rates together with weighting systems that try to put a value on the different kinds of exposure, and even the 'favourability' of the exposure. There are also statistical models that try to estimate the proportion of the target population that was exposed to the media coverage in question.

There are two main problems with these methods of 'valuing' exposure. The first is that they equate sponsorship exposure with advertising, while the second is that they are based on estimations that may not be valid. The assumption that sponsorship exposure and advertising have the same impact on consumers is unproven and questionable. When compared to sponsorship exposure, an advertisement is a targeted communication that is designed to convey a specific message to the consumer. The message that is conveyed to a consumer through a sponsorship alliance is more subtle and complex, requiring an understanding of consumers' attitudes and beliefs about the two brands, both separately and together. Furthermore, it is also unreasonable to assume that all consumers pay complete or even partial attention to a sponsor's logo while exciting sporting action is occurring. This does not mean that the sponsorship alliance is worthless, but it does imply that sponsorship exposure is not the same as advertising. The value of sponsorship is ultimately not found in the value of air time, but in the way that a match up of brand images can influence consumer attitudes and purchase behaviour.

To make the approach even more dubious, mathematical methods for putting a 'value' on exposure may be invalid. They may not accurately measure what they say they are measuring. What these formulas try to deliver is a 'best guess' based on assumptions and estimations. There is significant variability in the methods, rates and weighting systems that different approaches use, so it remains impossible to compare the results of one with another. There is also the tendency towards inflating the advertising rates against which sponsorship exposure is compared, making sponsorship appear better value than it really is. However, to make a business case for the commencement or maintenance of a sponsorship agreement, these kinds of calculations may be persuasive and have a role to play in evaluation. They are most useful if used on a continuing basis where results can be directly compared from one year to the next. Using the same method consistently can help establish whether there has been a change in exposure. There are specialised sponsorship evaluation consultancies that conduct media exposure measurement for a fee.

In concluding this discussion about measuring media exposure, it is important to remember that media exposure does not in itself reveal anything about consumer intentions. If a logo was seen on television for a total of 45 seconds, there is no information about the impact it had on the people watching it. For example, did it change or strengthen their awareness or attitudes towards the sponsor's brand? While it might be important that consumers are exposed to a sponsor's product or brand, this in itself may not be sufficient to change their attitudes or buying habits. However, if these limitations are taken into account, measuring media exposure can still be one important element of sponsorship evaluation, particularly if it is combined with other forms of evaluation. It can also be an important tool for small sporting organisations that may not have sufficient money to spend on more complex evaluations. The key points to remember about measuring media exposure are summarised in Table 10.7.

Consumer awareness

One of the common objectives of a sponsorship agreement is to increase the awareness consumers possess about a sponsor's product or brand. The most common method used to test consumers' awareness of a brand or a product is based on the ideas of recognition and recall. Testing recognition usually involves showing consumers a list of sponsors' names or logos, and asking which ones they recognise. Sometimes false companies may be added to the list (i.e. companies that are not sponsors) to test the degree to which consumers mistakenly associate brands with a sponsorship just because they are on a list. Testing recall is different because it involves asking consumers to recall sponsor brands spontaneously, without any cues. For example, a consumer may be asked to list the companies or sponsorships that he/she associates with a sport event, without receiving any prompting. Recalling a brand name without any prompting is obviously more difficult, so this is considered a better test of awareness than recognising a brand on a list once prompted.

When using recognition and recall tests, it is possible to test consumers' awareness of two different aspects of the sponsorship: (1) the individual brands (or products) of the sponsor and the sport property and (2) the link or association between the sponsor and sport property. In other words, it is possible to look at evaluating brand awareness as well as sponsorship awareness. Surveys looking at the link between the sponsor and sport property are called association measures.

There are a number of factors that may affect whether a consumer recalls a brand's sponsorship association. These include how long consumers have been exposed to the sponsorship, how strongly they associated previous sponsors with the sport property, how the sponsorship message is delivered, how interested and involved the consumers are with the sport property, the role of other promotional strategies used (such as advertising) to reinforce the sponsorship, and the size of the sponsor. It is also important to realise that recall of a sponsorship can change over time. For example, it may increase just before and during a big sport event, but may die away a few weeks after it has finished.

TABLE 10.7 Measuring media exposure

Measuring media exposure
At its most simple, media exposure can be measured by documenting the type, frequency and duration of media exposure, as well as readership/viewer statistics, and their demographic profile. There are many methods that try to put a monetary value on media exposure; these provide a 'best guess' based on assumptions and estimations, and their validity is therefore questionable (although it may still be persuasive)
Media exposure can be one important element of sponsorship evaluation, particularly if it is combined with other methods

The ability of consumers to recognise and recall sponsorship partners is typically tested during phone surveys and face-to-face surveys, although it is also possible to incorporate them into a focus group analysis. One of the important things to consider when designing a survey or focus group is how consumers will be selected to take part. This will be influenced by the objectives set for the sponsorship agreement. For example, if the aim is to increase awareness in the general public, then this would be best tested with a large, random sample, which of course can be an expensive and difficult undertaking. However, if the aim were to increase awareness within a more specific target group, then an alternative method for selecting participants such as purposeful sampling (e.g. approaching people at an event, or from a membership list) would be appropriate. Measuring consumer awareness is summarised in Table 10.8.

Consumer attitudes/image affects

While media exposure and consumer awareness evaluations are popular ways to assess the success of a sponsorship, they do not uncover anything about the impact of sponsorship on consumer attitudes. Finding out what consumers really think about a product, brand or sponsorship is not an easy task. It is easier to find out whether consumers can recognise and recall a brand, compared with finding out what beliefs they have about the brand, and what values they associate it with. However, discovering what consumers think can be extremely valuable. For example, consumers' attitudes are more likely to give an indication of their likely buying behaviour than awareness measures alone, although the link between attitudes and behaviour is not direct or causal.

Consumer attitudes are often measured through surveys with so-called 'Likert' scales ('agree' and 'disagree' items), and with short-answer questions that ask consumers to give an unprompted response. There are a number of different aspects of consumer attitudes that can be evaluated including (1) perceptions about positioning, (2) the fit between the sponsor and sport property, (3) the perceived sincerity of the sponsor, (4) purchase intentions and (5) affinity measures. Each is discussed in the following subsections and summarised in Table 10.9.

TABLE 10.8 Measuring consumer awareness
Measuring consumer awareness
Consumer awareness is most commonly measured by testing recognition and recall of a brand, product or sponsorship alliance
Recognition is when a consumer is able to identify the brand/product/alliance from a list. This means that he/she has been prompted to remember it
Recall is when a consumer remembers the brand/product/alliance without prompting or recognising from a list
Recognition and recall tests can measure brand awareness (of the individual partners in the sponsorship) as well as sponsorship awareness (the alliance between the partners)

TABLE 10.9 Measuring consumer attitudes
Measuring consumer attitudes
Consumer attitudes are the beliefs that a consumer has about a product or brand. There are a number of different types of consumer attitudes that are commonly evaluated including: (1) perceptions about positioning, (2) the fit between the sponsor and sport property, (3) the perceived sincerity of the sponsor, (4) purchase intentions and (5) affinity measures
Consumer attitudes are often measured on surveys with Likert scales using 'agree' and 'disagree' items, and short-answer questionnaires

Positioning perceptions

One important kind of consumer attitude evaluation involves trying to understand how consumers conceptualise a sponsor's brand compared to others. In order to uncover such complex issues, surveys and short-answer questionnaires ask consumers to indicate what they associate with the brand, such as values, features or symbols. For example, do they associate the brand with prestige, reliability or family values? A questionnaire may also ask how consumers compare the sponsor's brand to others. For example, do they see it as better value or more dependable than other brands? Obviously, before it is possible to design and implement a consumer attitude survey seeking to evaluate consumer beliefs about positioning, it is vital that there is clear information about how a sponsor sought to position its brand in the first place. The key questions are: What values, features and images do consumers associate with a sponsor's brand?; and, how do consumers compare a sponsor's brand to others?

Sponsor and sport property fit/sponsorship congruence

A sponsorship will be more effective if there is a strong fit or match up between the sponsor's brand and the sport property. The level of fit, or congruence, that consumers perceive relates to the degree to which they think that there is a logical connection between the two. For example, there is an obvious congruence between a sport event such as a tennis grand slam and a sponsor that manufactures tennis products. To explore whether consumers perceive a good fit between the sponsor and sport property, survey questions may be posed to determine the characteristics they associate with each, or what consumers think each symbolises or stands for. The researchers can then assess the similarity.

Sincerity of the sponsor

Consumers are more likely to think favourably about a sponsor if they believe that the sponsor is motivated by a sense of community and philanthropy rather than just financial gain.

Purchase intentions

It is often difficult to accurately measure sales that have resulted directly from a sponsorship. One of the ways around this problem is to find out whether consumers intend or plan to purchase the sponsor's product. Purchase intentions are therefore a proxy for actual sales, in that they represent a substitute, or a stand-in measure. Purchase intentions can also be considered a proxy for actual behaviour; that is, for actually buying and consuming a product. It is obvious, however, that planned behaviour and actual behaviour can be quite different.

Affinity measures

The word 'affinity' in the context of sponsorship evaluation refers to whether or not consumers feel an attraction to a sponsor's product or brand. More specifically, it refers to the degree to which consumers feel that a sponsor's product or brand is 'their kind of brand'. For example, does it give the consumer the sense of identity that they are seeking? Or, do consumers think that it suits other people that they would like to be similar to? Questions of this kind have a relationship to product and brand positioning because they are designed to find out whether the way that consumers think about a sponsor's product/brand reinforces the way that they would like to think about themselves.

Sales effects

Linking any promotional activity, including sponsorship, to an increase in sales is problematic. One of the main reasons is that a sponsor will usually implement a whole range of different promotional strategies, making it difficult to separate out which strategies have led to which sales. However, in some instances, it can actually be easier to track sales effects that have been stimulated by sponsorship, compared with other promotions. For example, food or beverage rights at a sport event give the sponsor exclusive or preferential sales rights to consumers at the event. It is a simple task to calculate the sales that have been made at the sponsored event.

It is more difficult, however, to determine whether there is an indirect increase in sales as a result of the event. For example, did more consumers choose to use a sponsored product after the event as a result of its affiliation with the sponsored property? These kinds of sales are sometimes called claimed sales because consumers may 'claim' that they bought a product as a result of being exposed to it in a certain way. Claimed sales can be measured through surveys asking consumers to indicate their awareness of the sponsorship, their exposure to the sponsor and their reasoning for purchase. Sometimes brief surveys may even be done at the point of sale to find out what has led the consumer to their decision.

It is also possible to estimate sales by proxy. This means trying to estimate sales by using a 'stand-in', such as a coupon or token that is redeemed at the point of sale. For example, if the coupon has been distributed at a sport event and the consumer uses it at the point of sale, then the sale can be associated with the sponsorship. One of the complicating factors of this method is that coupons and tokens often include an incentive for people to redeem them, like offering a discount. This makes it difficult to determine whether the sale was made as a result of the sponsorship or the discount promotion. However, while this may make it difficult to accurately estimate sales by proxy, it can be an effective way of leveraging a sponsorship programme. Table 10.10 summarises the important issues associated with measuring sales effects.

To review, three different types of *sales measures* are used in sponsorship evaluation. They are (1) actual sales, (2) claimed sales and (3) sales by proxy. Sales effects measures can make a contribution to a sponsorship evaluation, but they do have two major limitations. First, they do not accurately reflect the effect on sales flowing from a sponsorship. Second, the major benefit of sponsorship may actually be less related to sales and more relevant to the positive effects on consumer attitudes and therefore brand equity.

Satisfaction

The final area for evaluating sponsorships is related to satisfaction. A sponsor may aim to increase customer, staff or even shareholder satisfaction through the sponsorship. For example, the sponsor may offer staff corporate hospitality at a sporting event with the aim of improving staff morale and loyalty. It logically follows that if this is an objective, then measures using a satisfaction rating of some kind are required.

Establish benchmarks

Once a suite of evaluation tools has been selected to evaluate the sponsorship, it is important to establish a benchmark. Benchmarks are used to determine the 'status quo' before the sponsorship promotions commence. This is essential to find out whether an objective has been achieved over and above the original levels prior to the commencement of the sponsorship relationship. For example, if the objective is to increase brand awareness among a specific target market, then there must be evidence of what the awareness levels were before the sponsorship agreement began. A benchmark therefore works as a point of reference in the evaluation strategy.

Measure sponsorship outcomes and report

The final two stages of the evaluation process are to measure the outcomes of the sponsorship programme and then report these formally to the sponsor. Measuring the outcomes of a sponsorship means using the suite of evaluation tools again after a set duration during which the sponsorship has been in place. These results should be considered against the benchmarks obtained from the previous step to assess whether the desired goals have been realised. The results of the evaluation should be formally reported

---

TABLE 10.10 Measuring sales effects

Measuring sales effects
It can be difficult to directly attribute sales to the impact of a sponsorship agreement. Sometimes it may be possible to calculate actual sales, such as when a food or beverage company sponsors an event and makes sales at that event
If it is not possible to measure actual sales, it may be feasible to estimate claimed sales, by surveying consumers about why they purchased a product
Finally, sales can be measured by proxy, which involves estimating sales by using a 'stand-in' such as a coupon or token that is redeemed at the point of sale

to the sponsor, along with any recommendations about improvements that can be made or ways in which the sponsorship can be leveraged for even better results in the future.

> *Chapter tool 10.4 Sport sponsorship evaluation*: A step-by-step process of sponsorship evaluation should include: (1) review sponsorship objectives, (2) establish performance measures, (3) select evaluation tools, (4) establish benchmarks, (5) measure sponsorship outcomes and (6) reporting.

The tools that are chosen to evaluate the sponsorship programme should be directly related to the sponsorship objectives and performance measures originally set.

There are five main kinds of sponsorship evaluation to select from: (1) exposure, (2) consumer awareness, (3) consumer attitudes, (4) sales effects and (5) satisfaction. The most effective and informative sponsorship evaluation programme will use tools from many, if not all, of these five areas.

AMBUSH MARKETING

The word 'ambush' refers to a trap or a surprise attack on a competitor. In the sponsorship world, *ambush marketing* is a term used when a company creates the impression that it is associated with a sport property, whereas in reality they have no affiliation at all. Ambush marketing is planned to establish an artificial association with an event in order to obtain some of the benefits and recognition of an official sponsorship, without having to invest any money. Typically, ambush marketing involves an intrusion on the physical space of a sport property or sport event, making use of a particular diversion or grab for attention in order to wrestle the association away from the actual sponsor.

Ambush marketing occurs most often with large sporting events, where the ambushing company deflects attention away from the official sponsors and onto themselves, without having made the appropriate investment into the sport property. Ambush marketing is sometimes called 'parasitic' marketing because a company is 'free-loading', like a parasite, on the back of the official sponsor. In these situations, consumers can become confused and even believe that the ambushing company is an actual sponsor. Before more stringent legislation was introduced, the earliest attempts at ambush marketing were quite clumsy. For example, the ambush company would park a hot-air balloon with their logo on it above a competing brand's sponsored event, or would hand out free memorabilia at the event. Ambush marketing was popularised by the bitter rivalries of companies fighting for the same market, such as Coke and Pepsi, and Nike and adidas.

Ambush marketing attempts to undermine the brand equity of official sponsors at the same time as it aims to increase the brand equity of the ambusher. Ambush strategies can be effective. In terms of the recall and recognition of consumers, non-sponsors can often be perceived as genuine and official sponsors, and they may even become more memorable than the official sponsors because they have employed particularly unusual devices and tactics for stealing the attention of consumers.

> *Chapter principle 10.9*: Ambush marketing refers to a strategy where a company (other than an official sponsor, and often a competitor to the official sponsor)

creates the impression that it is associated with the sport property. This is achieved by attracting attention and by giving the false impression of a relationship with the sport property.

There are many ways in which ambush marketing can be undertaken. The most obvious is by the illegal use of official logos or merchandise, or by making false claims about being an official sponsor. Because there are clear laws in most countries that prohibit this kind of behaviour, legal action can be undertaken in response to it. However, some aggressive companies continue to mount ambushing campaigns in ways that may not cause a clear-cut breech in law, and even in ways that may be completely legal. There are five main ambush marketing strategies that companies may legally use, often with several approaches used at the same time. The five include the ambushing of advertising, broadcast, subcategories, athletes or promotions. Each is described in detail in the following subsections.

Advertising ambush: buying advertising time around an event

An advertising ambush can occur when a non-official sponsor implements an advertising campaign that coincides with the sport event. This could simply involve buying normal advertising time and space, and the ambusher may argue that it is well within its rights to promote its brand by purchasing legitimate airtime during sporting events. However, the official sponsor is more likely to believe that it has been ambushed. More aggressive advertising ambushes can even imply that there is a link between the ambusher and the event.

An advertising ambush can use any of the forms of advertising that have been detailed in Chapter 9. Some examples include television commercials, magazine and newspaper advertisements, radio spots, posters, billboards, Internet pop-ups, and advertisements on buses and bus stops. Virtual billboards at sporting events offer another avenue through which companies can attempt to ambush.

Broadcast ambush: sponsoring the broadcast of an event

By sponsoring the broadcast of a sport event, a company can create the impression that it is associated with the sport property. It has, in fact, paid for the right to be associated with the broadcast itself, but the awareness that this generates can spill over onto the sport event as well. Interestingly, a broadcast sponsor has the opportunity to associate itself with the sport to a much larger television audience than the event sponsor, who may only be reaching those people in attendance.

Subcategory ambush: sponsoring a subcategory of a sport event

It is common for sport events to offer different categories of sponsorship. In addition to an overall sponsorship of the event, they may also offer sponsorships of smaller categories in the event. An ambusher can invest less money by sponsoring a small element of the event, and then aggressively promote its association. This can even convince the public that the subcategory sponsor is actually a major event sponsor. As noted earlier, the key to success in this form of ambushing is effective sponsorship leveraging. With this tactic, the best approach is to invest only small amounts in the sponsorship itself, and support it with substantial investments in leveraging, giving the impression of a major event sponsorship. When this approach works, it is far less expensive than paying for a major sponsorship.

Athlete ambush: sponsoring an athlete or team

Sponsors may also support an individual athlete or a team who is usually allowed to seek his or her own endorsements.

Promotions ambush: using non-sponsorship promotion

An ambushing company can also use non-sponsorship promotional strategies that coincide with a sport event to create an association. Other strategies can include giving away branded T-shirts or temporary tattoos for spectators to wear, which will be seen on the television broadcast. There are limitless examples of promotional ambush strategies, so the list could go on: conducting competitions, giving away official merchandise as prizes without permission, unauthorised websites, live screenings, mobile phone content, unofficial corporate hospitality, unofficial merchandise, unauthorised publications, virtual advertising, advertisements that wish athletes good fortune or congratulate them, and promotions that show famous sporting landmarks in the background.

Chapter tool 10.5 Ambush marketing methods:

1 Buy advertising time during the event (advertising ambush)
2 Sponsor the broadcast of an event, not the event itself (broadcast ambush)
3 Sponsor subcategories of the event (subcategory ambush)
4 Sponsor a team or athlete (athlete ambush)
5 Use imaginative, non-sponsorship promotions during the event (promotions ambush)

Ambush prevention

The idea of ambush marketing probably appears unfair to most people. Whether or not it is illegal, however, often depends on the particular details of the ambushing campaign. Even if an ambushing campaign is clearly illegal, the time and costs of settling a dispute through the courts may be considered excessive, unreasonable and counterproductive. Some commentators have claimed that even when it is not illegal, ambush marketing constitutes an immoral practice, although this is a controversial position. Putting aside the legal and ethical issues of the practice, the fact remains that ambush marketing is a problem for both the official sponsors and the sport property, and it is vitally important to consider what strategies can be implemented to avoid the problem occurring in the first place. Thus, the professional sport marketer must know how to use forms of ambush marketing at some times, and defend against it at others.

Clearly ambush marketing has a detrimental impact on official sponsors. It can limit their ability to recoup their investment because it reduces positive impact on consumer awareness and attitudes. Ambush marketing can also negatively affect the sport property itself. This is because it can damage the relationship with the official sponsor, and make it more difficult to secure future sponsorships. It is therefore important to understand when ambush marketing is most likely to occur, and what strategies can be implemented to prevent it. It is generally considered to be more effective to block out ambushers than to instigate legal action because of the significant cost and difficulty in establishing that something illegal has occurred.

There are five major elements of an ambush prevention strategy: (1) control of intellectual property, (2) control of the event environment and locality, (3) control of the event partners, (4) design of the sponsorship programme and (5) leveraging official sponsorships. Each is described next.

Control of intellectual property

The intellectual property relating to a sport event can include names, logos, mascots and merchandise. Controlling the use of these properties is really only possible through legal avenues, such as contracts, copyright law, trademark registration and other specialised legislation. Logos and emblems are usually protected by copyright legislation as an original work of art. It is important with these works to negotiate with the designer to have the copyright transferred to the sport property. Names and logos can be protected legally in a given country if they are registered as a trademark. Different legislation and registration systems operate in different locations, so it can be difficult to track and protect these rights. In the case of large sport properties, such as the Olympics or the World Cup, governments in the hosting country may enact specific legislation to protect logos, names and slogans that are related to the event.

For the sport property, controlling intellectual property means ensuring that trademarks are registered in the relevant region and copyright ownership is clarified in contracts. Usually the sport property will also indicate that a trademark or copyright exists, such as through the use of the letters (tm) or (c) wherever the word or logo appears. However, while copyright, trademark and other legislation may deter ambushers from using a logo or other forms of intellectual property, it does not guarantee that they will not. It may be effective in some cases to use legal teams to put further pressure on ambushers to stop their use of a proprietary logo or name. Although it can be costly and difficult, the sport property may choose to settle the matter in court.

Control of the event environment and locality

To prevent an ambush at a sport event, the organisers need to plan for what is called a 'clean' venue. This means that no signage, promotions or advertising appear within the grounds that promote competitors of the official sponsors. This includes the stadium itself, bars and eating areas, toilets, buildings that are visible to the spectators or television cameras, or even the airspace above the stadium. In practice, there must be teams of workers monitoring the event and removing any ambushing material. The terms and conditions of admission can reserve the right for event organisers to refuse entry or eject patrons if they are seen to be participating in an ambush strategy.

The environment surrounding the event should also be controlled where possible, although the extent to which this can be achieved depends upon the available budget and cooperation of local authorities and media. For example, it may be feasible to prohibit promotions by competitors occurring at the event entry, or in nearby streets. Sport events that make use of a wide geographical area, such as marathons and other long-distance events, can pose significant problems.

Control of the event partners

In addition to the obvious partners of a sport event (athletes, teams, sponsors, suppliers and merchandisers), other partners can include licensed broadcasters, media and local authorities. Some of these partners will have a contract with the sport event (athletes, sponsors, broadcasters, suppliers and merchandisers), which should bind them to comply with anti-ambush strategies. The other parties such as local councils, police and local media are not necessarily obliged to support the anti-ambush strategies, but efforts should be made to inform and negotiate with them to play a role.

Controlling broadcasters

When a sport event organiser negotiates a contract with an event broadcaster, it is essential for it to consider the protection of its sponsors. For example, broadcasters can be contractually bound to give the event sponsors the first opportunity to purchase broadcasting rights as well as advertising time in and around the event. Broadcasters can also be contractually obligated to give the official event sponsors the right to veto their competitors from becoming broadcast sponsors, programme sponsors and/or buying advertising time during the event. It is common for event organisers to reduce the cost of a broadcast sponsorship in exchange for more control over whom the broadcasters subsequently sell advertising time to.

Controlling sponsors, suppliers and merchandisers

Sponsors, suppliers and merchandisers for a sport property or event could deliberately or inadvertently help an ambush to occur. For example, official merchandise could be provided to an ambusher who plans to use the goods as prize give-aways without permission. Similarly, official sponsors could facilitate an ambush by participating in joint promotions with non-sponsors. The contracts that are signed with these parties should therefore prohibit behaviour that may lead to ambushing. For example, sponsors can be prohibited from undertaking joint promotions related to the event, unless the organisation they intend to partner with is also an official sponsor. Sponsors can also be prohibited from sharing their sponsorship rights or from sub-licensing them to another, non-official sponsor. All promotional materials can be subject to prior approval by the event organisers.

The contracts that are signed between the sponsors and sport organisers can give the sponsors certain rights to protect their interests. For example, it can give them the right to approve the promotional material of other licensees and sponsors before it is distributed. Sometimes it can ensure them the first opportunity to advertise in official publications. These rights are often called 'rights of first refusal' because they give the sponsor the first opportunity to be involved, or to refuse if they so wish.

Controlling athletes, teams and sport associations

Ambushing can occur through the sponsorship of a team or athlete. On the one hand this is a legitimate agreement, and the athletes/clubs have the right to seek support and endorsement. However, problems can arise if this sponsorship clashes with the overall sponsorship of an event or property. The ability to control this problem will vary from event to event depending on variables such as the relative bargaining power of the event compared with the athletes/clubs, and the regulations of the event itself. However, there are restrictions that may be considered as part of the contractual agreement. Some examples include that (1) athletes may be restricted from wearing branded clothing or footwear; (2) all promotions related to the event may be subject to the event organiser's approval; (3) participants may be required to use specific products or services (those of a sponsor) at the event; and (4) there may be restrictions on participants filming or documenting events.

Design of the sponsorship programme

The way that a sponsorship programme is designed may have an impact on whether ambush marketing campaigns will occur. This is because ambush marketing is most likely to happen under certain circumstances. These situations can include when there is a wide variety of sponsorship categories and many sponsors per category, a high cost of official sponsorship, a strictly limited number of sponsors allowed into the event, or side events that are happening outside the main event. For example, if there are a broad variety of sponsorship categories, and/or there are many sponsors per category, it is harder for consumers to identify the official sponsors. This 'clutter' can lead to confusion about who is and who is not involved. It becomes easier for ambushers to take advantage of this confusion, and lead sport consumers to believe that they are officially involved in the event. However, it is also possible that the sponsorship agreement has strict exclusivity rules that limit the opportunity for companies to become legitimately involved, potentially leading them to unofficially try to grab some attention.

Leverage official sponsorships

Leveraging official sponsorships means getting the maximum amount of benefit and advantage from the agreement through planning additional and integrated marketing activities. If the official sponsors themselves are not promoting their involvement well enough, this may provide the opportunity for an unofficial sponsor to step in and fill the gap. Sponsors who make the most of their agreement can also minimise the impact of an ambush if it does occur. As outlined in the earlier section on leveraging sponsorships, sponsors and sport properties may use other elements of the promotions mix to complement and boost the sponsorship, as well as use the other elements of the marketing mix.

> *Chapter tool 10.6 Sport sponsorship evaluation*: There are five major elements of an ambush prevention strategy: (1) control of intellectual property, (2) control of the event environment and locality, (3) control of the event partners, (4) design of the sponsorship programme and (5) leverage official sponsorships.

PRINCIPLES SUMMARY

- Chapter principle 10.1: The term sport property refers to the recipient of the sponsorship. This could be an athlete, team, event, venue, association, cause or competition.

- Chapter principle 10.2: Sport sponsorship is a business agreement where one organisation provides financial or in-kind assistance to a sport property in exchange for the right to associate itself with the sport property. The sponsor does this in order to achieve corporate objectives (such as enhancing corporate image) or marketing objectives (such as increasing brand awareness).

- Chapter principle 10.3: Sport sponsorship generates goodwill among consumers. The amount of goodwill generated can vary depending on the kind of sport property being sponsored, the degree of involvement that consumers have with the sport property, the time at which the sponsor becomes involved, and when and how the sponsor ceases the sponsorship.

- Chapter principle 10.4: Fan involvement is an important consideration in sponsorship because a consumer's response to a sponsorship is driven by the level of involvement that he/she has with the sport property.

- Chapter principle 10.5: The objectives of sponsorship can vary greatly, depending on the size of the partners, the type of sponsorship and the type of sport property being supported. Some common objectives for the sponsor are to enhance sales, to promote the public image of its brand, to increase consumer awareness, to modify its brand image and to build business relationships.

- Chapter principle 10.6: The objectives of sponsorship for the sport property will vary. In addition to attracting financial support, objectives include increasing credibility, increasing awareness, and managing brand image.

- Chapter principle 10.7: Sponsorship affinity refers to whether there is a good fit or match between the sponsor and the sport property. Two factors are particularly important for ensuring a good match: (1) an overlap of target markets and (2) a match up of brand positioning strategies.

- Chapter principle 10.8: To be able to demonstrate that sponsorship has a positive outcome for corporations is the best way to legitimise it as a marketing technique, and to attract and retain sponsors.

- Chapter principle 10.9: Ambush marketing refers to a strategy where a company (other than an official sponsor, and often a competitor to the official sponsor) creates the impression that it is associated with the sport property. This is achieved by attracting attention and by giving the false impression of a relationship with the sport property.

TOOLS SUMMARY

- Chapter tool 10.1 Sponsorship proposal
- Chapter tool 10.2 Sport sponsorship rights
- Chapter tool 10.3 Sponsorship leveraging
- Chapter tool 10.4 Sport sponsorship evaluation
- Chapter tool 10.5 Ambush marketing methods
- Chapter tool 10.6 Sport sponsorship evaluation

REVIEW QUESTIONS

1   Identify all kinds of sport properties that can be sponsored.

2   What are the major reasons sport properties and sponsors decide to enter sponsorship agreements?

3   What are the variables that affect consumer goodwill about a sponsorship?

4   Provide a good example of a sponsor and sport property relationship that enjoys a high level of affinity.

5   Describe the process of sponsorship evaluation.

6   Explain why sponsorship leveraging is so pivotal to successful associations.

7   Outline the legal approaches to employing ambush marketing in sponsorship.

RELEVANT WEBSITES

www.kia.com.au/game-on   Kia Game On App
www.wtatennis.com   Women's Tennis Association
www.alpg.com.au   Australian Ladies Professional Golf
www.puma.com   Puma

FURTHER READING

Desbordes, M. (2012). *Marketing and Football*. London: Routledge.
Fortunato, J.A. (2013). *Sports Sponsorship: Principles and Practices*. Jefferson, NC: McFarland Publishers.

CHAPTER 11

Sport services

LEARNING OUTCOMES

At the end of this chapter, readers should be able to:

- define the term services marketing
- outline the differences between sporting goods and sporting services
- explain the term 'the service experience'
- identify the three elements of the services marketing mix
- discuss the key variables of quality service
- explain the difference between outcome and process quality
- discuss approaches for measuring service quality
- define the term customer satisfaction
- explain the concept of 'delighting the customer' and examine its strategic implications
- outline the six-step process of customer relationship marketing.

OVERVIEW

This chapter introduces readers to sport services marketing. It highlights the principles and tools for delivering first, quality service and second, establishing customer satisfaction. The chapter also explains the importance of developing strong relationships with sport customers in their roles as spectators, fans, players, participants, volunteer officials, and citizens in general. Finally, the services marketing mix is outlined, and its applicability to the delivery of services is explained.

SPORT SERVICES

This text has already introduced the four traditional elements of the sport marketing mix, which are product, price, place and promotion. It has also discussed the concepts of sponsorship and product endorsement as an extension of the promotional aspect of marketing. We are now in the position to add the idea of 'service' as a way of differentiating products. The chapter begins with a review of the characteristics of sport services before explaining the sport services mix, which covers services quality, customer satisfaction and relationship marketing. Figure 11.1 shows the elements of sport services within the Sport Marketing Framework.

Defining a sport service

Although sport is regularly packaged into tangible goods such as sport equipment, sport apparel, merchandise and memorabilia, most sport is actually experienced as a service. People attending an athletics meet are being delivered a service, and so too are people involved in exercise to music classes. Attending a coaching seminar, or having a rock-climbing lesson are also examples of service experiences. It may be useful at this point to review the differences between sport goods and services. Chapter 6 presented four ways in which sport goods and services can be differentiated. They are tangibility, consistency, perishability and separability. Each point of differentiation is explained in more detail below.

Tangibility

When a sport product is tangible, it is a physical thing that can be touched, seen, felt and sometimes even smelt. Sporting goods such as a baseball bat or badminton racket are tangible because they are physical, and are often objects that can be taken away – that is, transportable – such as a DVD or a team scarf. Some sport services are also intangible because unlike a tube of toothpaste, they cannot be seen, touched, or stored away for later use. They do not exist beyond the memory of their experience. Sport services are like a performance, where a team of players or an individual athlete do two interconnected things. First, they participate – or perform – in a physical contest. Second, this performance delivers fans and spectators – the consumers – an experience. The experience can be memorable, or it can be totally forgettable. Additionally, sport consumers do not actually own the service, and they cannot take it home to keep on a shelf next to their family photo album, unless of course, they photographed some incidents at the event. For the most part they will just experience it for a certain amount of time, and subsequently place it in their personal memory bank for later recall in moments of nostalgic reflection.

In fact, most sport goods and services are a mixture of tangible and intangible elements. This is because many physical sport products have a service or emotional element contained in them. For example, a canoe bought by a consumer is clearly a tangible good. However, whenever it is used on a stretch of water it delivers the participant a benefit, be it a good physical workout, a sense of achievement, or just a vague feeling of happiness. These benefits are, of course, intangible in nature. In addition, many sport services are sold together with something tangible. A membership to a football club may come with a subscription package including club stickers, badges, regular newsletters and discount vouchers for use at selected retail outlets. Sport consumption can thus involve a mixture of goods, services, benefits and experiences.

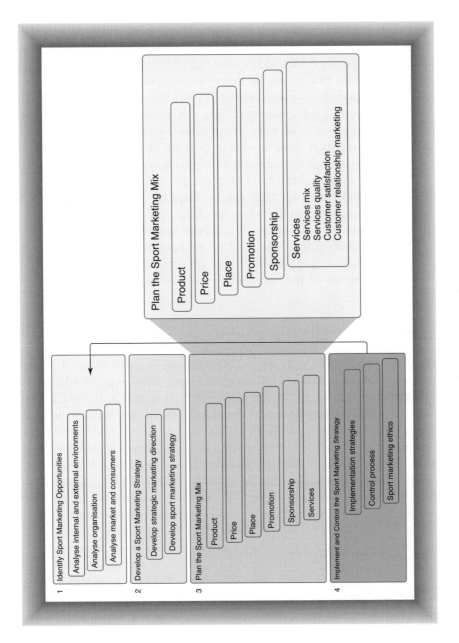

FIGURE 11.1 Sport services and the Sport Marketing Framework

Plan the Sport Marketing Mix

Product
Price
Place
Promotion
Sponsorship
Services
 Services mix
 Services quality
 Customer satisfaction
 Customer relationship marketing

1 Identify Sport Marketing Opportunities
 Analyse internal and external environments
 Analyse organisation
 Analyse market and consumers

2 Develop a Sport Marketing Strategy
 Develop strategic marketing direction
 Develop sport marketing strategy

3 Plan the Sport Marketing Mix
 Product
 Price
 Place
 Promotion
 Sponsorship
 Services

4 Implement and Control the Sport Marketing Strategy
 Implementation strategies
 Control process
 Sport marketing ethics

Consistency

Consistency is a second way in which sport goods and services can be separated. Consistency refers to the uniformity of quality from one time that a sport product or service is delivered to the next. Sporting goods usually have a high degree of consistency. For example, there is not much change in the quality of one sporting shoe compared with another of the same brand and style from one purchase to the next. And, there is no difference at all between two DVDs with a recording of the same sport content. On the other hand, sport services usually have far more variable quality. The quality of a sport experience may change depending on a range of factors including who is providing the service as well as the special conditions of its offering. For instance, a change in the weather can have a dramatic effect on consumers' experiences. So too can the performance of athletes and teams. Many sport services come in the form of a sporting competition set within the confines of an infrastructure, both of which can vary enormously from week to week. For example, in professional team sport the quality of the spectator experience will be shaped by the refereeing, the field, pitch or court, the catering service provided, the seating arrangements, and even the behaviour of surrounding spectators. And, to top it all off, there is always going to be enormous variability around the contest itself. It could be close, exciting and spectacular, on one hand, or one-sided, dull and banal on the other. Similarly, one Crossfit session may prove more enjoyable than another, for no other reason than the instructor, nature of the 'workout of the day', and who else turns up to participate.

Perishability

Perishability refers to whether a sport product or service can be stored and used at another time. Sporting goods such as clothing and equipment tend not to be perishable, although there are exceptions such as nutritional supplements that have a specific life span. Basketballs, cricket bats and bicycles can be stored and used many times over during their operating life. They can also be traded in the second-hand product markets. Sport services, such as a morning meal of coffee and croissants at a local café, cannot be stored and reused. For example, there is no way to store any unsold tickets to a sport event in order to sell them at another time. Additionally, once the game has been played, any seats that were not filled are lost forever. Similarly, if only five customers have arrived for an aerobics class in a leisure facility at a given time, the vacant positions represent unsold potential that can never be reclaimed. Of course, as observed in Chapter 6, many sport services are combined with sport products to make up for the perishability of sport services. An example is a DVD recording of a game, or more likely, the digital content placed online for members and fans to replay. Since the game or event has been converted to a digital file it can be viewed many times over. This gets over the perishability problem in sport services that can only be run once by offering something tangible at a low production cost.

Separability

Separability is a term that is used to describe the extent to which a product or service is consumed at the same time and at the same place it is manufactured. Canned groceries are often consumed months after they are manufactured, and their consumption can take place thousands of kilometres away from the place of manufacture. Sporting goods have the same features. For example, a hockey stick is made in a manufacturing plant, it is delivered to a wholesaler who then supplies it to a retailer. The retailer places the hockey stick on the hockey equipment shelf, and it is hopefully purchased by a consumer at some time in the future. This could be months or even years after its initial production. Another way of looking at this is that the quality of the hockey stick is separated from the quality of service at the sport store where it is bought. It is possible to separate the item from the person selling it, although as we will note later, sometimes one can affect the other.

Sport services, on the other hand, are usually made and consumed at the same time and in the same place. At a live sport event, the competition is both manufactured and supplied in the same space. And, anyone who wants to experience the event in real time and real space will have to attend the same stadium at which it is being supplied. Otherwise they will not be a spectator, but instead will be a radio listener, a television viewer, or just casual fans who might follow the game on their mobile phone. Similarly, if people want to participate in a swim carnival, then they must attend the nominated venue at the designated time. Otherwise they will 'swim alone', and the communal experience they were seeking will not be realised.

> *Chapter principle 11.1*: There are four characteristics that illustrate the difference between sport goods and services: tangibility, consistency, perishability and separability. Sport services are intangible because they exist only as an experience. Sport services tend to be inconsistent because they are affected by variables that are difficult to control. Sport services are perishable because they can only be offered and experienced once at any point in time. Sport services are inseparable because they are consumed at the same time as they are produced.

INTERACTIVE CASE

The service sector is the largest employer of people in every industrialised nation in the world. In most advanced industrial societies at least 70 per cent of the workforce is employed in the service sector. Services take every imaginable form. They include a teaching period in a school classroom, a haircut, a session with a dentist, train travel, a day at the local swimming pool, a visit to the local library, and a night at the cinema.

Questions

1 Services are sometimes explained in terms of what they are not. What does this statement mean, and what examples can be provided to support this statement?
2 In many service exchanges the suppliers of the service have physically close relationships with customers. What are some good examples of this 'close proximity' service exchange?

3   There are many service exchanges where other customers can heavily affect the quality of the customer experience. What sport-related experiences are especially impacted upon by the behaviour of other customers? Is this always a good thing?

4   In most service delivery situations the customer derives value from the experience, but ends up not owing any tangible good or object. In some instances it may actually involve the loss of a tangible element. Having rubbish removed from your garden is an example. Where does participating in an exercise class fit? And, what about attendance at a community sport event? Does the same issue emerge after physiotherapy treatment?

5   When it comes to understanding the sport experience, the question arises as to when sport is a tangible product, and when sport is an intangible service. It is a useful exercise to take a sample of consumption activities that have some connection to sport and lay them out on a continuum with high tangibility, high consistency, low perishability and high separability at one end, and low tangibility, low consistency, high perishability and low separability at the other end. So, where do the following sporting products and experiences fit along this continuum?

*   a visit to a sports museum;
*   a gym workout;
*   securing the services of a photographer to take photos of you playing in a basketball tournament;
*   getting a refit of your powerboat;
*   being treated by a chiropractor for a back injury that occurred while playing rugby;
*   having a mechanic service your racing bike;
*   purchasing memorabilia at the completion of a professional basketball game;
*   seeking the advice of a lawyer over your playing contract with a local football club;
*   consuming an energy drink prior to a tennis tournament;
*   having dental work done after being involved in an altercation at your sister's netball game;
*   having a parachute lesson;
*   'kitting' yourself out for the upcoming football season;
*   re-surfacing a tennis court;
*   coaching at a gymnastics club;
*   selling off old equipment at the local life-saving club.

6   The other issue that surrounds these exchanges is how to evaluate the quality of the above experiences. Which of these exchanges appear to be relatively easy to evaluate, and which of them appear to be difficult? What makes some of the above sport-related services so difficult to evaluate?

Points of interest

Services may be intangible, but they deliver something of value. They deliver an experience. This experience can be brief, routine and banal. An Internet banking transaction is a case in point. But it can also be prolonged, intense and memorable. Some people find that church attendance can go beyond the intense and the prolonged, and enter the transcendental. In sport these prolonged, intense and memorable experiences can take many forms. They can arise from playing a sport, but they can also come from watching someone else play a sport. A bad experience may come from poor treatment for an injury, but a good experience might result from a successful rehabilitation programme. It would not be an exaggeration to say that we live in the age of the big experience, with sport in the forefront.

SERVICES MIX

The special nature of sport services when compared with sport goods means that the marketing of services can be substantially different. This has led some commentators to argue that there is a need to augment the conventional sport marketing mix, which was originally devised with goods in mind. Although many supplementary ideas have been suggested to help marketers work directly with services, one approach has become popular. It involves the use of three additional 'Ps', which are (1) participants (staff and customers), (2) physical evidence (tangible elements of the service) and (3) processes (the system of service delivery). These additional 'Ps' are not just the concern of sport marketers, but are also influenced by the administration and human resources staff, therefore demanding an integrated approach from everyone in a sport organisation. In this respect, the three service mix 'Ps' can be seen as complementary equivalents to the four conventional marketing 'Ps' that are described in Chapters 6–9. As such they provide many useful clues as to how best to market sport services. The three Ps of the sport services mix are described next.

Participants

Because a sport service is consumed at the same time as it is produced, both staff and other consumers can influence perceptions of service quality. This is particularly true for 'high contact' services such as fitness centres and sporting competitions. In fact, the 'staff' in these examples is actually part of the service. For example, a sport masseur is part of the massage service, just as athletes are part of a sporting match. The quality and management of employees (and athletes) is therefore an important part of sport services marketing. Furthermore, in sport events other consumers are especially important elements to the service as they have a powerful impact on atmosphere. This means that for sport organisations, the ways in which they allow consumers to interact with one another is a fundamental consideration of the service structure.

Physical evidence

The physical evidence of a sport service includes the environment in which it is delivered, and any other visual or tangible elements. For example, the physical environment of a tennis competition includes the stadium, the food and beverage facilities, the seating and the scoreboard. Other tangible elements could include the design of tickets, programmes and merchandise. Not only are these characteristics important components of the service, they are significant because consumers use physical evidence as clues to the service quality. In fact, the more intangible a service, the more important it is to include physical elements to reinforce service quality.

Processes

Processes in sport services marketing refer to the steps that a consumer progresses through to receive a service, as well as those in which a service provider has to perform to deliver the sport service. For example, to attend a rugby match, a sport fan may have to queue for a ticket, travel on public transport, wait again in queues to enter the ground, submit to a security screening, find the right seat, locate some food and beverages and eventually exit. It is therefore important that consumers are educated to understand and anticipate what processes they have to experience to receive a service. It is also important for these processes to be conducted in an appropriate way so that they do not take away from customers' perceptions of the quality of the service.

> *Chapter principle 11.2*: The sport services mix is made up of participants, physical evidence and processes. Participants are those people involved in delivering and receiving a sport service. Physical evidence is the tangible or visual elements of a service such as a sport stadium. Processes represent the steps involved in delivering a sport service.

SPORT SERVICES MARKETING AND THE SERVICE MIX

Although the three services mix elements were originally developed for services marketing in general, they are relevant to the marketing of sport services as well. Chapter 6 showed that most sport products contain intangible elements, and that most sport services include tangible elements. This means that almost all sport marketing involves making decisions about both product and service elements. For example, although sport equipment, memorabilia and merchandise are tangible products, they are sold to consumers through service outlets that can have an influence over consumer perceptions of the product. This fact can be troublesome for manufacturers who do not have control over the sales-related service of their goods.

In addition, it is obvious that the three elements of the services mix interact in ways that make their independent management difficult. For example, those who deliver a sport service are constrained by the physical environment (evidence) that houses their services and by the processes they employ. As a result, it is difficult to develop tactics for the services mix (participants, physical evidence and processes) in a sport marketing plan in the same way as it is done for product, price, place and promotions (and sponsorship as a major part of promotions). In fact, sport services are really just a prominent part of a sport product strategy, and should therefore remain consistent with overarching product strategy. The challenge for sport marketers is to determine where to invest their limited resources to create the best service outcomes for consumers.

One way to approach this challenge is for sport marketers to decide *what* is to be done across the services mix that will lead to a better *quality* of service, stronger *relationships* with consumers and higher levels of their *satisfaction*. The remainder of this chapter explains how service quality, customer relationship building and customer satisfaction are the critical success areas behind the successful marketing of sport services.

> *Chapter principle 11.3*: There are three key principles behind the successful marketing of sport services: service quality, customer relationship building and customer satisfaction.

SERVICE QUALITY

Chapter 6 indicated that product quality is one of the central factors influencing the development of brand equity (brand equity is the added value that a product has because of its brand name). This is also true for service quality. Consumers are more likely to be loyal to a service (leading to greater brand equity) if they perceive that it is of high quality.

> *Chapter principle 11.4*: Sport consumers are more likely to be loyal to a service if they perceive it to be of high quality.

Because of the relative characteristics of sport goods and services, there are different aspects to their quality management. Chapter 6 introduced the elements of product quality, noting that they can be measured relatively easily in terms of whether the product conforms to specifications, how long it lasts and how quickly it is fixed when there are problems. Service quality, on the other hand, is more complex to define because it involves the assessment of an individual consumer's experience. Typically, five dimensions of service quality can be specified, as summarised in Table 11.1.

Service quality can be seen as a consumer's general judgement about the value, superiority or excellence of a service. However, it is difficult to measure this judgement because each consumer will have a unique idea about what a value, excellent or superior service involves. For example, one consumer might believe that the key quality feature of a service is staff courtesy, whereas another might think it more important that the service is delivered on time. To get around this problem, a useful way to understand service quality is to consider it the degree to which a service meets the needs and expectations of consumers. When a consumer's expectations are not met, they are likely to perceive that the service quality is low. When a consumer's expectations are met or exceeded, they are likely to perceive that the service quality is high. There are some obvious connections between service quality and customer satisfaction that are explored later in this chapter.

> *Chapter principle 11.5*: Service quality can be seen as the degree to which a service meets the needs and expectations of consumers.

TABLE 11.1 Five elements of sport service quality

Quality element	Explanation	Examples
Reliability	The ability to provide a service in a consistent and dependable way. Whether customer expectations of the service will be met every time	Is the service performed right the first time? If a service is promised within a certain time, is it delivered? Is the service the same quality regardless of the time of day or staff member who delivers it? Are reports or statements free of errors?
Responsiveness	The willingness to help customers, and to provide them with the service on time	Does the sport organisation respond to problems quickly? Are employees willing to answer customer questions? Are times for delivery/completion of service given to the customer?
Assurance	The level of confidence and trust that a customer holds in the service	Do employees appear to know what they are doing? Are employees able to use equipment and technology skilfully and quickly? Are the materials provided up-to-date?
Empathy	The ability to get to know customers and their needs, and to deliver a personalised service	Do employees try to get to know the needs of the customer? Is the organisation flexible enough to accommodate the customer's schedule? Do employees recognise regular clients and address them by name?
Tangibles	Physical features of the service (e.g. information booklets, equipment, appearance of staff, facilities, sport venue)	Are the facilities attractive? Does the equipment look modern? Are employees dressed appropriately? Are written documents attractive and easy to understand?

Outcome and process quality

When service quality is defined in terms of customer expectations it means that quality is determined by customers not sport organisations. It is whether the service conforms to customers' specifications rather than those of the sport organisation that will determine whether service quality exists. Customers will make a judgement about whether a service is meeting their expectations at two points in time: first, they will evaluate what the service delivered after it has been consumed (outcome quality); and, second, they will evaluate how the service is delivered during consumption (process quality). A customer's judgement about service quality does not therefore rely just on the outcome of a service, but also on judgements about how a service is delivered. In some instances it may be difficult for customers to judge the outcome quality of a service. For example, assessing the immediate results of a fitness or health consultation with a personal trainer or a sports medicine practitioner would be impossible without specific knowledge, or time to see whether the advice led to good results. As a result, when customers have difficulties interpreting outcome quality, they tend to rely on how the service was delivered (process quality) to make their judgements.

> *Chapter principle 11.6*: Customers will make a judgement about whether a service is meeting their expectations at two points in time: first, they will evaluate what the service delivered after it has been consumed (outcome quality); and, second, they will evaluate how the service is delivered during consumption (process quality).

Process quality (how a service is delivered) relates to how the service is delivered to the customer. For example, whether employees are willing to answer questions, whether they recognise customers, and whether they appear to use equipment quickly and skilfully, are features of how the service is being delivered to the customer. Service quality is more strongly related to outcomes. The physical quality of facilities, equipment, documents and staff appearance is not primarily associated with how a service is delivered, but is part of what is delivered. Furthermore, customers will usually make judgements about how reliable a service is after it has been delivered (such as whether a service is performed right the first time, on time, regardless of who is delivering it, see Figure 11.2).

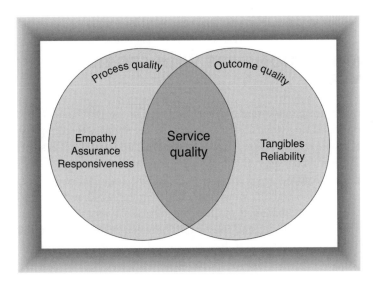

FIGURE 11.2 Sport service quality

INTERACTIVE CASE

There are always some areas that can be designated as the *core* areas of service quality. This will apply to any industry or organisation, including sport. Customers, however, may also have specific expectations about the ways in which certain industries and organisations should go about delivering their service products.

Questions

Provide an example of two sport services in which the service quality dimensions are quite different. What relationship is there between the service quality dimensions and the expectations held by customers?

Points of interest

Expectations can also vary from customer to customer. For example, members of a boxing gym may not be interested in 'modern' looking equipment, but desire, and expect 'back-to-basics' facilities that come with well-worn equipment and the stench of sweat. On the other hand, more professional 'types' who have caught the boxercise 'bug' would like their experience to be clean, neat, tidy and free from even the slightest hint of body odour. For this reason it is important to also understand the unique expectations that customers have about service products. This understanding might partly come from intuition and inspired guesswork, but it will have far more credibility and legitimacy if it comes out of carefully designed market research.

BUILDING RELATIONSHIPS WITH SPORT CONSUMERS

The idea of relationship marketing was first discussed in the 1980s and 1990s. Definitions of relationship marketing typically include statements about attracting, maintaining and improving customer relationships. The word relationship is used because of the fact that two parties are involved (most obviously a supplier and a customer) who interact with one another. Relationship marketing recognises the importance of keeping current customers, as well as attracting new ones, and emphasises that the relationship with customers needs to be managed well to encourage loyalty. It also recognises that organisations rely on networks, and interaction between many different people, not just consumers, to deliver a service and/or product. For example, relationships between suppliers and market intermediaries are also important.

Relationship marketing focuses on the one-to-one relationships between parties, often the buyer and seller, or sport fan and sport organisation. It is also concerned with the quality and long-term potential of this connection, and the fact that both parties can derive a benefit from it. The idea of relationship marketing has more recently been instrumental in the development of customer relationship management (CRM).

CUSTOMER RELATIONSHIP MANAGEMENT

Relationship marketing has made way for the concept of CRM. CRM involves using information technology to better manage customer relationships. More specifically, it involves using information technology to collect information about sport consumers to keep track of their consumption activities, and to create long-term relationships with them.

> *Chapter principle 11.7*: CRM involves the use of information technology to create and maintain ongoing, long-term relationships with sport consumers, leading to high levels of loyalty, and improved sales.

Like relationship marketing, the aim of CRM is to create stronger connections between sport consumers and sport organisations. It involves acquiring relevant information about current and potential sport customers, such as their buying patterns, preferences, consumption habits, motivations and purchasing triggers. Much of this information can be collected at the point of sale and is later used to stimulate communication with customers.

Shopping on Amazon provides a simple example. If a consumer were to search for this text, the Amazon CRM software will subsequently suggest that other consumers who bought this book also purchased others, which are listed, and will likely be associated with sport or marketing in some way. This example shows that CRM involves communicating with consumers on a one-to-one basis, in a way that is quite different to mass marketing. It helps an organisation to anticipate the behaviour of their consumers to improve sales and customer loyalty. In a sport context, most professional clubs and teams use CRM systems to enhance their contact with customers. A standard CRM system can be used to collect data relevant to creating new opportunities for contact with consumers. For example, the software can generate an automatic email message to the parents of a junior member of a club a few weeks before their birthday. The message might offer to sell the latest club merchandise at a 'birthday' discount. In general, the software is capable of analysing thousands of sales, looking for patterns that might help sport marketers to anticipate the needs of their customers. Among the most helpful information, the software can provide guidance on customer preferences, which customers purchase the most, patterns in demand at different times of the year and which products are the most successful.

According to forecasts based on current trends, by around 2017 companies will be spending more on technology to support marketing than they will to bolster infrastructure. We can expect a similar transition for sport enterprises as well. Not only will technology play a driving role in sport, its management as a tool for connecting fans with sport products will become instrumental to success, creating a proliferation of new jobs in sport around customer relationship marketing and data analysis. Any sport organisation operating without a sophisticated customer relationship management system will be left behind. Where CRM was initially just a technical name for a customer database filled with names, addresses and contact details, it now encompasses far more including intricate details on fan preferences, expenditures on merchandise, game attendances, downloads and social media contributions, and even such nuances as meal choices. In fact, any activity that can be logged and recorded can also be studied using CRM systems. It is now becoming the standard to use CRM systems to generate creative interaction with fans too. Some common options sport enterprises are currently experimenting with involve the development of online and social media communities, new and customised entertainment alternatives and add-ons such as games, music, statistics and athlete forums, and rewards schemes offering loyalty-based and highly customised returns to fans committed to engagement. Some new CRM systems can integrate with personalised applications downloaded to smart devices and tablets. As a result, data can be collected about every detail of fan engagement leading to new offerings that are personalised to the point of successfully predicting what an individual fan will want in the future.

CRM involves a six-step process to form the steps identified in Figure 11.3. It should be observed that the process has similarities to the overall Sport Marketing Framework that guides this text because it involves the basic processes of collecting information, segmenting consumers, and developing and implementing a strategy. Each is outlined next.

Develop customer profiles

Sport organisations gather a wide range of data for CRM including the buying patterns, online and application habits, browsing preferences, shopping and spending, motivations and purchasing triggers for both current and potential customers. Typically, such information is collected at the point of sale and is added to a consumer history 'file', which gives a picture of needs, values and behavioural patterns over time. It is also important to collect sales revenue information so that it can be linked with customer histories. This way it is possible to link specific customer profiles to specific consumption behaviour. It is also possible to keep track of what follow-up and support is requested by a customer after their purchase, as this can help sport marketers to more accurately calculate what it has cost to make the sale to that customer.

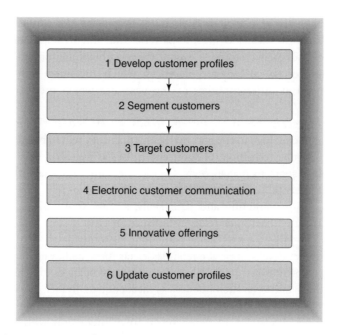

FIGURE 11.3 Six-step process of CRM

Segment customers

CRM software provides additional information that can be used in segmentation. This information can lead to sophisticated patterns of consumption that can provide the basis for specific segmentation categories. For example, consumers can be segmented according to their attendances, merchandise purchases, social club activities or even their online presence. Sport marketers can employ CRM data to help them make decisions about the most appropriate deployment of their marketing resources.

Target customers

Targeting customers involves choosing which sport consumers are going to be the focus of marketing efforts. With CRM, this process includes making a number of estimations about the sport organisation's relationship with the customer such as (1) the likely costs of delivering the sport product or service to that customer, (2) the likely revenue that will be generated through their purchases and (3) the likely value of that customer to the sport organisation over the lifetime of the relationship (this is called customer lifetime value, CLV).

Electronic customer communication

The basic vehicle of CRM is information technology, which of course develops with technological progress. Currently, CRM mainly makes use of database software, websites, mobile or cellular phones and call centres to get messages to consumers. For example, sport consumers may receive messages on their mobile (cellular) phones offering them live sport, scores, replays, tickets or discounted merchandise. However, the technology being employed by sport marketers to communicate with consumers is changing all the time. So important is the application of digital and social media that Chapter 12 is dedicated to it.

Innovative offerings

The key to this step is that sport consumers should be offered opportunities based on their demonstrated needs and buying habits. If the information collected in step one about customer preferences and habits is accurate, it should provide a guide as to what to offer customers next.

Update customer profile

Throughout the process of offering sport customers new products and services, it is important to continue to keep track of how they respond. Over time sport marketers can learn more about consumer habits and preferences, and any changes that occur can lead to an appropriate response.

Chapter tool 11.1 Customer relationship marketing process: The six-step process of CRM is briefly as follows:

1 *Develop customer profiles*: Information could include buying patterns, preferences, shopping habits, motivations for both current and potential customers, and revenue information. This gives a picture of customer needs, values and behavioural patterns over time.

2 *Segment customers*: Segmentation is usually based on buying habits, shopping patterns, preferences etc.

3 *Target customers*: Choose which customers are going to be the focus of marketing efforts. This usually involves estimating (1) the likely costs of delivering the sport product or service to those customers, (2) the likely revenue that will be generated through customer purchases and (3) the likely value of those customers to the sport organisation over the lifetime of the relationship.

4 *Electronic customer communication*: CRM uses information technology such as database software, websites, mobile and cellular phones, and call centres to get messages to customers.

5 *Innovative offerings*: Sport customers should be offered opportunities based on their demonstrated needs and buying habits.

6 *Update customer profiles*: Keep track of customer responses, and learn more about their habits and preferences over time.

CUSTOMER SATISFACTION

There are a wide range of emotional and psychological experiences associated with a sport service that are relevant to satisfaction. In fact, it is reasonable to identify at least five different states of satisfaction: satisfaction as contentment, pleasure, relief, novelty and surprise. These states are described in Table 11.2.

Whether a customer experiences one of the states of satisfaction recorded in the table depends on what they are expecting out of the service in the first place. A customer will evaluate how a service has performed after they have used it, and compare it with the expectations they had prior to consumption. If the customer judges that there is a difference or discrepancy between what they expected and what they received, they will experience a strong reaction to the service. The reaction may be positive or negative, depending on whether the service fell short or exceeded expectations. In other words, there are degrees of satisfaction and dissatisfaction.

> *Chapter principle 11.8*: Since service delivery can stimulate a diverse range of emotional responses, sport marketers must understand how each of their programs yields different satisfaction outcomes for different consumers. Customer satisfaction can take numerous forms including satisfaction as contentment, pleasure, relief, novelty and surprise. A thorough knowledge of this range, and the service delivery measures to generate them, remains essential in securing satisfaction for as many sport consumers as possible.

Satisfaction and quality

Satisfaction and service quality are strongly linked as they represent different sides of the same coin. Both ideas are concerned with what a customer expects from a service. It is important to realise, however, that although these concepts are connected, they are not

TABLE 11.2 Five states of satisfaction

Satisfaction as . . .	Characterised by . . .	Example
Contentment	Habit/continual consumption, low arousal	A leisure facility continues to offer a clean pool as part of their services
Pleasure or relief	Increased pleasure or decreased unpleasant emotions/perceptions (relief)	A sport physiotherapist may help to decrease pain and distress (relief)
		A close match where a consumer's team wins may stimulate positive emotions (pleasure)
Novelty	New performance/experience	A consumer's local fitness centre installs state-of-the-art equipment
Surprise	When the unexpected happens, or the expected does not	Spectators witness an unexpected, record-breaking performance
		When returning a pair of used, faulty running shoes a consumer expects the staff to decline to assist, but they are helpful instead

the same thing. One of the main ways in which they are different is that satisfaction relates to a specific experience (or series of experiences) of consuming a product or service, whereas a customer's perceptions about the quality of a service are not linked to one specific experience. Furthermore, it is also possible for a customer to believe that a service is high quality, even if they have never consumed it. For example, many sport fans would believe that the Wimbledon tennis event offers a high-quality service, although most would never have attended. It is also possible to feel satisfied by a service while still feeling that it is not a high quality. A good example of this may be a customer who is satisfied by a service because it was inexpensive, even if it was of low quality, such as cheap tickets to a sport event that are a long way from the action. Customers can be satisfied by a service that is low in quality if it meets their needs.

Service quality is also different from satisfaction in that customers usually judge quality based on service attributes, and their ideas of what an excellent service should entail. On the other hand, customer satisfaction is affected by many things (other than the service attributes), which are out of the control of the service producer, such as the weather, and parking availability. From this perspective it is likely that customer satisfaction, rather than customer perceptions of service quality, gives a better indication of the sport organisations that perform better in the marketplace.

If a customer experiences satisfaction repeatedly from a sport service, this can lead to a belief that the service is of a high quality. In addition, as service quality increases, satisfaction also tends to increase. In fact, satisfaction can be affected by a customer's perceptions of service quality. Even though satisfaction and quality are two different ideas, they influence each other.

Chapter principle 11.9: Focusing on customer satisfaction ensures that sport marketers make the needs and perceptions of their customers a priority, which in turn leads to stronger loyalty to the sport organisation and its products.

Critical incidents and satisfaction

Satisfaction is also a function of the number of times an incident associated with a sporting service is reported to be negative. Sequential incident techniques (SIT) are often used to capture 'customer experiences'. Within the assumptions of this model customers and fans are asked to identify favourable and unfavourable experiences for specific episodes and incidents that occur in the process of experiencing a sport performance. Episodes and incidents are incorporated into a customer experiential pathway (CEP). Take, for example, the sequence of events involved in attending a Formula 1 motor race meeting. The first thing to do is identify this experiential pathway that begins from leaving home, travelling to the event, attending the race, going through the race debrief, and returning home. This may involve the following ten-step process:

- Step 1: Travel to venue
- Step 2: Arrival and move to venue
- Step 3: Entry point to venue
- Step 4: Admission
- Step 5: Movement to seat
- Step 6: Seating and viewing
- Step 7: Event quality
- Step 8: Other fans and spectators
- Step 9: Exit from venue
- Step 10: Return home.

All negative and positive incidents are compiled, and the most frequently cited incidents are then highlighted and interrogated. When all the data have been complied, and evaluated, action is then taken to remedy the problem incidents, and thus improve the levels of satisfaction for consumers next time round. These remedies and recommendations can then be fed into the planning process for subsequent events.

CUSTOMER SATISFACTION AND SPORT MARKETING

Customer satisfaction is an important concept for sport marketers to understand for two reasons. First, it encourages sport marketing efforts to remain focused on the needs of customers, making these needs and associated perceptions of sport products a priority. As Chapter 1 stressed, the most basic idea in sport marketing is that of meeting the needs of consumers. Second, customer satisfaction can influence not only a customer's intention to purchase, but also their repeat purchasing over time. Simply put, a satisfied customer is more likely to be loyal than an unsatisfied one.

> *Chapter principle 11.10:* Customer satisfaction is a judgement that customers make after they have experienced a sport service where they compare what they expected from it with what they believe they actually received. When expectations are met or exceeded, customers are satisfied, and when expectations are not met, customers are dissatisfied.

Delighting the customer

An idea related to customer satisfaction is that of delighting the customer. It occurs when a customer's expectations are exceeded to a surprising degree, resulting in an extremely positive emotional state. In these circumstances, the customer is more than just satisfied. They may feel excited, exhilarated or other positive emotions that have a strong physiological element.

The importance of the concept of delight is best understood in the context of satisfaction. As the previous section established, customers compare what they expect from a service with how it actually performs. If the service performs worse than they expected they are likely to feel dissatisfied, but if it meets or exceeds their expectations they are likely to feel satisfied. It is the degree to which the service exceeds expectations that determines whether a customer experiences satisfaction or delight. If the service exceeds expectations within a normal range, a customer may simply feel satisfied. For example, if a parent receives a free coffee when waiting to pick up their child from a karate class at a leisure centre, then they might experience satisfaction slightly above the normal expectations. However, if a service performs to a surprisingly positive degree, then a customer might experience delight. The key here is that delight comes about when the service has performed to a level that the customer could not have reasonably expected. For example, if a sport fan's seat was upgraded at a sport event as the result of a loyalty programme, then they might experience delight. The difficulty for sport marketers is that eliciting delight can only occur if the service performs to a surprisingly high level, and this means that the sport organisation must put in substantial extra effort and resources. There is also the danger of resetting expectations to a higher and unsustainable level. There are three types of delight that are useful for sport marketers to manipulate.

> *Chapter principle 11.11*: Customer delight occurs when a customer's expectations are exceeded to a surprising degree, resulting in an extremely positive emotional state. Delight transpires when the customer is more than just satisfied. This can happen when a service exceeds a customer's expectations of what they think is normal or reasonable from that particular sport service.

Assimilated, re-enacted and transitory delight

A general principle is that when customers are delighted they are more likely to be loyal to a sport service than if they were merely satisfied. However, it is also true that delight can increase customer expectations, which will make customer satisfaction much more difficult in the future. How then can a sport organisation know whether it is beneficial to try to delight their customers? Three different types of delight – assimilated, re-enacted and transitory – help to answer this question as each has a different effect on customer experiences and expectations.

Assimilated delight

Feelings of delight do not stay permanently with a customer; they will not continue to feel the physical intensity of delight (such as excitement or exhilaration) indefinitely, although they are likely to remember the experience. If, for example, fitness centre customers remember being delighted the last time they used a service, their expectations may be raised well above normal. This may be termed assimilated delight, because the customer has incorporated the things that delighted them into their expectations of what is normal. The customer may even tell others about the features of the service, and as a result others may also come to expect a high level of performance as normal. Worse, competing organisations may hear about what is being offered and duplicate it themselves, which of course will mean that there is nothing unique about the original service. As a result, sport organisations have to carefully consider whether the cost of providing a delighting feature is worth it.

Re-enacted delight

Re-enacted delight occurs when a customer savours the memory of being delighted. A good example is a football fan who experienced serious delight when attending an exhilarating match where Christiano Ronaldo delivers one of his sublime performances. The delight doesn't stop there, since she then enjoys remembering and re-living the experience over and over again. She may watch replays, chat about it on the Internet or attend other matches at the same venue or between the same teams to recreate the original feelings. It is as if she re-experiences the original delight even though subsequent performances may be significantly inferior.

Re-enacted delight can happen when customers realise that the delighting experience is unique and cannot be easily recreated. They accept that they cannot reasonably expect it to happen on a regular basis. This is often true of experiences of sport participation and spectating. This has marketing implications since a sport organisation may encourage re-enacted delight by creating one-off or once-per-season special events that customers will remember fondly in the future. The organisation can also help customers and participants to develop strong memories through recreations, ceremonies and memorabilia related to the delightful event, as well as recordings or online content.

Transitory delight

The final type of delight, transitory delight, occurs when customers forget that they had once been delighted. This means that they will not expect the delighting features to be present when they use the service again in the future; they may be delighted all over again as if it is the first time! For example, if a customer attributes the delightful experience to pure chance or fate, they may decide that it is unlikely to happen again. They may also attribute good service to one particular staff member, not the organisation, and therefore not expect the same service again in the future. It is possible, in these scenarios that a customer's reaction to the experience is fleeting, and they forget about what delighted them after some time has passed.

Should delighting sport customers be a priority marketing goal?

At first glance it seems plainly obvious that the more we delight customers the more repeat business we will get. But once we dig deeper into this issue, we find that delighting customers will sometimes pay off, but other times may not. For example, with assimilated delight it is possible that customer expectations will be raised to another level, and that this will make it difficult to satisfy customers' desires in the future. Some critics of 'customer delight' theory argue that, although delighting the customer may help profitability in some situations, it is probable that customer dissatisfaction hurts a sport organisation more than delight helps it. This means that it is generally more effective to focus on reducing dissatisfaction and complaints (therefore increasing overall satisfaction), rather than focusing on trying to achieve the next level of 'delight'. The most important point to take away from these comments is that sport marketers must be aware of the situations in which delighting the customer can be profitable, and the times when it may be a counterproductive investment.

> *Chapter principle 11.12*: Providing customer delight in a sport service can lead to higher levels of loyalty, word of mouth promotion and an advantage over competitors. However, it is essential to know how customer satisfaction/delight influences customer behaviour. It is also important to consider how capable competitors are of copying any innovative service features. It is usually better to invest resources in decreasing customer dissatisfaction than in increasing customer delight.

INTERACTIVE CASE

Review the Sport England sport satisfaction and quality survey, paying careful attention to the categories of questions and the responses across the sector.

www.sportengland.org
(www.sportengland.org/research/about-our-research/satisfaction-with-the-quality-of-the-sporting-experience-survey/)

Questions

What kind of information will a survey of this nature provide about customer satisfaction? Would it tell a sport marketer whether his or her customers have been 'delighted'? Is this necessarily a service quality priority?

Points of interest

It is important to know whether customer satisfaction/delight has a strong influence on customer behaviour. For example, will delight result in loyalty, word of mouth promotion, or will it be overlooked as irrelevant? One way to find out this kind of information is through market research and pilot programmes. In addition, the role of competitors is important. For example, competitors with substantial resources will find it easier to imitate novel services. In this instance there may be limited advantage in raising expectations.

PRINCIPLES SUMMARY

- Chapter principle 11.1: There are four characteristics that illustrate the difference between sport goods and services: tangibility, consistency, perishability and separability. Sport services are intangible because they exist only as an experience. Sport services tend to be inconsistent because they are affected by variables that are difficult to control. Sport services are perishable because they can only be offered and experienced once at any point in time. Sport services are inseparable because they are consumed at the same time as they are produced.

- Chapter principle 11.2: The sport services mix is made up of participants, physical evidence and processes. Participants are those people involved in delivering and receiving a sport service. Physical evidence is the tangible or visual elements of a service such as a sport stadium. Processes represent the steps involved in delivering a sport service.

- Chapter principle 11.3: There are three key principles behind the successful marketing of sport services: service quality, customer relationship building and customer satisfaction.

- Chapter principle 11.4: Sport consumers are more likely to be loyal to a service if they perceive it to be of high quality.

- Chapter principle 11.5: Service quality can be seen as the degree to which a service meets the needs and expectations of consumers.

- Chapter principle 11.6: Customers will make a judgement about whether a service is meeting their expectations at two points in time: first, they will evaluate what the service delivered after it has been consumed (outcome quality); and, second, they will evaluate how the service is delivered during consumption (process quality).

- Chapter principle 11.7: CRM involves the use of information technology to create and maintain ongoing, long-term relationships with sport consumers, leading to high levels of loyalty, and improved sales.

- Chapter principle 11.8: Since service delivery can stimulate a diverse range of emotional responses, sport marketers must understand how each of their programs yields different satisfaction outcomes for different consumers. Customer satisfaction can take numerous forms including satisfaction as contentment, pleasure, relief, novelty and surprise. A thorough knowledge of this range, and the service delivery measures to generate them, remains essential in securing satisfaction for as many sport consumers as possible.

- Chapter principle 11.9: Focusing on customer satisfaction ensures that sport marketers make the needs and perceptions of their customers a priority, which in turn leads to stronger loyalty to the sport organisation and its products.

- Chapter principle 11.10: Customer satisfaction is a judgement that customers make after they have experienced a sport service where they compare what they expected from it with what they believe they actually received. When expectations are met or exceeded, customers are satisfied, and when expectations are not met, customers are dissatisfied.

- Chapter principle 11.11: Customer delight occurs when a customer's expectations are exceeded to a surprising degree, resulting in an extremely positive emotional state. Delight transpires when the customer is more than just satisfied. This can happen when a service exceeds a customer's expectations of what they think is normal or reasonable from that particular sport service.

- Chapter principle 11.12: Providing customer delight in a sport service can lead to higher levels of loyalty, word of mouth promotion and an advantage over competitors. However, it is essential to know how customer satisfaction/delight influences customer behaviour. It is also important to consider how capable competitors are of copying any innovative service features. It is usually better to invest resources in decreasing customer dissatisfaction than in increasing customer delight.

TOOLS SUMMARY

- Chapter tool 11.1 Customer relationship marketing process

REVIEW QUESTIONS

1   Identify the elements of the sport services mix. Provide an example of how each is relevant to the marketing of sport services.
2   Explain what sport service quality is and compare it with sport goods quality.
3   Provide an example of each of the five areas of service quality.
4   Explain how customer satisfaction and dissatisfaction come about.
5   What is the relationship between service quality and customer satisfaction?
6   How does CRM lead to opportunities for customer loyalty?
7   Under what circumstances is customer delight worth pursuing?

RELEVANT WEBSITES

www.sportengland.org   Sport England

FURTHER READING

Ko, Y.J., Zhang, J., Cattani, K. and Pastore, D. (2011). Assessment of event quality in major spectator sports. *Managing Service Quality*, 21(3), 304–322.

Lee, J.H., Kim, H.D., Ko, Y.J. and Sagas, M. (2011). The influence of service quality on satisfaction and intention: A gender segmentation strategy. *Sport Management Review*, 14(1), 54–63.

Theodorakis, N.D., Alexandris, K., Tsigilis, N. and Karvounis, S. (2013). Predicting spectators' behavioural intentions in professional football: The role of satisfaction and service quality. *Sport Management Review*, 16(1), 85–96.

CHAPTER 12

Sport digital marketing and social media

LEARNING OUTCOMES

At the end of this chapter, readers should be able to:

- understand the terms digital and social media marketing
- define the advantages and disadvantages of digital and social media marketing
- describe how digital and social media marketing relate to the Sport Marketing Framework
- identify the six key principles of social media marketing
- describe the six-step process of engaging consumers with social media marketing
- outline the five broad categories of digital marketing technology
- differentiate between available social media tools and their appropriate deployment in sport marketing
- study digital and social media examples by interacting with cutting-edge existing sites and through brief cases.

OVERVIEW

The purpose of this chapter is to explain the application of digital and social media approaches to sport marketing, including the new kinds of thinking they require. It explores the kinds of technologies and tools that are available to sport marketers and considers the influence that digital marketing and media have on the sport marketing mindset.

INTRODUCING THE DIGITAL REVOLUTION

It is easy enough to understand digital sport marketing as any form of marketing that utilises technology, which of course means a focus on the Internet and all the devices, channels and media that it implicates. At the same time, this broad definition no longer helps distinguish digital marketing from other forms in an era when just about every marketing activity involves a digital aspect. Even conventional printed flyers rely on print-on-demand technologies, while even modest sporting events utilise digital ticketing in order to save money. The simple act of watching sport live cannot escape the digital era either. Most surveys suggest that around half of sport fans refer to their smartphones for extra content during events. At the same time as the technologies and tools of the digital era have become entrenched in our marketing expectations, sport marketers must come to terms with a new way of looking at their offerings. In short, sport digital marketing and social media demand a new kind of mindset where the conventional distance between sport properties, their marketing representatives, and fans is completely blurred, and where success means constant adaptation. No longer are digital and social media tools just 'add-ons' to the standard marketing methods. Today, a digital world needs a digital message.

Digital marketing is often described as electronic marketing and is usually associated with the Internet, computers, and forms of mobile communications. To phrase this more generally, digital marketing refers to communications that are generated by electronic means or through recent (non-analogue) technological platforms. Digital marketing refers to technologically sophisticated platforms or vehicles for transmitting and communicating information. In this chapter, we describe how all of these digital platforms are revolutionising sport marketing and have justifiably become essential tools in the toolkit. By implication of the escalation of digital channels, as a secondary goal of this chapter, we also explain how social media must become a central element in a sport organisation's digital profile. The term 'social media', like the term 'marketing', can mean different things depending on the context. We take a broad view in referring to social media as any instrument or means of communicating information that relies on the interactions between networked groups of individuals. It is important to take a broad view like this because technology has provided the sport marketer with so many innovative ways of communicating with the general public that they no longer have to rely only on traditional 'media' organisations.

> *Chapter principle 12.1*: Digital sport marketing refers to communications that are generated by electronic means, or through recent technological platforms. It refers to technologically sophisticated platforms or vehicles for transmitting and communicating information, including social media channels, which utilise the interactions of networked individuals.

Today, digital content is delivered through many devices such as smartphones, PDAs, tablets and MP3 music players. The information can even be transferred seamlessly from one digital technology to another and from one digital format to another (for example from a mobile phone to a computer). Another feature of digital media is that data, or information, is accessible in real time. Digital media is especially important in sport marketing because it permeates all aspects of consumers' lives.

> *Chapter principle 12.2*: Digital media is flexible, transferable and can be customised.

Not long ago, digital media, and especially social media, were seen as the latest technological trends, but it has now become indisputable that they have significant and permanent implications for sport marketing. Digital media is more than technology and tools; it requires a different style of marketing where sport marketers can communicate in novel ways with sport consumers. It is also important because it creates additional opportunities in sport, such as new assets and revenues (such as website and mobile digital rights, as well as new sales channels), and new possibilities in licensing and merchandising (such as computer games). Although the types of technologies that are available continue to change and develop, the principle remains the same: sport marketers can use advanced technology to communicate with their customers and sell them extra products and services that are associated with sport. Perhaps more importantly, the social media dimension of the digital revolution allows marketers and sport organisations an unprecedented connectivity with their customer and fan base.

The popularity and prevalence of digital and social media technology mean that it provides sport marketers with innovative ways of communicating with consumers. Many of these communication approaches are far more rapid, responsive and interactive than other marketing strategies. For example, compare the one-way content of television with the opportunity to customise a replay directly to a consumer's smartphone. Not only are digital media platforms fast and direct, they are also inexpensive compared with traditional techniques of sport marketing. Even more importantly, digital media enables sport organisations to develop messages that are personalised to key target audiences.

Chapter principle 12.3: Digital and social media technologies provide sport marketers with new ways of communicating with consumers, and novel approaches to their marketing activities. Many of these approaches are far more rapid, responsive, interactive and inexpensive when compared with other marketing strategies; they are also more easily customised to key target audiences.

INTERACTIVE CASE

In one memorable digital marketing campaign launched by baseball equipment manufacturer, Louisville Slugger, the company leveraged the 2013 success of the newly crowned World Series champions, the St Louis Cardinals, by using a scavenger hunt.

Questions

Visit the Louisville Slugger website: http://slugger.com
In considering the content, look at the Twitter, Facebook and Instagram platforms that the company maintains as a core part of its digital marketing strategy. What do you notice about the social media presence the company maintains? How is it distinguished from other sporting equipment manufacturers' websites?

Points of interest

Using Facebook and Twitter as promotional channels, Louisville Slugger orchestrated a scavenger hunt, hiding 45 baseball bats around the city with clues periodically posted as to their locations. An immediate runaway success, Louisville Slugger's Facebook followers skyrocketed from 755 followers to more than 7,000. Facebook likes escalated by nearly 150 per cent at the same time as its Twitter following increased by a similar margin.

DIGITAL SPORT MARKETING: RETHINKING SPORT MARKETING

At its most simple, digital sport marketing refers to the use of electronic media technologies, tools and channels in marketing programmes. However, digital marketing means more than just using up-to-date technology within a traditional marketing programme. It also refers to a novel marketing approach that recognises the complex social and technological world that sport consumers occupy. To be effective, digital marketing must do more than just use new technology. It also has to respond to the changing lifestyles and expectations of sport consumers.

Sport consumers are inundated with marketing messages. Despite the technological options, sport marketers must compete with a vast range of entertainment and communication technologies. There is an enormous amount of 'clutter' in the marketing environment, and sport marketers must find ways to cut through it. In this new environment, conventional marketing strategies are becoming less effective. As a result, sport marketers must be aware of the ways in which sport consumers' lives have changed, and the corresponding new expectations they have of sport products and marketing programmes. For example, sport consumers have limited discretionary leisure time, consume more media from a greater variety of media outlets, belong to numerous virtual networks, and tend to be fragmented as an audience (leading to the erosion of mass media effectiveness). Sport consumers also possess new expectations including personalised experiences, interactivity, choice and control, the opportunity to multitask (Generation M) and access to user-generated content.

Digital sport marketing recognises that consumers are exposed to an immense amount of marketing and have a wide range of sport product choices at their fingertips. As a consequence, sport consumers are less likely to be convinced by mass media sales pitches. In fact, consumers can be resistant to traditional marketing strategies such as advertising campaigns. It is important to note that the digital marketing approach does not render the standard principles of marketing obsolete, but it does give the sport marketer new principles to wield that are particularly relevant to the current environment. The presence of new technological tools should therefore sharpen sport marketers' thinking about the pace of marketing and the nature of interaction and communication with consumers.

Chapter principle 12.4: Digital sport marketing demands customised communication with targeted sport consumers, generated by electronic means or through technologically sophisticated platforms that facilitate the transmission of information.

There are six key dimensions that summarise the thinking that must underpin digital sport marketing that can be employed by sport marketers to engage better with consumers. These are customisation, modularity, sticky branding, networked communication, inclusivity and permission. The principles are illustrated in Figure 12.1 and are described next.

Chapter principle 12.5: Digital sport marketing involves targeted and personalised interactions based on the principles of customisation, modularity, sticky branding, networked communication and permission.

Customisation

As opposed to a mass marketing approach, digital sport marketing is targeted and customised. New media technology gives marketers specific information about the behaviours and preferences of their consumers. As a result, marketing can become more specialised and nuanced, directed precisely towards the personal needs and choices of customers. Digital options are instrumental in converting scattered mass marketing into surgical direct marketing.

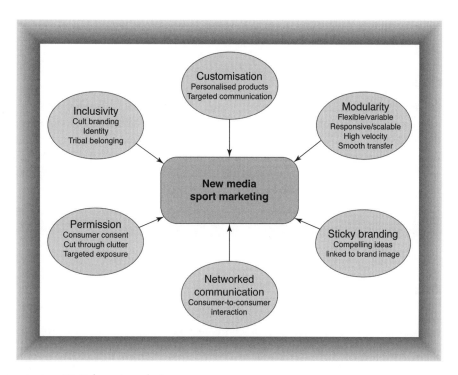

FIGURE 12.1 Digital sport marketing

The concept of behavioural targeting through social media profiling is one example of potential customisation. New technology is also changing the way in which sport products are designed and personalised. Nike, for example, allows customers to design their own customised footwear. In the 1990s, the technological sophistication required to offer reasonably priced, customised footwear to the general public was not available. Now, however, Nike is able to capitalise on technology, and is able to cater to consumers' demands for individualised products that give them a sense of personal identity and control.

Chapter principle 12.6: Customisation: Digital sport marketing messages should be customised or targeted and adapted to specific consumers and their needs.

INTERACTIVE CASE

A great example can be seen in the digital marketing strategy developed by the NHL team, the New Jersey Devils. In 2011, the franchise broke new ground by establishing the first professional sport social media centre.

Questions

Go to the New Jersey Devils website and explore the content under the 'Fanzone' tab: http://devils.nhl.com

What is a 'Fanzone'? How does it seem to work? In what ways would a sport marketer be able to capitalise on the connections made through the Fanzone?

Points of interest

Unashamedly ambitious in stature and name, the 'Mission Control Center' was distinguished by its use of fans at the hub of the model. Given the task of stimulating and monitoring online 'chatter' connected to the team, 25 committed fans delivered a sense of authenticity and independence that resonated with other fans. In addition to winning the team numerous awards for social media engagement, the approach has suggested a new model for customising social media cultivation.

Modularity

A modular object is composed of elements or units that conform to a regular standard and can stand alone in functionality or combine with other modules to provide new functionality. This allows flexibility and variety in the way the elements are used. For example, Lego blocks can be joined and arranged in an incredible variety of constructions. Digital marketing technology is often structured in a modular fashion, such as sports betting websites that provide a set format (or 'unit') for setting up a betting account and standardised systems for using its interactive services. Another simple example is email. It can stand alone as an independent form of communication, or it can be linked into other forms such as mobile devices, Facebook, electronic newsletters and automated databases.

From a digital sport marketing perspective, modularity means that communication with consumers can be fast, responsive, simple and flexible. It is important that the marketing message is fast because the more quickly an idea passes from one consumer to another, the larger the number of consumers who will come into contact with it before it dies out. Velocity is also important in dealing with customer enquiries, orders and demands. Sport consumers expect services to operate responsively and products to be delivered almost instantaneously.

Digital sport marketing can provide fast and responsive solutions to consumers, and allows an unprecedented level of responsiveness to changing demand levels. A modular system can be scaled up and down easily, meaning that it can easily adjust to servicing small or large numbers of people as demand changes. A club's Internet message board, for instance, may need to be able to receive and organise increased traffic after a significant event such as a season final win or a player scandal.

Modularity should also enable smoothness of information transfer between consumers. Being able to access and spread ideas through the click of one button is an ideal example. The ideal scenario is to have an idea or product that is so smooth that once someone is exposed to it, they are instantly hooked. Examples of functions that make ideas effortless to transfer are 'Tell-a-friend' tools on websites; 'save to my web' and 'email this page' icons; 'furl this site' links; and 'forward to a friend' functions. Presently, the most powerful method for spreading information quickly is through Twitter.

> *Chapter principle 12.7*: *Modularity*: A modular digital marketing programme (including product design) is standardised and automated incorporating flexibility, responsiveness to changes in demand, and ease of transfer.

INTERACTIVE CASE

Examples are springing up all the time with major sport properties partnering with serious social media players to offer modular platforms for engagement. One method that does not require a commercial partnership was utilised by Major League Baseball. The league developed what they called the 'MLB Fan Cave' incorporating Tweets from bloggers aiming to engage fans with play-by-play accounts of every game.

Questions

Log on to Major League Baseball's Fan Cave: http://mlb.mlb.com/fancave
Why was the Fan Cave strategy so successful? Using an example from another sport with which you are familiar, explain how you would introduce a Fan Cave.

Points of interest

In another example, NASCAR teamed with Twitter to deliver a television commercial unveiled via a conventional hashtag, but also incorporating an exclusively customised micro social networking site.

Sticky branding

An idea or product has to stand out from the crowd to last or even to be noticed at all. People will respond to an idea if it is compelling or gripping in some way. In the case of sports, what the sport marketer ultimately wants is for an idea to stick that says something about the sport brand. An all-male professional sport league, for example, may wish to attach ideas of masculinity, drama and physical power to their brand to attract male viewers. This could be achieved by posting game highlights and physical clashes on YouTube or through posting imagery on their website of heavily muscled players captured in dramatic poses.

The key point here is that the sport brand must be linked with ideas that are 'sticky' – or that take hold in consumers' minds – and that are consistent with the positioning strategy for the brand image. As consumers may respond to many different kinds of ideas, the key is to identify those that are consistent with the marketing strategy. Some of the more effective 'sticky' ideas are funny, sexualised, thought-provoking, offering financial profit, horrible, shocking, beautiful, hyper-real, attention-grabbing, involving sensory bombardment, unconventional and unpredictable. A sticky idea may also be one that meets a niche need or fills a market gap. There are many effective digital tools that can be used to propagate sticky content, such as social networking sites, web pages and social bookmarking/photo-sharing services. Following are a number of activities that offer the opportunity to explore and reflect on the marketing potential of these networking hubs. First, consider the essential social networking site, Facebook. It allows consumers to read blogs, participate in conversations, and communicate interactively with sport organisations, players and other fans.

> *Chapter principle 12.8: Sticky branding*: Occurs when digital sport marketing content takes hold in consumers' minds in ways that are consistent with the positioning strategy for the brand, and as a result are readily passed on digitally.

Networked communication

The fourth principle of digital marketing is networked communication, which refers to the use of digital platforms and social media to facilitate communication between consumers. It allows a network of communication to develop, rather than just a one-way projection of information to the customer. Put very simply, it means getting consumers to talk to each other. The idea of networked communication is based on the idea that instead of telling consumers about certain products, it is more productive to get consumers to talk to each other about the products. This is easier than ever before because social media platforms allow an interactive approach where marketers can organise consumers to communicate with one another. For this reason, digital sport marketing tends to be focused on marketing activities that bring consumers together, such as online communities, blogs, podcasts and message boards. Digital marketing is not just a set of tools for communication, but is also a hub of consumer interaction and commercial activity.

Networked communication provides consumers with a personalised experience, and because of this it is sometimes called engagement marketing. It stresses the importance of fostering the interaction between consumers in a way that encourages word of mouth (word of mouse) communication to facilitate their interest in the sport product. This is based on the premise that consumer-to-consumer (C2C) marketing is more powerful than business-to-consumer (B2C) marketing as occurs with traditional advertising.

Viral marketing is a prominent example of networked communication using digital and social media technologies. A virus is an infectious agent that replicates itself and spreads from one living thing to another. Although it may start out in small numbers, in the right environment a virus will grow exponentially. Viral marketing is a term that describes any marketing message that is designed to be passed on from one consumer to another. Like a virus, the aim of viral marketing is to encourage rapid communication from one person to another, until thousands, or even millions of people have been 'infected'. Viral marketing is therefore a systematic approach that aims to encourage people to share a marketing message with their personal contact network.

> *Chapter principle 12.9: Networked communication*: Networked communication is based on the idea that instead of telling consumers about products, it is more productive to get consumers to talk to each other about them.

Inclusivity

The principle of inclusivity in digital and social media marketing is closely related to the idea of networked marketing. Because digital channels can provide sport consumers with a platform for communication and interaction, it lends itself to offering them something to belong to. Sport consumers are motivated by a psychological need to feel as if they 'belong' to a group. In particular, digital sport marketing can be conducted in such a way that sport consumers feel 'included' in virtual groups.

> *Chapter principle 12.10: Inclusivity*: Refers to the use of digital marketing to fulfil the need to 'belong', which in turn fosters the development of identity and a stronger connection to the sport brand.

Permission

The sixth principle of digital marketing is permission. Some traditional approaches to marketing are based on the idea of 'interruption', or marketing at consumers. For example, an advertisement on television can be seen to 'interrupt' a viewer with an unanticipated message as they watch a programme. Marketers hope that even though the viewer was not expecting to see their advertisement, it will nevertheless influence their brand perceptions and purchase intentions. Another simple example of interruption marketing is Internet banner advertising, where a banner unexpectedly appears on a computer screen in an attempt to entice the operator to click through to a website. In both of these examples, the communication of information is one way: from the marketer to the consumer. Many consumers are resistant to these kinds of advertising campaigns. In addition, such advertising strategies are largely ineffective because the market is flooded with them and consumers have learnt to tune out to their invasive messages.

In contrast to 'interruption' marketing, better digital sport marketing is based on the idea of 'permission', which leads to deeper engagement. This is often referred to as permission marketing and refers to the use of digital content to communicate with sport consumers who have given their permission to receive customised messages, usually via email, smartphones, social media sites and applications, and PDA devices. Not only can permission-based approaches help to overcome the problem of consumers' inboxes overflowing with spam, they also help marketers to segment and target consumers more accurately and therefore cut through the advertising clutter. Usually consumers will sign up to receive the messages and communications they actually want, which in turn drives engagement and deeper levels of sport brand identification. For example, subscription-based short message service (SMS) instant messaging may be an option where a sport stadium could message members to inform them about parking, short queues, half-time food and beverage specials, merchandise deals, games results on other courts/arenas and perhaps in the future instant video replays. Requiring fans to complete a simple registration to receive this content means that relevant messages are sent to interested recipients.

> *Chapter principle 12.11*: *Permission*: Refers to the effectiveness of communicating with consumers who have consented to receive customised messages, rather than sending random, untargeted and uninvited marketing communications.

Compared with traditional marketing, digital sport marketing can help sport organisations to spread messages quickly to a large but targeted audience at a relatively low cost. However, there are disadvantages as well. First, it is not possible to control the content that is generated through networked communication and interaction. This exposes sport properties to the risk of negative opinions and public perceptions. In some cases as we will describe in the social media section later in this chapter, sometimes it is athletes and players who generate unwanted attention through inappropriate and occasionally scandalous blogs, tweets and uploads. Second, it is often difficult to control the timing of some aspects of the digital marketing campaign. Technological innovation creates both opportunities and challenges for sport organisations. It is also important to note that digital sport marketing should not replace traditional marketing principles. In fact, digital marketing should be considered a (potentially powerful) marketing strategy that can be used within the Sport Marketing Framework. A summary of the digital sport marketing principles appears in Table 12.1.

TABLE 12.1 Summary of digital sport marketing principles

Principle	Description
Customisation	The marketing message, as well as the products themselves, should be targeted and customised to specific consumers and their needs
Modularity	The marketing programme (including product design) should be structured in a standardised and automated way that allows it to be flexible, responsive to changes in demand, and quick and easy to pass from one person to another
Sticky branding	The brand must be linked with ideas that are 'sticky' – or that take hold in people's minds – and that are consistent with the marketing plan for the brand image
Networked communication	Digital content allows a network of communication to develop between consumers, as well as between consumers and the organisation. Networked communication is based on the idea that instead of telling consumers about your products, it is more productive to get consumers to talk to each other about your products
Inclusivity	Through networked communities and user interaction, digital technologies can fulfil the need to 'belong', which in turn fosters the development of identity. Digital marketing can be conducted in such a way that people feel 'included' in virtual groups
Permission	This refers to the fact that it is often more effective to communicate with customers who have given their permission to receive customised messages, rather than to send random, untargeted and uninvited information

THE DIGITAL SPORT MARKETING PROCESS

To review, the six elements of digital sport marketing are *customisation, modularity, sticky branding, networked communication, inclusivity* and *permission*. When these ideas are understood as a package, they suggest that there is a process involved in engaging consumers through digital marketing. First, sport organisations must make *contact* with consumers using compelling ideas to capture their attention and the features of modularity to ensure the contact is fast, flexible and smooth. Once contacted, consumers may respond to the customised offerings and engage in *conversation* via the networked and interactive capabilities of the platform. Conversation leads consumers to make social *connections* with other users, with whom they can share *content*. Over time this interaction leads to the development of a deeper sense of *community* and belonging to the other users, the platform, and the sport property.

A sport consumer may then become a *convert*: someone convinced of certain beliefs and ideas that are shared through the platform, which, in the best-case scenario, include the sticky ideas that have been attached to the brand image. This process is represented in the diagram in Figure 12.2.

Even though sport consumers may not be receptive to some traditional marketing strategies, they still want to participate in sport-related consumption in both traditional

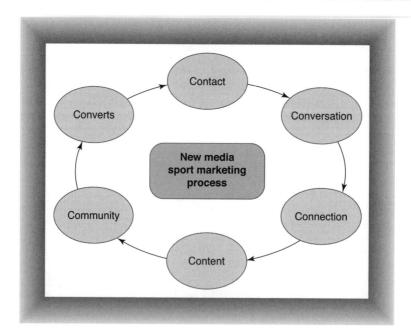

FIGURE 12.2 Digital sport marketing process

and novel ways. This means that sport marketers must engage the sport consumer and find ways for them to identify and belong to the sport product and organisation. Sport marketers must utilise personalised strategies in their marketing programmes. Fortunately, new technology allows sport marketers to develop an unprecedented combination of consumer interaction and marketing customisation. The tools of digital sport marketing are available to almost all sport organisations and therefore represent an unprecedented level of access to consumers that has conventionally been the purview of only the most well-resourced sport organisations.

DIGITAL SPORT MARKETING TOOLS

The digital sport marketing principles outlined in the previous section can be used to help achieve the positioning strategy specified as an outcome of following the Sport Marketing Framework. In this section, some technological tools for implementing digital sport marketing principles are outlined.

The introduction of digital marketing into the sport marketing realm means that the context of marketing is changing and that there are more tools for communicating with sport consumers than there have ever been before. In general, the most popular tools of marketing, such as advertising, are only available to those organisations with plenty of resources. However, with the use of new digital tools, any sport organisation can be seen and heard. Sport organisations may also be able to collect market research data more easily than ever before and therefore understand their customers better. There is software, for example, that sport marketers can use to monitor blogs written about their brand that will report on certain keyword or phrases. This potentially enables sport marketers to monitor positive, negative and incorrect information that is being published about them, and also to learn about the attitudes and needs of their consumers. Similar software add-ons such as RSS enable the search and retrieval of news headlines or stories. These examples exemplify how important it is for sport marketers to understand the different types of digital tools that are at their disposal, and to continue to keep up-to-date with developments in new technologies, software and applications. In this section, the central, available digital tools are outlined. This leads into the final section of the chapter, which examines social media as the most powerful integrative tool in the digital sport marketing space.

Digital technologies can be classified into five tools, although some overlap between categories is inevitable. They are (1) Internet-driven platforms, (2) mobile communications, (3) upgraded conventional technologies, (4) hardware and (5) software. These categories are illustrated in Figure 12.3.

Following are some further examples of each digital tool. These lists are not exhaustive and, given the pace of development, new devices will continually be added. Despite the likelihood that these examples will become dated soon after the printing of this text, they will continue to provide a useful starting point for thinking about each category.

Internet-driven platforms

Internet-driven platforms include the increasingly sophisticated methods of communicating that the World Wide Web supports, such as blogs and social networking sites, email, web

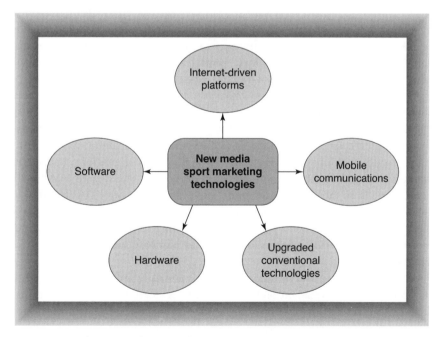

FIGURE 12.3 Digital sport marketing technologies

video, podcasts, vodcasts, websites, pop-ups, spam, virtual worlds, wikis, electronic commerce (such as online and mobile payments), Twitter and Facebook. The use of YouTube and other similar user-generated video sites is another popular example of Internet-driven technology being used in sport marketing. By broadcasting snippets of compelling content to an audience eager for thrills and entertainment, leagues, clubs and athletes eager for sponsorship and fame are hoping to reach larger audiences than they have ever been able to access before.

> *Chapter tool 12.1 Internet-driven platforms*: Include methods of communicating that the World Wide Web supports, such as blogs and social networking sites, e-mail, web video, podcasts, vodcasts, websites, pop-ups, spam, virtual worlds, wikis, electronic commerce, Twitter, Facebook and YouTube.

Mobile communications

Mobile communications include the communication tools that are associated with mobile or cellular phones and any wireless communication system. Examples include Bluetooth, smartphones and tablets, PDAs, wireless, SMS, multimedia messaging service (MMS), 4G mobile/cellular phones and PS2, all of which are free from the restrictions of traditional land-based connections. Mobile communications such as these can be used to distribute information using either a push or pull strategy. A push strategy involves sending unsolicited communications to consumers, such as through a SMS. A pull strategy involves providing free information, such as weather reports, game updates and news headlines that the consumer has given permission to receive.

The use of SMS technology provides an example of how mobile communications can be used to market goods and services. An SMS message can do much more than simply convey information. An emerging trend is the use of mobile phone coupons (much harder to lose than paper coupons) where a barcode can be sent to a consumer and scanned at the point of sale. Using this technology, sport leagues, events and retailers can offer exclusive promotions to consumers who have given permission to receive regular deals. Competitions can also be designed to make use of mobile phone technology, such as competitions for game tickets.

In addition to the potential for messaging information to consumers, mobile communications are increasingly capable of delivering personalised content and even streaming broadcasts. Mobile communications can be used to access information, replays, live footage and statistics about prominent sport events and games from anywhere in the world, including from the game venue itself. Some venues rent out PDAs for this purpose at games, but it is more likely that consumers will use their own devices. Of course, the same system can be used to send personalised marketing communications to consumers. Consumers can even decide whether they want to purchase something on offer on the spot via smartphone.

The wireless feature of mobile communications allows roaming connectivity between different portable and permanent technologies such as smartphones and tablets, laptops, handheld computers and diaries, and the Internet. This integration will make portable real time and recorded sport viewing from virtually any location in the world a possibility in the short term and an inexpensive one in the medium term. Handheld, wireless computers are already available and are cheap and pervasive enough for displaying sporting events, replays and highlights. It is also likely that they will be employed during events for similar functions.

Chapter tool 12.2 Mobile communications: Include the communication tools that are associated with mobile or cellular smartphones, tablets and any wireless communication system. Examples include Bluetooth, smartphones, PDAs, wireless, SMS, MMS, 4G mobile/cellular phones and PS2, which are free from the restrictions of traditional land-based connections.

Upgraded conventional technologies

Upgraded conventional technologies refer to the technological advances that have been made with devices such as televisions, radios and video data recorders. Examples include digital television broadcasts, interactive television, digital video recorders, TiVo (the TiVo device stores television programmes onto non-removable hard disk storage much like all digital video recorder devices), graphical user interfaces, satellite radio and electronic kiosks.

In addition to the benefits of interactivity, there are several ways in which digital data can be used to enhance the conventional sport watching experience. First, it can be viewed like ordinary video or television transmissions and it also offers increased flexibility so that events may be watched over the Internet. As wireless connectivity to the Internet improves in quality, cost and convenience, the option of watching a sporting event on the run through a personal computer, smartphone, diary or pad will become more common. Second, digital can be used to cover specific players or aspects of the sporting event. The viewer can be the director if they choose, selecting camera angles, players, activities or replays at their discretion. Third, digital can be employed to create new statistics associated with the event. The technology provides more options for measuring and monitoring. These statistics can also be stored for each player or team and revisited later for analysis or even for use in game play. Fourth, digital technologies enable real-time interaction such as gaming. As viewers watch the big game, they can link in to play in direct competition through their home gaming console or computer interface. As data are stored historically, game players will be able to create their own teams based on real game performances.

Chapter tool 12.3 Upgraded conventional technologies: Refer to the technological advances that have been made with devices such as televisions, radios and video recorders. Examples include digital television broadcasts, interactive television, digital video recorders, TiVo (the TiVo device stores television programmes onto non-removable hard disk storage much like all digital video recorder devices), graphical user interfaces, satellite radio and electronic kiosks.

Hardware

Hardware refers to the physical objects and equipment that make digital technology possible, such as computer systems, mobile devices, portable equipment, game consoles and multimedia (CD, DVD). New technology has already produced prototype pocket

PCs with sufficient processing power to access and replay almost every sporting moment ever broadcast. For most of us, this is nothing spectacular; merely an expectation that comes with owning a recent smartphone. Another trend in information technology hardware is the increasing ability for devices to perform multiple tasks and to interact seamlessly with other equipment.

> *Chapter tool 12.4 Hardware*: Refers to the physical objects and equipment that make up new media technology, such as computer systems, mobile devices, portable equipment, game consoles and multimedia (CD, DVD).

Software

Where hardware refers to the physical equipment involved in digital technology, software enables that equipment to operate. Software includes both the systems software enabling the technology to function (such as the operating system and the utilities), as well as the applications that run the users' programs. Software (and mobile applications) is therefore the interface that ultimately makes all digital media technologies function. In addition to the proliferation of mobile applications for sport, and for social media engagement that are relevant to sport, virtual reality software is an example that promises to dramatically change the way spectators view sport in the future. The virtual nature of spectatorship will offer spectacular opportunities for sport enterprises to improve their revenues, particularly if they are a genuinely international property. For example, virtual reality will allow remote users to 'sit' anywhere in the stadium. Like pay-per-view television, the number of virtual reality participants will determine profitability, except virtual reality provides more opportunities for discriminatory pricing. Used in combination with social media and through mobile applications, the latest software is bringing sport experiences closer to the consumer all the time.

> *Chapter tool 12.5 Software*: Includes both the systems software that enables the technology to function (such as the operating system and the utilities), and the applications software that runs the users' programs, including mobile applications.

SOCIAL MEDIA: THE NEW HUB OF DIGITAL SPORT MARKETING

You want to know how your team performed. Forget about the TV or the newspaper, and even the online news is a bit slow and cumbersome. Go directly to Twitter for your live sports ticker, and for more information, and perhaps a conversation about the results, go directly to the sport fans' hub, Facebook. And, hyperlinks to YouTube can offer the footage within moments of the big play. All of this on the run; on your smartphone, iPad, or any other WiFi or mobile device. In fact, most surveys in North America, Western Europe, and the Asia Pacific report that between two-thirds and 85 per cent of fans use social media during games, while up to half check scores or watch highlights after the event using smartphones. By the time you read this text, the figures are likely to have climbed even higher. However, as we shall discuss in this section, savvy digital sport marketers know that while data and updates are compelling services for fans, the real power of social media lies in its unprecedented ability to create close, personal engagements between sport properties and their followers. In the end, like all marketing, we aim for better relationships, experiences, feedback and advocacy. One conclusion is absolutely undisputed: the use of social media has become an essential investment rather than an interesting experiment at the periphery of sport marketing.

Few could argue that the contemporary sport consumer has changed radically in just a few, short years. We want sport content at our convenience, which typically means on the run, and often comes with the expectation of updates from our favourite and most trusted sources of social networking insight. In short, we want to know what is going on, and we want to be able to find out '24/7'. In a world rapidly heading towards two billion smartphone owners, the implications for digital sport marketing are prodigious. To start with, sport consumers want instant access. Next, that access must be customised, or at least 'customisable', in order to meet the fickle preferences of each fan. Access must also arrive seamlessly. That means both a smooth download as well as through an integrated platform where the sport fan needs only engage with a single or a few locations for their updates. Integration plays a central role in effective digital marketing because consumers are using their smartphones and mobile devices for Internet browsing almost as much as through computers. In addition, they check email and social networking messages and sites, post photos and comments, listen to voice messages, consult their calendars, check the weather forecast, use apps, and play music and games. Although it varies depending on the region, some studies suggest that consumers within certain demographics pick up their phones more than 100 times a day. No wonder hardware manufacturers and app developers are so focused on providing an interface that captures the user's demand for intuitive functionality. Because sport consumers are so well educated about sport and technology, they expect more than the garden-variety results. Rather, content must be accompanied by novelty, entertainment and insight. Finally, attending sporting events can be prohibitively expensive leading sport consumers to find alternative ways of engaging with game content as well as looking for new ways of generating the excitement and buzz of the contest. Enter social media.

Chapter principle 12.12: Social media: Can be used as a pivotal tactic in a sport digital marketing campaign for cultivating closer consumer engagement, leading to better relationships, experiences, feedback and advocacy.

INTERACTIVE CASE

Major sport events create an astonishing convergence of social media activity. Recently, for example, the Australian Open Tennis Championship recorded up to 15,000 tweets per second at the culminating moments of key matches. The event has acquired nearly 100,000 Twitter followers and 750,000 Facebook fans.

Questions

How might a small sporting event stimulate Twitter followers? Do you think that every sporting event needs a Facebook site as a must-have?

Points of interest

The Australian Open social media volume pales in comparison to the 150 million tweets posted during the London Olympic Games and the 15–20 million for the US Superbowl. Other events such as the UEFA Cup Final and the EURO 2012 final generated hundreds of thousands of tweets. The 2014 World Cup exceeded the Superbowl effortlessly, and even eclipsed the 2014 Sochi Winter Olympics.

Social media options

At present, three social media platforms dominate, although there is always a proliferation of competitors on the rise. Most sport marketers should be using a variety of platforms, where a focus on one or two can be used to seed others. The key lies with using each platform for a different purpose. For example, Facebook allows sport properties to connect with fans, as well as to help fans connect with each other. Facebook is therefore the place for sharing photos, event details, news, comments and links. Increasingly, Facebook is being employed as a merchandise hub as well. Meanwhile, Google+ offers the main competition with the added benefits of integration with other Google features, tools and applications. Twitter, however, takes the lead for mobile connectivity and instant communications. It established the microblogging trend with a compelling restriction of 140 characters per post. Most serious sport fans 'follow' at least one high-profile athlete or player in order to receive the latest inside information. Fans can also follow clubs and teams to access live scores or specialist updates about player injuries, team tactics or club promotions. Finally, YouTube should be employed by sport properties to upload and share video content. Many larger sport organisations develop their own 'television station' and broadcast snippets, highlights or even live events.

Of course, there is a suite of additional platforms available for sport marketers to experiment with. Some examples include Flickr, Instagram and Pinterest to post and comment on sporting images, while Tumblr has combined microblogging with imagery. Location-based social media applications such as Foursquare present another interesting avenue for sport marketers to explore. These platforms use downloadable applications to allow users to register their visits to specific venues and even receive discounts or giveaways for their activity. Obviously recreation and sporting venues have much to gain from location-based social media in driving attendance, participation or even retail merchandise sales. Social media is no longer the exclusive purview of major sport venues. One study commissioned by Sport England found that more than a third of participants would be more active in their sports if they could access a web tool to search and review opportunities locally.

All social media channels can support and leverage more 'traditional' online blogs. In addition, feed column platforms such as Hootsuite or Tweetdeck can help manage the clutter of different channels by allocating or redirecting content across a range of outlets automatically. It is also increasingly common for sport properties or sport media and entertainment companies to provide their own proprietary mobile applications, or 'apps', which allow sport fans to access information, content and commentary through a unique avenue. Bringing together a social hub for consumers has become known as social 'curation'. Typically through the sport enterprise's website, all of its social media accounts can be accessed in a sleek and interactive manner, likely in the near future to also include live event broadcasts.

Chapter principle 12.13: Social media platforms: Encompass a wide variety of sites and applications including the big three, Facebook, Twitter and YouTube, where each plays an essential role in a digital sport marketing strategy.

INTERACTIVE CASE

With the radical popularity of YouTube, sport organisations are expected to post content either using embedded YouTube videos, or for larger organisations, establishing their own YouTube channels.

Questions

Two sport channels worth visiting are Wimbledon's YouTube Channel (www.youtube.com/user/Wimbledon), and Barcelona FC YouTube Channel (www.youtube.com/channel/UC14UlmYlSNiQCBe9Eookf_A – or search for Barcelona FC in YouTube). Examine the structure and content. How could such a channel be developed for a less sizable sporting organisation?

Points of interest

Consider what Barcelona FC posted on their YouTube site:

FC Barcelona is the first sports club anywhere in the world to be able to boast more than 100 million followers on its social networks, thus consolidating its position as a global phenomenon in the digital world. Sporting and social excellence has led to leadership in the 2.0 market, where FCB is the top club on all the world's major networks. In fact, the club is gaining about 100,000 new followers a day on its different social networks, and is the number one sports club on each of Facebook, Twitter, Instagram, Google+, Tencent Weibo and YouTube, the biggest platforms in the world.

The other screens

Most of modern life is spent within close proximity to several screens including the television, computer, pad and smartphone. In fact, most of us take at least one device with us everywhere we go, and sport viewing is no exception irrespective of whether it is live or through a broadcast. Sport marketers have grasped the opportunities that go with constant connectivity to draw fans more deeply into the game, its players, and all the intrigue, excitement and hype that occurs via the seemingly personalised communications that smartphones deliver. A sporting experience no longer means just viewing a game or event. Sport fans have at their fingertips a smorgasbord of information, statistics, live feeds, replays, messages and insider observations with which to engage. Twitter feeds and Facebook posts can integrate with broadcasts. Venues and media channels can provide customised apps with real-time updates to enhance the viewing experience. It has now also become common for major sporting venues to provide enhanced WiFi in stadia to encourage fan use of social media and content highlights.

Of course, from the sport marketer's viewpoint, there is also unprecedented opportunity to utilise competitions and prizes for augmenting engagement. For example, clubs such as Toronto FC run live competitions as part of their Twitter feed. Marketers select the best tweets from fans using designated club hashtags (Twitter address) and award prizes. Other forms of engagement involve question and answer sessions with players, managers or coaches.

In addition, an increasing number of major sport properties are partnering with social media and broadcasters to channel customised advertising and merchandise to sport fans. At the time of writing, 'Twitter Amplify' has taken an early position as a powerful new channel to generate advertising revenue. The platform works by teaming with content providers, such as ESPN, which provide short video highlights very shortly after their live broadcast. Numerous stakeholders have an interest including the social media platform, sport properties, advertisers, sponsors and broadcast content-owners.

New business models

Social media's impact has not just affected business models around branding, commercialisation, sponsorship and broadcasting, it has also propelled some athletes further into the spotlight as social networking superstars and immense brands in their own right. Even more daunting, some high school players have become the subjects of social media trends as college recruiters tweet about their nascent talents. For some broadcasters and franchises, social media can be employed to amplify pre-season hype and maintain fan interest during times when sponsor awareness and merchandise sales can flag. During the 2013 National Football League (NFL) draft, for example, the Atlanta Falcons manufactured their own social media content in the absence of games. They broadcast statistics and other analytical commentaries and highlights about each prospective draft pick and provided the data for fan commentary on the club website. A similar approach was wielded by ESPN in augmenting their 2013 NFL draft broadcast. We can expect a lot more of this form of engagement where social media and conventional broadcasting content become integrated through social media, customised apps and leveraged, cross-promotional advertising and sponsorship campaigns. The sky is the limit for new forms of social networking ambush marketing too.

Fame and followers can happen sharply as well. For example, some new college drafts, particularly in football and basketball have found themselves sudden celebrities, their every move scrutinised with interest from fans, including the now infamous examples of posted MRI results for injury diagnosis, not to mention the repercussions from inappropriate comments and details of questionable exploits. Herein lays the double-edge of the social media opportunity. Vast reach brings with it serious brand management consequences when athletes make poor tweeting decisions about personal opinions or activities. As a result, rigid team, league and event policies around tweeting are escalating in an attempt to control brand image, and in some cases, diminish the likelihood of gambling related information distribution. For example, the US Open Tennis Grand Slam has banned all courtside tweets including those relating to player participation or performance, weather, court conditions, or any other aspect of the game unknown to the live observer. Similarly, the NFL has banned tweets from 90 minutes before and after games. Not only are players under scrutiny, but coaches, support staff, officials and the media must remain tweet silent as well.

Chapter principle 12.14: Social media integration: Social media and conventional broadcasting content can be integrated through social media, customised apps and leveraged, cross-promotional advertising and sponsorship campaigns.

INTERACTIVE CASE

Most remarkable are the followers flocking to hear about the daily, and sometimes even hourly, observations of European footballers and other superstar athletes. Footballer Ronaldo has surged past 50 million Facebook fans while Usain Bolt's London Olympics 200 metre final stimulated 80,000 tweets-per-minute.

Questions

How can small, parochial organisations and clubs leverage the popularity of tweets and other social media content from superstar players and athletes from the same sport? Can a suburban basketball club benefit from LeBron James's Twitter popularity?

Points of interest

Of the top ten Facebook team profiles in sport, eight are European football clubs. For example, Barcelona and Real Madrid command towards 40 million 'likes', while Manchester United has exceeded 30 million. The highest number of likes attracted by a US-based team belongs to the NBA's LA Lakers. At the same time, Ronaldo can tweet to more than 20 million followers compared to less than 10 million for NBA star LeBron James. Although European football dominates, ahead of the NBA and NFL, a handful of other athletes have remarkable social media profiles. As a genuinely global sport, tennis hosts Roger Federer, Rafael Nadal and Maria Sharapova can reach around 10 million followers. Usain Bolt enjoys similar exposure, as does the Indian national cricket team.

Social media lessons for digital marketing

Social media works best when marketers focus on creating high quality, 'native' experiences in the platforms – such as Facebook – rather than trying to use them to drive traffic elsewhere. Context remains instrumental. Sport fans will go to Facebook in order to have a great Facebook experience, but will become irritated if they simply get shunted from one site to another. As a result, sport marketers need to abandon the lingering idea that social media provides a channel for directing consumers towards other content. For the most part, the better tactic involves committing to the quality of each social media platform being employed so that it provides a unique and fulfilling experience with each engagement. One example can be seen through English Premier League club Manchester City and their Facebook site. The club has created an engaging and one-stop location for interaction with a constantly revolving suite of content available, such as advent calendars, 'fancam', live streaming, question and answer sessions with players, and a variety of competitions. To give the site greater authenticity, the club also developed specific pages for the captain to offer his own personal comments in response to fan posts. Links also connect 'friends' to Facebook accounts for other players.

Sport marketers should keep in mind that social media does not magically create new fans, but it does deliver an unprecedented opportunity to connect with them, and to help them connect with each other. In this respect, social media helps cultivate relationships that can lead to stronger affiliation, brand identification, and ultimately, more spending. First comes connection, then comes the commercial realisation of a sporting brand's connection value. Some sport enterprises are even using social media to crowdsource ideas for new marketing collateral. Social media is redefining market research with sport consumers. Some essential starting points could be to:

- promote a hashtag on all marketing collateral and tweet consistently with at least daily updates on events, players, commentaries, media links, giveways and promotions, or just retweet interesting tweets from high-profile sources in the same sport. Provide match/game updates and live results where possible. Use software platforms (such as RSS) to leverage content between the club website and its twitter feed;
- set up a Facebook page as a community building and information distribution method. Promote and sell merchandise, tickets and events;
- post video content on YouTube. Consider forming a YouTube channel for the sport or sport organisation;
- post regularly to a photo-sharing application such as Instagram with team and player imagery. Cross promote using Facebook and tweets;
- use a website as a central hub to blog and link all social media connections.

Chapter principle 12.15: Social media native experiences: Social media works best when marketers focus on creating high quality, 'native' experiences in the platforms, rather than using them to drive traffic elsewhere.

INTERACTIVE CASE

Some noteworthy social media campaigns have involved sponsors as well. In one illuminating example, Roland Garros (The French Open Tennis Grand Slam) celebrated their 40-year sponsorship with BNP Paribas by using a novel and first-time-ever-tried combination of social media and real-world action called 'Tweet & Shoot'.

Questions

Search for other examples where sport events, organisations or clubs partnered with their sponsors to deliver a social media experience to fans. Choose one example and explain how the partnership operated and how it engaged with fans to create a novel interaction. Is there a way in which this strategy can be adapted for use on a much smaller scale?

Points of interest

Through 'Tweet & Shoot', fans using social media were able to 'train' the top French seed Jo-Wilfried Tsonga. Through a custom developed website using a game mechanic system, fans could specify the location of machine-fired balls to Tsonga. Each decision a fan made on the virtual tennis court was translated into a coded Tweet directing the aim of the shots directed at Tsonga during a training session. For the first time ever, a ball-firing robot was instructed by tweets delivered by fans. More than 5,500 fans recorded tweets, while the website received nearly 200,000 views.

From now to the future of digital and social media sport marketing

In looking at the pivotal developments of 2014 from a digital sport marketing viewpoint, our forecasts begin with the lessons writ large on the back of three major, global sporting events: the US Super Bowl, the Sochi Winter Olympics and the World Cup. These three events signposted several exploding trends in digital sport marketing that have immense implications for all sport and leisure organisations irrespective of size.

First, there is no such thing as 'appointment' television anymore when it comes to sport. Live, on-demand highlights, replays, streaming video and tweets are all expected parts of the sport consumption experience. For example, right now fans of some clubs can download the iPod playlist of their favourite player's pre-game music.

Second, the actual event represents only a portion of the available content for sport fans. Viewers can engage through contests, forums, blogs, gaming consoles, tablets, smartphones, smart TVs, and a growing range of social media and networking sites and applications. With specialisation comes fragmentation. While the dominant social media giants seem likely to prosper, a new second tier of social media networking sites and applications will emerge. Each will be highly customised and designed to meet niche market demands.

Third, new business models designed to convert fan following into commercial revenue are exploding. We can expect a proliferation of new media entities organised around the confluence of social media, broadcasting, sponsorship and sport property franchises. New smartphone and mobile device apps will lead the way. For example, Apple has released a new platform called iBeacon that allows retailers, including sport enterprises, to deliver messages directly to a user's mobile device if they have the Apple Store application installed. Major League Baseball adopted the application in 2014 and uses it to provide customised information to fans, such as the location of available seats in a stadium. Of course, we can expect fans to also be directed to merchandise stalls, food and beverage stands, and a raft of digital 'point of sale' opportunities from media downloads to sponsored products.

Just as we have seen on a modest scale in the form of YouTube content, such as the Wimbledon television channel, there will be more aggressive moves to integrate high-profile sport enterprises with broadcasting. As large sport enterprises come to terms with their immense, potential global audiences, they will become more reluctant to forge partnerships with existing broadcasters beyond television, instead creating their own content through inexpensive, fluid, virtual, digital news and replay stations. With this unprecedented ownership of novel content, sport enterprises will pursue new revenue opportunities from selling online advertising to direct sales channels with their fans. Revenues from digital sites are increasingly radically. For example, for the Australian National Rugby League, website revenue doubled between 2012 and 2013. Similarly, visits to NBA.com are increasing by more than 100 per cent a year, every year.

Finally, the convergence of hardware technology, software development and application, digital channels and social media will create new opportunities for mobile devices to become more seamlessly connected to the human senses. Google Glass foreshadows the appetite for wearable media technology, which will soon be joined by a new glut of smart watches, microchipped armbands, and remote hardware integrated into phones providing everything from heart rate monitors to predictive software capable of anticipating the needs of the user. Before the next edition of this text has been printed, most serious sport fans will watch their favourite content on the move through wearable glasses, and perhaps in a few more years still, contact lenses. In addition, we can expect high-profile players and athletes to wear devices that will allow fans to monitor physiological performance and even to experience the same sights and sounds players experience during the big moments of a game.

There are numerous imminent and promising technologies that are almost certainly going to have an impact on sport marketing in the future. Many of them will diminish the gap between the most powerful and well-resourced sport organisations, and those that have traditionally struggled for exposure. Smaller sports will find that web broadcasting and all its digital opportunities are their best bet for finding a stable niche. Other exciting developments are being seen in the development of state-of-the-art cameras that can be embedded in eyeglasses and even contact lens style cameras that fit over the retina. With athletes wearing such devices, the data could be transmitted directly to viewers who could choose an athlete to follow as well as choose angles and replays.

While new media technologies can offer significant advantages for sport marketers, there are also dangers associated with digital and social media marketing. Sport organisations must have the tools to ensure that the relationships they cultivate with fans bridge the gap between commerce and community. In turn this necessitates the careful management of customer input into products and services. Sport enterprises will have to work hard to ensure that experiences are created for sport consumers that are superior to those they might receive through other discretionary leisure pursuits. Technology has the sometimes unwelcome potential of converting services or customer experiences into commodities. To fortify the sporting experience, sport organisations must continue to focus on understanding the feelings of belonging in sport supporters.

PRINCIPLES SUMMARY

- Chapter principle 12.1: Digital sport marketing refers to communications that are generated by electronic means, or through recent technological platforms. It refers to technologically sophisticated platforms or vehicles for transmitting and communicating information, including social media channels, that utilise the interactions of networked individuals.

- Chapter principle 12.2: Digital media is flexible, transferable and can be customised.

- Chapter principle 12.3: Digital and social media technologies provide sport marketers with new ways of communicating with consumers, and novel approaches to their marketing activities. Many of these approaches are far more rapid, responsive, interactive and inexpensive when compared with other marketing strategies; they are also more easily customised to key target audiences.

- Chapter principle 12.4: Digital sport marketing demands customised communication with targeted sport consumers, generated by electronic means or through technologically sophisticated platforms that facilitate the transmission of information.

- Chapter principle 12.5: Digital sport marketing involves targeted and personalised interactions based on the principles of customisation, modularity, sticky branding, networked communication and permission.

- Chapter principle 12.6: *Customisation*: Digital sport marketing messages should be customised or targeted and adapted to specific consumers and their needs.

- Chapter principle 12.7: *Modularity*: A modular digital marketing programme (including product design) is standardised and automated incorporating flexibility, responsiveness to changes in demand, and ease of transfer.

- Chapter principle 12.8: *Sticky branding*: Occurs when digital sport marketing content takes hold in consumers' minds in ways that are consistent with the positioning strategy for the brand, and as a result are readily passed on digitally.

- Chapter principle 12.9: *Networked communication*: Networked communication is based on the idea that instead of telling consumers about products, it is more productive to get consumers to talk to each other about them.

- Chapter principle 12.10: *Inclusivity*: Refers to the use of digital marketing to fulfil the need to 'belong', which in turn fosters the development of identity and a stronger connection to the sport brand.

- Chapter principle 12.11: *Permission*: Refers to the effectiveness of communicating with consumers who have consented to receive customised messages, rather than to send random, untargeted and uninvited marketing communications.

- Chapter principle 12.12: *Social media*: Can be used as a pivotal tactic in a sport digital marketing campaign for cultivating closer consumer engagement, leading to better relationships, experiences, feedback and advocacy.

- Chapter principle 12.13: *Social media platforms*: Encompass a wide variety of sites and applications including the big three, Facebook, Twitter and YouTube, where each plays an essential role in a digital sport marketing strategy.

- Chapter principle 12.14: *Social media integration*: Social media and conventional broadcasting content can be integrated through social media, customised apps and leveraged, cross-promotional advertising and sponsorship campaigns.

- Chapter principle 12.15: *Social media native experiences*: Social media works best when marketers focus on creating high quality, 'native' experiences in the platforms, rather than using them to drive traffic elsewhere.

TOOLS SUMMARY

- Chapter tool 12.1 Internet-driven platforms
- Chapter tool 12.2 Mobile communications
- Chapter tool 12.3 Upgraded conventional technologies
- Chapter tool 12.4 Hardware
- Chapter tool 12.5 Software

REVIEW QUESTIONS

1   Describe the key characteristics of the digital sport marketing approach.

2   Provide a sport example of each of the following principles: customisation, modularity, sticky branding, networked communication, inclusivity and permission.

3   What implications do digital sport marketing principles have for conventional sport marketing techniques?

4   Provide some examples of how mobile communications might be pivotal to the future of marketing communications within venues.

5   Speculate on the future of sport marketing related software and applications. Provide an example that you think might be developed in the future.

6   Describe how to employ different social media platforms at the same time for maximum marketing impact.

RELEVANT WEBSITES

www.flickr.com	Photo-sharing website
www.youtube.com	YouTube video-sharing
http://slugger.com	Louisville Slugger
http://devils.nhl.com	New Jersey Devils
http://mlb.mlb.com/fancave	Major League Baseball 'Fancave'
www.youtube.com/user/Wimbledon	Wimbledon YouTube Channel

FURTHER READING

Abeza, G., O'Reilly, N. and Reid, I. (2013). Relationship marketing and social media in sport. *International Journal of Sport Communication*, 6(2), 120–142.

Newman, T., Peck, J., Harris, C. and Wilhide, B. (2013). *Social Media in Sport Marketing*. Scottsdale, AZ: Holcomb Hathaway Publishers.

Wilson, S. (2012). *Sports Marketing on a Shoestring: How to Make More Money and New Fans*. Amazon Digital Services, Amazon.

CHAPTER 13

Sport marketing implementation and control

LEARNING OUTCOMES

At the end of this chapter, readers should be able to:

- describe the importance of implementation and control strategies in a sport marketing strategy
- explain how implementation differs from planning sport marketing strategies
- identify the key concepts behind successfully transforming a sport marketing strategy into action
- outline the steps of a control process
- understand how to link the control process to improved strategic decisions
- debate the ethical and social responsibilities of sport marketers.

OVERVIEW

This chapter presents the final stage of the Sport Marketing Framework, the process of implementing and controlling the sport marketing strategy. It introduces the strategies available for enhancing the success of the implementation process. The chapter explains how to develop a control process for implementation, and shows how its use can help evaluate and improve a sport marketing strategy. The final section of the chapter provides a summary of the philosophy, process, principles and tools of sport marketing highlighted in the text.

INTRODUCTION

The first three stages of the Sport Marketing Framework – (1) identify sport marketing opportunities, (2) develop sport marketing strategy and (3) plan the sport marketing mix – have been explained. It is now time to outline the final stage of the Framework, which is to *implement and control* the sport marketing strategy. The implementation and control process is shown in Figure 13.1, within the Sport Marketing Framework.

Implementing a sport marketing strategy means putting the plans that were devised into action. Controlling a sport marketing strategy means keeping the implementation of marketing activities consistent with the plan and the measures that were put in place to indicate success. In practice, control is all about ensuring that a plan's objectives are going to be achieved, and taking action to correct any problems if it looks as though things are not going as they should. As a result, a central function of control is to evaluate implemented marketing activities to see whether they have achieved what they were supposed to. To evaluate a sport marketing plan means to assess it, or to weigh up its positive and negative outcomes to reach a view on its performance. In the end, it is essential to determine how successful a sport marketing strategy has been, or else there is no way of knowing what worked and what did not, and no way of improving in the future. This chapter provides the principles and tools underpinning the successful development of an implementation and control process.

> *Chapter principle 13.1*: Implementing a sport marketing strategy means putting the plans into action.

IMPLEMENTATION STRATEGIES

When it comes to executing a sport marketing plan, it might seem simple enough to follow the plan, but many sport organisations find that it is much harder than it sounds. A marketing plan may be innovative, but if it is not implemented properly it will fail. While it is common for sport marketers to discover that executing a strategy is more difficult than they anticipate, there are five sport marketing implementation tools that greatly increase the probability of success, as illustrated in Figure 13.2.

> *Chapter principle 13.2*: The implementation success of a sport marketing plan is enhanced through the use of five implementation tools: (1) leadership and commitment, (2) communication and delegation, (3) teamwork and projects, (4) rewards and reinforcement and (5) control and feedback.

Leadership and commitment

A sport marketing plan is more likely to be successful if there is a clear leader or group of leaders who take responsibility for its implementation. In practice this ensures that the sport organisation is committed to the plan it has devised. The role of the leader is to coordinate and organise marketing activities, as well as to manage the control process.

There are a number of levels at which leadership or initiative is required in the implementation of a sport marketing plan. Implementation begins with senior management leaders who have to develop and oversee the timeline associated with the marketing plan and every activity within it, along with the allocation of whatever resources are needed to take action. Any marketing plan will need resources to make it a reality. Every activity in a sport marketing plan will have a corresponding cost for implementation such as staff

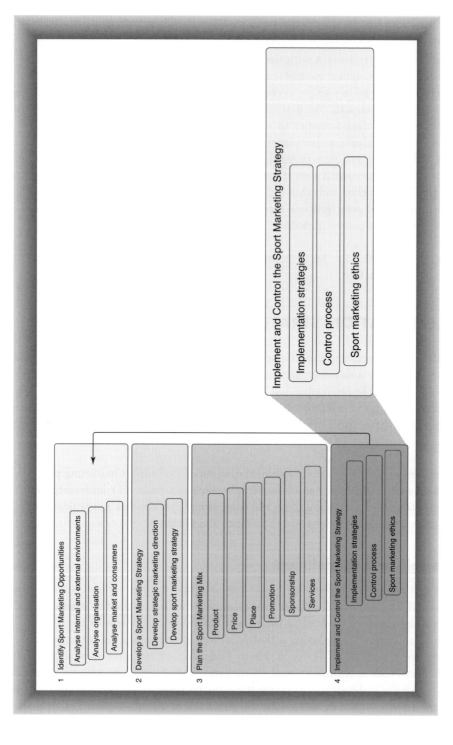

FIGURE 13.1 The Sport Marketing Framework

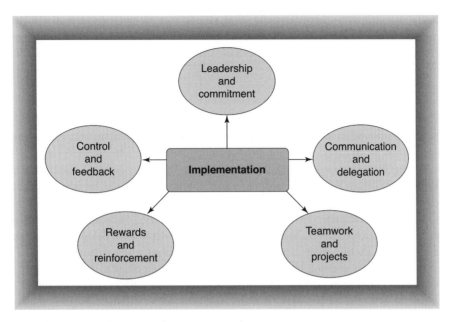

FIGURE 13.2 Sport marketing implementation tools

time and training, the research and development of products and promotions, and even the need to pay for specialist consultants or external contractors if the right expertise is not available internally. It is important not to underestimate the investment in staff time that will be needed. Developing and implementing a marketing plan will not only need the time of marketing staff, but also administration staff and management.

> *Chapter tool 13.1 Leadership and commitment*: A sport marketing plan is more likely to be successful if there is a clear leader or group of leaders who take responsibility for its implementation. Leadership and commitment involves the designation of a timeline and the allocation of resources.

Communication and delegation

It is important that all members of the sport marketing team have a good understanding of the marketing plan. Rather than just telling everyone about the plan after it has been developed, it is more effective to involve them along the way. Sport marketing strategies are more likely to be supported by the sport marketing team if all of its members have made a contribution.

Marketing leaders have to make decisions about how marketing activities should be delegated and what information should be provided to those empowered and responsible for tasks. Teams may need to be created, individuals may be given specific assignments and outside contractors may be engaged. The delegation of decision-making authority is delicate for sport marketers. Because of their centrality to the functioning of sport organisations, it is important that volunteers are given sufficient levels of responsibility to challenge and stimulate them. Equally, they should not be given roles that will burden them, or cause serious anxiety and stress. Most of all, volunteers should not be given tasks and responsibilities for which they do not have the authority to fulfil, or the accountability to answer for. The delegation of decision making for marketing activities is therefore complex. A number of issues should be considered that are strongly connected with effective communication.

There are four preconditions to successful delegation. Delegation of marketing tasks can only work if leaders are: (1) receptive to the ideas of subordinates and volunteers, (2) prepared to let go of tasks, (3) willing to let others make mistakes and (4) ready to trust subordinates. However, even if marketing leaders are ready to delegate the performance of planned marketing tactics, subordinates and volunteers may not be ready. Resistance to delegation may arise from: (1) the fear of criticism over possible mistakes, (2) lack of confidence, (3) inadequate resources to do the job properly, (4) lack of an incentive and (5) already too much to do. If these concerns can be alleviated then delegation is workable. Since a sport marketing plan cannot be deployed without a significant amount of help from employed staff and volunteers, there is really no choice but to make it work.

Delegation is not just a way of involving more people in the implementation of sport marketing, it is a way of accessing a wider range of skills and abilities from those who want to contribute. Effective delegation will also lead to greater clarity about what needs to be done since the delegation process requires a clear statement of the jobs and responsibilities involved. It will also lead to faster decisions since those actually involved in the activity do not need to seek approval before they take action. Delegation allows staff and volunteers to act responsibly when dealing with fans and consumers to improve customer satisfaction.

All activities within a sport marketing plan should be delegated or allocated to specific staff members or teams. If duties are not delegated, it becomes easy to assume that someone else is doing it. It is best to have a detailed job assignment that is put in writing after the marketing leader and the staff member or volunteer have agreed on the details. A detailed job assignment should address the following issues:

- name: name of the person responsible for the project (job);
- marketing plan: short description of the relevant objective of the marketing strategy;
- project title: short, clear description of the specific project (job) being delegated;
- project description: detailed description of each part of the project;
- methods: statement of *how* the staff member is expected to carry out the project (e.g. processes and techniques they should use);
- reporting systems: who the staff member should report their progress to, how they should communicate it and how often they should do this;
- performance measures: indicators of performance;
- timeline: timeline for each stage of the project;
- resources: what resources the staff member is able to use (e.g. money, materials, administration staff time, training).

It is also important to regularly communicate with other people in the organisation who are not in the marketing team. The more the employees and volunteers of a sport organisation who support the marketing plan, the more likely it is to succeed. This underpins the relevance of communicating the marketing plan internally within the organisation. Internal promotion and marketing means educating every staff member, volunteer and stakeholder about the contents of the plan.

> *Chapter tool 13.2 Communication and delegation*: Marketing leaders have to make decisions about how marketing activities should be delegated and what information should be provided to those empowered and responsible for tasks. Delegation of marketing tasks can only work if leaders are: (1) receptive to the ideas of subordinates and volunteers, (2) prepared to let go of tasks, (3) willing to let others make mistakes and (4) ready to trust subordinates. Resistance to delegation may arise from: (1) the fear of criticism over possible mistakes, (2) lack of confidence, (3) inadequate resources to do the job properly, (4) lack of an incentive and (5) already too much to do. A detailed job assignment should be created for every major marketing project or activity within the plan.

Teamwork and projects

The successful implementation of a sport marketing plan requires the involvement of a combination of staff and volunteers who have the right mix of skills, experience and attitudes. One of the most effective ways of ensuring that implementation is effective is to make project teams responsible for certain projects or groups of activities. Project teams are an indispensable tool for achieving quality service outcomes and sporting clubs in particular can make use of project teams because of the need to conduct events with a combination of paid and volunteer staff. A project team structure also has a fixed life and involves delegation, and is therefore a useful device for the organisation of special one-off functions at both the local level and for larger, more complex events. For example, if a marketing plan includes a promotional barbeque, marketing leaders may decide to establish a special project team to conduct the event. The project team operates as long as it takes to organise, conduct and evaluate the event, after which time it disbands.

Not all marketing teams will produce high quality outcomes in implementing their set projects and activities. However, the chances of a project team fulfilling its potential are dramatically increased when the following are in place:

- agreement that the project is vitally important to the success of the marketing strategy;
- the project team has a guaranteed and appropriate lifespan;
- the team has a shared purpose;
- realistic and concrete goals are agreed upon by the team;
- there is a common understanding on exactly what has to be done;
- agreement that the rewards and accolades for successful completion will be shared;
- unimpeded flows of communication, both within the team, and with marketing leaders;
- strong working relationship with other related teams.

Part of building a team is choosing the right members who provide a mix of skills and abilities so that a team can tackle different kinds of marketing tasks. A mix of the

TABLE 13.1 Team knowledge and skills	
Knowledge of	*Skills in*
The sport industry and marketplace	Communicating with staff, consumers and other groups
Marketing principles and concepts	Talking with the media
General business and management principles	Public speaking and hosting events
The target consumers, and sport consumers in general	Generating and developing ideas
The range of goods and/or services being offered	Problem-solving and negotiation
Specialist areas (e.g. contacts, sponsorship, event management and budgeting, risk management, facility development)	Organisation, time management and project coordination
	Personally promoting the value of the product and organisation
	Understanding market research and statistics

knowledge and skills as shown in Table 13.1 is a good start for most marketing implementation teams.

> *Chapter tool 13.3 Teamwork and projects*: The successful implementation of a sport marketing plan requires the involvement of a combination of staff and volunteers who have the right mix of skills, experience and attitudes. Implementation teams work best when: (1) there is agreement that the project is vitally important to the success of the marketing strategy, (2) the project team has a guaranteed and appropriate lifespan, (3) the team has a shared purpose, (4) realistic and concrete goals are agreed upon by the team, (5) there is a common understanding on exactly what has to be done, (6) agreement that the rewards and accolades for successful completion will be shared, (7) there is an unimpeded flow of communication, both within the team, and with marketing leaders, and (8) a strong working relationship with other related teams exists.

Rewards and reinforcement

Whether the implementation of marketing strategy will be successful depends on the individual and team efforts of staff and volunteers. It can be helpful to put rewards into place for those who do a good job with implementing the strategy. Rewards can include positive feedback (e.g. praise, recognition), money (e.g. commissions, bonuses, raises) or other rewards such as stock options or promotions and special assignments. It can be useful to offer smaller rewards along the way, as well as bigger rewards when major targets are achieved. Irrespective of their composition, the purpose behind all rewards is to reinforce the kinds of behaviours and actions that are conducive to effective plan implementation.

Chapter tool 13.4 Rewards and reinforcement: It can be helpful to put rewards into place to reinforce the kinds of behaviours and actions that are conducive to effective plan implementation. Rewards can include positive feedback (e.g. praise, recognition), money (e.g. commissions, bonuses, raises) or other rewards such as promotions, days off and special assignments.

Control and feedback

The final part of implementing a marketing strategy is to review and evaluate its outcomes on a regular basis. It is vital to keep track of how well the plan is going, and to make changes if things are not going as intended. This is such an important part of implementation that the next topic, the control process, is dedicated to it.

Chapter tool 13.5 Control and feedback: Regular evaluation of the performance of a marketing plan is necessary in case corrections need to be made. This is achieved through the introduction of a control process.

CONTROL PROCESS

Controlling a sport marketing strategy involves six steps, which are summarised in Figure 13.3.

Chapter principle 13.3: Controlling a sport marketing strategy means keeping it on track, making sure that it is achieving what it set out to, and making changes

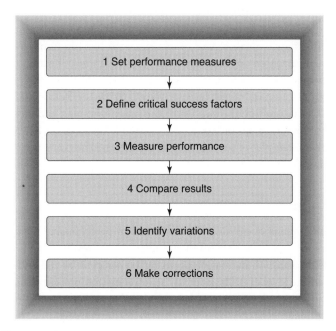

FIGURE 13.3 The control process

to correct variations and problems. The control process involves six steps: (1) set performance measures, (2) define critical success factors, (3) measure performance, (4) compare results, (5) identify variations and (6) make corrections.

Set performance measures

Setting performance measures is the first step of the control process. Because setting performance measures is part of the strategic process, they should have already been determined in stage two of the Sport Marketing Framework. It might be advisable to re-read the section on setting performance measures in Chapter 5.

Define critical success factors

Critical success factors (CSFs) represent those marketing projects and activities most influential to the successful implementation of a marketing plan. CSFs are the critical actions in marketing that when appropriately implemented have the most impact on the success of the plan. CSFs are determined by asking the question, 'what must go right for the marketing plan to be successfully implemented?' The key to using CSFs is to prioritise them, thereby showing which areas demand the greatest implementation attention. For example, after some prioritisation it might become clear that the most important CSF is a new sponsorship deal. If this is the case, resources can be allocated towards the development of a proposal and the staff to personally sell it.

Measure performance

The next step is to put the performance measures identified in step one into action. How performance is measured will depend on the nature of the measures that were set. For example, if a performance measure was to increase membership numbers by 10 per cent in one year, then information on membership rates needs to be collected. If a performance measure was to increase merchandise revenue to $120,000 by June 2016, then the relevant financial information needs to be acquired. With the before and after measures it is a simple task to determine the success of the marketing plan and its implementation in the next step. Obviously, an outcome of step two is to focus on the measurement of CSFs. Some further examples of performance measures and the corresponding information needed are given in Table 13.2.

Compare results

Comparing results means examining the outcomes of performance measurement *before* the marketing strategy was implemented and *after* it was implemented. For example, if the performance measure of 'increasing profit by 10 per cent by the end of the financial year' was set, then the level of profit prior to the implementation of the marketing strategy (the previous year's profit level) should be considered against the measurements made at the end of the financial year in which the strategy was deployed.

TABLE 13.2 Performance measures and required information

Examples of performance measures	Examples of required information
To increase membership from 70 to 100 members by January 2016	Membership numbers
To increase the number of people who use our service to 50 customers per month by July 2008	Numbers of people who use the service
To increase spectator levels to an average of 25,000 spectators per game, by December 2016, as measured by ticket sales	Spectator numbers (e.g. ticket sales)
To increase customer satisfaction levels to 7/10 as rated by them on a customer satisfaction survey	Customer satisfaction levels (in this example a customer satisfaction survey is used)
To increase profit to $120,000, calculated at the end of the 2016 financial year	Profit figures
To increase the number of people who have heard of our club in this area to 1,000, as measured by a phone survey	Survey responses of who has heard of the club

Identify variations

To ensure that the objectives of the marketing plan are being achieved, it is necessary to find out whether there are any variations between what was planned and what actually happened. Sport marketers usually call this *variance*. Sometimes the variance is positive because something beneficial occurred that was not planned. For example, it is common in sport to sell more merchandise if a team performs unexpectedly well during a season. On the other hand, at other times the variance may be negative such as the sudden emergence of a scandal involving the behaviour of a prominent athlete. Variance can also been seen in the light of whether something can be done about it or whether it is unavoidable.

Once variation has been determined it can be classified as either acceptable or unavoidable. For example, membership numbers might actually increase to 25 per cent in a year even though the performance measure set was an increase of 10 per cent. Clearly, this is an acceptable variation as it has a positive impact on the achievement of marketing objectives. Other examples of acceptable variations could include good publicity that was not expected, or an offer of sponsorship that was unsolicited.

An example of an unavoidable variation might be a circumstance where membership numbers dropped by 8 per cent because of a particularly bad season. Unavoidable variations are often random or infrequent events that cannot be foreseen or are difficult to plan for. Other examples of unavoidable variations could include negative publicity from alcohol overuse by players, or financial mismanagement. Part of the control process is to learn from these experiences and to try to improve them in the future. It is advantageous to measure performance as often as is practical to have time to take corrective action if something is going wrong.

Make corrections

The final step in the control process is to make changes if they are needed. This will depend on the types of variations noted in the previous step. If the variations are within acceptable limits, then no action may be necessary. But, if variations are significant enough, then corrective action will be needed to adjust the original plan to the new circumstances. For example, imagine that a performance measure reflected a goal to increase customer satisfaction ratings to 7/10 on a customer satisfaction survey by the end of June 2016. However, when June 2016 arrives, a new survey reveals that satisfaction actually dropped to 4/10. Naturally, this would constitute an unacceptable variance and it would be essential to immediately study the survey results to determine exactly what customers are unhappy about in order to take remedial action.

INTERACTIVE CASE

It is one of the more important goals of a sport organisation to instil trust from its many stakeholder groups. Implementing reliable policies and procedures that reflect the spirit of the game, the respect of its participants, interest groups, and the wider society is the responsibility of all sporting organisations at all levels. The Australian Institute of Sport (www.ais.gov.au/supporting/integrity_in_sport) commissioned research into a range of ethical and integrity issues. A number of problems recur within sport including verbal abuse, inequality in skill and physicality between competitors, and inappropriate administrative and officiating practices. As sports become increasingly exposed across multiple markets, there are many ethical challenges to address such as substance abuse, equality, exploitation, corruption or violence. The need to maintain high ethical standards that reflect accountability to the majority of stakeholders is essential.

Questions

The 'good old days' where sport was more recreation than profession seem long gone. But are they? Is sport generally more corrupt or unethical in today's environment? Or is the scrutiny placed upon sport so great that we are more aware of its limitations than ever before? Gamesmanship and sportsmanship are two terms that reflect the very core of sport participation. A simple search of the daily news can reveal numerous examples of gamesmanship or sportsmanship occurring across the globe. But how inappropriate is this form of behaviour? What constitutes unethical behaviour across an entire sport organisation?

Points of interest

Ethical marketing is about making decisions with integrity that enhance the organisation's reputation. Each individual brings their own set of morals to decision-making and outcomes may vary from situation to situation. There are three general ways ethical decisions can be viewed:

- the greater good for the majority of interest groups;
- morally right or wrong;
- fairness and equity across all interest groups.

The public outfall from unethical practices can be immense and choosing the right pathway is problematic. It may damage the organisation's reputation in the short term but not necessarily destroy them for good.

SPORT MARKETING ETHICS

While the implementation of a sport marketing plan should align with an organisation's objectives, it should also fit within the broader boundaries of ethical behaviour. Ethics in sport marketing typically refers to whether the traditional four Ps of the marketing mix are deployed within a moral and professional code. Mostly these include issues associated with unsafe or poor quality products, deceptive or predatory pricing, misleading or dishonest promotions and exploitative or collusive distribution. In the sporting world, other major marketing issues are concerned with publicising the private lives of athletes, exploiting passionate fans and children who idolise sport stars through athlete endorsements of commercial products, the use of venues with unsafe facilities, unrealistic promises associated with health, fitness and weight loss products, and the overpricing of high-profile matches and special sport events.

One helpful view of marketing ethics proposes that there should be three basic tenets against which behaviour must be matched: (1) the buyer and seller must both be fully informed as to what is being purchased and what is being paid in exchange, (2) neither the buyer nor seller is compelled or coerced in their choices and (3) both buyer and seller are capable of making a rational decision concerning the transaction. In short, informed, autonomous decisions based on the faithful representation of the product features and its price lie at the core of responsible sport marketing.

> *Chapter principle 13.4*: There are three basic tenets against which sport marketing behaviour must be matched: (1) the buyer and seller must both be fully informed as to what is being purchased and what is being paid in exchange, (2) neither the buyer nor seller is compelled or coerced in their choices and (3) both buyer and seller are capable of making a rational decision concerning the transaction.

Sport marketers and organisations might elect to follow a professional code of ethics, which can be employed as a guideline for dealing with uncertain situations. In general, professional codes contain rules about norms of behaviour, ethical values and core principles such as honesty, responsibility and fairness. Table 13.3 provides a set of common professional guidelines for sport marketers.

TABLE 13.3 Professional code of conduct for sport marketers
1 Products and services should be safe. Sporting venues and their facilities should meet all health and safety legislation requirements
2 All marketing communications honestly represent the products offered
3 The product-price exchange should represent fair value
4 Prices are transparent and clearly associated with products
5 Product features are clearly demonstrated and honestly represented
6 Sport marketers should not engage in price fixing or collusion outside of regulated practices
7 Marketing communications should not be coercive or manipulative
8 Athletes' and participants' private lives should not be used for marketing advantages without permission
9 Minors should not be exploited for marketing messages
10 Supply of sporting products should not be manipulated to influence pricing

INTERACTIVE CASE

The American Marketing Association (AMA) provides a *Statement of Ethics*, which provides an excellent example of professional guidelines on what the AMA considers 'Ethical Norms and Values for Marketers'.

Questions

Log on to the following website to review the major elements.
https://archive.ama.org/Archive/AboutAMA/Pages/Statement%20of%20Ethics.aspx
To what extent do you think they can be applied to the sporting context?

Points of interest

It is probably reasonable to suspect that most sport marketers do not consider ethics directly in their daily activities until they are faced with a moral dilemma or an issue with ambiguous elements. For example, should a sponsor be told that a prominent player has tested positive to banned drugs? Is it right to sell a single ticket to a sport event for hundreds of dollars just because demand far exceeds supply? Are there circumstances in which ambush marketing is acceptable? Should a sport event accept sponsorship funding from a tobacco company?

SPORT AND SOCIAL RESPONSIBILITY

Sport brands such as Nike, Patagonia and Asics have incorporated a 'green' lens in their branding strategies in response to a growing concern about the environmental damage caused by sport and as a way of augmenting their brand images. Environmental sustainability is not only making sporting events more marketable, but is attracting corporate sponsors who are keen to gain public approval to enhance their corporate reputations. As a result of innovative branding techniques such as corporate/non-profit partnerships, social awareness is playing an increasingly important role in consumers' brand perceptions, prompting questions about the best ways for 'green branding' to be married with marketing and issues of social responsibility. The result is that sport organisations are faced with the challenge of communicating their social branding messages to consumers in an attempt to positively influence perceptions about the brand and its associated causes without stimulating a cynical consumer backlash.

In order to reap the benefits of social branding from both the organisation and cause perspectives, a sport enterprise needs to increase its social exposure while still connecting with its fans and consumers. This is easier said than done, as there is a fine line between exposing and over-exposing a social message to consumers. An obvious risk is that sport brands run the risk of undermining their images through what is seen as gratuitous social promotion. Nike, for example – with a history of perceived labour improprieties in developing countries suffered from an 'anti-sweat shop' campaign that forced the company to change its outsourcing practices – has now developed rigorous social responsibility policies. At the other end of the continuum, some sport organisations have begun incorporating CSR into their branding outlooks, yet are relatively silent about their engagement. For example, in the surf-fashion context, an increase in the popularity of surfing, along with technological advances in equipment, has seen the emergence of a profitable global surf industry. Numerous parochial surf brands have developed into multinational corporations selling surfwear and sporting equipment to consumers globally, sponsoring professional surfers and staging international competitions.

Increasingly, sport organisations are applying a 'green' lens together with a drive towards sustainability in their branding approaches in response to growing consumer awareness about sport's impact on the environment. Social awareness is therefore a relevant variable in the way consumers' brand perceptions are forged, suggesting that sport brand managers need to understand how environmental or social messages can be embedded in branding without creating cynicism. Some more entrepreneurial sport brands are seeking innovative ways to differentiate themselves beyond more traditional sport sponsorships through the use of social, green or other cause-related marketing. In fact, an increasing number of sport organisations have been proactive and entrepreneurial in their approach to branding, incorporating social messages into their mission, vision and value statements, engaging in innovative branding techniques such as partnering with non-profit organisations in order to secure a competitive edge.

Like many terms in business and marketing, social responsibility has been variously interpreted. However, a consensus has emerged suggesting that sport organisations are accountable not only to shareholders (when in a profit-making business model such as a franchise) in the form of economic returns, but also to stakeholders and fans in the form of greater responsibility for social and environmental footprints. Nevertheless, irrespective of whether social responsibility is a thinly veiled attempt to convince consumers that companies care about them beyond the contents of their wallets, is a sophisticated version of philanthropy, or part of a larger agenda towards brand image, managing consumer perceptions remains the central issue.

In considering the dimensions associated with social responsibility in sport, it should be acknowledged that we seek those characteristics that are distinguished in sport. In other words, if we are to use sport as a means to deal with social issues, it is up to sport organisations to clearly identify and communicate what they perceive their social responsibilities to be. This does not mean that the generic elements of social responsibility for organisations should be overlooked. For example, relevant issues include internal (e.g. policies on non-discrimination in the workplace), external (e.g. policy on labour standards of suppliers), accountability (e.g. commitment to reporting on social activities) and citizenship (e.g. educational programmes for the promotion of social initiatives) elements guided by sources such as the UN Declaration of Human Rights, the UNESCO Project on Technical and Vocational Education, the UN Global Compact, the International Labour Standards Convention, the International Programme on the Elimination of Child Labour. There are, of course, social issues that are exacerbated by elite and/or professional sports people and organisations and hence are of direct relevance to the conduct of sport. These issues involve, but are not limited to, performance enhancing drug taking, crowd violence, racial vilification, gender inequality, sex and alcohol offences, anti competition legislation regarding the structure of sporting competitions, and general role modelling. Not only are all of these issues pertinent in terms of sport's social responsibilities, but they also offer a unique and powerful angle for sport branding and health promotion.

> *Chapter principle 13.5*: Social awareness and social responsibility are variables in the way consumers' brand perceptions are forged, suggesting that sport brand managers need to understand how environmental or social messages can be embedded in their activities to achieve social outcomes, and into their branding without creating cynicism.

INTERACTIVE CASE

The cross-cutting agenda of exposure to sport in tandem with the exposure to a social issue is gaining increasing attention. Supported by the UN General Assembly's adoption of the Millennium Development Goals by 2015, fostering an atmosphere of human rights tolerance through sport is of major importance in society today.

Questions

The Homeless World Cup (www.homelessworldcup.org) or the Right to Play (www.righttoplay.com) are exemplars for pursuing social goals through sport. Identify another prominent example. How has it mobilised political and economic resources towards its aims? Do you think it has worked? How should we measure the success of a social sport organisation?

Points of interest

Sport becomes a means to an end and events such as these are about leveraging social issues via the sport platform. Arguably, it may be impossible to prove the link between sport and social change is effective but it is possible to examine different programmes that exist around the world to identify the common features or conditions that foster successful programme implementation. Market research has a range of tools and methods to help the sport marketer better understand the markets they are targeting and the social message to be delivered.

FUTURE CONNECTIONS

The future of sport marketing will be determined by the impact of numerous powerful platforms and media distribution channels that are converging to forge a new level of technological integration. Sport spectators will wield unprecedented freedom of choice as well as new levels of interaction and engagement, in the process becoming sport participants. However, sport spectators and participants will also become more fragmented as the interactive, participative aspects of technologically driven sport offer customised possibilities that undermine collective fandom. With this 'new' form of virtual (and/or online) participation comes significant competition for the traditional meeting place of the amateur sport participant, the sporting club. It can be argued that significant social changes are occurring as fans connect 'virtually' rather than in a face-to-face environment.

Technological convergence refers to the merging of computing characterised by a combination of connectedness and ease of access. In practice it means that computing technology with different functionality is capable of integration so that it can work together seamlessly and with unprecedented levels of customisation. For example, wireless networks, roaming connectivity between different portable and permanent technologies such as phones, laptops, handheld computers and diaries and the Internet, are instrumental in allowing sport to be viewed on demand from almost anywhere and with a range of different devices. Not only does convergence make portable real-time and recorded sports viewing from virtually any location in the world an inexpensive possibility, it opens the door to a suite of new sport products packaged for instant experience. A central pillar in this process comes about in consequence of the availability of digital transmissions through free to air and fee or pay television.

There are several ways in which digital data is being used to diversify the sport watching experience. First, it can be viewed like ordinary video or television transmissions, but is more flexible and easily manipulated so that content may be streamed over portable devices via the Internet or smartphones. The implication here is that more sport will be packaged in modular forms for on-sale; niche sporting content will be available where it has never been before and popular sport content will increasingly be subject to a fee for service access. The demand for convenience will drive commercial offerings. As a result, watching sport through a personal computer, phone, diary or pad is becoming quite common. In fact, technological convergence means that a single portable device can serve all computing, entertainment and communications needs. Second, digital can be used to cover specific aspects of a sporting event. A viewer can act as a director if they choose, selecting camera angles, players, activities or replays at their discretion. Third, digital can be employed to create new statistics associated with sport content, allowing for enthusiasts to have more options to interact with and participate in online sport. Finally, digital convergence allows sport fans to connect easily with each other through forums and social media, often augmented by, or facilitated through, sport brands.

Perhaps the most radical possibilities for sport experiences will accompany content that employs sport as a theme rather than in its original form. The separation between spectator and participant is diminishing as a consequence of virtual sport experiences. The real power of virtual technologies is their increasing ability to intersect with the real world and blur the distinction between virtual reality and enhanced reality. A good example can be found in online virtual worlds where consumers' virtual participants – avatars – live, play, work and engage in commercial transactions that have value in the real world. Virtual sporting worlds are readily available, with many new applications devised with sporting brand affiliations.

Not only can sport be experienced in virtual worlds through avatars, but also through first person, physical, virtual reality. Already, for example, leading labs have designed interactive, three-dimensional virtual environments where users can physically participate in sport simulations. Virtual reality programs seek to create realistic but usually fictional environments using sophisticated software in real time and with responsiveness to the actions of a user. An inevitable combination of virtual reality and technological convergence will be the opportunity to engage in virtual sporting environments through the Internet from almost anywhere with portable devices. Temporarily the interaction will be physically superficial. For example, numerous game consoles employ controllers with positioning systems that detect spatial orientation, allowing a correspondence between the physical actions of the user and their gaming activity. Add to this the opportunity to personalise the appearance of the characters in line with the user's image, as well as the introduction of artificial intelligence in the software, and the cyber athlete becomes an evolving, unique character. Shortly, entertainment-based sport games will become even more real as wireless connections and LCD screens are replaced by goggles, contact lenses, sensor-detection feedback suits, and images projected directly onto the retina. Online cybersport is already so popular that it is developing a professional circuit where real leagues and teams are reproduced in a cyber world, complete with genuine prize-money, sponsorships and real-time audiences.

The traditional spectator is no longer a passive viewer, but a player in their own right. In fact, sport itself is changing, sport marketing along with it. How many recreational sport enthusiasts would play from their own consoles if they could get their exercise and fun in front of immense virtual crowds in replications of the most famous stadia in the world? There is no reason why the same group of Sunday players could not link up in the virtual world and play in the virtual game of their choice, followed by a collective trip to a virtual bar of their choice. Virtual sporting clubs may well become a realistic alternative to the 'real' thing. For the more leisure-minded, hours on the keyboard interacting with players and other fans is time well spent.

In the future, virtual spectators may be 'placeless'; the distribution of sport entertainment through conventional stadia and venues less important as a result of digitally changeable environments. As a result, future sport consumption will move away from the geographic focus of a city or region, instead revolving around the construction of artificial hubs through which supporters can become attached in vast networks. Virtual sporting clans will determine their own preferred virtual environments for sports watching and will create their own virtual geographic replacement. In a way, professional sport will best be described as media content, deliverable through a range of distribution services, but probably available via any multifunctional portable device. This will also encourage the further fragmentation of fans whose tribal affiliations will differ depending upon their method of access and interaction. In other words, sophisticated technological options will offer sport marketers access to a bigger market and it will offer the sport consumer more variety, more access flexibility (on demand), and more and richer information. It will also create new 'places' where sport enthusiasts view, perform, meet, congregate and participate in sport experiences. New virtual communities may well harness the potential to create meeting places, togetherness, and social cohesion analogous to traditional meeting places such as the sporting club. All of these developments will be augmented by sport brands and their marketing teams. The progress of media technology will encourage increased fan engagement and integration with sport.

INTERACTIVE CASE

About seventy per cent of major global brands have adopted Instagram as a means of promoting their products. Instagram is a successful social media application that takes advantage of photos to say more than promotional words could possibly achieve. There are few mediums that can deliver a visual communication as clearly as the combination of sport and a social media platform. Social media is proficient in spreading images and messages to the wider audience faster than any mainstream medium. With over 90 million Instagram users, 40 million photos shared daily, and an average of 8,500 likes per second, sport organisations should capitalise on this growing phenomenon. An Instagram badging strategy is a means by which an organisation can link users or fans from website to blog to Instagram site quickly. Embedding a badge on the organisation's website helps fans or new followers to navigate efficiently to the sport organisation's Instagram account where a more personal engagement can ensue. The advantage of Instagram badging applications lies with the ease in which they are developed and their minimum costs to employ.

Questions

How effective is the use of Instagram badging in marketing a sport product and growing its community? How can sport organisations employ Instagram for best effect? What basic guidelines would you recommend?

Points of interest

Sport organisations large or small can use Instagram effectively if a few guidelines are followed. There is more in marketing a sport than game day action shots. While they may capture live action, they do not necessarily reflect the whole organisation. A sport is able to draw on its fans for content and Instagram enables fans to contribute photos to the sport's archives. This is also a way to understand the club from a fan's perspective. Sport is more than the action pertaining to the actual competition. A look behind the scenes, for example, often appeals to fans, staff and other supporters as it can show the camaraderie, professionalism or quirkiness of the sport, which in turn highlights its culture and reinforces a sense of belonging. Instagram supports a social media strategy and is a powerful tool for delivering specific campaign promotions or newsworthy content. The creative opportunities are limitless, while linking opportunities to corporate brands can help to foster stronger relationships.

CONCLUSION

This text has explored sport marketing over four levels. The most fundamental level describes the philosophy of sport marketing: to satisfy the needs of sport consumers. One of the features that makes sport marketing unique is the range and diversity of sport consumers' needs. Not only can sport products be offered in the form of goods and services, but sport itself can be both the target of marketing and a vehicle for marketing. Furthermore, sport consumers may be involved personally in the delivery of sport products, such as with sporting competitions, or may be passive recipients of an experience, such as spectators at a sporting contest.

At the next level – the process of sport marketing – this text has reviewed and explained the four stages of the Sport Marketing Framework. Stage one requires the identification of sport marketing opportunities. This is achieved through the assessment of the internal and external environment, the sport organisation, and the sport market and its consumers. After this information has been collected and analysed, it is possible to undertake stage two of the Sport Marketing Framework, and develop a sport marketing strategy. To construct a sport marketing strategy, sport marketers must make a series of decisions about the direction of the marketing programme, culminating in the formulation of marketing objectives and performance measures. Stage two also involves deciding on the core of the marketing strategy. This involves deciding exactly what products and services will be marketed to consumers (segmentation), and how the brand will be positioned in the marketplace against competitors. With a target market and a positioning strategy in place, stage three of the Sport Marketing Framework, planning the sport marketing mix, can begin. Here, tactics for marketing the sport product, price, distribution (place), promotion, sponsorship and sport services are established. It is imperative that these tactics are integrated and consistent with the chosen positioning strategy. Finally, stage four can be introduced, which requires the implementation and control of the sport marketing strategy. This means that plans are put into action using implementation strategies, and kept on track through a control process. Part of the control process re-engages the objectives and performance measures set in stage two, to see whether or not the targets set were achieved. In this final stage of the process it becomes transparent which parts of the marketing plan have been successful, and which parts require remedial action.

At the third and fourth levels of sport marketing are principles and tools, respectively. The principles of sport marketing represent the general rules and guidelines of good practice, while the tools of sport marketing are techniques that can be used to execute the principles. The principles and tools highlighted in the text are summarised in the Appendix. The combination of the philosophy, process, principles and tools articulated in this text forge the relationship a sport brand enjoys with sport consumers.

PRINCIPLES SUMMARY

- Chapter principle 13.1: Implementing a sport marketing strategy means putting the plans into action.

- Chapter principle 13.2: The implementation success of a sport marketing plan is enhanced through the use of five implementation tools: (1) leadership and commitment, (2) communication and delegation, (3) teamwork and projects, (4) rewards and reinforcement and (5) control and feedback.

- Chapter principle 13.3: Controlling a sport marketing strategy means keeping it on track, making sure that it is achieving what it set out to and making changes to correct variations and problems. The control process involves six steps: (1) set performance measures, (2) define critical success factors, (3) measure performance, (4) compare results, (5) identify variations and (6) make corrections.

- Chapter principle 13.4: There are three basic tenets against which sport marketing behaviour must be matched: (1) the buyer and seller must both be fully informed as to what is being purchased and what is being paid in exchange, (2) neither the buyer nor seller is compelled or coerced in their choices and (3) both buyer and seller are capable of making a rational decision concerning the transaction.

- Chapter principle 13.5: Social awareness and social responsibility are variables in the way consumers' brand perceptions are forged, suggesting that sport brand managers need to understand how environmental or social messages can be embedded in their activities to achieve social outcomes, and into their branding without creating cynicism.

TOOLS SUMMARY

- Chapter tool 13.1: Leadership and commitment
- Chapter tool 13.2: Communication and delegation
- Chapter tool 13.3: Teamwork and projects
- Chapter tool 13.4: Rewards and reinforcement
- Chapter tool 13.5: Control and feedback

REVIEW QUESTIONS

1   What is the difference between implementation and control?

2   Provide an example for each of the five implementation tools.

3   Outline the steps of the control process.

4   How can critical success factors be used to enhance the success of a control strategy?

5   Do you think there are any aspects of sport marketing that make the development of a code of professional marketing ethics different to mainstream marketing? If so, what are they and how should they be incorporated into a code?

RELEVANT WEBSITE

www.ama.org

FURTHER READING

Galician, M.L. (2013). *Handbook of Product Placement in the Mass Media: New Strategies in Marketing Theory, Practice, Trends, and Ethics*. London: Routledge.

Schlegelmilch, B.B. and Öberseder, M. (2010). Half a century of marketing ethics: Shifting perspectives and emerging trends. *Journal of Business Ethics*, 93(1), 1–19.

Appendix

- Chapter principle 2.3: Sport organisations measure their success both on and off the field of play. On-field success refers to achievement within sport competition. Off-field success refers to financial stability and profitability

- Chapter principle 2.4: Sporting organisations that compete in leagues and competitions rely on the health of their competitors for their own success. Sport consumers are more attracted to attend games where there is a balanced competition

- Chapter principle 2.5: Sport leagues and competitions implement policies to encourage competitive balance. Policies often include salary caps for players, rules about sharing revenues and regulations regarding how players are to be shared between teams

- Chapter principle 2.6: Unpredictability can be advantageous in the competitive sport product because it makes sport more attractive

- Chapter principle 2.7: In competitive sport there is a low cross elasticity of demand where it is difficult to substitute (or replace) one sport league, team, brand or competition for another

- Chapter principle 2.8: Product loyalty is strong due to the emotional attachments that sport consumers develop to sport products and brands

- Chapter principle 2.9: Sport consumers identify with teams, clubs, brands and athletes, and see them as extensions of themselves

- Chapter principle 2.10: The competitive sport product is restricted by a fixed supply schedule making it difficult to change production rates in order to meet the demand of customers, but can be overcome through alternative distribution channels

Chapter 3 Sport consumers

- Chapter principle 3.1: A sport consumer is an individual who purchases sporting goods, uses sport services, participates or volunteers in sport, and/or follows sport as a spectator or fan

- Chapter principle 3.2: Sport fan motives for consuming sport products and services can be summarised into three categories:(1) psychological motives, (2) socio-cultural motives and (3) self-concept motives

- Chapter principle 3.3: Psychological motives for sport fans include the opportunity for stimulation, escape, aesthetic pleasure, and a sense of dramatic entertainment

- Chapter principle 3.4: Socio-cultural motives for sport fans include the opportunity for family and social interaction, cultural connections and even economic benefit

- Chapter principle 3.5: Self-concept motives for sport fans include the opportunity for belonging and group affiliation, tribal connections and vicarious achievement

- Chapter principle 3.6: Fan motives for consuming sport are affected by their age, education, income, gender and race, but these demographic variables do not always influence motivation in a uniform or predictable way

- Chapter principle 3.7: Sport fans can be classified according to the sources and dimensions of their attraction to the sport, and their frequency of attendance

- Chapter principle 3.8: Fans' decisions to attend or view sport may be influenced by external factors, such as the type of sport involved, the balance of the competition, how uncertain the outcome is, the likelihood of their team winning, the venue and facilities, weather conditions, prices, personal income levels, special experiences that are being offered, promotional factors and the availability of alternative activities

Stage 1: Identify sport marketing opportunities

Chapter 4 Sport marketing opportunities

• Chapter principle 4.1: The Sport Marketing Framework describes the four stages of sport marketing including identifying sport marketing opportunities, developing a sport marketing strategy, planning the sport marketing mix, and implementing and controlling the sport marketing strategy	• Chapter tool 4.1: SWOT and external environment analysis
• Chapter principle 4.2: The first step in identifying sport marketing opportunities is to analyse the internal and external environment using the tools of SWOT analysis (with external environment analysis) and competitor analysis (with the Five Forces Analysis)	• Chapter tool 4.2: Competitor and Five Forces Analysis
• Chapter principle 4.3: The second step in identifying sport marketing opportunities is to conduct an analysis of the organisation. This requires four tools: mission statement; vision statement; organisational objectives; and stakeholder analysis	• Chapter tool 4.3: Mission statement
• Chapter principle 4.4: The third step in identifying sport marketing opportunities involves acquiring information about the sport market and consumers. Market research is the process of collecting information in order to learn about the marketplace and what consumers in general, and a sport organisation's customers specifically, want. It involves two kinds of information: quantitative or numerical, and qualitative or non-numerical	• Chapter tool 4.4: Vision statement
• Chapter principle 4.5: A market opportunity is a situation where a new or modified product or service can be introduced that meets an unfulfilled sport consumer need	• Chapter tool 4.5: Organisational objectives
	• Chapter tool 4.6: Stakeholder analysis
	• Chapter tool 4.7: Quantitative market research
	• Chapter tool 4.8: Qualitative market research
	• Chapter tool 4.9: Product-Market Expansion Grid

Stage 2: Develop a sport marketing strategy

Chapter 5 Sport marketing strategy

• Chapter principle 5.1: The second stage of the Sport Marketing Framework is to develop a sport marketing strategy. This requires two	• Chapter tool 5.1: Marketing objectives

steps: (a) to develop a strategic marketing direction, and (b) to develop a sport marketing position

• Chapter principle 5.2: Developing a strategic marketing direction involves constructing marketing objectives and setting performance measures	• Chapter tool 5.2: Performance measures
• Chapter principle 5.3: Developing a sport marketing position involves four steps: market (1, 2), market positioning tactics (3) and devising the marketing mix (4)	• Chapter tool 5.3: Market segmentation • Chapter tool 5.4: Market positioning

Stage 3: Plan the sport marketing mix

Chapter 6 Sport products and branding

• Chapter principle 6.1: Sport goods may be differentiated from services on the basis of four factors: tangibility, consistency, perishability and separability	• Chapter tool 6.1: Sport product continuum
• Chapter principle 6.2: A sport product is the complete package of benefits presented to a sport consumer in the form of physical goods, services and ideas, or a combination of these to produce a sport experience	• Chapter tool 6.2: New product development
• Chapter principle 6.3: Sport products should be seen as a bundle of benefits comprising the core benefits, actual product features and augmented product. These three variables of the product are interrelated and should be manipulated as a group	• Chapter tool 6.3: Product life cycle stages
• Chapter principle 6.4: In sport marketing, a new product can take many forms such as the improved performance of an existing product, new functions added to an existing product, a new way to use an existing product, combining existing products, or a new look or design for a product	
• Chapter principle 6.5: The term *product life cycle* refers to the stages that a product goes through from first being introduced onto the market to its decline. There are four stages of the product life cycle: introduction, growth, maturity and decline	
• Chapter principle 6.6: A sport brand is the symbolic representation of everything that a sport organisation seeks to stand for, leading to expectations about its value and performance. A brand can be portrayed as an identifying badge that triggers consumers to remember a product or an organisation. It can be a name, a design, a symbol (or logo),	

an image or a combination of these things. Branding is one of the key strategies that marketers use to help their product to stand out from the crowd by positioning it through associated ideas and concepts

- Chapter principle 6.7: Building a brand is a process made up of four steps including (1) establish brand awareness, (2) develop and manage a brand image, (3) develop brand equity, and (4) develop brand loyalty

- Chapter principle 6.8: Brand equity increases when consumers rate products as high quality. There are different elements of product quality for goods compared with services. There are five elements of *service* quality: (1) reliability, (2) assurance, (3) empathy, (4) responsiveness and (5) tangibles. There are eight elements of goods quality; these are (1) features, (2) performance, (3) reliability, (4) conformity to specifications, (5) durability, (6) serviceability, (7) aesthetic design and (8) product warranty

Chapter 7 Sport pricing

• Chapter principle 7.1: Pricing communicates an important symbolic positioning message to consumers abut a sport product	• Chapter tool 7.1: Pricing goals
• Chapter principle 7.2: The value of a sport product is the relationship between its price and the benefits a consumer believes they will receive from it	• Chapter tool 7.2: Price sensitivity analysis
• Chapter principle 7.3: The price of a product is the amount of money a consumer must give up in exchange for a good or service. However, price is not the same as value, since value is the difference between price and the anticipated benefit. Although price is usually viewed in monetary terms, it may also include other consumer sacrifices in order to acquire a sport product, such as time or social cost. Additionally, in some instances the value secured from a sports product can be well in excess of its purchase price. This is a good position for a product to be in, since the expectation of getting more value for money will be an incentive to purchase the product	• Chapter tool 7.3: Break-even analysis
• Chapter principle 7.4: *Revenue* is the price that consumers pay for a product, multiplied by the number of units sold. *Profit* is revenue minus the costs of producing and selling the product	• Chapter tool 7.4: Assess pricing variables

- Chapter principle 7.5: The strategic pricing process provides a structure for setting price. The process involves: (1) setting a pricing goal, (2) determining price sensitivity, (3) conducting a break-even analysis, (4) assessing pricing variables, (5) selecting pricing tactics and (6) setting a price point

- Chapter tool 7.5: Select pricing tactics
- Chapter tool 7.6: Select price point

Chapter 8 Sport distribution

- Chapter principle 8.1: A sport distribution channel is an organised series of organisations, suppliers and individuals that move products from the producer to the final consumer

- Chapter tool 8.1: Distribution issues analysis

- Chapter principle 8.2: There are both direct and indirect distribution channels that vary in length. A direct distribution channel is short where the producer sells the product directly to the consumer. An indirect distribution channel is a long channel where there are a number of intermediaries involved along the way

- Chapter tool 8.2: Seating

- Chapter principle 8.3: A channel member is any organisation or individual that is involved in the sport distribution channel. Channel members may include wholesalers and retailers, as well as producers and consumers

- Chapter tool 8.3: Scoreboards and signage

- Chapter principle 8.4: The sport facility is the most important distribution channel for sport activity services and professional sport events

- Chapter tool 8.4: Lighting and sound systems

- Chapter principle 8.5: Sport marketers must consider four main aspects of sport facilities in which they can maximise the sport consumer experience: (1) location and accessibility, (2) design and layout, (3) facility infrastructure and (4) customer service

- Chapter tool 8.5: Transport

- Chapter principle 8.6: Ticket sales are one of the most important sources of revenue for sport organisations that conduct competitions or events. The smooth distribution of tickets is essential to the satisfaction of consumers and the maximisation of sales

- Chapter tool 8.6: Media and broadcasting
- Chapter tool 8.7: Childcare facilities
- Chapter tool 8.8: Merchandise
- Chapter tool 8.9: Food and beverages

Chapter 9 Sport promotion

- Chapter principle 9.1: Promotion can be defined as the way that sport marketers communicate with consumers to inform, persuade and remind them about the features and benefits described by a sport product's positioning

- Chapter tool 9.1: Advertising

- Chapter principle 9.2: The promotions mix consists of four marketing tools: (1) advertising, (2) personal selling, (3) sales promotions and (4) public relations

- Chapter tool 9.2: Personal selling

- Chapter principle 9.3: Promotional elements should be combined in order to complement one another in order to achieve a promotional goal that is consistent with the overall marketing and positioning strategy

- Chapter tool 9.3: Sales promotions

- Chapter principle 9.4: There are three main objectives of promotion: (1) to inform, (2) to persuade and (3) to remind

- Chapter tool 9.4: Public relations

- Chapter principle 9.5: Promotions that *inform* aim to communicate the product's existence, its benefits, its positioning, and how it can be obtained. Promotions that aim to inform consumers are usually undertaken during the early stages of the product life cycle

- Chapter tool 9.5: Align with marketing objectives

- Chapter principle 9.6: Persuasive promotions are utilised when trying to give consumers good reasons to buy a sport product. Persuasive promotions are more common when a product enters the growth stage of the product life cycle

- Chapter tool 9.6: Consider the target market

- Chapter principle 9.7: Reminder promotions aim to keep a product or brand name prominent in consumers' minds. Reminder promotions are most common during the maturity stage of the product life cycle

- Chapter tool 9.7: Set promotional objectives

- Chapter principle 9.8: A promotional strategy is a plan that aims to use the elements of the promotions mix for the best results. The promotions planning process involves five steps: (1) align with marketing objectives, (2) consider target market, (3) set promotional objectives, (4) set promotional budget and (5) develop promotional mix

- Chapter tool 9.8: Set promotional budget

- Chapter tool 9.9. Develop promotions mix

Chapter 10 Sport sponsorship

- Chapter principle 10.1: The term sport property refers to the recipient of the sponsorship. This could be an athlete, team, event, venue, association, cause or competition

- Chapter tool 10.1: Sponsorship proposal

- Chapter principle 10.2: Sport sponsorship is a business agreement where one organisation provides financial or in-kind assistance to a sport property in exchange for the right to associate itself with the sport property. The sponsor does this to achieve corporate objectives (such as

- Chapter tool 10.2: Sport sponsorship rights

enhancing corporate image) or marketing objectives (such as increasing brand awareness)

• Chapter principle 10.3: Sport sponsorship generates goodwill among consumers. The amount of goodwill generated can vary depending on the kind of sport property being sponsored, the degree of involvement that consumers have with the sport property, the time at which the sponsor becomes involved, and when and how the sponsor ceases the sponsorship	• Chapter tool 10.3: Sponsorship leveraging
• Chapter principle 10.4: Fan involvement is an important consideration in sponsorship because a consumer's response to a sponsorship is driven by the level of involvement that he/she has with the sport property	• Chapter tool 10.4: Sport sponsorship evaluation
• Chapter principle 10.5: The objectives of sponsorship can vary greatly, depending on the size of the partners, the type of sponsorship and the type of sport property being supported. Some common objectives for the sponsor are to enhance sales, to promote the public image of its brand, to increase consumer awareness, to modify its brand image, and to build business relationships	• Chapter tool 10.5: Ambush marketing methods
• Chapter principle 10.6: The objectives of sponsorship for the sport property will vary. In addition to attracting financial support, objectives include increasing credibility, increasing awareness, and managing brand image	• Chapter tool 10.6: Sport sponsorship evaluation
• Chapter principle 10.7: Sponsorship affinity refers to whether there is a good fit or match between the sponsor and the sport property. Two factors are particularly important for ensuring a good match: (1) an overlap of target markets and (2) a match up of brand positioning strategies	
• Chapter principle 10.8: To be able to demonstrate that sponsorship has a positive outcome for corporations is the best way to legitimise it as a marketing technique, and to attract and retain sponsors	
• Chapter principle 10.9: Ambush marketing refers to a strategy where a company (other than an official sponsor, and often a competitor to the official sponsor) creates the impression that it is associated with the sport	

property. This is achieved by attracting attention and by giving the false impression of a relationship with the sport property

Chapter 11 Sport services

- Chapter principle 11.1: There are four characteristics that illustrate the difference between sport goods and services: tangibility, consistency, perishability and separability. Sport services are intangible because they exist only as an experience. Sport services tend to be inconsistent because they are affected by variables that are difficult to control. Sport services are perishable because they can only be offered and experienced once at any point in time. Sport services are inseparable because they are consumed at the same time as they are produced

- Chapter principle 11.2: The sport services mix is made up of participants, physical evidence and processes. Participants are those people involved in delivering and receiving a sport service. Physical evidence is the tangible or visual elements of a service such as a sport stadium. Processes represent the steps involved in delivering a sport service

- Chapter principle 11.3: There are three key principles behind the successful marketing of sport services: service quality, customer relationship building and customer satisfaction

- Chapter principle 11.4: Sport consumers are more likely to be loyal to a service if they perceive it to be of high quality

- Chapter principle 11.5: Service quality can be seen as the degree to which a service meets the needs and expectations of consumers

- Chapter principle 11.6: Customers will make a judgement about whether a service is meeting their expectations at two points in time: first, they will evaluate what the service delivered after it has been consumed (outcome quality); and, second, they will evaluate how the service is delivered during consumption (process quality)

- Chapter principle 11.7: CRM involves the use of information technology to create and maintain ongoing, long-term relationships with sport consumers, leading to high levels of loyalty, and improved sales

- Chapter tool 11.1: Customer relationship marketing process

- Chapter principle 11.8: Since service delivery can stimulate a diverse range of emotional responses, sport marketers must understand how each of their programs yields different satisfaction outcomes for different consumers. Customer satisfaction can take numerous forms including satisfaction as contentment, pleasure, relief, novelty and surprise. A thorough knowledge of this range, and the service delivery measures to generate them, remains essential in securing satisfaction for as many sport consumers as possible

- Chapter principle 11.9: Focusing on customer satisfaction ensures that sport marketers make the needs and perceptions of their customers a priority, which in turn leads to stronger loyalty to the sport organisation and its products

- Chapter principle 11.10: Customer satisfaction is a judgement that customers make after they have experienced a sport service where they compare what they expected from it with what they believe they actually received. When expectations are met or exceeded, customers are satisfied, and when expectations are not met, customers are dissatisfied

- Chapter principle 11.11: Customer delight occurs when a customer's expectations are exceeded to a surprising degree, resulting in an extremely positive emotional state. Delight transpires when the customer is more than just satisfied. This can happen when a service exceeds a customers' expectations of what they think is normal or reasonable from that particular sport service

- Chapter principle 11.12: Providing customer delight in a sport service can lead to higher levels of loyalty, word of mouth promotion and an advantage over competitors. However, it is essential to know how customer satisfaction/delight influences customer behaviour. It is also important to consider how capable competitors are of copying any innovative service features. It is usually better to invest resources in decreasing customer dissatisfaction than in increasing customer delight

Chapter 12 Sport digital marketing and social media

- Chapter principle 12.1: Digital sport marketing refers to communications that are generated by electronic means, or through

- Chapter tool 12.1: Internet-driven platforms

recent technological platforms. It refers to technologically sophisticated platforms or vehicles for transmitting and communicating information, including social media channels, that utilise the interactions of networked individuals

• Chapter principle 12.2: Digital media is flexible, transferable and can be customised	• Chapter tool 12.2: Mobile communications
• Chapter principle 12.3: Digital and social media technologies provide sport marketers with new ways of communicating with consumers, and novel approaches to their marketing activities. Many of these approaches are far more rapid, responsive, interactive and inexpensive when compared with other marketing strategies; they are also more easily customised to key target audiences	• Chapter tool 12.3: Upgraded conventional technologies
• Chapter principle 12.4: Digital sport marketing demands customised communication with targeted sport consumers, generated by electronic means or through technologically sophisticated platforms that facilitate the transmission of information	• Chapter tool 12.4: Hardware
• Chapter principle 12.5: Digital sport marketing involves targeted and personalised interactions based on the principles of customisation, modularity, sticky branding, networked communication and permission	• Chapter tool 12.5: Software
• Chapter principle 12.6: *Customisation*: Digital sport marketing messages should be customised or targeted and adapted to specific consumers and their needs	
• Chapter principle 12.7: *Modularity*: A modular digital marketing programme (including product design) is standardised and automated incorporating flexibility, responsiveness to changes in demand, and ease of transfer	
• Chapter principle 12.8: *Sticky branding*: Occurs when digital sport marketing content takes hold in consumers' minds in ways that are consistent with the positioning strategy for the brand, and as a result are readily passed on digitally	
• Chapter principle 12.9: *Networked communication*: Networked communication is based on the idea that instead of telling consumers about products, it is more productive to get consumers to talk to each other about them	

- Chapter principle 12.10: *Inclusivity*: Refers to the use of digital marketing to fulfil the need to 'belong', which in turn fosters the development of identity and a stronger connection to the sport brand

- Chapter principle 12.11: *Permission*: Refers to the effectiveness of communicating with consumers who have consented to receive customised messages, rather than to send random, untargeted and uninvited marketing communications

- Chapter principle 12.12: *Social media*: Can be used as a pivotal tactic in a sport digital marketing campaign for cultivating closer consumer engagement, leading to better relationships, experiences, feedback and advocacy

- Chapter principle 12.13: *Social media platforms*: Encompass a wide variety of sites and applications including the big three, Facebook, Twitter and YouTube, where each plays an essential role in a digital sport marketing strategy

- Chapter principle 12.14: *Social media integration*: Social media and conventional broadcasting content can be integrated through social media, customised apps and leveraged, cross-promotional advertising and sponsorship campaigns

- Chapter principle 12.15: *Social media native experiences*: Social media works best when marketers focus on creating high quality, 'native' experiences in the platforms, rather than using them to drive traffic elsewhere

Stage 4: Implement and control the sport marketing strategy

Chapter 13 Sport marketing implementation and control

• Chapter principle 13.1: Implementing a sport marketing strategy means putting the plans into action	• Chapter tool 13.1: Leadership and commitment
• Chapter principle 13.2: The implementation success of a sport marketing plan is enhanced through the use of five implementation tools: (1) leadership and and delegation commitment, (2) communication and delegation, (3) teamwork and projects, (4) rewards and reinforcement, and (5) control and feedback	• Chapter tool 13.2: Communication and delegation
• Chapter principle 13.3: Controlling a sport marketing strategy means keeping it on track, making sure that it is achieving what it set out to, and making changes to correct	• Chapter tool 13.3: Teamwork and projects

variations and problems. The control process involves six steps: (1) set performance measures, (2) define critical success factors, (3) measure performance, (4) compare results, (5) identify variations and (6) make corrections

• Chapter principle 13.4: There are three basic tenets against which sport marketing behaviour must be matched: (1) the buyer and seller must both be fully informed as to what is being purchased and what is being paid in exchange, (2) neither the buyer nor seller is compelled or coerced in their choices and (3) both buyer and seller are capable of making a rational decision concerning the transaction	• Chapter tool 13.4: Rewards and reinforcement
	• Chapter tool 13.5: Control and feedback
• Chapter principle 13.5: Social awareness and social responsibility are variables in the way consumers' brand perceptions are forged, suggesting that sport brand managers need to understand how environmental or social messages can be embedded in their activities to achieve social outcomes, and into their branding without creating cynicism	

Index